HITLER
and His
Secret Partners

Books by James Pool

Hitler and His Secret Partners
Who Financed Hitler

Published by POCKET BOOKS

HITLER
and His
Secret Partners

Contributions, Loot and Rewards, 1933–1945

James Pool

POCKET BOOKS
New York London Toronto Sydney Tokyo Singapore

POCKET BOOKS, a division of Simon & Schuster Inc.
1230 Avenue of the Americas, New York, NY 10020

Library of Congress Cataloging-in-Publication Data

Pool, James, 1948–
  Hitler and his secret partners : contributions, loot and rewards,
  1933–1945 / James Pool.
     p.   cm.
  Includes bibliographical references and index.
  ISBN 0–671–76081–5
  1. Hitler, Adolf, 1889–1945—Friends and associates. 2. Political
corruption—Germany—History—20th century. 3. World War,
1939–1945—Confiscations and contributions. 4. Germany—Politics
and government—1933–1945. I. Title.
  DD247.H5P62   1997
  943.086′092—dc21   97-15506
                                                             CIP

ISBN: 0-671-76081-5

First Pocket Books hardcover printing October 1997

10 9 8 7 6 5 4 3 2 1

POCKET and colophon are registered trademarks of
Simon & Schuster Inc.

All photos courtesy of the National Archives except
where otherwise noted

Printed in the U.S.A.

Dedicated to all those who were
plundered by Hitler and his secret
partners,
    to all the victims who
were forced to work as slave laborers,
    and especially to all the
victims of the Holocaust.

May they one day be justly compensated.

Contents

Preface

Adolf Hitler caused more suffering, deaths, and destruction than any other man in history with the possible exception of Joseph Stalin. Since the crimes Hitler and his partners committed were so numerous, historians have naturally focused on the more serious ones: the waging of aggressive warfare on peaceful nations, the extermination of six million Jews, the murder of hostages, civilians, and prisoners of war. While thinking of major crimes, it is almost easy to forget the looting and plunder the Nazis engaged in.

But to ignore these seemingly less important crimes would be a mistake because new evidence indicates that looting and plundering were the primary motives of Hitler and the pro-Nazi industrialists and generals who were his secret partners. It made little difference to them if they had to kill, make war, and exterminate to get the wealth and natural resources they wanted. Even the Holocaust of six million innocent Jews must be reexamined in these terms. An abundance of evidence is presented to prove that Hitler, Nazi bosses, and pro-Nazi industrialists grew rich off robbing Jews and using them as slave labor. This is not to say that Hitler and the Nazis didn't hate Jews; they obviously did, but in the Third Reich ideology was often a cover for greed.

Robbery was elevated to a state policy in Hitler's Germany. However, the financial motives of Hitler and his partners have never been examined. This is unfortunate. By examining their financial motives, which often provided their primary reason for

ix

doing things, we can explain questions about Hitler and the Nazi period that have never been completely answered. What were Hitler's goals? Why did he start World War II? Why did the Nazis kill six million Jews? The answers to these and other questions about the very nature of Hitler's regime depend, in part, on discovering who Hitler's secret partners were, because their ambitions played a big part in all decisions in Nazi Germany.

Hitler's need for money did not end once he came to power. It increased. He had promises to keep and almost one million storm troopers to support. It was the middle of the depression and there was no extra money in the government budget, so Hitler asked Gustav Krupp, the munitions tycoon, to help collect the money from industry. Krupp immediately wrote pro-Nazi fellow industrialists telling them urgently: "Whoever helps quickly, helps doubly!"

Many pro-Nazi industrialists continued to contribute until 1945. For Hitler, these contributions had a big advantage over funds raised by taxes because records were kept on where tax money was spent. Contributions, on the other hand, could go to finance secret projects like concentration camps, Salon Kitty (the Gestapo's bugged brothel), or simply provide graft for Nazi leaders.

The money given to Hitler is only half the story of this book. The other half is about what the contributors got in return. In Nazi Germany those who financed Hitler were well rewarded with enormous war profits, confiscated Jewish property, loot from the conquered countries, and most important, power.

Hitler rewarded his financiers better than any king or dictator in history. Many received a 1,000-to-1 return on the money they gave. One of Hitler's largest financiers was rewarded with properties valued at over sixty billion dollars.

After the war, Hitler's supporters in business and the army tried to minimize the role they had played in the Nazi government. But this book will prove they ruled Germany along with Hitler as almost equal partners, and even though they remained behind the scenes, they were equally responsible for the crimes of the Third Reich.

In 1933, when Hitler first became chancellor, he was the junior partner in a coalition government with most of the power in the hands of conservative Vice-Chancellor von Papen and the generals. But Hitler's relationship with his partners was not always to be a peaceful one. They wanted a front man who would be their puppet. Instead they got one of the most charismatic leaders in history, who was much more difficult to control than they had ever imagined. They did not understand the awesome power of Hitler's personal magnetism and his appeal to the masses.

Hitler's partners should not have had any doubt about his hold over the German people if they saw the kind of reception he got in Nuremberg on September 4, 1934. "Like a Roman emperor Hitler rode into this medieval town at sundown today, past solid phalanxes of wildly cheering Nazis who packed the narrow streets," wrote American journalist William Shirer.

Tens of thousands of Swastika flags blot out the Gothic beauties of the place, the facades of the old houses, the gabled roofs. The streets hardly wider than alleys, are a sea of brown and black uniforms. About ten o'clock tonight, I got caught in a mob of ten thousand hysterics who jammed the moat in front of Hitler's hotel, shouting: "We want our Fuehrer." I was a little shocked at the faces, especially those of the women, when Hitler finally appeared on the balcony for a moment. They reminded me of the crazed expressions I saw once in the back country of Louisiana on the faces of some Holy Rollers who were about to hit the trail. They looked up at him as if he were a Messiah, their faces transformed into something positively inhuman. If he had remained in sight for more than a few moments, I think many of the women would have swooned from excitement.

After old President von Hindenburg's death, Hitler's power increased. But even by 1938 he still was not strong enough to challenge the army openly, so the Nazis used several well-timed sex scandals to try to weaken the power of the generals. The reason the partnership was maintained was because the pro-Nazi generals and industrialists had basically the same goals as Hitler. They were extreme nationalists who wanted to escape from the restrictions of the Versailles Treaty, rearm Germany, break out from the encirclement of Britain, France, and their allies, expand into Eastern Europe, where they would have access to grain and oil, and eventually dominate Europe.

Considering the very aggressive plans of Hitler and his partners, one of the most surprising things is that a number of prominent British individuals and Americans were willing to help them. The king of England did more than any other single individual to help Hitler rearm Germany. After he was forced to abdicate for his pro-Nazi attitude and become the Duke of Windsor, he and his wife, the duchess, continued to help promote the Nazi cause. Although not an admirer of Hitler, like the Duke and Duchess of Windsor, Prime Minister Neville Chamberlain tried to trick Britain into cooperating with the Nazi dictator. Chamberlain went to Munich with a secret agenda to help Hitler and betray the Czechs and the French.

One of Chamberlain's principal allies in working to appease Hitler was the United States ambassador to Britain, Joe Kennedy, who made statements that led Hitler to believe America wouldn't care if he killed the Jews. This belief of Hitler's was further reinforced by anti-Semitic statements from people like Colonel Charles A. Lindbergh and the American government's heartless refusal to admit Jewish refugees fleeing Nazi persecution.

Once Hitler started his conquests, his tactic of blitzkrieg was more a technique of looting conquered countries than a strictly military strategy. Only by plundering one victim after another were the Nazis able to get the resources to continue to wage war. Although Hitler is sometimes portrayed as an uncontrollable megalomaniac bent on conquering the world, his territorial ambitions in World War II were almost exactly the same as the kaiser's in World War I. This was because Hitler was above all else a German nationalist, and the same group of nationalistic military officers and industrialists who backed the kaiser were backing Hitler. These generals and industrialists had been plotting another expansionist war long before Hitler became their chief spokesman in 1933. Both Hitler and his partners saw World War II as a continuation of World War I. Hitler's major military objective in the war was to acquire grain and oil in the Ukraine and Russia.

The most extreme pro-Nazi businessmen and industrialists, and the list sadly included executives of some of Germany's largest companies, sank to the lowest depths of depravity by participating in the plunder and eventual extermination of six million innocent Jews. The Holocaust of European Jewry was planned jointly by Hitler, his henchmen, and Nazi "economic experts," with the idea of destroying their hated enemy and at the same time making a profit. In the first phase the theft of Jewish property was used by Hitler to reward his big financiers and to a lesser extent the middle-class Nazi party members. During the second phase of the Holocaust, Nazi industrialists grew rich off Jewish slave labor. Auschwitz, for example, was intended to be not just a concentration camp, but also the world's largest synthetic gasoline and rubber factory, which functioned by exploiting Jewish slave labor. Jews too weak to work were immediately exterminated. Several major German companies built factories at Auschwitz, and their Jewish slave laborers were subjected to beatings, starvation, and literally "worked to death."

This book will put the Holocaust in its proper perspective, showing just how important it was to Hitler and his partners. It was not only the central focus of Hitler's ideology but also a critical part of the economic program of the Third Reich he planned with his financiers and the generals.

It should be pointed out that most German industrialists did not support Hitler or anti-Semitism. The Communists claimed Hitler was a puppet of the capitalists. In reality, the German businessmen who were among the advocates of free market capitalism were among the most determined anti-Nazis, because totalitarianism was repugnant to them and because Hitler favored a planned economy and a welfare state. In contrast the industrialists who supported Hitler wanted government contracts and state protection to maintain industries that were having trouble competing in world markets. Partners like Hitler's financiers, who were to a great extent motivated by greed, could be counted on to remain loyal only as long as he enriched them with confiscated loot and the spoils of war.

After the invasion of Normandy, most of Hitler's partners turned against him and wanted to end the war as quickly as possible. Hitler's own physical and mental powers were failing. No one has ever known exactly why. New evidence presented here will show that Hitler's illness was caused by his abuse of drugs. He frequently had drastic mood swings and uncontrollable drug-induced rages. This further undermined whatever confidence the generals and industrialists still had in him.

There were three plots against Hitler's regime during the last year of the war. The first, the July 20 plot, failed, but the next two succeeded. Very little has ever been written about these two conspiracies against Hitler because the people involved in them, many of whom were Hitler's former partners, didn't want to be held responsible for Germany's defeat after the war. The one plot turned the Ruhr industry over to the Allies, intact. The other, during the battle of Berlin, sealed Hitler's fate when the army abandoned him and retreated to the west.

Introduction

The World of Hitler's Youth

Although it has been over fifty years since Hitler's death, hardly a day goes by without his name being mentioned in a newspaper, a book, or on television. Yet, biographers and historians still do not understand why he behaved the way he did. How did he captivate the German people? Why did he start World War II? Why did he commit such unspeakable atrocities?

In his youth, it seemed unlikely that Hitler would ever accomplish anything. Indeed it remains one of the great mysteries of history how such a loser without a profession or much of an education was able to take over a great nation. Some light will be shed on this mystery when we learn that he was sponsored by a wealthy, powerful secret society. Later some of the most important industrialists in Germany helped finance him, and high-ranking officers in the army protected him time after time. But why did these powerful well-educated people choose him? In 1939, these same people helped him start a world war and went on to participate with him in some of the worst crimes against humanity in history. What was the real relationship between Hitler and his financiers and partners? Were they his mesmerized followers or was he their puppet?

To understand Hitler it is useful to see the historical background from which he emerged. It is doubtful that he would

1

have been able to acquire the powerful patrons he did at any other time in history. Things that he learned in his youth later helped him get the support of some of the most prominent people in Germany.

Adolf Hitler was born in the small town of Branau on the River Inn, between Germany and Austria, on April 20, 1889. His father, Alois Hitler, was a fifty-two-year-old customs inspector in the Austrian customs service. Both his father and mother came from peasant families that had inhabited the Waldviertel region of Austria for centuries. Socially the family belonged to the lower middle class. Adolf's father earned about double the salary of the average factory worker at the time.

Alois Hitler retired from the customs service about the time his son started school. He received a very generous pension, so money was never a problem; however, the family moved a number of times while Alois looked for a place to settle down. As a result, young Adolf attended a number of different grade schools. He was an average pupil and seemed to be a normal boy who enjoyed playing "cowboys and Indians" more than going to school.

Finally, the family moved to Leonding, a suburb of Linz, which was the provincial capital of Upper Austria and located on the Danube, one of Europe's great rivers. Adolf lived in Linz between the ages of ten and eighteen and always considered it his hometown. Linz, at the turn of the century, was almost an idyllic place for a young boy to grow up. The town was just large enough to have some cultural life, with an opera house, a new cathedral, and a garrison; but it had none of the social problems of a large city. The countryside around Linz overlooking the Danube was quiet and beautiful. Adolf played outside a lot with the local children in the fields and meadows near his home.

Although some authors have tried to find the seeds of Hitler's later, tyrannical character in his youth, the truth is the Hitlers were a very ordinary family. True, his father had been illegitimate, was much older than his mother, and was said to be a stern disciplinarian, but none of these things were unusual in Austria at the time.

Adolf and his father seemed to get along well enough until the teenaged boy decided he wanted to become an artist. The old man insisted he prepare for a career as a civil servant. Partly in rebellion against his father, Adolf began to spend more time with his drawings than his schoolwork, and his grades naturally suffered. He began to hate school and had a low opinion of all his teachers except one, his history teacher, Leopold Poetsch, a fervent pan-German. Poetsch captured the imagination of his young students with heroic tales of the ancient Teutons and German victories.

This was young Adolf's first introduction to politics. His country, the Austro-Hungarian Empire, was a state made up of many diverse nationalities ruled by an Austro-German minority and an Austrian emperor of the Hapsburg dynasty. The empire was really a holdover from earlier centuries when states were based more on dynastic loyalties than national linguistic groups. In order to hold the empire together the Austro-Germans had to make increasing concessions to the Hungarians, Czechs, and other nationalities, as the passions of nationalism were beginning to stir in Eastern Europe. Many Austro-Germans, like Hitler's teacher Leopold Poetsch, wanted to see the old empire break up and Austria join Germany, to the north. Although the whole area around Linz was a hotbed of pan-German nationalism, Hitler's father remained loyal to the Austro-Hungarian Empire and its Hapsburg rulers. There is no indication that there were ever any political arguments between Hitler and his father. Adolf may have been inspired by Leopold Poetsch's classes, but he was not moved enough to become involved in politics. His only obsession was to become an artist.

When Adolf was fourteen, his father died suddenly. The principal obstacle to his becoming an artist was now removed. He continued school for two more years, but his heart was not in it, and at the age of sixteen, he dropped out without graduating. He spent the next two years studying art on his own. He would get up late, walk along the banks of the Danube looking for an isolated spot where he could sit for hours undisturbed sketching the landscape or the ruins of an old castle. At night he would read or attend the opera. Although a loner, he had one close friend who shared his interest in art and music.

Although not handsome, Hitler was always neat and clean and reasonably well dressed. For a time he even carried an ivory-handled cane, which was the custom of young gentlemen of the day. Obviously he was trying to put on airs and probably didn't impress anyone. Physically, he looked somewhat frail. His shoulders were narrow and his chest sunken. He had a pale complexion that was all the more noticeable because of his dark black hair. Because he was thin, he looked taller than his height of five feet nine inches. When he was seventeen or eighteen, he started to grow a mustache and a small goatee. His eyes were his only attractive physical feature. They were large and light blue. Even when he was an unknown teenager, many people found them hypnotic and compelling.

Adolf's mother was certainly overindulgent, and although she tried to urge her son to get a job, he continued to live at home idling away his time, dreaming about the day when he would become a great artist. According to Hitler, these years in Linz were the happiest of his life.

Without having graduated from high school and without a trade or profession, it was obvious to almost everyone but Adolf himself that he was destined for some hard times. However, at this point in his life, about the worst thing that could be said about him was that he was a dreamer and idler. Although he was sympathetic to the pan-German nationalists, so were most other young men in Linz. There were some Jews who lived in Linz and a few Jewish students attended Hitler's school, but there is little evidence that he was openly anti-Semitic at this time. He probably had some anti-Semitic prejudices typical to Austria of the period, but there is no record indicating that he was ever a member of any anti-Semitic group.

In the spring of 1906, the seventeen-year-old Hitler made a brief visit to Vienna. It was the most exciting thing that ever happened in his life. At the turn of the century, Vienna was one of the major capitals of Europe, as splendid as Paris or London. It was a city of cafés and glittering shop windows. Vienna had a reputation for charm and frivolity. Mention of the city produced images of the waltz, the court balls, the opera, and the *Blue Danube*. Naturally court balls and fine shops were beyond Hitler's budget, but many pleasures, such as the parks, the public gardens, and the art museums, were available to the ordinary people of Vienna. However, it was the great architecture that captivated Hitler. He went in awe from one magnificent building to another.

He returned to Linz full of enthusiasm for Vienna. He finally decided how he would realize his ambition of becoming a great artist. He would go to Vienna and study at the world famous art academy. Full of high hopes he set out for Vienna again in the fall of 1907 to take the entrance exam for the Academy of Fine Arts. His failure to pass the exam was a severe shock. The director of the Academy kindly explained to him that the test indicated his talent lay in the field of architecture rather than painting. Hitler reluctantly acknowledged that this was true, as his best paintings and drawings were always pictures of buildings rather than of people. However, a new problem presented itself, because it was very difficult to get into the School of Architecture without having graduated from high school.

While Hitler was brooding about his artistic career, he received an urgent letter from Linz saying that his mother was very ill. He returned home at once to find that she was dying of breast cancer. With selfless devotion, he nursed her through the last months of her life. Hitler had dearly loved his mother and was devastated by her death. After her burial, he was anxious to get away from the painful memories in Linz, so he returned to Vienna determined somehow to succeed as an artist or an architect.

Hitler suffered from a lack of sense of direction. He wanted to be an artist or architect, but he wasn't sure how to go about it and was too proud to seek advice. So he continued his "studies." He sat in the parks and sketched buildings and palaces; he spent hours at the library reading about obscure topics; he visited all the major museums regularly. In order to be able to afford the opera he had to skimp on food for a week, but to him the sacrifice was worth it.

When Hitler's money from home ran out, he quickly became desperate. He could no longer afford to pay his rent. He had to pawn his belongings, and his clothes became shabby and worn. Before long, he was in the ranks of the homeless, forced to accept charity just to survive. As he wrote in *Mein Kampf*, his autobiography, these were "years of hardship and suffering during which Hunger was my faithful companion. It never left me for a moment."

He got a job as a laborer on a construction project, but when he refused to join a socialist labor union some of the other workers who were Marxists beat him up and kicked him off the job. This was his first encounter with socialism (the Social Democratic party) and Marxism. Marxism was repugnant to Hitler because it rejected all his middle-class values and the nationalistic beliefs he had picked up from the pan-Germans while living in Linz. He could not understand how Austro-German workers could reject their own nationality and embrace the idea of international solidarity. One day, while walking through the city, Hitler witnessed a huge Marxist parade. There was a sea of red flags and red banners. Marching workers alternately sang songs and shouted slogans. "For nearly two hours," said Hitler, "I stood there watching with bated breath the gigantic human dragon slowly winding by. Oppressed with anxiety I finally left and went home."

In an effort to understand more about Marxism and the Social Democratic party, Hitler began to read about politics. Although his initial dislike of the Social Democrats did not change, he soon came to respect their use of propaganda to win over the workers. While reading Social Democratic newspapers, Hitler noticed that many of the party's leaders were Jewish. He considered this a very important discovery.

Precisely when Hitler became an anti-Semite is difficult to say. Thousands of Jews from Eastern Europe were streaming into Vienna every year, seeking an opportunity for a better life. Since most of them were poor, Hitler encountered them daily in the lower-class neighborhood where he lived. In his autobiography, he admitted he found their appearance objectionable; their "strange facial features, the black caftans . . . the black side-locks" disturbed him. He thought they looked "unclean" and "unheroic."

As an artist, Hitler should have been able to appreciate human diversity and the picturesque traditional dress of Orthodox Jews. However, as a boy, Hitler was taught to admire nationalism, militarism, order, and discipline. The Jews didn't fit into that rigid mold. Hitler conveniently seemed not to notice that many Jews, like Sigmund Freud and Gustav Mahler, were among Vienna's most creative and brilliant citizens.

Hitler's confrontation with Marxist socialism seems to have been what set him off down the path of anti-Semitism. In other words, he began to hate the Jews because they were the leaders of the Marxist Social Democratic party. He started to read anti-

Semitic pamphlets. Some of the worst lunatic fringe anti-Semitism in the world could be found in Vienna at the turn of the century. Hitler read the pamphlets of Lanz von Liebenfels, who wrote of a struggle between blond Aryan heros and dark hairy ape-men of inferior races who were trying to seduce blonde women. As an insignia Liebenfels used the swastika, which he claimed was the sign of racial purity.

It is possible that Hitler was partially converted to anti-Semitism even before he came to Vienna. While still in Linz, he became an ardent admirer of Richard Wagner's operas. When he first read Wagner's writing, however, is not known. But the question is important because Wagner was a fanatical anti-Semite. The composer was also an extreme German nationalist who saw it as his mission to purge German music of all foreign influences, particularly Jewish influence. In a pamphlet he wrote in 1850 entitled *Judaism in Music* he ridiculed Jewish music. In a more general political attack, Wagner said, "the Jew is the plastic [formative] demon of the decline of mankind."

Even though critics pointed out that Wagner's anti-Semitism was the result of a persecution complex, Hitler considered the composer a credible source, something that could not be said for the gutter pamphlets of Lanz von Liebenfels. If Hitler did not read Wagner's writings while still in Linz, he probably read them during the many hours he spent in the libraries of Vienna. In a revealing comment made later in his life, Hitler said, "Whoever wants to understand National Socialism must first know Wagner."

Wagner's stature as a German intellectual meant that many people besides Hitler read his writing. Moreover Wagner was not the only German intellectual who was propagating anti-Semitism and rabid nationalism. Other respected scholars like Paul Lagarde and Julius Langbehn were just as bad. The people who were exposed to this type of thinking were the educated middle and upper classes. Thus many of the people who would finance Hitler in the 1920s and 1930s were reading the same kind of nationalistic literature he read shortly after the turn of the century.

During most of the time he lived in Vienna, Hitler earned his living by painting watercolors that he sold to tourists and merchants, who used them to fill cheap picture frames. He lived in one of the poorest neighborhoods of the city in a cheap men's hostel. He did, however, have a small private cubicle, and the place was reasonably clean.

Hitler still lacked any self-discipline. As soon as he would sell a painting, he would take several days off and either go to the library or sit in a café eating cream puffs and reading newspapers. Although he still took no part in politics he carefully followed the struggle between three of the major new political parties in Vienna; the Pan-German party, the Christian Social party, and the Marxian Social Democratic party.

At first Hitler sympathized with the Pan-German party. It was extremely nationalistic and anti-Semitic. He found such ideas acceptable because they were similar to the pan-German nationalism he had been exposed to in Linz as a schoolboy. Growing up on stories of heroic Germanic battles and conquests naturally made him an admirer of nationalism, militarism, and racism. However, Hitler was intelligent enough also to notice the weakness of the Pan-German party. They made little attempt to appeal to the workers' economic and social problems, so they remained primarily a middle-class party.

After living in Vienna for a while, Hitler gradually came to respect the Christian Social party and its charismatic leader, Karl Lueger, the mayor of Vienna. Lueger was a dynamic orator who knew how to sway a crowd. The popularity of the Christian Social party was based on its social welfare program and its anti-Semitism. Hitler admired the way Lueger won votes by making economic promises to the working class and the poor. He objected, however, to Lueger's anti-Semitism—because it was not extreme enough. Lueger's anti-Semitism was based on religious prejudice. Like the Pan-Germans, Hitler considered the Jews an inferior race, not just a different religion. A Jew could always escape religious anti-Semitism, at least theoretically, by converting to Christianity. There was no escape from racial anti-Semitism because it was a matter determined by birth and ancestry.

The only outward signs that Hitler was interested in politics were occasional arguments he would have with other residents of the men's hostel. Since he did much of his painting in the recreation room of the hostel, he would often discuss politics and paint at the same time. But once the Jews were mentioned in the discussion, he would become very excited, raise his voice, and gesture wildly, paintbrush in hand. It is said that he once became so agitated he knocked over his easel during an argument. However, there is no record of Hitler's ever succeeding in winning anyone over to his point of view. He was regarded as something of a curiosity even among the odd assortment of characters who inhabited the men's hostel.

In the spring of 1913, fed up with his continual failure to accomplish anything, Hitler, who was then twenty-four years old, left Vienna and moved to Munich. He said he decided to move to Germany because he could no longer stand "the conglomeration of races" in Vienna. There was probably another reason he left Vienna. He was fleeing Austrian military service. But whatever his reason for leaving Austria, he had learned a great deal in Vienna. He later wrote that Vienna was "the hardest, though most thorough school" of his life, where he developed the foundations of a "philosophy . . . and a political view" that remained with him forever.

This statement was certainly true. Hitler always remained more an Austrian than a German. Nationalism and anti-Semitism were more extreme in Austria because the Austro-Germans felt threatened by the rising aspirations of the people they had long dominated. The problem of national hatred was simmering in the Austro-Hungarian Empire years before it erupted in the rest of Europe in 1914. While the old dynastic order held on longer in Austria-Hungary, it was very obvious by 1900 that it was about to collapse. Hence, people like Hitler were already thinking about what kind of government would follow. In contrast no one in Germany thought the Hohenzollern monarchy was about to collapse. Finally, Hitler's poverty in Vienna led him to experience Marxism and the politics of class warfare with an intensity he would never have encountered if he had lived among the middle class in Germany. In a sense, his life in Vienna gave Hitler a preview of what Europe would be like in 1918 after the end of World War I.

In Munich, Hitler lived a very quiet life. As he had in Vienna, he earned his meager living from selling his paintings. He rented a room above a tailor's shop in the Schwabing district where many artists lived. He had no close friends. The tailor and his family remembered Hitler as a "nice man" who was "very polite" but always kept to himself.

Hitler's solitary life, which was seemingly going nowhere, was suddenly transformed by world events. In August of 1914, World War I broke out. At last his German nationalism would have an outlet. He gathered with thousands of other patriots in the Odeonplatz in Munich to cheer the declaration of war. He believed Germany would at last have a chance to assert her military might on the battlefield and claim her rightful place as the dominant power in Europe. As much as he had tried to evade service in the Austro-Hungarian army, because he didn't want to serve in the same army as Slavs, he now volunteered for the German Army.

Like most people, Hitler had little knowledge of the real reasons for the war. The average person was so emotionally involved in national pride and honor that they failed to see that the development of great historic and economic forces made war almost inevitable. Behind all the nationalist rhetoric was the industrial rivalry among Germany, Britain, and France. German industrialization had progressed steadily in the latter half of the nineteenth century. By 1871, German industrial production exceeded that of France, and by 1900 it was greater than Britain's. Not only was Germany the greatest industrial power in Europe, but its factories were also more modern and efficient than its rivals. Germany's problem was that it did not have access to world markets and raw materials equal to its productive capacity.

A large part of the world's markets and sources of raw materials was dominated by the colonial empires of Britain and France. Germany's leaders had often complained that Germany was being economically encircled and strangled. German industrialists seeking more access to world markets were the financiers of the extreme nationalist parties in the pre-1914 era. Some of the same industrialists who financed the prowar forces prior to 1914 would later help finance Hitler.

A few days after the declaration of war, Hitler was training with the List Regiment and was on his way to the front. The List Regiment went into battle in Flanders and suffered heavy casualties, but Hitler was not even wounded. After a short time as an ordinary infantryman, Hitler became a dispatch runner. His job was to carry messages forward from regimental head-quarters to the men in the trenches. It was a dangerous job that required a great deal of courage and initiative. The runners often had to go forward during artillery barrages, running a few hundred yards, taking cover in one shell hole after another, finally crawling on their stomachs through the mud to the forward trenches while enemy bullets whizzed over their heads.

Hitler won the Iron Cross second class in 1914. He was wounded in the leg in 1916. In August of 1918, he won the Iron Cross first class, Germany's highest honor, which was rarely given to enlisted men. The medal was awarded for his single-handedly capturing fifteen French soldiers. It is, however, some-thing of a mystery that in spite of his excellent military record Hitler never rose above the rank of corporal.

This may have been due to several factors. First of all, Hitler's job as a runner was vital and he was good at it. If he had been promoted he would have been replaced by an inexperienced man. There was also the fact that he remained a loner. He didn't fit in. The uneducated working-class soldiers thought he was an aloof bookish intellectual. Yet, he lacked the formal education of middle-class young men who were usually promoted to junior officers. His officers must have thought such a strange fellow didn't seem to have the authority to command men.

Whenever there was a lull in the fighting and Hitler had a free moment, he would find a quiet spot to sit and read. He went to war with a copy of Schopenhauer's *Will to Power* in his knapsack. Besides reading elitist philosophers like Schopenhauer and Nietzsche, he spent a great deal of time reading the political and military news in newspapers. He made a very thorough study of the differences between German and British war propaganda. The British propaganda was far more effective, he concluded. He was open-minded enough to have considerable admiration for the rhetorical skill of the British prime minister, Lloyd George.

In spite of the fact that Hitler recognized the cleverness of enemy propaganda he remained a fervent German nationalist. In the later days of war when Germany was doing poorly, he often argued with the men in his regiment who expressed "defeatist sentiments." He was a patriot to the last.

The war had a decisive effect on Hitler's character. As military service does for many young men, it gave him a sense of discipline and self-confidence. Up to the war, Hitler had so lacked personal self-discipline that in spite of his intelligence he was incapable of accomplishing anything. But the war also had a negative effect on him. The violence and carnage he saw all around him brutalized him. Death and destruction were now commonplace in his world. His regiment had one of the highest casualty rates in the German Army. He watched friends having their bodies blown apart only a few yards away. Of course this is no excuse for the murderous crimes Hitler later committed, because after all, many men who experienced the same brutalities of World War I reacted by later becoming pacifists. But it is an explanation for how he learned to use violence to get what he wanted. Before the war, Hitler's anti-Semitism and fanatical German nationalism were all talk and theory. He never tried to physically assault any Jews or incite a pogrom because he didn't know how. World War I educated him in violence. He now knew how to kill. In later years, when trying to convince his hesitant partners to participate in the Holocaust, he would often refer to the war, saying, "If two million of Germany's best youth were slaughtered in the war, we have the right to exterminate subhumans who breed like vermin."

By the end of 1917, the British naval blockade of Germany was beginning to have a decisive effect. In peacetime, Germany imported much of the food consumed by her people. Now, cut off from the rest of the world, there were severe food shortages throughout the country. There was almost no milk and no coffee. The only fresh vegetables available were turnips and potatoes, and bread was made from potato peelings. The revolutionary Marxist underground tried to take advantage of the situation by organizing strikes against the war. On January 28, 1918, there was a general strike throughout Germany. Thousands of munitions workers in Berlin walked off their jobs demanding peace, increased food rations, and worker representation in negotiations with the Allies.

The news of the strike had an effect on the morale of the troops at the front. Many of the soldiers were tired of the war and wanted peace. But others, like Hitler, felt they were being betrayed by the civilian strikers. "What was the army fighting for if the homeland itself no longer wanted victory?" he asked. "For whom were all the immense sacrifices and privations? The soldier is expected to fight for victory and the homeland goes on strike against it!" He called the strike "the greatest villainy of the war."

After the failure of the great Ludendorff offensive in the summer of 1918, there was a serious drop in morale. Discipline began to break down in some places. Desertions increased. Red agitators among the troops encouraged rebellion. There were disorders on troop trains taking men to the front.

On August 8, the Allied troops broke through the German front line. General Ludendorff said it was "the black day of the German Army." He now realized victory was no longer possible. By September, the military situation had deteriorated so much that the high command told the government to seek an armistice.

While the government tried to open peace negotiations with the Allies, the fighting continued as the Germans gradually pulled back. On the night of October 13, 1918, Hitler's regiment was dug in on a low hill south of Ypres in Belgium. Earlier in the day, the hill had been heavily bombarded by Allied artillery. The Germans crouched in their trenches as the exploding shells turned the earth around them into a pock-marked moonscape. Just after sunset, one of the German soldiers shouted the warning: "Gas! Gas!" Hitler and the others hurriedly put on their gas masks. A deadly fog of chlorine gas slowly enveloped the battlefield. The gas attack lasted until midnight. After several hours the gas was able to penetrate the primitive gas masks worn by the German soldiers. By morning, Hitler's eyes felt "like burning coals." Slowly he began to stumble toward the rear, carrying with him his last dispatch of the war.

Hitler was soon on board a hospital train, with hundreds of other gas victims, heading eastward back to Germany. He was taken to the military hospital at Pasewalk near Berlin where he was treated for gas poisoning. Responding well to the treatment he regained some vision within a week and could distinguish shapes and outlines. He was, however, depressed because he was afraid he would never be able to see well enough to paint again. He was also uneasy about Germany's military situation. Things were not going well at the front, and there were signs and rumors of antiwar activities at home.

13

During the latter part of October, the German military position was becoming desperate. Rather than face the prospect of defeat, the commanders of the navy decided they wanted to attempt to break the British blockade in one final sea battle. But when the fleet was ordered to sea, the crews of several battleships in the port of Kiel mutinied. The sailors broke into armories then imprisoned their officers. A sailors' soviet was established, and most of the ships in Kiel harbor ran up the red flag of revolution.

While the Kiel mutiny was taking place, another uprising broke out in Munich, led by a Socialist named Kurt Eisner. By the evening of November 7, the revolutionaries were in control of the city. Trucks manned by revolutionaries waving red flags patrolled the streets. The major military posts in Munich were seized when a number of soldiers joined the uprising. Some of Eisner's men set up machine guns at strategic intersections. There was no resistance when the revolutionaries occupied government buildings. The defenders of the old order, including the king of Bavaria, simply faded away without a fight.

The revolution quickly spread throughout Germany. On November 9, the German public learned the kaiser had abdicated and Friedrich Ebert, a moderate Social Democrat, had become chancellor. But Ebert was not radical enough to satisfy many of the revolutionaries; they wanted a Communist government like Soviet Russia. A group of about three thousand mutinous sailors occupied the kaiser's palace and looted everything in sight. When the Ebert government ordered them to leave they refused.

Hitler was in the military hospital at Pasewalk when a truckload of sailors arrived waving red flags and calling for revolution. According to Hitler, the red sailors were led by "a few Jews." He wondered why they were not arrested for treason.

A few days later, an elderly pastor came to the hospital to speak to the wounded men. He told them the news of the kaiser's abdication, that Germany was now a republic, and the government was seeking an armistice with the Allies. As he spoke the pastor began to weep. Hitler was dumbfounded at the sudden realization that Germany had lost the war. "It was impossible for me to listen any longer." Hitler later wrote, "Everything began to go black again before my eyes, stumbling, I groped my way back . . . to my cot and buried my head in the pillows. I had not wept since the day I had stood at my mother's grave."

For days, Hitler was severely depressed. He brooded on all the sacrifices that had been in vain and all the comrades and friends who were lost. He believed the German Army had not been defeated on the field of battle but betrayed, "stabbed in the back" by a gang of Communist traitors led by Jews. His depression turned to rage. He was determined to do something about it and no longer be a passive observer of the political situation. It was the critical turning point of his life. He made up his mind to become a politician.

Like Hitler, most Germans were stunned by their country's sudden defeat. After all, they had defeated Russia, and German troops still occupied enemy soil in France and Belgium. Only the generals of the high command knew how close the German line was to complete collapse. Consequently, in later years, most Germans, like Hitler, honestly believed their army had never been defeated but was stabbed in the back by traitors.

By Christmas, Berlin was on the verge of anarchy as fighting erupted between the moderate forces supporting Chancellor Ebert and the Communists, who called themselves Spartacists, in honor of the slave who led the rebellion against Rome. On January 5, the streets of Berlin were turned into a battlefield when armed Communists seized the railway station and a number of important government buildings. Many of the revolutionaries were supplied with money and weapons by sympathizers at the Soviet embassy. The Russian Communists saw a chance to spread their revolution to Germany.

In desperation, Chancellor Ebert called on the army for help. Units of loyal anti-Communist troops, called Free Corps, were sent to try to retake Berlin. The Communists had set up machine gun nests at the Brandenburg gate and other important intersections. They fought the Free Corps troops from behind barricades in the streets. Heavy fighting continued until January 12, when the Free Corps gradually got the upper hand. A few days later, the Free Corps captured and shot the two most important Communist leaders, Karl Liebknecht and Rosa Luxemburg. Communist uprisings spread to the Ruhr, Leipzig, Hamburg, and Bremen; but they were suppressed everywhere by loyal army troops.

In Munich, on February 22, a nationalist officer assassinated Kurt Eisner, the left-wing socialist leader of the Bavarian government. A month of turmoil followed. Finally the Communists and radicals gained control and proclaimed Bavaria a Soviet Republic. The revolutionary forces in Munich were little more than an undisciplined mob made up of Communist workers, radical intellectuals, and the unemployed. They robbed banks, looted homes, and terrorized the population.

During much of the unrest in Munich, Hitler was serving as a guard at a remote prisoner-of-war camp at Traunstein. He had volunteered for the duty at Traunstein just to get out of Munich, because he was so disgusted by the revolutionary atmosphere. But in the spring the prisoner-of-war camp was closed when the last of the Russian soldiers were sent home. Hitler was forced to return to Munich. Because he had given a speech in the barracks urging his fellow soldiers not to support the revolution, the Communists sent three men to arrest Hitler. When he confronted the three with a rifle, they departed and never returned.

The days of Communist government in Munich were numbered as anti-Communist Free Corps troops, sent on order of Chancellor Ebert, advanced on the city from several directions. When the troops learned the Communists were shooting hostages, they made preparations to attack the next day.* On May 1 the Free Corps troops moved in on the Communists. There was some heavy fighting but the undisciplined Reds were no match for trained soldiers. In Moscow, Lenin was hailing the birth of a Soviet Bavaria while Free Corps troops were slaughtering Communists as they surrendered. Although fighting lasted another two days, as the Free Corps cleaned out the last nests of resistance, there was never any doubt about the outcome.

The fact that Germany had almost gone Communist was to play a decisive role in Hitler's rise to power. More than anything else, it explains why many upper-class and upper-middle-class people financed and supported him. The German upper classes were terrified by communism. In spite of the fact that revolutionary uprisings had been suppressed the threat continued for the

---

*Most of the hostages killed belonged to a right-wing secret group, called the Thule Society, that would later play a decisive role in financing Hitler.

next thirteen years. A militant German Communist party, supported by about 20 to 30 percent of the working class, survived the failed uprising of 1919 and kept on agitating for revolution. The Russian Soviets also continued their efforts to stir up working-class unrest in Germany. Against this background were the horror stories that poured out of Soviet Russia about what Lenin's "workers' paradise" was really like—how private property had been confiscated and outlawed; how people were starving and the economy was in ruins and ultimately how thousands of upper-class men, women, and children including the czar and his family, had been butchered by Communist fanatics.

The Communist revolution in Germany in 1918 played an important part in the rise of German anti-Semitism. Some of the principal leaders of the revolution—Eisner, Liebknecht, and Luxemburg—had been Jewish. This led anti-Semites like Hitler to make the accusation that the Jews were the "secret force" behind communism. In retrospect, such an idea is obviously ridiculous, but the German middle and upper classes were traumatized and seeking answers as to why their society had suddenly collapsed. Such people were vulnerable to conspiracy theories. If it had not been for the Communist uprisings in Germany, Hitler would probably never have found a receptive audience for the anti-Semitic garbage he had learned in Vienna. Moreover he would not have found so many industrialists, aristocrats, and officers willing to contribute to his cause.

Part I

Chapter 1

Financing the 1933 Elections

On the cold winter weekend of January 28, 1933, Germany was officially without a government. Chancellor Kurt von Schleicher and his cabinet had resigned on Saturday afternoon, and eighty-six-year-old President von Hindenburg had not yet appointed a new chancellor. A nervous tension spread over Berlin. Everyone waited for news; most felt Germany was at an historic turning point.

Who would be the next chancellor? Hitler—the leader of the largest party, the Nazis, who pledged to destroy democracy? Papen—the aristocratic horseman who had been chancellor before Schleicher, but who had no popular following? Perhaps Schleicher again, if he could persuade the Social Democrats, the second largest political party in the country, to join him in a coalition? Governing Germany in the middle of an economic depression with nine million unemployed was not an enviable task. The country had just had three different chancellors in rapid succession. By tradition, the leader of the largest party was usually appointed chancellor.* But the Nazis had been the

---

*In Germany, the president was elected by popular vote. He was responsible for appointing the chancellor, who was either the leader of the largest party or the leader of a coalition that had a majority in the Reichstag. However, if no one could form a majority in the Reichstag, the president had the power, under Article 48 of the German constitution, to appoint a chancellor to rule by decree.

largest party for over a year, and so far intrigues and political maneuvering had succeeded in keeping Hitler out of power. Everyone guessed what a Hitler government would mean. He had not kept his militarism, anti-Semitism, and dictatorial ambitions a secret.

Political intrigues were so numerous that weekend that no one really knew what was going on. Sensational rumors were being spread throughout the city. Some said an army coup was imminent, that Schleicher and the generals were about to abduct President von Hindenburg and declare martial law. There were also rumors of an armed Nazi uprising and a general strike by the socialist workers.

Hitler and Hermann Goering, the second most powerful man in the Nazi party, stayed up all night on Sunday, January 29, trying to figure out what Hindenburg might do. It was not until after 10 A.M. on Monday that Hitler received a summons to the president's office. Even at that point, the Nazis were not certain whether Hitler would be appointed chancellor or Hindenburg would ask him to serve as vice-chancellor.

Across the street from the Chancellery, in the Kaiserhof Hotel, Hitler's lieutenants were waiting, unsure of what was going on. Goebbels, the Nazi propaganda chief, said:

In the street the crowd stands waiting between the Kaiserhof and the Chancellery. We are torn between doubt, hope, joy and despair. We have been deceived too often to be able, wholeheartedly, to believe in the great miracle. [S.A.*] Chief of Staff Roehm stands at the window (with binoculars) watching the door of the Chancellery from which the Fuehrer [the leader, Hitler] must emerge. We shall be able to judge by his face if the interview was a success. Torturing hours of waiting. At last, a car draws up in front of the entrance. The crowd cheers. They seem to feel that a great change is taking place. . . .

A few moments later, he is with us. He says nothing. . . . His eyes are full of tears. It has come! The Fuehrer is

*The S.A. men were the Nazi party's private army of brown uniformed thugs. They were also called storm troopers or Brownshirts.

appointed Chancellor. He has already been sworn in by the President of the Reich. All of us are dumb with emotion. Everyone clasps the Fuehrer's hand. . . . Outside the Kaiserhof, the masses are in a wild uproar. . . . The thousands soon become tens of thousands. Endless streams of people flood the Wilhelmstrasse. We set to work . . . at once.[1]

Hitler's victory was not a complete one by any means. He had been appointed chancellor in a coalition government. Papen was to be his vice-chancellor, and all the powerful cabinet posts were held by Papen's conservative allies, rather than the Nazis. But at the moment, Hitler's followers weren't worried about the details; for them the only thing that mattered was that Hitler was chancellor. They had come to power! All day, crowds gathered in the square outside the Kaiserhof Hotel and the Chancellery.

At dusk Nazi storm troopers in their brown uniforms gathered in the Tiergarten park, along with men of the Stahlhelm, an ultranationalistic veterans' organization, for a torchlight victory parade through the center of Berlin.[2] As soon as it was dark, they came marching by the thousands through the Brandenburg Gate, carrying swastika flags and the black, white, and red flags of the German empire. Bands marched between the units, beating their big drums as the men sang old German military songs. But as each band came to the Pariser Platz, where the French embassy was located, they stopped whatever they were playing and, with an introductory roll of drums, broke into the tune of the challenging war song "Victorious We Will Crush the French."[3]

The torches carried by the marchers glowed hypnotically in the darkness. To foreign witnesses, it was a frightening sight. "The river of fire flowed past the French Embassy," Ambassador François-Poncet wrote, "whence, with heavy heart and filled with foreboding, I watched this luminous wake."[4] Liberal Germans found it an "ominous sight." It was, wrote one German reporter, "a night of deadly menace, a nightmare in . . . blazing torches."[5]

As the marchers came by the Chancellery, there were tumultuous cheers for Hitler, who stood in an open window saluting them. He was so excited that night, he could hardly stand still. He was raising his arm up and down heiling, smiling, and laughing so much, his eyes filled with tears. "It was an extraordinary experience," recalled Papen, who was standing behind Hitler. "The endless repetition of the triumphal cry: 'Heil, Heil, Sieg Heil!' rang in my ears like a tocsin." When Hitler turned to speak with Papen, his voice choked with emotion. "What an immense task we have set for ourselves, Herr von Papen—we must never part until our work is accomplished."[6] Hitler and Papen were much closer allies than anyone at the time imagined.

It was after midnight when the parade ended. Being too excited to sleep, Hitler, Goering, Goebbels, and a few other Nazis sat up talking for hours. They could hardly believe it had actually happened: they were in the Chancellery at last. That evening, Hitler said to Goebbels, "No one gets me out of here alive." It was one of the few promises he kept.

On the morning of January 31, Hitler's storm troopers gave the German people a glimpse of what Nazi rule would be like. All over Germany, thugs in brown shirts took possession of the streets and roughed up Communists, socialists, and Jews; they chased socialist mayors and officials out of government buildings and even broke into the private homes of their political enemies. When people complained to Papen, he laughed. "Let the storm troopers have their fling." Among his friends at the Herrenklub, an exclusive gentlemen's club, he boasted: "We've hired Hitler." To a skeptic he replied: "What do you want? I have Hindenburg's confidence. Within two months we will have pushed Hitler so far in the corner that he'll squeak."

The facts seemed to support Papen's optimism. Not only did Papen have Hindenburg's confidence, but in fact the old president had promised never to receive Hitler unless he was accompanied by his vice-chancellor. Papen also held the important post of minister-president of Prussia, Germany's largest and most powerful state. From the composition of the cabinet, it seemed all the real power was in the hands of the conservatives: the aristocratic General von Blomberg was minister of defense, Baron von Neurath, a career diplomat, was foreign minister, and the old archreactionary Hugenberg was both minister of economics and minister of agriculture. The Nazies were outnumbered six to two.

The two Nazis in the cabinet, Wilhelm Frick and Goering, held posts that were thought to be insignificant. Frick was minister of the interior, but he did not control the police, which in Germany was under the jurisdiction of the individual state governments. Goering was made minister without portfolio, but with the promise that he would be minister of aviation as soon as Germany had an air force. He was also named minister of the interior of Prussia, an office that did not receive much notice by the public but did control the Prussian police.

The aristocrats and gentlemen of the Right who made up the majority of Hitler's cabinet hated the concept of democracy even more than the Nazis did. These men belonged to the old ruling class of the kaiser's Germany. They wanted to regain their old position of supremacy, lost in 1918. They wanted to restore the monarchy, suppress the socialist unions, avenge the loss of World War I, and make Germany the dominant power in Europe. It was obvious why such reactionary nationalists helped put Hitler in power: their goals and his were very similar.

Few people knew the full extent of Papen's collaboration with Hitler. Historians have said he "did more than anyone else outside the Nazi party to help Hitler to power."[7] Papen helped Hitler because he was trying to control him and use the Nazis for his own aims.

Papen was a handsome aristocratic-looking man with distinguished gray hair and an officer's mustache. From an impoverished family of the Westphalian nobility, he became a General Staff officer, a skillful horseman, and a man of great charm. After a successful marriage to the daughter of a wealthy Saar industrialist, he bought a large block of shares in the Center party's newspaper, *Germania*.* For a short time in 1932, Papen was chancellor, but his government had no popular support. Papen believed it would be rather easy for an aristocratic officer like himself to manipulate a former corporal, like Hitler, and

---

*The Center party was Germany's Catholic political party. Most of its members were lower-middle-class moderates. The few upper-class Catholics who belonged to the right wing of the Center party had limited influence.

thus be able to use the Nazi's mass following to accomplish the aims of the upper-class conservative nationalists.

Hitler immediately began to outmaneuver his conservative colleagues. He reported to the cabinet that the Center party was making impossible demands and could not be counted on to form a coalition with the Nazis and the Nationalists that would have a majority in the Reichstag. Because of this situation, Hitler argued he would have to call for new elections. The only "demand" the Center party made was that Hitler promise to govern constitutionally, but none of the other members of the cabinet bothered to check Hitler's statement. They agreed to new elections on the condition that Hitler promise that the composition of the cabinet would not change regardless of the outcome of the voting.

New elections would provide Hitler with a chance to improve on the poor results the Nazis had received at the polls the past November. If the Nazis won a clear majority in the elections, they might be able to get rid of their coalition partners. Hitler had every reason to believe the election campaign would be a big success. The entire machinery of government, including the radio, was now under Nazi control and could be used for campaigning. The party had been flooded with new applicants for membership since he had become chancellor. In the cabinet meeting on February 2, Hitler discussed his preparations for the elections. Wilhelm Frick, the Nazi minister of the interior, proposed that the government set aside a million marks for the election campaign. Count von Schwerin von Krosigk, the minister of finance, rejected this suggestion. Hitler did not force the issue. He would have to get the money elsewhere.

The theme of the Nazi election campaign was to be the fight against communism. Hitler opened the attack in a late-night radio broadcast to the nation on February 1. He blamed the hard times Germany had gone through since 1918 on the Social Democrats, which had been the largest party in the Reichstag during most of those years. The Social Democrats, he reminded his listeners, were actually a Marxist party. "Fourteen years of Marxism," he said, "have ruined Germany; one year of bolshevism [communism] would destroy her. The richest and fairest territories of the world would be turned into a smoking heap of ruins. Even the sufferings of the last decade and a half could not be compared to the misery of a Europe in the heart of which the red flag of destruction has been hoisted." He went on to promise to put the unemployed back to work and save the peasants from bankruptcy.

On his fourth day in office, just after opening the election campaign, Hitler took time off to attend a very important dinner. He had been invited to the home of General von Hammerstein, chief of staff of the army, to meet the leading officers of the army and navy. In a speech that lasted almost two hours, Hitler explained his plans for rebuilding German military power.[8]

The generals were the real power in Germany during the Weimar period. After World War II, many Germans tried to cover up the role certain members of the Officer Corps had played in helping to put Hitler in power. Many historians naively accepted this view, but the real story is quite different. Traditionally, the German Army ruled from behind the scenes and had the final "power to veto" any important issue. After the loss of World War I, the Versailles Treaty severely restricted the size of the German Army. The only way the generals could maintain mass training and develop new weapons was to finance private paramilitary units, like the Free Corps, with secret army funds.

Hitler not only began his career as an army agent, but even in the 1930s he was supported by a powerful faction in the army. Over several years, General von Schleicher, who was in charge of a secret informal political department of the army, funneled over ten million marks to Hitler.[9] Why? Many military officers wanted an authoritarian government that could unify the nation. The people needed to be infused with a new spirit of patriotism because powerful interests were planning a war of revenge against the Allies. Naturally there was a division of opinion among the generals as to how much power to give Hitler.

Hindenburg originally had strong reservations about appointing a man from a lower-class background, like Hitler, chancellor.[10] However, the aggressive action the Nazis took against Communists was admired by Hindenburg, and his relationship with Hitler rapidly improved.

One day, Hindenburg summoned Hitler when Papen was away from Berlin. Hitler informed the president that Papen was out of town and reminded him of the rule he (Hindenburg) had made, that the chancellor could visit him only when accompanied by the vice-chancellor. "The old gentleman [Hindenburg]," said Hitler, "replied that he wished to see me alone, and that in the future the presence of Papen could be regarded as unnecessary. Within three weeks, he had progressed so far that his attitude towards me became affectionate and paternal. Talking of the elections fixed for the 3rd of March, he said, 'What are we going to do if you fail to get a majority? We shall have the same difficulties all over again.' "[11]

At the beginning of the election campaign, Hitler and Papen persuaded old President von Hindenburg to sign an emergency decree to protect law and order. The decree gave Nazi officials the right to prohibit public meetings. Newspapers could be suppressed if they "incited" civil disobedience or published "false" reports. The decree gave Hitler and Papen a very useful weapon in the election campaign.

There was certainly plenty of election violence. The Nazi storm troopers invaded the beer halls and bars where the Communists and Social Democrats held their meetings. There were fistfights and bloody street brawls with clubs and razor blades. During the election campaign, from January 30 to March 5, over seventy people were killed in political violence.

Where the use of violence was involved, Hermann Goering was the expert. Thus he played a decisive role in the first year of Hitler's government. Without Goering's drive and ruthlessness, Hitler might never have been able to transform his position as chancellor to that of dictator.[12]

During the war, Goering had been a fighter ace in the Richthofen Squadron and won the *Pour le Mérite* (Blue Max), Germany's highest decoration. He succeeded his famous commander Baron von Richthofen (the Red Baron), and was himself appointed commander of the Richthofen Squadron. After Germany lost the war, Goering became bitter. For a short time, he commanded Hitler's storm troopers, but his most important job for Hitler was as fund-raiser. Being from an upper-class background, Goering had access to princes, industrialists, and bankers. During the 1920s and early 1930s, he obtained millions of marks for Hitler. In 1918 Goering had been a handsome, slender man; but during the 1920s he put on weight. By 1933, he was very fat. But in spite of his size, Goering had enormous energy.

Goering's political power was based on his position as Prussian minister of interior, which controlled the police in almost two-thirds of Germany. As soon as he was appointed, he moved quickly to dismiss all senior police officials with Social Democratic or moderate sympathies and replace them with storm trooper officers or other Nazis.

In mid-February, Goering issued an order to the Prussian police: "With Communist terrorism . . . there must be no trifling, and when necessary revolvers must be used without regard for the consequences. Policemen who fire their revolvers in the execution of their duties, will be protected by me . . . but those who hesitate to shoot will be punished according to regulations."

On February 22, Goering took a major step toward turning the Prussian police into his private Nazi Army by recruiting S.A. and S.S. men into the police force as "auxiliaries."* Insisting that the resources of the regular police were stretched to the limit and in urgent need of reinforcements, he drafted fifty thousand storm troopers into the force. As soon as they put a white armband marked SPECIAL POLICE on their brown shirts (S.A.), or black shirts (S.S.), they represented the law. In election violence and the resulting street fights, Goering's auxiliary police used their nightsticks to help their Nazi comrades "give the Reds a good beating." Also, they often intimidated the general public by marching into restaurants and trying to force the frightened patrons to buy photographs of Hitler or Goering at exorbitant prices. Goering's auxiliary police plus the Nazified regular Prussian police made Goering one of the most powerful men in Germany, second only to the minister of defense in the number of armed men he could command.[13]

Why did Papen give such power to Goering? Journalists at the time and later historians contended that when the Hitler-Papen cabinet was formed, the fact that the Prussian minister of interior controlled the Prussian police was simply overlooked. This argument makes no sense. Papen was a master of political intrigue who certainly knew which office controlled the police

---

*The S.S. was Hitler's black-uniformed elite bodyguard unit. The number of men in the S.S. was rapidly expanded from 1933 until 1945.

force. He could have stopped Goering at once if he had wanted to. But Papen did nothing, apparently because he had made a deal with Hitler and Goering at the time the cabinet had been sworn in. This appears to have been just the first step of a three-phase plan Papen, Hitler, and their coconspirators had concocted to turn the democratic government of Germany into an authoritarian regime. Goering was entrusted with such power because he was more of an upper-class officer of the old school than he was a Nazi. In fact, the conservatives saw him as a counterbalance to Hitler. Papen thought he could use Goering to help control Hitler and the more radical Nazis.

While Goering's police were enforcing the authority of the Nazi regime, Hitler was busy enacting emergency laws to restrict the freedom of his opponents. Although initially he had some difficulty getting Hindenburg to approve his decrees to limit the freedom of the press, eventually his persuasive ability won over the old president. Hitler later bragged about how he had accomplished this: "I played a little trick on him and addressed him not as a civilian with 'Mr. President,' but as a soldier with 'Field Marshal,' and developed the argument that in the Army criticism from below was never permitted . . . for what would happen if the N.C.O. passed judgement on the orders of the Captain, the Captain on those of the General and so on? This the old gentleman [Hindenburg] admitted and without further ado, approved of my policy saying, 'You are quite right, only superiors have the right to criticize!' and with these words the freedom of the press was doomed."[14]

By mid-February the Nazis were running short of money for the election campaign. Hitler's strategy, which called for a whirlwind propaganda extravaganza, would have to be canceled if new funds were not obtained somehow. The Nazi party rank and file had been called on to give and give again, but no further money could be extracted from ordinary people in the middle of a depression.

Goering and Hjalmar Schacht, a pro-Nazi banker, sat down together and tried to come up with a plan to help Hitler out of his financial difficulty. These men were familiar with raising funds from industry; as they saw it, the industrialists needed the Nazis and the Nazis needed the industrialists. Since the voters had entirely deserted the traditional moderate parties financed by industry, the industrialists suddenly found themselves without political influence. Up to this time, most industrialists had not contributed to Hitler.

The industrialists now had an excellent opportunity to gain influence over the Nazi party by providing Hitler with the desperately needed campaign financing. Little risk was involved, since the Nazis were already a part of the government. On the other hand, if the industrialists didn't give any money to the Nazis, it would be very risky to have no influence over the largest party in the country. Goering and Schacht had talked with their numerous contacts among the industrialists and determined there was at least a good chance the majority of non-Nazi industrialists would come over to Hitler or at least help finance him if approached properly.[15]

Goering sent out telegrams to twenty-five of the most prominent industrialists in Germany, inviting them to Berlin on February 20 to meet with Chancellor Hitler. The meeting took place in the early evening at Goering's residence, the palace of the Reichstag president. The "palace" itself was a large old baroque building with a somber dark interior and heavy Renaissance furniture. Almost all of the invited industrialists attended.

Among those present were Gustav Krupp, the largest armaments manufacturer in the world; Georg von Schnitzler, and two other directors of I.G. Farben, the chemical cartel that had become one of the largest industrial organizations in Europe, and Albert Voegler of United Steel. Also present were several leading bankers and chief executives from other firms in the metal, iron, textile, and automobile industries. The guests sat in chairs that had been carefully arranged according to the power and wealth of their firms. In the front row sat Gustav Krupp, von Schnitzler, two other I.G. Farben directors, and Albert Voegler, of United Steel. Goering spoke first to introduce Hitler. Most of those present had never before met him personally.

With the brief preliminary remarks over, Hitler stood up and began a speech to reassure his audience that he would encourage private enterprise and respect the sanctity of private property. "An impossible situation is created," said Hitler, "when one section of a people favors private property while another denies it. A struggle of that sort tears a people apart and the fight continues until one section emerges victorious. . . . It is not by

31

accident that one man produces more than another; the concept of private property is rooted in this fact. . . . Human beings are anything but equal. As far as the economy is concerned, I have but one desire, namely, that it may enter upon a peaceful future. . . . There will, however, not be a domestic peace unless Marxism has been exterminated."

When Hitler finished speaking the industrialists gave him warm applause. Goering then told the audience that the purpose of the meeting was to finance the election campaign. As far as the money he was asking them to contribute was concerned, Goering said, "The sacrifice asked for from industry will be easier to bear if it is realized that the election of March 5 will be the last for ten years, in all likelihood, indeed, for one hundred years."[16]

Goering was certainly not trying to hide what the Nazis were planning. The audience seemed relieved at the prediction. No more elections would mean no more campaign contributions.

Hjalmar Schacht then announced: "And now gentlemen, your contributions." For several moments there were hushed conversations as the industrialists talked among themselves. Then Krupp stood up and pledged one million marks to the election campaign. Schnitzler of I.G. Farben pledged 400,000 marks. One by one, Schacht got commitments from most of the other members of the audience. By the time the evening was over, he had managed to raise three million marks for the campaign.[17] Naturally this money was to be divided between the Nazis and their coalition partners.

On February 21, the day after Hitler's meeting with the industrialists, the Communists began to take a more aggressive stand in street fights with Nazi storm troopers. The Union of Red Fighters urged the workers to "disarm" the S.A. and the S.S. "Every comrade a commander in the coming Red Army! This is our oath to the Red soldiers of the Soviet Union."[18]

The most violent exhortations were coming from fringe Communist groups rather than the official party leaders. There were, however, still at least six million Communists in Germany, and many working-class neighborhoods in Berlin were solidly "Red." A Communist uprising was certainly a possibility.

Hitler and Goering believed that a Communist revolution was

imminent and they might soon be fighting a civil war. Their strategy, which had already been determined at the first cabinet meeting, was to let the Communists make the first move and then crush them with a strong counterattack.[19] Goering took the increasingly radical Communist rhetoric as an indication that the Red uprising was in the offing and decided to try to provoke them into acting prematurely.

On February 24, Goering's Prussian police raided the Karl Liebknecht House, Communist headquarters in Berlin. No prominent Communists were captured because they escaped from the building through a secret underground tunnel while the police were crashing in the front door. In fact, many Communist leaders had gone into hiding or had quietly slipped out of the country to Russia a week or so earlier. The police did, however, find plenty of Communist literature that was stored in the basement. Along with propaganda pamphlets summoning the masses to armed revolt, Goering said he found the plans for the Communist insurrection. Government buildings were to be set on fire, vital factories sabotaged, Hitler and other political figures assassinated, food and water supplies poisoned, and general looting ordered once the uprising had begun. These were probably just "contingency" plans. The official leadership of the Communist party seemed determined to lay low and not be provoked by the Nazis.

On the evening of February 27, Hitler was taking a night off from campaigning and enjoying dinner with Goebbels and his family in the suburbs. Suddenly the telephone rang at Goebbels's residence. It was Ernst Hanfstaengl, Hitler's foreign press chief. In a very agitated voice he said the Reichstag was on fire.

Meanwhile at the Herrenklub, just a few blocks from the Reichstag, Papen and President von Hindenburg were having dinner. "Suddenly," Papen later recalled, "we noticed a red glow through the windows and heard sounds of shouting in the street. One of the servants came hurrying up to me and whispered: 'The Reichstag is on fire!' which I repeated to the President. He got up and from the window we could see the dome of the Reichstag looking as though it were illuminated by search lights. Every now and then a burst of flame and a swirl of smoke blurred the outline."[20]

A small crowd of people gathered in the Tiergarten Park

across from the Reichstag to watch the firemen fight the blaze. Two large black Mercedes came speeding up to the police cordon around the building and were waved on through. As soon as the first car came to a stop outside the main entrance of the Reichstag building, Hitler jumped out and ran up the broad front steps two at a time with the tails of his trench coat flying. Goebbels and a bodyguard followed him. Once inside, Hitler found Goering, whose face was flush from the heat of the fire. Around him were firemen, fire hoses, and policemen.

Goering came over to Hitler saying: "Without a doubt this is the work of the Communists, Herr Chancellor. . . . We have succeeded in arresting one of the incendiaries." "Who is he?" Goebbels asked. Turning to him, Goering replied: "We don't know yet, but we shall squeeze it out of him."

"Are the other public buildings safe?" Hitler asked.

"I have taken every possible precaution," answered Goering. "I have mobilized all the police. Every public building is guarded. We are ready for anything."

Outside one of the policemen told a reporter: "They got one of them who did it, a man with nothing but his trousers on. Seems to have used his coat and shirt to start the fire."[21]

The man the police captured was Marinus van der Lubbe, a twenty-four-year-old eccentric Communist from Holland. He was stocky, very nearsighted, and awkward, which gave him the appearance of a "half-wit"; but he was not stupid by any means. He had left the Dutch Communist party because it was not radical enough and joined a Communist splinter faction. He had accurately seen Hitler's becoming chancellor as a key turning point in history. Deciding that the Communists and socialists had to do everything they could to resist Hitler, he immediately set out on foot from Leyden, Holland, to Berlin. Hitchhiking part of the way, he arrived in Berlin in a few weeks and went around attending Communist and socialist rallies. Finally he decided the German workers would start a revolution only if they were motivated by some great event. He thought a bold act of terrorism would inspire the masses to revolt.[22]

On the evening of February 26, van der Lubbe had started fires in the Berlin City Hall, the former Imperial Palace, and a government welfare office. The fires were all discovered and put out before they had done any significant damage. The next day, February 27, he bought more matches in the afternoon and then headed for the Reichstag. The weather was bitter cold and there was a frigid wind. He stopped in the Alexander Platz post office for half an hour to get warm. It was dark by the time he reached the Reichstag building. Dressed in a peaked cap and the worn clothes of a manual laborer, he went unnoticed as he circled the Reichstag building several times trying to find the best way in. At about nine in the evening, he found the western entrance to the ornate old building deserted and climbed over the wall. The Reichstag was not in session, so security precautions were minimal.

Once inside the dark empty building, van der Lubbe found his way to the debating chamber, which had wooden deputies' seats and wood-paneled walls and thus was an ideal place to start a fire. It took him only a few minutes to set several fires throughout the chamber. The flames took hold and began to spread. The heat from the blaze broke the circular glass dome overhead and created an updraft, which turned the debating chamber into an inferno. A policeman alerted by a passer-by called the fire department. Van der Lubbe was arrested about twenty minutes later, still hanging around outside the burning building with incendiary material on him. He made a defiant confession saying he did it "as a protest."

Although van der Lubbe's confession was relayed to Goering immediately, he was convinced that the fire was the result of an organized Communist plot and the work of a number of men. Hitler, Goering, and fire department officials began a tour of the building to inspect the damage. They had to step over charred debris and puddles of water. In a hallway Goering found a rag that smelled of gasoline on the floor by one of the half-charred curtains. "Here you can see for yourself, Herr Chancellor," he said, "how they started the fire. They hung rags soaked in gasoline over the furniture and set it on fire."

Turning to Sefton Delmer, a British reporter who was accompanying them, Hitler said: "God grant that this is the work of the Communists. You are witnessing the beginning of a great new epoch in German history. This fire is the beginning." Tripping over a fire hose, he quickly recovered his balance. "You see this

35

building," he went on, "you see how it is aflame? If the Communists got hold of Europe and had control of it for . . . two months, the whole continent would be aflame like this building."[23]

While they were still in the Reichstag building, one of the police inspectors had told Hitler and Goering that the arson looked like the work of a single man. "This is a cunning and well-prepared plot," Hitler scoffed. The more he and Goering talked, the more they sold themselves on the idea of a Communist conspiracy. Hitler was also beginning to realize the great propaganda opportunity the fire offered him. "Now we'll show them!" said Hitler as he became more excited. "Anyone who stands in our way will be mowed down! The German people have been soft too long. Every Communist official must be shot. All Communist deputies must be hanged this very night. All friends of the Communists must be locked up, and that goes for the Social Democrats as well."

After Hitler calmed down, he and Goering drafted more practical orders for the police. By midnight, emergency broadcasts were going out all over Germany on police radios, calling for the arrest of all Communist Reichstag deputies and all local Communist leaders. All Communist newspapers were to be shut down.

After Hitler and Goering parted, Hitler headed for the Berlin offices of the *Völkischer Beobachter*, the Nazi party newspaper, to see how the editors were going to cover the fire. "It took half an hour before I could find anyone to let me in," recalled Hitler. "Inside the editorial offices were empty. The only writer in the building was down in the proof room, hastily writing a short article on the fire for the 'local news' page the next day." Hitler was furious.

"An occurrence like this must go on the front page," he shouted. "Surely your instinct as a journalist should make you realize that!" Someone was sent to get the head editor out of bed. When he arrived, Hitler cursed and raged at him: "Your article ought to be humming through the presses now! All I can say is that it's a masterpiece of inefficiency!" Throwing his trench coat and hat over a chair, Hitler sat down and began to write a lead article for the next day's paper. The front-page headline read "COMMUNISTS SET FIRE TO THE REICHS-TAG!" Hitler stayed at the newspaper offices until he could examine the first issues coming off the presses. By that time it was dawn.[24]

Hitler got no sleep that night. By the time he returned to his quarters in the Chancellery, there was just time to take a bath, change clothes, and eat something before getting ready for the cabinet meeting that morning. He sometimes seemed possessed by an almost demonic energy that enabled him to go without sleep for several days. The more he had time to think, the more he recognized the tremendous opportunity the Reichstag fire offered him. The fear of communism had been the major issue of his election campaign. The fire offered visible proof of the danger that could help terrify middle-class voters. The fire would weaken any resistance the army officers and aristocrats might have to granting him full power.

The excitement of the fire the night before made Hitler bold. He opened the cabinet meeting and began to rant against the Communists. The present danger, he said, called for "a ruthless settling of accounts" with the Communists. He proposed an emergency decree that he and Frick, the Nazi minister of the interior, had hastily written that morning before the cabinet meeting. The decree called for the suspension of all civil liberties: the right of freedom of speech, free press, freedom of assembly. The Weimar constitution, which had granted the rights of a democratic society to Germans since 1919, was to be wiped out in one blow.

There were, however, objections from some other members of the cabinet, particularly the reactionary Hugenberg, who was the leader of the Nationalist party. He agreed with Hitler about the Communist danger and even the need to suspend civil liberties. But he argued that Hitler's decree did not go far enough! He wanted an immediate military dictatorship; a state of military emergency, rule by a group of generals; mass arrests of all Communist and Social Democrat leaders; the outlawing of both the Communist and Social Democratic parties; and the indefinite postponement of the Reichstag elections.

A military dictatorship would have destroyed everything Hitler had worked for. Power was about to slip from his grasp just as he was laying his hands on it. Hugenburg and the conservatives had a majority in the cabinet and could easily outvote Hitler and the two other Nazis.

Just when it seemed Hitler was trapped, General von Blomberg came to his rescue. Blomberg, the minister of defense, said the army was not interested in assuming dictatorial power or declaring martial law. After all, General von Blomberg and his clique had conspired to help make Hitler chancellor to avoid the need for a military dictatorship.* By tradition the German Army wanted to avoid involvement in politics—at least avoid involvement in the everyday business of governing. They wanted to remain the power behind the throne and above all they wanted to avoid being involved in a civil war.

The cabinet meeting went on for hours. Once General von Blomberg refused to accept power on behalf of the army, Hitler was able to persuade the reluctant cabinet to go along with his original decree with some slight modifications. A civil state of emergency was thus substituted for martial law, with the cabinet holding the power usually given to a commanding general.

With the new emergency decree "For the Protection of the People and State," Goering's police became even more powerful.[25] Truckloads of storm troopers and police roared through cities all over Germany, arresting Communists in the middle of the night, dragging them out of bed, and taking them to an S.A. barracks where they were savagely beaten. Sometimes the victims were shot and thrown into a river or lake, or dumped by the roadside. The tremendous hostility between the Nazis and the Communists had been brewing a long time. For years, Communists had beaten up their political opponents and disrupted business and industry with violent strikes.

Far from disapproving of the brutal way the Nazis were treating the Communists, most upper- and middle-class businessmen were relieved to see the "Reds" crushed. The owner of a small factory in northern Germany who was interviewed by a foreign reporter said he was glad the Nazis had taken action

---

*Most generals were not Nazis. The pro-Nazi members of the Officer Corps were still a small minority. General von Hammerstein, a staunch anti-Nazi, was commander in chief of the army until February 1934.

against the Communists. This man was not a Nazi and disapproved of many of Hitler's methods, but in the fall of 1932 some of his loyal employees told him that his name was on the death list of the Communist party. When the Red uprising began, he was to be executed, his wife and children taken hostage, and his factory burned. For months he lived in fear. He kept a car secretly waiting near his home so that he could be ready to escape across the border when the Communist revolution began. It would certainly be understandable if the purge of the Communists came as a great relief to such a man.

Were the Communists really planning a revolution in Germany in 1933?[26] Hitler and Goering probably believed that a Communist uprising was imminent. They both had lived through the Communist revolution in 1918 and knew many people who had lost everything in the Russian Revolution. The approximately six or seven million Communists in Germany would have been difficult to suppress without a bloody civil war.

The day after the fire, Goering, as Prussian minister of the interior, addressed the nation by radio, describing the burning of the Reichstag as one part of a Communist plan to commit acts of terror throughout the country. In Germany Goering's explanation of the fire was widely believed. In fact, peasants in the Brandenburg countryside around Berlin were so frightened they took turns as sentries at the village wells to prevent Red terrorists from poisoning their water supply.

However, outside Germany, where people were not so naive, the Communist conspiracy story was discounted. Soon there was a growing sentiment that the Nazis had burned the Reichstag themselves as a pretext for suppressing the Communist party. In order to quiet the international uproar, Hitler agreed to a public trial for van der Lubbe and three other Communists accused of being conspirators. Fortunately for Hitler the trial would not begin until after the elections.

The Reichstag fire worked to Hitler's advantage by winning over a number of middle- and upper-class voters terrified by the thought of a Red revolution in Germany. Hitler was clever enough not to outlaw the Communist party until after the election so the lower-class vote would remain divided between the Communists and the Social Democrats.

As the election day neared, the Nazis finished up with a

whirlwind campaign. There were torchlight parades and mass rallies. On the hills above the Rhine valley, Nazi bonfires lit up the night. The Communist danger was Hitler's main campaign theme.

While Hitler spoke in lofty terms of self-sacrifice, Goering was speaking with more brutal frankness. He told an audience in Frankfurt: "My measures will not be crippled by any bureaucracy. I won't have to worry about justice, my mission is only to destroy and exterminate [Marxism]."[27] At a private dinner party for wealthy Nazi supporters, Goering spoke openly of the things he intended to do. "I know exactly what is happening all through the Reich. . . . The remotest hideout of the Communists is known to us. There were eight million Communist votes at the last election. We won't forget them. We're building concentration camps now." His fat chest glittered with medals and a blood lust flickered in his eyes as he went on: "You must not be shocked by what some people call excesses. Flogging, general cruelty, even deaths . . . these are the inevitable in a forceful, sweeping young revolution."[28] No one objected or contradicted.

The German people went to the polls on March 5, 1933, for the last free elections Germany would have in years. In spite of all the propaganda, intimidation, and millions of marks contributed to Hitler's campaign, the majority of Germans voted against him. True, the Nazis received more votes than any other party, 17,277,180 or 44 percent of the total vote. Hitler had won five million more votes than the last election, but he was still unable to get a decisive majority. The Communists received 4,848,100 votes, even though most of their leaders were in jail. The Social Democrats maintained their position as the second largest party with 7,181,600 votes. The Nationalist party, led by Hugenberg, was very disappointed with its showing of only 3,136,760 votes.

Although the Nazis openly boasted of their "victory," secretly Hitler was also disappointed. He had a bare majority in the new Riechstag with 288 Nazi seats, plus 52 Nationalist seats, out of a total of 647. This was enough to remain in office and perhaps carry out the everyday business of government, but it was far from the two-thirds majority he needed to vote himself dictatorial powers.

President von Hindenburg was pleased with the election

results. At last, he had a nationalistic government that had a majority in the Reichstag. When the election returns came in he was visibly excited and boomed out in a satisfied voice: "Hitler wins!" After the election results were confirmed, Hitler said Hindenburg "told me straight out that he had always been averse to the parliamentary game, and was delighted that the comedy of elections was now done with once and for all."[29]

Chapter 2

Steps Toward Dictatorship

Because the results of the elections were inconclusive, it was more important than ever for Hitler to strengthen his ties with the upper class. President von Hindenburg, the army, the aristocrats, and the industrialists all wanted a restoration of the monarchy. But they were afraid to impose a king on the country. They wanted the monarchy to have popular support among ordinary people. Hence the need for Hitler, who in turn manipulated these conservative elements, leading them to believe that he too favored an eventual restoration of the Hohenzollerns. Actually, nothing was further from his mind. But he needed the conservatives because they still held the real power and controlled the army, the foreign office, and the economy. Even President von Hindenburg alone could have overruled him if he had really wanted to. Also, princes and aristocrats were now contributing large sums to the Nazis, not as large as the industrialists, but significant sums nevertheless.

Hitler's eagerness to be in the good graces of the princes became the social gossip of Berlin. He made it his business to attend a number of elegant society parties, although he was always uncomfortable at such affairs.

He would bow deeply and kiss the hands of the titled ladies. Sometimes he would even personally dash off to bring some duchess or baroness a drink, which was unheard of for a chancellor to do. He did not, however, indulge with them in caviar, pheasant, or champagne but contented himself with some orange juice and occasionally nibbled on a lettuce leaf. Beaming with a servile smile, he would stand in respectful silence listening to the pointless chitchat of senile old aristocrats and their wives.

Of all the German princes the six sons of the former kaiser were the most important because their attitude and behavior influenced other conservative Germans. However, most of the kaiser's sons had no use for Hitler. Only Prince August Wilhelm was a devoted Nazi. Goering had persuaded him to join the Nazi party several years before Hitler became chancellor. The prince, who had the dark piercing eyes of his ancestor Frederick the Great was seen frequently with Hitler in the 1930s. He served as a Nazi member of the Reichstag and with his great wealth gave generous contributions to Nazi causes.[1] Hitler deviously hinted and started rumors that he was grooming August Wilhelm to be the next kaiser after the monarchy was restored.

Even those princes who were pro-Nazis would probably have not been so enthusiastic in their support of Hitler if the former kaiser, living in exile in Holland, had objected. But not only did he not object, he had become pro-Nazi himself. His motives for backing Hitler were summed up by his grandson Prince Wilhelm: "You know, Grandfather really lives in the illusion that the Nazis are going to restore our throne!"*

To further ingratiate himself with the monarchists and convince them he was a traditional nationalist rather than a dangerous radical, Hitler needed a supreme gesture of conciliation. A current predicament provided an answer.

The opening session of the newly elected Reichstag was scheduled for March 21. But with the Reichstag building burned, where were the deputies to meet? Hitler chose the Potsdam

---

*The name Wilhelm was very popular with the German royal family. The former kaiser was Kaiser Wilhelm II. His first-born son was Crown Prince Wilhelm. The kaiser named his fourth son Prince August Wilhelm. Crown Prince Wilhelm also named his eldest son Prince Wilhelm. This prince was the kaiser's grandson.

Garrison Church. In the crypt of the church lay the tomb of Frederick the Great. The church was a shrine of German nationalism and military spirit.

There was a heavy downpour all night on March 20, but on the morning of the twenty-first the clouds scattered and the sun came out. The bells of the old church rang loud and clear in the brisk spring air as the officials and audience assembled.

The central gallery of the church was reserved for the royal family. In the front stood an empty chair symbolizing the place held for the exiled Kaiser Wilhelm II; behind it stood the Crown Prince and his brothers. The nave was occupied by members of the Reichstag with the exception of the Communist deputies, who were in prison, and the Social Democrats, who chose not to come. At the appointed hour, President von Hindenburg and Hitler entered the church, and the audience rose to their feet. Wearing his field marshal's uniform and spiked helmet, Hindenburg walked slowly down the center aisle leaning heavily on his cane. Although the years had taken their toll, he still stood tall and possessed the calm dignity of a veteran leader. When he reached the Royal Gallery he turned and raised his marshal's baton to salute the empty seat of his sovereign. Hitler, dressed in a formal black tail coat and gray-striped pants, walked at Hindenburg's side. The French ambassador said he "looked like a timid newcomer being introduced by an important protector into a company to which he does not belong."[2]

Hitler made a short speech about Germany regaining her place among the great powers of the world. To conclude the ceremony there was an army parade outside the church. In the front row of spectators stood the Crown Prince, who looked as if he were reviewing his own troops.

On March 23, the newly elected deputies of the Reichstag assembled at the Kroll Opera House, which had been chosen as the temporary site of the Reichstag. The atmosphere was tense. S.A. and S.S. men patrolled the aisles and corridors, and a huge black, white, and red swastika banner hung behind the stage.

The bill the Nazis had just submitted to the house was the so-called Enabling Act. The proposed bill took the power of legislation, including control of the budget, away from the

Reichstag and gave it to the cabinet for a period of four years. The bill also stated that the laws enacted by the cabinet could deviate from the constitution. The powers of the president were to remain undisturbed. Passage of the bill would move Hitler one step closer to dictatorial powers.

Intense negotiations on the bill had been going on for several days. Hitler needed a two-thirds' majority to pass such a measure, and he did not have the votes even with Communist deputies absent. The 120 Social Democratic deputies were strongly united against the bill. The only significant block of votes for Hitler to win over was the ninety-two deputies of the Catholic Center party.

Since the days of Bismarck, the Center party had traditionally played on the balance of power in German politics. They had thus been able to negotiate deals to preserve the independence of the Catholic Church. It was clearly in the best interests of the Center party to vote against the Enabling Act.

Hitler was busy with intrigues behind the scenes to put pressure on Center party politicians. Hitler had two powerful sources of influence he was attempting to use on the Catholic deputies: the authority of the pope and threats from the financial backers of the Center party.

Hitler's agents had been negotiating with papal representatives for several weeks. Why was the pope willing to deal with Hitler? Pope Pius XI was adamantly anti-Communist and pro-Fascist. He was pleased with Mussolini's Fascist government in Italy.

It was assumed by many, including Pope Pius XI, that the Nazis were just the German variety of fascism. When the pope met with Papen later that year, he expressed "his pleasure that at the head of the German state was a man like Hitler, on whose banner the uncompromising struggle against communism . . . was inscribed."[3]

Pope Pius XI also disapproved in principle of Catholic political parties. In Italy, he had preferred the Fascists over the Catholic Popular party.

Through his agents, Hitler offered the pope concessions on the issue of religious education in return for the withdrawal of Vatican support from the Center party. On the other hand, if the pope continued to back the Center party, Hitler said he would not be able to control "forces" in the Nazi party that wanted to close Catholic schools and abolish the Catholic Youth movements.

The pope decided to withdraw his support from the Center party. Monsignor Pizzardo, the Vatican undersecretary of state, later told a foreign diplomat: "The Holy See is not interested in the Center party. We are more concerned with the mass of Catholic voters in Germany than in the Catholic deputies who represent them in the Reichstag."[4] For a movement like the Catholic Center party, which was based on religious allegiance, the lack of the pope's support was a terrible blow.

There were, however, some members of the Center party, like former chancellor Bruening, who were still opposed to voting for Hitler's bill regardless of what the pope thought. To break down this resistance, Hitler also applied pressure and threats to the financiers of the Center party.

There was still some doubt on March 23 how the deputies of the Center party would vote. Before the vote was taken, Hitler marched up to the podium to speak. There were shouts of "Sieg Heil! Sieg Heil!" and wild applause from the boisterous Nazi deputies in their brown shirts. The Social Democrats looked nervous as they sat quietly. The deputies of the Center party seemed worried and undecided.

Hitler's speech was moderate at first. He promised to respect private property and individual initiative—to aid the peasants and the unemployed—and to seek peace with France, Britain, and even Russia. He gave reassurances to the Reichstag, the president, the states, and the churches that none of their rights would be infringed upon by the Enabling Act. However, he blamed Germany's problems on the Versailles Treaty and the "breed of traitors" who had ruled Germany. "Sedition and treason," he shouted, "will in the future be burned out with barbaric ruthlessness." In closing, he implied that it would be smarter for the Reichstag to give him the powers of the Enabling Act voluntarily rather than compel him to seize them by force. "Now, gentlemen," he concluded, "you may yourselves decide for peace or war."

After a short recess the leader of the Social Democrats, Otto Wels, stood up to speak against the bill. It was a courageous speech, considering the circumstances. Wels affirmed his faith in democracy. The right to criticize the government, he said, was beneficial to a nation, and its critics should not be persecuted.

Thanks to Nazi spies, Hitler had seen a copy of Wels's speech before it was delivered. His rebuttal was well prepared. It seethed with all the resentment that had built up inside him during the years in opposition. In spite of Papen's attempt to restrain him, Hitler rushed back to the podium as soon as Wels had finished.

In a savage and mocking voice he began: "You talk about persecution. I think there are only a few of us [Nazis] here who did not have to suffer persecution and prison from your government. . . . You say that criticism is beneficial. You should have recognized the benefits of criticism during the time we were in the opposition. . . . In those days our press was forbidden time after time, our meetings were forbidden, and I was forbidden to speak, for years on end.

"I do not want your votes," he thundered to the Social Democrats in concluding. "Germany will be free, but not through you. The star of Germany is ascending, yours is about to disappear. Your death knell has sounded."

There were prolonged applause and shouts of "Heil" from the galleries. The speech not only demonstrated Hitler's well-known ability to crush an opponent in debate but it also gave the world a glimpse of his psychology. The hatred with which the Nazis fought, pummeled, and persecuted their own opponents contained all the bitterness and savage brutality of an abused underling who finally rises to the top and is determined to avenge himself.

When the speakers were finished, Goering, as president of the Reichstag, prepared to call for a vote. The atmosphere was at a boiling point. From the corridors came the chanting of the storm troopers: "We want the bill—or blood and murder!" The square outside the Kroll Opera House was packed with Nazis shouting and howling.

When the vote was taken, Monsignor Kass, the leader of the Center party, stood and announced that his party would vote for

47

the bill.* Goering quickly tallied the votes—441 for it and 94 against. The Nazis leaped to their feet shouting and "heiling." Then they sang the "Horst Wessel Song." In the square outside, the crowd roared its approval. Hitler had his victory. He would no longer be restrained by the Reichstag and democracy.[5]

Although free of the Reichstag, Hitler's powers were still limited by the cabinet. He explained his difficulties to some provincial Nazi leaders who were visiting Berlin: "The reactionary forces believe they have me on a leash. They will set as many traps for me as they can. I know that they hope I will achieve my own ruin by mismanagement. . . . But we shall not wait for them to act. Our great opportunity lies in acting before they do. And we have no scruples. I have no bourgeois hesitations. . . . I have had to accept harsh conditions. [A cabinet dominated by conservatives.] I shall observe them as long as I am forced to do so."

As he spoke he got up from behind his desk and prowled restlessly up and down his small Chancellery office. "I have sown fear and apprehension in the hearts of those old women Hugenberg and company. . . . They regard me as an uneducated barbarian," he exclaimed. "Yes, we are barbarians! We want to be barbarians! It is an honorable title. We shall rejuvenate the world! This world is near its end. It is our mission to cause unrest. Barbarian forces," he said, "must break into decadent civilizations in order to snatch the torch of life from their dying fires."[6]

Anti-Semitism was unquestionably the most barbaric aspect of Hitler's character. Once Hitler became chancellor, the Nazis were determined to make life in Germany unpleasant for Jews. A new wave of anti-Semitism swept across the land. Jews were ridiculed, cursed, and slandered; some were even physically attacked on the streets of Berlin. In the smaller towns and countryside, beatings of Jews were common occurrences. The racial persecution and anti-Semitic hatred that had suddenly

---

*To get the votes of the Center party, Hitler had personally promised Kass that he would guarantee in writing political and civil liberty. But it was just another one of his tricks and lies.

exploded in Germany did not go unnoticed by the international press. People in America and Britain had not paid much attention to stories of beatings and murders of Communists, because many people felt they were getting what they deserved. The Jews, on the other hand, were a defenseless minority.

Articles in the foreign press about the mistreatment of Jews in Germany infuriated the Nazis. Instead of acting as a restraint on Hitler, the publication of such articles was like waving a red flag in front of a bull. He was determined to make the Jews in Germany pay for what he called "the atrocity propaganda" of the American and British Jews.

Hitler carefully mapped out the next step in his attack on the Jews with his newly appointed minister of propaganda, the vicious, clubfooted, little Dr. Goebbels. In his diary entry for March 26, Goebbels wrote: "Travel to Munich by night, and from there to Berchtesgaden, where the Fuehrer had summoned me. He has thoroughly thought over the situation up in the solitude of the mountains, and has made up his mind. We shall only be able to combat the falsehoods abroad if we get at those who have originated them . . . namely, the Jews living in Germany. So we must proceed to an extensive boycott of Jewish business in Germany. Perhaps the foreign Jews will think better of it, when they see their racial brethren hard pressed."[7]

The boycott was scheduled to begin on April 1. The evening before, Italian ambassador Cerruti met with Hitler and urged him to call it off. Cerruti said Mussolini felt anti-Semitic persecutions would only discredit the Nazi movement. Hitler was not to be deterred. He told Cerruti that since there were only a small number of Jews in Italy, Mussolini did not understand "the Jewish question." But he said he had studied it "for long years, from every angle, like no one else."[8]

On the morning of April 1, brown-shirted storm troopers were posted outside all Jewish-owned shops and department stores. The Nazis carried signs with anti-Jewish slogans and painted Stars of David on some shop windows. In general, there was little violence. Customers were allowed to enter the stores, if they had the courage to walk past the storm troopers' picket lines. Most people preferred to watch from a distance.

In the center of Berlin, there was the stamping of heavy Nazi boots on the sidewalk outside the offices of the Ullstein Publishing Company, which published several of Germany's leading newspapers and was Jewish owned. In chorus the Brownshirts shouted, "To hell with Jews!" Then they sang the Nazi anthem, the "Horst Wessel Song." At the train stations in Berlin, companies of Brownshirts were also marching back and forth shouting: "To hell with Jews! Death to the Jews! Jews get out!"

Hitler and Goebbels were congratulating themselves. They thought they had discovered a way to paralyze the business of all Jewish stores and destroy them economically. However, Hitler soon received complaints against the boycott from an entirely different quarter than he had expected. His newly appointed president of the Reichbank and longtime financier, Hjalmar Schacht, rushed in to see him, demanding the boycott be called off at once. Schacht told Hitler that the economic destruction of the Jews would create an economic vacuum that would inevitably suck in a large number of German businesses as well. A number of bank failures would be unavoidable. If Hitler refused to call off the boycott, Schacht said he would resign.

No sooner had Hitler finished talking to Schacht, than he received another protest, this time from Hindenburg. The president sent Hitler a special letter by courier condemning the mistreatment of the Jewish war veterans. "If they were worthy of fighting and bleeding for Germany, they must be considered worthy of continuing to serve the Fatherland in their professions."[9]

In the face of such pressure from all sides, Hitler backed down and instructed Dr. Goebbels that the boycott would not be resumed on April 2. Outwardly it looked as if reason had triumphed; Hindenburg and the industrialists were still able to control Hitler. But those who believed Hitler would abandon his anti-Semitic campaign were mistaken. They completely underestimated the intensity of his hatred of the Jews.

On April 7, Hitler enacted a decree removing all Jews from the civil service. Then in rapid succession a number of laws were passed limiting the rights of Jews to practice law, medicine, and dentistry. Local governments began dismissing Jewish judges or "suggesting" they "retire." In some cases, the Brownshirts marched into the local courthouse, physically threw the Jewish judges and lawyers out in the street, and warned them never to return if they valued their lives.

Although Hindenburg had at first opposed Hitler's more extreme anti-Semitic measures, his resolve was gradually weakened by Hitler's lie that the Jews monopolized 80 percent of the professions of law and medicine. "One of the major reasons the old Prussian State was such a clean one was that the Jews were granted only a very limited access to the civil service," said Hitler. And "the Officer Corps kept itself almost entirely pure." Evidence of Hitler's success in turning Hindenburg into an anti-Semite was seen at a dinner at the Swedish legation in Berlin. The king of Sweden, who was present, expressed certain criticisms of Germany's persecution of Jews. Hindenburg denied there was any persecution and in his deep bass voice grumbled that the treatment of the German Jews was a purely domestic problem and hence the responsibility of the German chancellor alone.

In April, a member of Gustav Krupp's board of directors told a friend that the anti-Jewish boycott was very unpopular among his business associates. Most of his colleagues had refused to take part, he said. From the tone of his conversation it was clear this man had no sympathy for Hitler or anti-Semitism. Prior to 1933, Gustav Krupp had not been an admirer of Hitler. However, once Hitler became chancellor, he helped fund his March election campaign. But he was not yet fully committed to Hitler. True, Krupp wanted a chancellor who would push rearmament and crush Marxism; but Hitler was still unproven. The Nazis might not last.

When Krupp went to Berlin on business a week before the Enabling Act was passed, he conferred with some of the top generals and the men close to Hindenburg. From them he learned that some of the most important army officers and the president stood solidly behind Hitler. That removed many of Krupp's doubts.[10]

The Enabling Act seemed to be a milestone for Krupp. After the Reichstag abdicated its powers to the Hitler cabinet, Gustav Krupp became an outspoken Nazi. The day after the passage of the Enabling Act he wrote a formal letter to Hitler stating that he and the other industrialists of the Ruhr agreed that Germany finally had "the basis for a stable government. Difficulties which arose in the past from constant political fluctuations, and which

obstructed economic initiative to a high degree, have been eliminated."[11]

On April 1, the very day of the anti-Jewish boycott, Krupp had
a private meeting with Hitler at the Chancellery. Krupp had
come to Berlin not to complain about the Jewish boycott but to
cement an alliance between himself and Hitler. At the meeting
Krupp agreed to become Hitler's chief fund-raiser, and Hitler in
turn promised to appoint Krupp the fuehrer of German industry.

In April, Krupp began his job as chairman of the Adolf Hitler
Fund. He approached Germany's leading industrialists, requesting contributions for Hitler. He told them the situation was
urgent: "Whoever helps quickly, helps doubly!"[12] Why was the
need for money so urgent? The Nazi party was an enormous
organization with heavy daily expenses. In 1933 approximately
25 percent of the members were unemployed and couldn't even
pay the nominal party dues. The S.A. now numbered over one-
half million men, a force larger than the armies of most nations,
indeed five times the number of men in the German Army itself.
The expenses for the upkeep of the S.A. were astronomical. The
unemployed storm troopers had to be clothed, fed, and housed
at the party's expense.

Gustav Krupp voluntarily served as chairman of the Adolf
Hitler Fund for a number of years until he was succeeded by his
son, Alfried. The fund was the largest source of private contributions to the Nazi party. The stated purpose of the Adolf Hitler
Fund was "to support the S.A., S.S., Hitler Youth, and political
organization of the Nazi party."

There was, however, another purpose for the Adolf Hitler
Fund—to organize industry's contributions into one central
fund and thus free industrialists from the numerous solicitations
of Nazi organizations. By April of 1933, all sorts of Nazi
organizations and groups, the S.A., the S.S., local party leaders,
even the Nazi women's organization, were pestering the industrialists with incessant requests for money. The situation was
getting out of control.

How much money actually went into the Adolf Hitler Fund?
Krupp helped develop a proposal by which German companies
would give a definite monthly contribution to Hitler. All
branches of the economy—industry, banking, retail trade, agriculture, and insurance—would contribute on the basis of one-

half percent of the 1932 payments made by each contributor for salaries and wages.* Over thirty million marks were contributed to the fund in 1933.[13]

Over the years, Gustav Krupp contributed six million marks of his own money to the Adolf Hitler Fund. If his correspondence is any indication, he seemed to enjoy thoroughly his job as chairman of the Fund.[14]

Why would a businessman take pride in his support for an authoritarian regime that had just suppressed democracy in his country? Many German industrialists, particularly weapons manufacturers like Krupp, were not advocates of the free-enterprise system. Industry had traditionally sought political favors and regarded the government as an ally. They were actually eager for an authoritarian regime, especially one that would abolish the Marxist labor unions. The more government contracts a company could get, the greater its profits.

When Hitler met with people, including industrialists, he usually made a favorable impression. If he wanted to he could appear to be a rational, intelligent politician. Some businessmen found him so persuasive, his appeal was difficult to resist. One wealthy woman said there was something about him that made you feel compelled to help him. "Did he impress you as a criminal or maniac?" people often asked British journalist Sefton Delmer, who interviewed him on numerous occasions. "Neither," said Delmer. "The truth is that the very first impression he made on me was that of a rather ordinary fellow."[15]

Hitler's two extraordinary physical characteristics were his voice and eyes. No one, said Delmer, "spoke with the passion, the volubility and the concentration of Hitler." When asked a question, his reply would swell into an oration as more and more ideas flowed into his "imaginative and highly articulate mind."[16]

While Hitler was talking with a person, he would fix them in the gaze of his large, blue hypnotic eyes. Almost everyone who met him mentioned his strangely compelling eyes. Martha Dodd, the daughter of the American ambassador, found his eyes

---

*It is not known how many businesses contributed to the fund. However, the contributions were almost compulsory.

"startling and unforgettable." His eyes had been his most outstanding feature since youth. His eyes, a boyhood friend recalled,

> were so outstanding that one didn't notice anything else. Never in my life have I seen any other person whose appearance was so completely dominated by the eyes. They were the light eyes of his mother, but her somewhat staring, penetrating gaze was even more marked in the son and had even more force and expressiveness. It was uncanny how those eyes could change their expression, especially when Adolf was speaking. . . . In fact, Adolf spoke with his eyes. When he first came to our house and I introduced him to my mother, she said to me in the evening, "What eyes your friend has!" And I remember quite distinctly that there was more fear than admiration in her words.[17]

The magnetism of his eyes seemed to be something Hitler could turn on and off at will. He used it as a persuasive tool on crowds as well as individuals. On one occasion Hitler was sitting in a train compartment talking with Sefton Delmer after a Nazi rally in Coblenz. A few minutes before the train was ready to leave the station, Hitler's adjutant Bruckner opened the compartment door and told Hitler that two girls had run all the way from the stadium where the rally was held to shake hands with him. Hitler got up and went out into the train corridor to meet the girls. They were almost hysterical, kissing his hand, shrieking, and crying.

When Hitler returned to his seat, it was obvious he was extremely moved. His face was in a "trancelike" expression. He opened the window and looked out at the people on the station platform. "He gazed at them," said Delmer, "with his mesmeric stare turning in an arc like a searchlight from left to right, exposing everyone within sight to the emotion the two girls had inspired in him and which he was now throwing back into the crowd. Then with the men and women on the platform still cheering and clapping, he slowly raised the window again, drew the curtains and sat down to resume our conversation. And he resumed it at the exact point where he had broken off."[18]

Hitler's popularity wasn't just due to his charisma or Nazi

propaganda; he was riding the crest of a wave of nationalist hysteria. In many ways the mood was like that in Germany in 1914, when people cheered the declaration of war and rushed off gladly to fight their neighbors. The Germans were going through another period of superchauvinism, bullying, and conformity. Everyone was "Heiling" everyone else to prove they were "good Germans." Some of these very same people contemptuously referred to Hitler as "that man" before January 30.

The millions of marks Gustav Krupp raised for the Adolf Hitler Fund were a great help to the Nazis, but Hitler was surprised to learn from the party treasurer, Schwarz, it was not enough. Roehm needed more money for the S.A. In spite of every effort to put storm troopers and party members on the government payroll in every capacity from police to clerks, there were still thousands of unemployed S.A. men the Nazis had to support. Hitler worried that the allegiance of the unemployed could be fickle. Many of them had only recently dropped out of the Social Democratic or Communist parties to join the Nazis, and if they were not supported, they could easily swing back to marxism. The financial situation was so tight that even the guards at the concentration camps were underpaid, overworked, and threatened to mutiny.*

Hitler tried to come up with some scheme to raise money. Goering and Schacht assured him that no more funds could be squeezed out of industry or wealthy party sympathizers this year. Schwarz, a skilled accountant, was doing everything possible to cut down on corruption and economize on the party budget.

Dr. Robert Ley, the short, fat alcoholic who was in charge of the Nazi Labor Front, had a suggestion. The labor unions were loaded with money. They had built up their strike funds for years. They even had their own banks for the workers. There were union newspapers and buildings, and it was all worth hundreds of millions of marks. Why not take over the unions, Ley argued, and confiscate their money?

---

*The first concentration camps were established in the spring of 1933 to hold the overflow of prisoners arrested after the Reichstag fire. At this time most of the prisoners were Communists or socialists.

Realizing he would have to break the power of the socialist labor unions sometime if he was to establish an authoritarian state, Hitler decided it might as well be now. He knew his financiers were anxious to see the unions crushed so they would be freed from disruptive strikes and demands for higher wages. However, the Nazis had to be careful. The unions had over four million members. A general strike by these same unions had caused the conservative Kapp putsch to collapse in 1922. The unions still had the power to paralyze the entire country.

Hitler and his propaganda chief, Dr. Goebbels, hatched a brilliant piece of trickery. For over fifty years, May Day had been Marxism's traditional day of celebration for the worker. In order to deceive the union leaders and the socialist workers and lull them into a false sense of security, the Nazis proclaimed May Day a national holiday. The government assured the union leaders that their participation in the festival planned for May 1 would not be political, but rather a sign of solidarity among all Germans who worked.

Meanwhile Hitler and Goebbels were busy working together planning a May Day spectacle that would surpass anything the workers had seen at the traditional Marxist rallies. The main feature of the Nazi demonstration was to be a huge rally at Tempelhof airfield at night, concluding with a massive fireworks display.

May 1 turned out to be a beautiful sunny day. Church bells rang all over Berlin. In the late afternoon hundreds of thousands of people began streaming out of Berlin toward Tempelhof field on the outskirts of the city. Some walked with their families, others marched in formation with the other workers from their factory or office.

Out at Tempelhof field, the huge dirigible *Graf Zeppelin* flew overhead. It made a majestic sight as it circled in the late afternoon sunset. The rows and rows of grandstands, hung with bright swastika banners, were already packed hours before dark. The bands played martial music, and the crowd, which numbered a half-million, enthusiastically sang patriotic songs.[19]

At dusk the weather changed. A chilly wind stirred up, and it started to sprinkle rain. But at last, the waiting was over. There was a distant murmur and then tumultuous applause as Hitler, standing in his car, his arm raised in the Nazi salute, made his appearance. It was soon dark and searchlights pointing up in the night sky were turned on, their gentle bluish light setting off contrasting gaps of darkness. After a few introductory comments by Goebbels, Hitler stood up to speak. A hushed silence fell over the multitude. Suddenly most of the searchlights were turned off, except for a few near Hitler that were turned up. Their beams, after reaching high in the dark sky overhead, met and formed a giant cone or magic tower of light over his head.

Hitler began by praising labor and the role of the worker in the framework of society. This May Day, he said, was a symbol of rebirth, of national unity instead of division, an end of domestic class warfare. He outlined a program by which the nation would be rejuvenated by work. There would be public works on a large scale to end unemployment. The new Germany would no longer be subject to social conflict.

Hitler's voice was amplified by loudspeakers all around the field, and he spoke first with warmth and then built up to a fierce passion as he concluded. Free of class conflict Germany would once again become a powerful and respected nation, he shouted; once again she would follow her true destiny of glory and grandeur.

When Hitler finished there was a tremendous ovation. The bands then struck up the German national anthem, "Deutschland Über Alles" ("Germany Above All"). Skyrockets then signaled the beginning of a magnificent fireworks display, ending with thunderous explosions in the distance that sounded like the hellish artillery barrages of World War I.

This great spectacle left the masses spellbound just as Hitler had intended. At ten the next morning, May 2, he struck. S.A., Brownshirts, and police seized and occupied all labor union offices, newspapers, cooperative centers, and lodging houses. Eighty-eight union leaders were arrested. Special units under the direction of Dr. Ley seized the labor union banks, files, and bank accounts. Total union assets seized amounted to over 184,000,000 marks.[20] It would be enough money to support the Nazi party for over a year. It was over sixty times the amount of money the industrialists had given the Nazis for the March elections, and it was over six times the thirty million Gustav Krupp had raised for Hitler.

From the powerful unions there was no resistance and hardly

any protest. Decapitated, the giant organizations were powerless. In an effort to reassure the workers, Hitler promised to protect their rights.

Hitler's true labor policy became very clear less than a month later when he issued a decree ending collective bargaining. Henceforth, labor disputes were to be settled by Nazi "labor trustees" whose decisions were legally binding. There would be no strikes in the new Germany. The Nazi Labor Front pledged not to disrupt business. Ley further promised "to restore absolute leadership to the natural leader of a factory—that is the employer . . . only the employer can decide."

His triumph over the labor unions did not satiate Hitler's appetite for power; on the contrary, it was only part of a process the Nazis called "coordination" (i.e., Nazification).

By the summer of 1933, Hitler had made great strides on the road to dictatorship. He had firmly established Nazi control throughout Germany by controlling the police. The Communists had been suppressed. He had abolished democracy with the Enabling Act. He had taken over the labor unions and seized their great wealth. Finally he had outlawed all opposition political parties, by using the powers granted to him in the Enabling Act.[21]

But dangerous problems lay ahead for Hitler. He had come to power on a coalition of three forces—mass popular support, financial support from certain business interests, and support from a powerful group of pro-Nazi officers in the army. Now this coalition was threatening to break apart. The S.A. and the left-wing Nazis were beginning to call for a second or "true socialist" revolution against big business and the Junkers, the Prussian landed aristocracy. Naturally this alarmed Hitler's financiers and they demanded that such "revolutionary" advocacy be stopped. To make matters worse, rivalry was developing between Ernst Roehm, the leader of the rapidly growing, two-million-strong S.A., and the army. Hitler might be forced into the uncomfortable position of having to choose sides between his own Nazi S.A. and the army. He would lose either way.

Chapter 3

Hitler Was Given His Orders

Sunday, July 1, 1934, was a warm summer day in Berlin. The temperature was over eighty degrees. On the outskirts of the city, thousands of people were enjoying themselves on the shores of Berlin's lakes. In the city, Hitler was giving an afternoon tea party in the Chancellery gardens for diplomats and government officials. Waiters with polished brass buttons and white gloves served drinks from silver trays. Surrounded by a group of attractive women, Hitler was smiling and seemed to be enjoying himself. A careful observer, however, would have noticed that he was tense. When there was a sudden noise from a tray dropping, he jumped but immediately regained his composure.[1]

Hitler had good reason to be tense that day. At the Lichterfield Cadet School, only a few miles away from the Chancellery, his Nazi comrades were being lined up against a wall in the courtyard and shot. Some of the men shouted a defiant "Heil Hitler!" before the bullets riddled their bodies. The shooting had been going on all morning at about thirty-minute intervals. All over Germany, men were being murdered that weekend. Some were close friends and associates of Hitler, while others were men who had personally opposed him.

In Munich, at about ten o'clock on Saturday morning, two

automobiles pulled up outside the villa of Ritter von Kahr, a retired Bavarian politician who had opposed Hitler during the 1923 putsch. The seventy-three-year-old von Kahr was still in his robe and slippers when he answered the door. Before he had a chance to say a word, the three men on his doorstep grabbed him and hustled him off toward one of the waiting cars. It was broad daylight, but his neighbors did nothing to help. Later, Kahr's body was found in a marsh near the little town of Dachau, hacked apart by pick axes.[2] Other men had been murdered in their offices, on their doorstep, or shot and pushed from speeding cars on the highway.

No one attending Hitler's party at the Chancellery seemed to be aware that anything unusual was going on. Hitler moved easily among the diplomats and ladies. Occasionally he sipped on a glass of lemonade. While the party was going on, one of Hitler's adjutants came up to hand him a note. As he read it, he turned pale. He quickly said good-bye to some of his guests and left the party. What was in the note that had so visibly upset Hitler? It said that Ernst Roehm had been executed. Ernst Roehm had been one of Hitler's closest friends and the second most powerful man in the Nazi party.

In the turbulent days at the end of World War I, it was Ernst Roehm, then an army captain, who had "discovered" Hitler. Roehm was really the cofounder of the Nazi party. If he had not extended the army's protection over the fledgling movement, it would never have gotten off the ground. The first significant sums of money Hitler received were given to him by Roehm from the secret Free Corps (anti-Communist paramilitary units) slush funds. Roehm also organized the first storm troopers from unemployed Free Corps men. He introduced Hitler to prominent people and taught him how to behave among officers and wealthy people.

Historians have explained the bloody Roehm purge, which took place on Saturday, June 30, and Sunday, July 1, 1934, as a personal power struggle between Hitler and Roehm. Indeed, Hitler himself later presented it this way. But Roehm was loyal to Hitler; they only differed on the path to be taken toward a goal they both agreed upon.

The Roehm purge was much more than a personal rivalry between two men. It was an extremely complex power struggle with many forces, some representing powerful economic interest groups intriguing against one another. There were three main rivalries: (1) the socialist Nazis, who were allied with Roehm and the S.A., were against Papen and the conservatives; (2) they were also against rightist Nazis like Goering and his industrialist patrons; and (3) Papen and the conservatives, along with some anti-Nazi generals, were plotting on their own to get rid of both Roehm and Hitler and reestablish the monarchy.

Hitler was trying to play all these forces off one against another. In the power struggle, in the spring and summer of 1934, he demonstrated his agility as a politician and manipulator, fending off threats from the Left and Right, from within the Nazi party, and from his conservative "allies." However, the crisis was precipitated by Hitler's inability to control his own storm troopers.

The S.A., or storm troopers, were originally organized to protect Nazi meetings and to break up the gatherings of rival political parties. Hitler had recruited the storm troopers largely from the ranks of unemployed war veterans. In 1931, Captain Ernst Roehm was appointed commander of the S.A. Roehm was a professional soldier who had been wounded in the war; he was an adventurer and mercenary by nature. "Since I am an immature and wicked man," said Roehm, "war and unrest appeal to me more than good bourgeois order." Hitler gave Roehm and the S.A. the task of winning the streets of German cities from the Communists. In 1932, the year before Hitler came to power, there were 400,000 storm troopers; by the summer of 1933, there were almost three million.

The storm troopers were disillusioned with the compromises Hitler had made to become chancellor. Most S.A. men were from the impoverished lower middle class or working class; many were unemployed. They still took the anticapitalist ideas in the Nazi party program seriously. Most had hoped they would have at least gotten a job when Hitler took over. Although Hitler had made significant progress in finding work for the unemployed, and said it was his number one priority, there were still almost five million Germans without jobs.

A government job was the answer for many Nazis. New openings were being created by the dismissal of Social Democrats and Jews from the civil service. Storm troopers who had fought and bled for Hitler for years felt they were entitled to these posts. Unfortunately for them, there were far too few positions to go around. The offices of every Nazi party boss from Hitler down were crowded with eager job seekers. Herman Rauschning, the gauleiter of Danzig, recalled how one Nazi job seeker shouted at him: "I won't get down and out again. Perhaps you can wait. You're not sitting on a bed of glowing coals. No job, man, no job! I'll stay on top no matter what it costs me. We won't get a second chance to get on top again."[3]

The dissatisfaction among the S.A. was growing, and many were openly calling for a second revolution. The enemy in this revolution would be Hitler's allies in the coalition government. Goebbels, who was the known enemy of the conservatives, wrote in his diary: "Everyone among the people is talking of a second revolution which must come. . . . Now we must settle with the reactionaries." All the dissatisfied elements that wished to perpetuate the revolution began to rally around Roehm and his three-million-strong S.A. Brownshirts.

Secretly Roehm was disappointed that Hitler had come to power without bloodshed. For him, no revolution would be complete without the final insurrectionary phase. "One victory on the road of the German Revolution has been won," said Roehm. "The S.A. and the S.S., who bear the great responsibility of having set the German revolution rolling, will not allow it to be betrayed at the halfway mark. . . . If the Philistines believe the national revolution has lasted too long . . . it is indeed high time that the national revolution end and become a National Socialist one. . . . We shall continue our fight with them or without them. And if necessary, against them."

As an attempted compromise with Roehm and the left-wing Nazis, Hitler offered to remove Hugenberg, the arch-conservative, from the cabinet. Hugenberg held two posts, minister of economics and minister of agriculture. As a representative of the Junker landlords, Hugenberg was unpopular with both the socialist-minded followers of Roehm and with the industrialists. Hugenberg finally yielded to Hitler's financial threats to ruin his heavily indebted media empire and resigned from the cabinet. In Hugenberg's place, Hitler appointed two men who were more sympathetic to Roehm and the S.A.: Walther Darre, a radical Nazi agrarian socialist, became minister of agriculture, and Dr. Kurt Schmitt, the director of an insurance company, became minister of economics. Dr. Schmitt was certainly not a socialist, but he favored an economy that would emphasize raising the workers' standard of living over spending on rearmament.

Encouraged by Roehm's call for a second revolution, the socialist elements within the Nazi party became more aggressive. Hitler's new minister of agriculture called for a moratorium on farm debts and a cut in the interest rate. The Nazi Small Shopkeepers Association stepped up their attacks and picketing of department stores. Radical members of the Nazi Labor Front passed out pamphlets calling for a second revolution to workers outside factories. Nazi economic cranks like Gottfried Feder demanded the nationalization of major industries and the abolition of "unearned" incomes.

With Germany still in the grip of a worldwide depression, the attacks against business and people accused of being "reactionaries" by left-wing Nazis began to take on a momentum of their own. All over Germany, self-appointed Nazi commissars were invading businesses and factories and trying to take them over. The procedure was rather simple: a dissatisfied Nazi, usually an ignored clerk or foreman, would get the support of the local S.A. and then burst into a directors' meeting backed up by half a dozen Brownshirt thugs. He would declare himself commissar and appoint a new board of directors with himself in charge. It did the owners of the business little good to call the police, because the police were afraid to touch the S.A. Firms with a Jewish partner or Jewish owner were particularly vulnerable to this tactic.

Before long, Hitler, Goering, and Papen were receiving hundreds of complaints from businessmen about the disruptive tactics of the left-wing Nazis and the S.A. A number of Hitler's big contributors threatened to cut off their financial support if something wasn't done immediately.

Hitler was put in the uncomfortable position of having to make a difficult decision. On the one hand, he had little love for the upper class and was reluctant to try to discipline the S.A., but on the other hand, he had sense enough to know that socialistic economic experiments could threaten the whole economic recovery. He was counting on the recovery to accomplish his two priorities, which were to end unemployment and to begin rearmament.

Hitler made it very clear that he was opposed to a "second revolution" when he spoke to Nazi state governors who were summoned to the Chancellery on July 6. "The revolution is not a permanent state of affairs," said Hitler. "We must therefore not dismiss a businessman if he is a good businessman, even if he is not yet a National Socialist, and especially not if the National Socialist who is to take his place knows nothing about business. In business, ability must be the only standard.

"History will not judge us according to whether we have removed and imprisoned the largest number of economists, but according to whether we have succeeded in providing work."

The speech left no doubt that Hitler was still respecting the original agreement he had made with his coalition partners, namely the conservatives would control the army, the economy, and foreign policy. Lest there be any doubt that he would back up his words with action, he moved swiftly against leftist Nazi organizations.

The Nazi Small Shopkeepers Association was dissolved and its members were forbidden to take any further action against department stores. Walther Darre, the minister of agriculture, was instructed to quietly drop his demand for a moratorium on farm debts and a reduction of the interest rate. There was little resistance from the leftist Nazis. They retreated temporarily, biding their time until the conflict between Roehm and the conservatives would erupt into the open.

Roehm's physical appearance gave a hint of his toughness. He was a short fat man with a pudgy face and a military haircut so short that the sides of his head were almost shaved. The bridge of his nose had been shot away during the war, and there were deep scars from wounds in his chin and cheeks.

Decorated for bravery in combat, Roehm was an excellent officer and a born leader of men. "I am a soldier," he said, "and I look at the world from a soldier's point of view. It is the military element in any situation that interests me." In spite of his self-proclaimed one-sided military mind, he had an understanding of political subtleties that was rare for a soldier. Most Nazi leaders were arrogant bullies even when off duty. In contrast,

Roehm was known for his instinctive courtesy, diplomatic tact, and savoir faire.

Although Roehm's name was widely known in Bavaria because of his role in Hitler's failed putsch in 1923, the first time most Germans had heard of him was in association with several well-publicized scandals. Roehm never made much effort to keep his homosexuality a secret.[4]

In an attack on Hitler and the S.A., General Ludendorff, the World War I hero who had been Hitler's ally in 1923, wrote: "I have in my possession documentary evidence that Herr Hitler was acquainted, as early as 1927, with grave abuses inside the organization [the S.A.], stemming from the homosexual proclivities of his subordinates, Roehm and Heines [the S.A. leader in Silesia], and in particular with the corruption of the Hitler Youth by Heines."[5]

Under Roehm's command, the S.A. leadership was said to have become a haven for homosexuals. It was true that Roehm surrounded himself with handsome young men who served on his staff. There were also rumors of wild orgies at Roehm's headquarters. More serious charges alleged that Heines was using the Hitler Youth as a network to recruit boys to be lovers for homosexual S.A. leaders.

Hitler always defended Roehm no matter what the charges. Although the two men were very different in social background and character, they were very close friends. There were some stormy quarrels, separations, and reconciliations, but the friendship survived. Roehm may have been Hitler's closest friend. He was one of the few people allowed to address the Fuehrer with the familiar *du*. There is no evidence to indicate, however, that there was a homosexual relationship between the two men. In fact, Roehm once commented on Hitler's sexual tastes in front of several witnesses: "He [Hitler] is thinking about the peasant girls. When they stand in the fields and bend down at their work so you can see their behinds, that's what he likes, especially when they've got big round ones. That's Hitler's sex life. What a man." Hitler didn't move or say a word, but simply stared at Roehm with compressed lips.[6]

Knowing Hitler as well as he did, Roehm had a unique insight into some of the weaknesses in his friend's character. "What worries me as much as anything," Roehm told another Nazi, "is that Hitler really is no executive. He hates details now as much as he always did. . . . The truth is that he's incapable of them; only when it's a question of outright propaganda or when his immediate interests are involved does he look after details himself. In everything else, it is still the same Austrian sloppiness." However, Roehm was aware of the strengths of Hitler's personality as well as his weaknesses. "You know as well as I do," he went on, "how Hitler can wear you down—he's incomparable in the art of making people believe in him."[7]

In spite of Hitler's persuasive powers, there was one major issue where he never succeeded in winning Roehm over to his point of view: the question of incorporating the S.A. into the regular army. It was an old quarrel between the two men. Since the early days of the Nazi party, Hitler had intended for the S.A. to be an organization of bouncers to intimidate political opponents. Roehm, on the other hand, wanted the S.A. to become a true fighting force, capable of a coup if necessary. Now that Hitler had become chancellor legally, Roehm hoped that if his huge force were amalgamated with the much smaller regular army, he would come out on top. Incorporating the S.A. into the army would also provide prestige and much needed government paychecks for the unemployed Brownshirts. Roehm's lieutenants were all looking forward to the day when they would be generals. Seeing himself as the new German Bonaparte, Roehm dreamed of building after the revolution a mass army with a new spirit like the French citizen army. Roehm complained to another Nazi leader:

The basis [of the new army] must be revolutionary. You can't inflate it afterwards. You only get the opportunity once to make something big that will turn the world upside down. But Hitler keeps putting me off. He wants to let things drift and keeps counting on a miracle. That's Adolf for you. He wants to inherit a ready-made army. He'll leave it to the "experts." When I hear that word, I blow my top. He'll make it [the army] National Socialist later on. But first he'll leave it to the Prussian generals. I don't know where he's going to get the revolutionary spirit from. They're the same old fogies, and they'll certainly lose the next war.[8]

Hitler's view had never changed. He was as firmly opposed as ever to Roehm's idea of merging the S.A. with the regular army to form a new "people's" army. He was afraid of alienating the generals. The memory of his failed 1923 putsch, when he had opposed the army, was something he would never forget. Prior to the putsch, he believed the army would not dare fire on nationalist forces. When they did so, it gave him a healthy respect for the ruthlessness of the generals in defending their own interests. In contrast, things had gone so smoothly on January 30, 1933, when he had come to power with the support of a powerful army faction. Also the simple fact remained that the army had the power to remove him if it chose to do so.

Looking ahead Hitler had two additional reasons for wanting to cooperate with the army. First of all, old president Hindenburg was in poor health and could die at any time. The generals would ultimately determine who would be his successor. Second, Hitler's foreign policy goal was rearmament—to put Germany back on an equal level with the great powers militarily. For this, he would need the technical expertise of the generals. The S.A. could become an armed mob, not a modern army.[9]

Some historians have contended that Hitler understood better than any other Nazi leader how dependent his government was on the goodwill of the army. Roehm, too, must have known what the true situation was. After all, he had been the first officer to employ Hitler as an army agent. He was familiar with the vast secret sums of money the army maintained to spend on clandestine rearmament and covert political operations. If anyone understood the role of the army as the power behind the throne in Germany, Roehm did. The difference between Roehm and Hitler was that Roehm was willing to fight a civil war against the army and Hitler was not.

To reassure the generals of his loyalty, Hitler enacted a law freeing the army from the jurisdiction of the civil courts, thus restoring the military to their pre-1918 privileged position. At a political rally before a mixed audience of Nazis and their nationalist allies, Hitler tried to give the generals further reassurance when he said: "On this day we should particularly remember the part played by our army, for we all know that if in the days of our revolution [January 1933] the army had not stood on our side, then we would not be standing here today. We can assure the army that we shall never forget this and that we see in them the bearers of the tradition of our glorious old army."[10]

On the other hand, Hitler continued to try to work out a compromise with Roehm. On December 1, he appointed Roehm to the cabinet. This satisfied a long-standing S.A. demand for a representative in the government.

But Roehm was not about to let Hitler put him off with a few token honors.[11] He began at once using his position in the cabinet to push for greater powers. He submitted a detailed proposal calling for the S.A., the army, and all paramilitary organizations to be put under the control of a new combined ministry of defense. It was obvious from the details of the proposal that as chief of the largest organization, Roehm himself would be the new minister of defense.[12]

The generals were horrified at the thought. The army had only tolerated Hitler on the condition that they would control military affairs. With an air of haughty disdain, General von Brauchitsch, the commander of the First Division at Königsberg, said, "Rearmament was too serious and difficult a business to permit the participation of peculators, drunkards and homosexuals." Confronted with such firm opposition from the army, Hitler did not support Roehm's proposal.

When Anthony Eden, the British diplomat, arrived in Germany in February for disarmament talks, Hitler secretly agreed to reduce the size of the S.A. by two-thirds and set up a system of verification to ensure that they received no military instructions. In return, Hitler wanted Britain to allow Germany to increase the size of its regular army.

When news leaked out about Hitler's offer to Eden to cut the S.A., Roehm was furious. In an attempt to make a compromise between the S.A. and the army, Hitler summoned the leaders of both groups to a conference at the Ministry of Defense. He asked the generals and the S.A. leaders to forget their differences in the interest of national defense. He said a "people's" army, such as Roehm proposed, would not be capable of swift offensive action. Only an expanded modern regular army would guarantee German power. Thus the army would be the only bearer of arms in the nation, and the S.A. would be responsible for premilitary (unarmed) training.[13]

The generals applauded while the S.A. leaders sat in angry silence. At Hitler's insistence, Roehm did get up and shake hands with General von Blomberg, the minister of defense and supreme commander of the armed forces, at the conclusion of the conference. Roehm was not very worried. He dismissed Hitler's speech as "just so much talk."

After the conference, Roehm invited the generals to a reconciliation breakfast with the S.A. leaders. Although accustomed to privilege, the army officers were uncomfortable with the excessive luxury of Roehm's dining hall. The fine china, silver, tapestries, and original oil paintings seemed out of place with the S.A. rowdies. The champagne flowed freely, but there was little conversation. After the generals had departed, Roehm asked his S.A. chiefs to remain. Pouring himself another glass of champagne, he released his pent-up anger: "That was another Versailles Treaty. . . . I have no intention of keeping this agreement," he grumbled. "Hitler is a traitor and at the very least must go on leave. . . . If we can't get there with him, we'll get there without him."[14] Hitler, he said, was nothing but an "ignorant corporal." Sitting among the S.A. bosses was Viktor Lutze, who was still loyal to Hitler. He remained quiet while Roehm spoke but in time reported everything that was said to the Fuehrer.

Before long, General von Blomberg was complaining to Hitler that Roehm was not keeping his bargain, which was not to train the S.A. with weapons. The S.A. was secretly arming elite units called "staff guards" with heavy machine guns. This was not only a threat to the army, but also jeopardized the covert rearmament program the generals were trying to keep secret from the French and British. To complicate matters, Hitler and General von Blomberg were notified that President von Hindenburg's health was failing rapidly. Hitler knew the monarchists and the conservatives around Papen were planning to reinstate the Hohenzollern monarchy on Hindenburg's death. Hitler had to prevent this at any cost. The generals would have the final say on who succeeded Hindenburg. So when General von Blomberg invited Hitler to go on naval maneuvers in the Baltic and North Sea with the commanders of the army and navy, he jumped at the chance, in spite of his well-known aversion to the sea.

69

On April 10 Hitler flew north to Kiel on the Baltic Sea to board the pocket battleship *Deutschland*. As the boatswains' whistles sounded, he walked up the gangway to be greeted by Admiral Raeder, the commander in chief of the German Navy, Generals von Blomberg and von Fritsch, respectively the supreme commander of the armed forces and the commander in chief of the army, and a naval honor guard in dress blues.

The next day the great gray steel hulk of the *Deutschland* turned and slowly headed out into the Baltic and up the Norwegian coast. Cruising through the foggy northern waters, the *Deutschland* provided the perfect isolation for Hitler and the military leaders to hold a secret conference. Exactly what was said during this conference has never been known, however, according to William Shirer, Hitler agreed to reduce the strength of the S.A. on the condition that the army would permit him to succeed President von Hindenburg as head of state.* By the time the ship returned to Wilhelmshaven, Hitler and General von Blomberg had concluded an agreement. Roehm's days were numbered.

On May 16, the senior generals of the army held a secret conference at the little Bavarian resort of Bad Nauheim to decide on a successor to President von Hindenburg. There were three possible candidates: the Crown Prince, General Ritter von Epp, a World War I officer who had been an early supporter of the Nazis, or Hitler. After General von Blomberg explained the agreement he had reached with Hitler, the choice of Hitler was almost unanimous.[15]

During the spring of 1934, tension was building in Germany. The radical elements in the S.A. were growing more vocal in their demands for a second revolution. On the other hand, industrialists who had been heavy contributors to Hitler were fed up. They wanted the S.A. suppressed and Roehm silenced. Through their secret contacts with the military in the clandestine rearmament program, they urged the army to take a stand against the S.A.

* * *

---

*There is no documentary proof of what took place at the conference aboard the *Deutschland*. However, Shirer's description of events seems reasonable.

The industrialists decided the best leverage they could exert against Roehm and the S.A. would be through Goering. He had been the recipient of more money from business and industry than any other Nazi. Consequently he was the most likely to do the industrialists' bidding. He was also one of the most powerful men in Germany, because he commanded the Prussian police, the second largest legal armed force in the country and almost half the size of the regular army.*

There was a bitter rivalry between Goering and Roehm. Considering Goering's upper-class background and connections, it was natural that he would side with the conservatives. President von Hindenburg had recently made him a general in the regular army, and he seemed to prefer the prestigious dress green-gray uniform to the common brown shirt.

The S.A. called Goering a "reactionary swine" and his girlfriend, the actress Emmy Sonnemann, "the slut."** In turn, Goering made fun of Roehm and his "gang of fairies."

When Goering planned a day of pageantry to celebrate his opening session of the Prussian Council of State, the S.A. decided he needed to be taught a lesson. Goering was in his glory in a splendid uniform covered with gold and silver medals, reviewing the police parade. The final unit in the parade was the S.A. band. When they approached the reviewing stand, they stopped playing and slovenly sauntered by Goering and his guests of honor. Goering, whose enormous vanity was insulted easily, was enraged. He determined then and there to get his revenge.

Where Hitler stood in the feud between Goering and Roehm was not clear. Although both men were his key lieutenants, they both were also his possible rivals. Hitler was afraid the conservatives might see Goering as a possible compromise candidate to succeed President von Hindenburg. For months, Hitler had been trying to exert his authority on behalf of the central government over Goering's Prussian State government. Goering rebuffed

---

*Although the S.A. was much larger than either the army or the Prussian police, they technically were not a legal armed force. They did have some weapons, but their training was poor.

**Goering's first wife, Carin, died in 1931.

every attempt Hitler made to get control of the Prussian police.

On April 1, 1934, Goering suddenly gave in and appointed
Heinrich Himmler, the commander of the black-uniformed S.S.,
chief of the Gestapo, which up to then had been a part of the
Prussian police.[16] Goering had lavished great attention on build-
ing the Gestapo into the most feared secret police unit in
Germany.

Some observers contended that Goering turned the Gestapo
over to Himmler to have an ally in the fight against Roehm.[17]
After April 1, Goering and Himmler began to plot together
against Roehm.

Goering and Himmler were encouraged in their conspiratorial
role by highly placed officers in the army. The most prominent
army officer directly involved with Goering and Himmler was
General von Reichenau, who was General von Blomberg's chief
of staff. Reichenau was extremely ambitious and had a Machia-
vellian mind. He thought the Nazis could be used to strengthen
the power and position of the army. At a secret meeting of army
leaders in February of 1933, he stated that the political chaos in
Germany and particularly the danger of Marxism could only be
remedied by a dictatorship. But Reichenau did not plan to hand
over power to Hitler. The army would remain the real power
behind the throne. Hitler the "dictator" would be something of a
figurehead. The dictator would be in charge of domestic politics,
but the army would always have a veto power.

The huge size of the S.A. paramilitary organization was the
only threat to Reichenau's scheme.[18] At any rate, Reichenau's
involvement in the intrigues against the S.A. was a great
encouragement for Goering and Himmler and their shadowy
financial backers. Knowing they could count on the prestige and
power of the army made them bolder.

In April Goering and Himmler launched a joint investigation
of the S.A.[19] They hoped to gather sufficient evidence to prove to
Hitler that Roehm was planning a coup. That spring, Berlin was
full of rumors of coups and plots. Thousands of Brownshirts
were conducting "secret" field exercises with weapons on the
outskirts of the capital, right under the noses of the army high
command. Even passers-by on the road reported seeing large
numbers of armed men in the khaki uniforms of the S.A.

crawling through the underbrush. On a higher level, Himmler learned that General von Schleicher, the former chancellor with leftist sympathies, was meeting with Roehm, talking about the prospects of a new government.

Hitler decided to personally confront Roehm and see if he couldn't defuse the crisis. He summoned the S.A. chief to the Chancellery for a private meeting. The meeting lasted nearly five hours and dragged on until midnight. Hitler said it was his "last attempt" to reach an understanding with his old comrade: "I informed him that I had the impression from countless rumors and numerous declarations of faithful old party members and S.A. leaders that conscienceless elements in the S.A. were preparing a national Bolshevist uprising that could bring nothing but untold misfortune to Germany. . . . I implored him for the last time to voluntarily abandon this madness and instead to lend his authority to prevent such a development that . . . could only end in a catastrophe."

People in the waiting room outside Hitler's office said they heard the loud voices of the two men "bellowing" at each other for hours.

What Roehm said to Hitler is not known. At any rate, Hitler later claimed that by the time Roehm left, he promised he would try "to put things right."

Two days after this meeting with Roehm, Hitler ordered the S.A. to go on leave during the month of June. The storm troopers were not to wear their uniforms or to take part in any exercises or demonstrations while on leave. This was something Hitler and Roehm must have agreed upon at their meeting as a way to defuse the crisis. On June 7 Roehm announced that he would be going on sick leave.[20] He would spend his leave resting at the Bavarian resort of Bad-Wiessee and then would address a conference of S.A. leaders there, on June 30. Hitler had also agreed to come and speak at the conference.

Goering and Himmler were continually supplying Hitler with information indicating the S.A. was planning a coup. Hitler said everybody "brought to light more and more disquieting facts." Evidently Hitler did not believe a coup was imminent because on June 14 he flew to Venice to hold his first meeting with Mussolini.

No sooner had Hitler returned home than he found his regime under attack from an entirely different quarter than he had expected. The peaceful old university town of Marburg, unchanged since the Middle Ages, was suddenly the center of a crisis when Vice-Chancellor von Papen gave a speech there that was the most scathing public attack ever on the Nazi regime by one of the members of the cabinet. Papen openly criticized the Nazis for corruption, the restriction of personal freedom, and interference with religion. But the main point of his speech was a veiled threat to Roehm and Goebbels and other left-wing Nazis. "There is no end to talk of a second wave which is to complete the revolution. . . . He who threatens with a guillotine might be its first victim." The speech was wildly cheered by the audience.

Goebbels, who had become minister of propaganda in March, banned the speech as soon as he heard about it, but he acted too late to keep it out of the early evening edition of many major newspapers. Hitler was furious. As he soon learned, Papen's speech was part of a well-coordinated conservative attack. Copies of the speech had been printed up beforehand and distributed to the press and foreign journalists.

"The situation is absolutely dynamite," Walter Bochow, one of Papen's assistants, told a British journalist. "Now we are right in the middle of the war for Hindenburg's succession. On the one side is Hitler, who wants to take over from the old man and make himself the absolute dictator of Germany. On the other hand, are Papen and his fellow conservatives in the cabinet. They want to stop Hitler. They reckon the moment has come for the Crown Prince to take over a kind of regency as a first step to the restoration of the monarchy. President von Hindenburg, himself, supports them."[21]

Papen thought the time was right to strike because of Hindenburg's rapidly failing health and the rivalry between Hitler and Roehm. He was preparing for a showdown with Hitler at the next cabinet meeting scheduled for July 3. Papen would demand that Hitler immediately suppress any S.A. members calling for a "second revolution." If Hitler refused or tried to stall, then Papen and all the other conservatives would resign together. President von Hindenburg had promised that in this event, he would dismiss Hitler and give the army executive powers.

Enraged over Goebbels's banning of his speech, Papen decided to seize the opportunity of the moment and not wait until the cabinet meeting on July 3. The vice-chancellor stormed in to see Hitler and threatened to resign and to report the matter to President von Hindenburg. Although Hitler would have been glad to get rid of Papen, he acted cautiously. He had heard some of the rumors that Hindenburg was planning to declare martial law. Hitler stalled Papen and decided to go to Neudeck to find out for himself what old Hindenburg was up to.

On June 21, Hitler traveled to East Prussia to the president's estate. On the steps of Hindenburg's villa, he was met by General von Blomberg and Goering, who was also wearing an army general's uniform. "Having been informed of events by Vice-Chancellor von Papen," said von Blomberg, "President Hindenburg summoned General Goering, in his capacity as commander of the Prussian police, and myself to Neudeck. Our instructions are to consult with you on the measures to be taken to ensure internal peace. If a complete relaxation of tension does not immediately take place, martial law will be proclaimed. The president, being ill, deeply regrets being unable to receive you."[22]

Hitler was stunned! Blomberg, the supreme commander of the armed forces, who had long been a pro-Nazi, was no longer the congenial yes-man everyone had nicknamed "the rubber lion." And Goering, who owed his position to the Nazi party, was now taking the side of the generals and reactionaries. "But it is absolutely essential that I see the president," Hitler insisted. Blomberg went away and returned a few minutes later. "Please follow me," he said to Hitler.

President von Hindenburg looked like a combination of an avenging god and the grim reaper. He was dressed in a black coat that made a stark contrast with his deathly pale, wrinkled face, his snow white hair and white mustache. The old man didn't even bother to try to rise out of his chair for Hitler. When General von Blomberg presented the chancellor, Hindenburg grumbled: "You will either get rid of Roehm and reduce his storm troopers to order, or you will get out! I am not going to tolerate the existence of a party state within the state or a private army beside the regular army!"[23]

The situation suddenly looked serious for Hitler. Not only his succession to the presidency was in jeopardy, but if the army also took over, the Nazi government would be out. All the years of struggle and election campaigns would be for nothing. All lost! Hitler realized he now had no choice but to fulfill the agreement he had made with General von Blomberg.*

Still in the last week of June, Hitler was reluctant to act. As he later admitted, he hesitated "again and again before making the final decision. . . . I still cherished the secret hope that I might be able to spare the movement and my S.A. of the shame of such a conflict and that it might be possible to solve the problem without a severe crisis."

Goering and Himmler were working frantically, issuing orders, assembling loyal men, and preparing to purge the S.A. At the same time, they were still trying to convince Hitler that Roehm and the S.A. were planning a coup. In the end, it was the evidence prepared by Himmler that convinced Hitler that Roehm was really a traitor.[24] His agents had discovered that Roehm had purchased heavy machine guns in Belgium and was stockpiling weapons at a number of key locations.

On June 25, General von Fritsch, the commander in chief of the army, put the army on a state of alert. All troops were confined to their barracks and all leaves were canceled. Sentries were reinforced outside all military installations and defensive machine gun positions were put in place behind sandbags and barbed wire. On June 28, Roehm was expelled from the Officers' League. The next day, General von Blomberg published a most unusual article in the *Völkischer Beobachter*.

"The army's role is clearly determined. . . . It must support the leaders who have given it back its noblest right to be the bearer of arms with the unlimited confidence of the people. . . . The army stands loyal and disciplined behind the rulers of the State, behind the President Field Marshall von Hindenburg, its Supreme Commander and behind the leader of the Reich, Adolf Hitler, who came from its ranks and remains one of ours."[25]

---

*It is most likely that the agreement General von Blomberg made with Hitler did not specify exactly how Hitler was to "reduce the power of the S.A." If Hitler decided to kill the S.A. leaders the responsibility was his alone.

Just what did General von Blomberg mean by the phrase "Hitler remains one of ours?" Obviously Hitler was not "one of theirs" simply because he was a veteran of World War I. Millions of Social Democrats and even Communists were veterans of the war, and the army was not claiming them as part of its family. Hitler was never an officer or even a professional soldier.* Obviously Hitler had made a deal with the pro-Nazi faction of the Officer Corps in 1933. Now, Blomberg wanted to remind Hitler of his obligations and give Roehm a clear warning about which side Hitler would choose in the conflict.

Hitler left Berlin to fly to Essen on June 28; the purpose of his trip was ostensibly to attend the wedding of Gauleiter Josef Terboven. The real reason for the trip was to have a last-minute secret meeting with Gustav Krupp. In early June, four S.A. men had forced their way into the Krupp factory, shut down the assembly line, and delivered a speech to the workers on the "second revolution." This was the last straw for Gustav Krupp. He contacted Hitler and demanded immediate action.

On June 29, Hitler toured the labor service camps in Westphalia. In the late afternoon he returned to Godesberg, where he was staying in the hotel Dresesen. The hotel had a spectacular view of the Rhine and the river valley with its peaceful vineyards and castles dotting the hillsides.

Hitler and his staff had dinner at 8:00 P.M. He was quiet throughout most of the meal. At 8:20, Goebbels was called to the telephone. When he returned to the table, he told Hitler that Sepp Dietrich, a trusted S.S. officer, had arrived in Augsburg with several companies of Hitler's S.S. bodyguards. Hitler replied: "It's best that way." He and Goebbels both seemed as if they were waiting for more important news. There was a feeling of tension in the air.

Shortly after 9 o'clock, a group of girls from the League of

---

*In 1919, Hitler was an army agent. General von Blomberg's statement could be interpreted to mean that Hitler remained an army agent throughout his political career. However, there is little additional evidence to support this conclusion. If it were correct, it would radically alter our understanding of German history and World War II.

German Maidens arrived to serenade Hitler on the hotel terrace. They sang patriotic and marching songs as Hitler leaned on the rail of the terrace to listen.

In the growing darkness the barges on the river below had turned on their navigation lights. There was the smell of rain in the air and in the distance were jagged bolts of lightning. As Hitler stood at the balcony railing alone, his pilot, Hans Baur, noticed that he was crying: "Although he could very easily slip into a soft, sentimental mood, I found no explanation for his behavior. All too soon it was to become clear to me."[26] Realizing that he couldn't put off the decision much longer, Hitler knew he was going to have to kill his old friend, Roehm.

At last the storm broke with thunder, lightning, and a brief downpour. A motorcycle dispatch rider brought an important message from Goering at about 11 P.M. Apparently several well-known Berlin doctors had been called to the president's bedside. If old Hindenburg died before Hitler suppressed Roehm and the S.A., General von Blomberg might call off the deal he had made and instead declare martial law. Hitler would have to act fast. He looked tense; his skin was pale and there were bags under his eyes, as if he hadn't slept the night before. He asked his pilot, Baur, to check on the weather between the Ruhr and Munich and to have his crew stand by to leave for Munich on short notice.

Shortly after 1:00 A.M. Hitler received two messages, one from Munich and one from Berlin. His loyal party boss in Munich, Adolf Wagner, reported that rebellious S.A. men were gathering in the streets for an uprising. Almost at the same time word came from Himmler that he had definite proof the S.A. was planning to strike the next day and occupy government buildings. "In these circumstances, I could only make one decision," Hitler said later. "Only a ruthless and bloody intervention could halt the spread of this revolt."[27] Suddenly Hitler's indecision vanished and he began to bark out orders. He seemed full of self-assurance. Accompanied by his staff and bodyguards, Hitler quickly left Godesberg by car for the Bonn airport, where he boarded his private plane and took off for Munich.

It was almost dawn by the time Hitler's plane neared Munich. The sky was a pale gray. The red and blue airport runway lights still stood out in sharp contrast to the ground where the darkness was just lifting. As the plane approached the runway, a small group of people and several vehicles were visible below.

Hitler was the first out of the plane. The people waiting turned out to be his loyal supporters—the local party boss Wagner and some of his men. There were also two army officers who immediately came up to report to Hitler. They said General von Blomberg had placed two armored cars and troops at Hitler's disposal. The armored cars and several trucks full of soldiers sat parked nearby. Getting into an automobile with his bodyguards, Hitler gave orders to drive to the Ministry of Interior, where several S.A. leaders were being held by Wagner's men. In the Ministry building, Hitler confronted August Schneidhuber, the chief of police of Munich and the highest ranking S.A. man in the city. Wagner had arrested Schneidhuber a few hours earlier on Hitler's instruction by phone. Hitler shouted at Schneidhuber that he was a traitor and then in a frenzy tore off his insignia and party badge.[28]

At about 6:00 A.M., Hitler and his men set out for Bad-Wiessee. They traveled in a convoy of six cars, of which at least three were full of S.S. detectives in civilian clothes. Following the automobiles were the two armored cars General von Blomberg had sent.

Outside of Munich the road ran through open country and farmland. In the distance there was the dark green forest. Thirty-five miles south of Munich was Bad-Wiessee, where Roehm and his S.A. leaders were still asleep in their beds in the Hotel Hanselbauer. The conference of S.A. leaders was scheduled to take place there at noon.

Hitler sat slumped in the front seat of the lead car alongside his personal chauffeur, Erich Kempka. His face was slightly swollen and puffy; his eyes were red from the sleepless night. At the last bend in the road before Wiessee, Sepp Dietrich was waiting for Hitler with several army trucks full of armed S.S. bodyguards. The plan was going according to schedule. Lake Tegernsee came into view. The shore of the lake was still in early morning shadow from the surrounding mountains, but higher slopes were already bright with sunlight. Hitler's convoy drove down the road alongside the dark waters of the lake. Wiessee was less than a mile away. As they entered the little town of Wiessee, Hitler told his driver, Kempka, "When we come to the

Hotel Hanselbauer . . . if you see S.A. guards in front of the hotel, don't wait for them to report to me; drive on and stop at the hotel entrance."[29]

Luckily for Hitler there were no S.A. guards outside the hotel. The cars drove right up to the front entrance; Hitler, his bodyguards, and staff jumped out with their revolvers in hand. A few drowsy S.A. guards in the lobby of the hotel were taken by surprise and quickly disarmed. Accompanied by two S.S. men, Hitler headed straight for Roehm's room and pounded on the door.[30]

"Open the door!" he shouted.

Roehm answered sleepily, "Who is it?"

"It's me—Hitler! Let me in!"

"What! You already! I thought you weren't coming until noon," said Roehm as he opened the door.

Hitler rushed into the room and began shouting accusations of treason at a dumbfounded Roehm. The half-naked, fat, flabby body of the S.A. chief was an unpleasant sight. Not yet completely awake, he at first stood in silence as Hitler berated him. Finally, he began to grasp what was going on and began to protest and shout back at Hitler.

"You are under arrest," Hitler said, ending the argument abruptly. He then left the room and turned Roehm over to the two S.S. men.

The hotel corridors were now full of noise and confusion. Doors were being kicked open by S.S. men with revolvers drawn. Half-asleep S.A. leaders were being handcuffed and pushed along at gunpoint. Edmund Heines, the S.A. leader from Breslau, was found naked in bed with a teenage boy. He refused to cooperate and get dressed. When the S.S. detectives reported this to Hitler, he went to Heines's room and shouted: "Heines, if you are not dressed in five minutes, I'll have you shot on the spot."

Everything went smoothly; the S.A. leaders were all being herded into a laundry room, where they were held until they could be taken to Munich. Only Heines caused trouble. Hitler became so furious with him that he ordered some S.S. men to take Heines and his young lover outside and shoot them. No one even noticed the two shots that killed them.

Suddenly there was trouble; a truck full of Roehm's S.A.

bodyguards pulled up to the front of the hotel. Hitler's adjutant, Captain Bruckner, ordered the commander of the S.A. troop to return to Munich. The S.A. officer refused. He said he would take orders only from Roehm. Now there'll be some shooting, thought Hitler's chauffeur, Kempka, who was standing outside watching. Hitler came out of the hotel and walked up to the S.A. officer. "What's the matter?" Hitler barked. "Didn't you hear Captain Bruckner? Return to Munich at once!" The S.A. officer hesitated then saluted, and got back in the truck. If Roehm, who was in the hotel lobby at the time, had cried out for help, the situation could have ended differently.

With their mission accomplished, Hitler and his convoy, which included their prisoners, returned to Munich. The prisoners were taken to the Stadelheim prison.

Late in the afternoon, Hitler headed for the airport and then boarded his plane to return to Berlin.[31]

Meanwhile in Berlin, Goering and Himmler were busy arresting S.A. leaders and carrying out the purge in the capital.[32] A number of people in addition to the S.A. men were arrested or murdered. General von Schleicher, the former chancellor and former minister of defense, who was involved with Roehm, was murdered along with his wife in their own home. Papen's assistant who had written the Marburg speech was killed. The Nazis also used the purge as an excuse to even old scores or silence people who knew too much.[33] Goering thought Papen needed to be humbled, so he was placed "in protective custody" at his home with his phone cut off and isolated from the rest of the world.

Hitler's plane arrived at Tempelhof airfield just as the sun was setting. Appropriately the sky was blood red. The airfield was surrounded by Goering's private police regiment in their blue-gray uniforms. Once the plane was on the ground, Hitler was the first one out the door. He was wearing his uniform brown shirt, black tie with a dark brown leather jacket, and black army boots. His very pale face stood out in contrast to his dark clothes. He was unshaven and looked gaunt. Goering and Himmler had been waiting at the airport for over an hour. They rushed up to greet him. The three walked together toward the waiting cars; the staff and bodyguards followed at a discreet distance.

Hitler walked slowly, as if every step was an effort. He

listened closely as Goering and Himler reported what had been going on in Berlin. Himmler pulled a list out of his pocket and handed it to Hitler. His finger moved down the piece of paper. Several times he paused to ask Goering or Himmler a question; they would whisper something into his ear. The list obviously contained the names of those arrested or shot.[34]

But Hitler had an unpleasant surprise for Goering and Himmler—Roehm was still alive; Hitler had given orders to spare his old friend. This made both Goering and Himmler nervous. As long as Roehm was alive, nothing had really been accomplished. If he got back into Hitler's good graces, the tables could be turned against them. Both men went with Hitler to the Chancellery, where they continued to recommend Roehm's execution. Hitler hesitated; he said he was too tired to make a decision. He would discuss the matter with them in the morning.

The next day, Goering and Himmler argued with Hitler for hours about Roehm's fate. At one o'clock on the afternoon of July 1, Hitler gave in. He telephoned Munich. Roehm was to be given a revolver and permitted to commit suicide; if he didn't, he was to be shot.

When the S.S. guards placed a revolver in Roehm's cell, he told them: "If Adolf wants me dead, let him do it himself." After ten minutes, the S.S. men returned. Roehm had not used the revolver, so they shot him three times at point-blank range. He was dead in seconds.[35]

When the bloody massacre was over, Hitler received not a word of criticism from the traditional forces of law and order in Germany. There were no protests from the police, the judiciary, the churches, the scholars, and above all no complaints from the army. (Only two generals protested General von Schleicher's murder.) In fact, General von Blomberg, the commander of the army, congratulated Hitler. On July 1, he informed the army: "The Fuehrer has personally attacked and wiped out the mutineers and traitors with soldierly decision and exemplary courage. The army as the sole bearer of arms in the Reich remains aloof from internal political conflict but pledges anew its devotion and its fidelity."

The results of the purge accomplished just what many generals wanted—Roehm was out of the way and the S.A. was no longer a rival. The generals had never soiled their hands. All the dirty work was done by the S.S. and Hitler. To further reassure the German people that the traditional forces stood behind Hitler, President von Hindenburg sent the chancellor a telegram praising his action. "I learned that you, by your determined action and gallant personal intervention, have nipped treason in the bud. You have saved Germany from a serious danger. For this I express to you my profound thanks and sincere appreciation."

Hitler gave no public explanation of the events of the purge until thirteen days later when he addressed the Reichstag. Hitler accused Roehm and the S.A. of plotting a coup. They were, he said, "Revolutionaries who favored revolution for its own sake and wanted revolution established as a permanent condition." To defend himself against charges in the foreign press that he took the law into his own hands, he said, "If anyone reproaches me and asks why I did not resort to the regular courts of justice . . . then all that I can say to him is this: in this hour, I was responsible for the fate of the German people, and thus I became the supreme judge of the German people. . . . I gave the order to shoot those who were the ringleaders in this treason."[36]

As usual, some of the things Hitler said in his speech were true and some were not. The speech was a brutally frank but frightening warning of the lawlessness and government-sponsored terrorism that was to come to Germany. On the main issue of Roehm planning a coup, Hitler was not as truthful, unless he still believed everything Goering and Himmler had told him. It is probable that on June 29, he really thought an S.A. revolt was imminent, especially considering the "evidence" given to him by Himmler. However, by the time he made his Reichstag speech about the purge, thirteen days later, he should have learned the truth. Of course, by then he had no choice but to cover up.

One police official, Hans Gisevius, became suspicious when a plane carrying Karl Ernst, who had been arrested in Bremen, landed at Tempelhof airport shortly before Hitler's plane arrived from Munich on July 1. Karl Ernst was commander of the Berlin S.A. and supposedly one of the key men in Roehm's conspiracy. But what was Ernst doing in Bremen, Gisevius asked himself, if the S.A. was planning a coup that evening? As it turned out, Ernst was getting ready to board a ship to Madeira for his honeymoon. A curious action for a revolutionary.[37]

On June 24 General von Kleist, the army commander in Silesia, had been warned that an attack by the S.A. on the army was imminent. There were a number of rumors and small incidents that increased the tension between the S.A. and the army. The situation was so dangerous, General von Kleist said, "only a spark was needed to touch off the explosion." Kleist decided to take a bold step. He met with Edmund Heines, the local S.A. commander in Silesia, and asked him what was going on. Heines said the S.A. had heard rumors and had information that they were about to be attacked by the army. Both men agreed not to take any rash action before trying to find out what was going on.

On June 29, Kleist flew to Berlin to see General von Fritsch, the commander in chief of the army. He told him about his conversations with Heines and said, "I have the impression that we—the army and S.A.—are being egged on against each other by a third party."[38] General von Fritsch asked General von Reichenau (General von Blomberg's assistant) to join the discussion. Of course, General von Reichenau was coordinating the army "defensive" measures against the S.A. After hearing General von Kleist's suspicions, Reichenau calmly replied: "That may be true, but it is too late now."*

Of course it wasn't too late, but General von Kleist was telling the wrong man. General von Reichenau was working with Goering and Himmler. Reichenau and his boss, General von Blomberg, had both been very active behind the scenes manipulating forces against the S.A.[39] On the day of the purge, while Hitler was arresting Roehm in Munich, General von Reichenau was working along with Goering and Himmler as they issued orders for arrests and executions in Berlin and the rest of Germany. In fact, General von Reichenau stayed at Goering's villa, the Berlin command center of the purge, until all the grisly

---

*Although most generals hated Roehm and the S.A., only a few were actively involved in the intrigues against the S.A. It is not clear if General von Fritsch was involved or not.

work was done. A year later, General von Reichenau boasted to a Berlin police official of his role in the purge; he said it had really taken considerable skill to make it appear as if the Roehm affair was simply a dispute between Roehm and Hitler.[40]

If an S.A. uprising was to have taken place on the afternoon of June 30, as Hitler contended, it is strange that Roehm and his S.A. leaders were caught asleep with no guards posted that morning. It is also strange that they were at an inaccessible resort with no special communication facilities. There wasn't even a nearby airfield. The large stores of weapons taken from the S.A. by the army after the purge do seem to indicate that the S.A. was planning some sort of revolution, but probably not in the immediate future.

After the execution of Roehm, the army emerged stronger than ever. They were the only armed force in Germany (with the exception of the police, who were no threat), a position they had not enjoyed since 1918. The Communists had been crushed, and now Hitler had been forced to emasculate his own paramilitary force, the S.A. Furthermore, Hitler had promised to increase the size of the army from 100,000 to 300,000. General von Reichenau's plans to use the Nazis to strengthen the position of the army seemed to be working.

Hitler was not to stand by idly and let the generals use him. True, he had suffered a setback with the purge, but he was not about to give up. Hitler wanted to gain control over the army just as Roehm had, but he realized it would take time. Hitler and Roehm had shared similar goals. That was why it was such a difficult decision for Hitler to choose between Roehm and the army. However, unlike Roehm, Hitler was not willing to risk a military confrontation between the S.A. and the army, which might lead to civil war and endanger everything he had gained through years of struggle.

Several weeks after Roehm's death, Hitler spoke candidly to Herman Rauschning, the Nazi leader from Danzig:

Anyone who gets out of step will be shot. Have I not implored these people [the S.A.] a hundred times to follow me? At a moment when everything depends on the party being a single, close entity, I must listen to the reactionaries taunting me with the inability to keep order and discipline in my own house! I must accept the accusation that the party is a hotbed of insubordination, worse than the Communists! . . . But they are mistaken. . . . They underestimate me because I have risen from below, from the "lower depths," because I haven't had an education, because I haven't the manners that their sparrow brains think right! . . . The insubordination of my S.A. has deprived me of a great many trump cards. But I hold plenty of others. . . . They can't pass over me when the old gentleman [Hindenburg] dies. . . .

The people don't want a Hohenzollern monarchy. Only I could induce them to accept it. . . . But I will not do it! They're at their wits' end, these miserable busybodies. . . . I have spoiled their plans. . . . They saw me already wriggling in their net. They thought I was their tool. And behind my back they laughed at me and said I had no power now that I had lost my party. I saw through all that long ago. . . . If I call on the people today, they will follow me. If I appeal to the party, it will respond more closely knit than ever. . . . They have tried to estrange me from the party in order to make me a weak-willed tool in their hands. But I stand here stronger than ever before.[41]

He did not have to wait long for his big opportunity. On August 2, 1934, at nine o'clock in the morning, President von Hindenburg died at his estate of Neudeck in East Prussia. The day before, Hitler flew from Bayreuth to Neudeck to sit at the bedside of the dying president. Old Hindenburg, fading in and out of consciousness, did not recognize Hitler and addressed him as "Your Majesty." Hitler did not wait for the president to die but returned to Berlin immediately to persuade the cabinet to pass a new law combining the offices of president and chancellor. This was the moment of truth for Hitler. Would the generals honor the deal they had made with him? Everything went smoothly.

When General von Blomberg, the minister of war, agreed to sign the new law, the other conservative members of the cabinet, including Papen and Foreign Minister von Neurath, followed his example. Hitler was, according to the new law, "head of state" and assumed the title "Fuehrer and Reich chancellor," which he preferred to the more democratic-sounding title of "president." Hitler's powers as head of state included all the power formerly held by President von Hindenburg, including that of commander in chief of the army.

Most historians mark Hindenburg's death as the final turning point on Hitler's road to absolute dictatorship. Some have said that by allowing Hitler to assume both the office of president and chancellor, the conservatives "acquiesced in their own defeat." However, looking behind the scenes, it is obvious that this was not the case. Hitler's gain was significant but not overwhelming. Although he was now nominally commander in chief of the army, the secret cabal of senior officers still controlled the army. After all, every president of the Weimar Republic had nominally been commander in chief of the army, but their authority over the generals was limited. As far as other aspects of government were concerned, Hitler maintained the original agreement he had made with his partners and financiers when the coalition Hitler-Papen government had been formed, i.e., he would not interfere in economic and military matters. Traditional conservatives continued to control the ministries of economics, finance, foreign affairs, and defense.[42]

On the afternoon of August 2 the armed forces throughout Germany took a new oath of loyalty not to the constitution or the nation, but to Hitler personally: "I swear unconditional obedience to Adolf Hitler, Fuehrer of the German Reich." In later years some German officers made much of this oath. They used it as an excuse for everything. But that was just what it was, an excuse. German officers had taken an oath and were honor bound to their Lord and Sovereign, Kaiser Wilhelm II, but when the generals thought the kaiser was more of a hindrance than an asset, he was simply asked to leave, and there was no wringing of hands over breaking a sacred oath.

In 1934, the oath to Hitler meant little to the men of the armed forces; very few officers protested the wording. Contrary to popular belief, the oath was not something Hitler demanded of the army. It had actually been written by General von Blomberg and was given to Hitler in exchange for his written pledge that the army would be the sole bearer of arms in the nation. In a letter addressed to General von Blomberg, Hitler said, "I want to thank you and through you, the army for the oath of loyalty taken to me. . . . Just as the officers and soldiers . . . have pledged themselves to the new State in my person, so will I always regard it as my most important duty to intercede on behalf of the stability and inviolability of the army . . . as the sole bearer of arms in the nation."[43]

There were two weeks of national mourning after President von Hindenburg's death. Instead of holding new elections for the presidency, as was required by the constitution, Hitler decided to call a plebiscite to prove that a majority of the German people approved of his assumption of Hindenburg's office as head of state. On August 19, over forty-five million Germans went to the polls; thirty-eight million voted "yes" in favor of Hitler's assumption of supreme power. Only four million had the courage to vote "no." Almost one million deliberately spoiled their ballots. The overwhelming vote in the plebiscite was just what Hitler needed to convince the generals and the conservatives that they had made the right choice in making him Hindenburg's successor. Only Hitler had the confidence of the German people. Only he could whip up the necessary patriotism to begin the massive tasks of rearmament and the preparation for a new war.

Chapter 4

Did the King* of England Help Hitler Rearm?

In January 1933, Germany was, militarily, the weakest large nation in Europe. Just four years later the German Army was the strongest fighting force on the continent. Hitler's success in rapidly rearming Germany was an almost unbelievable story. Initially Germany's enemies had all the advantages. By an uncanny understanding of his opponents' weaknesses and a series of brilliant diplomatic coups, Hitler succeeded in dividing Germany's foes. He eventually even persuaded one of the Allies, Britain, to abandon the Versailles system of collective security and tolerate Germany's drive for rearmament.

Incredibly Hitler's staunchest advocate in Britain was King Edward VIII. But Hitler had to know just how far the king would let him go in rearming Germany. Hitler's agents needed an inside source of information about the king's true opinions. They discovered that someone was already encouraging Edward's pro-German sentiments. That person was Wallis Simpson, who was involved in a romance with the king and who was suspected by some members of the British intelligence community of being a security risk.

---

*King Edward VIII, later the Duke of Windsor.

Before Edward VIII became king, Britain and France had generally cooperated in enforcing the Versailles Treaty. Although the Versailles system kept Germany weak and incapable of waging another aggressive war, secret German rearmament had been going on long before Hitler became chancellor. Almost as soon as the ink was dry on the Versailles Treaty, Germany began a clandestine effort to evade the treaty's restrictions. The army, industrialists, and even officials of the Weimar Republic were involved in this evasion. In neutral countries through subsidiary companies German firms developed new submarines, tanks, bombs, and other weapons forbidden by the treaty. By a secret agreement with Moscow, the army then tested these weapons in Soviet Russia beyond the watchful eyes of the Allied inspectors. Although the army was limited to 100,000 soldiers, several hundred thousand men were given illegal military training in the so-called Free Corps and other paramilitary organizations like the Nazi S.A.

There was little question that the Versailles Treaty was unjust. When Woodrow Wilson first saw the treaty, he said "If I were a German, I think I should never sign it."[1] Herbert Hoover was horrified at its severity. However, Hitler's task of freeing Germany from the treaty was not an easy one.[2] The first period of rearmament would be the most dangerous. While Germany was still weak, she would have to avoid any action that would provoke her neighbors, particularly France or Poland. They could use any breach of the treaty as an excuse to invade Germany. And rearmament itself was of course a violation of the treaty. So all of Germany's actions would have to be kept secret.

By 1935, it was obvious to everyone that the German economy was steadily improving. Unemployment, the most visible problem of the depression, was reduced from six million in 1932 to less than three million. Factories that had long been idle were busy again. Nazi propaganda credited Hitler's public works projects, particularly the construction of the autobahn, for putting people back to work, but the real basis of the economic recovery was the rearmament program. The budget for the public works was five billion marks and the secret rearmament budget was twenty-one billion marks.[3]

Naturally there was a problem concealing such a huge expenditure. In spite of Hitler's efforts to maintain secrecy, the transformation of German industry was too big for the Gestapo to hide. Visitors returning from Germany reported that industry there seemed to have a new vitality. All the metal factories were busy. Steel output was up 25 percent in just a year's time. Machine tool factories were working overtime and were said to be months behind in deliveries. New construction was visible on many plant sites. Obviously the owners were anticipating even further increases in business if they were adding to the size of their factories. Even though there were still some men unemployed, there was a growing shortage of skilled labor, especially machinists and construction workers. In fact, some machine factories were retraining bakers' assistants and textile workers.

Although journalists and curious foreigners might be able to find out that a metal factory had added a third shift and anyone could hear the hammers and great presses working day and night, it was not so easy to find out exactly what the factories were producing. Most plants were now surrounded by high barbed wire fences, and armed guards checked workers in and out at the gates. Employees were instructed not to talk about their jobs to anyone, even their own families. The censors of the propaganda ministry carefully watched newspapers to be sure no industrial information was revealed inadvertently.[4] Hitler had personally instructed General von Blomberg, the supreme commander of the armed forces, and Admiral Raeder, the supreme commander of the navy, that all rearmament orders were to be given verbally to the industrialists involved; nothing was to be put in writing for fear of Allied spies.[5]

An increasing number of innocent foreigners were arrested by the Nazis for espionage. Some had simply taken a photo with a factory in the background. Others were "guilty" of asking too many questions about what kind of work a German did. The Gestapo and Nazi party busybodies were ever vigilant. Still information leaked out. One American, driving in the countryside, saw a large squadron of planes maneuvering overhead with military precision (Germany was forbidden by the Versailles Treaty to have an air force). Suddenly the planes disappeared, apparently landing in a patch of woods. The American's curiosity was aroused, so he drove toward the forest. When he reached its fringe, he encountered a roadblock, and a policeman shouted at him to halt. *"Verboten,"* (forbidden) barked the policeman as he signaled for the American to turn around.

What was really going on in German factories? Hitler had ordered 100 new tanks by March 1934 and 650 one year later, in spite of the fact that Germany was forbidden by the Versailles Treaty to have any tanks at all. Companies also began receiving orders for armored cars and other military equipment as early as the fall of 1933. The army ordered 3,000 new heavy trucks. Aircraft factories were working day and night in three shifts to build fighters and bombers for Goering's Luftwaffe. Hitler also gave an order to produce a submarine a month; and heavy 26,000-ton battle cruisers were secretly being built in Germany's northern ports.[6]

To throw up a smoke screen around his rearmament activities, Hitler's strategy was to talk peace while he prepared for war. He calculated correctly that the desire for peace was very strong among the British and French people. Appealing to this public opinion, he took the position that Germany had been unjustly and unfairly treated by the Versailles Treaty. There was enough truth in this argument to arouse some sympathy, particularly in Britain. Hitler insisted that all he was asking for was for Germany to get equal treatment like any other nation and thereby to be able to possess enough arms to defend herself.[7]

After several months of consolidating Nazi rule in Germany, Hitler felt he was strong enough to make a bold move in foreign policy. As the first public step toward rearmament he wanted to withdraw Germany from the League of Nations and the Disarmament Conference.[8]* This would be a good way to determine how Britain and France were likely to respond to German rearmament.

On October 14, in a radio broadcast to the German people, Hitler announced that Germany was withdrawing from the Disarmament Conference and the League of Nations. The reason for this move, said Hitler, was that other nations were still not treating Germany as an equal, especially in the matter of

---

*The delegates of sixty nations had been meeting at intervals from 1932 to 1934 to bring about a reduction in arms.

armaments. Hitler's action was largely a symbolic protest against the Versailles Treaty. There was very little risk involved for Germany because public opinion in Britain and France was very divided on the issue so it was unlikely that the League would invoke sanctions.[9]

To demonstrate to the Allies that he had the support of the people for his foreign policy, Hitler called a plebiscite to vote on Germany's withdrawal from the League. The results of the plebiscite were impressive; 95 percent of the German people voted in favor of Hitler's foreign policy.

In the Secret Defense Law of 1935, Hitler appointed the minister of economics, Dr. Hjalmar Schacht, as plenipotentiary for war economy, with orders to direct the economic preparation for war. This law made Schacht the economic dictator of Germany.[10] Schacht was a tall thin man who always dressed in a dark suit and white shirt with a high, stiff, old-fashioned collar. He wore small, round wire-rim glasses that, together with his gray hair parted in the middle of his head, gave him an owlish look. His influence was such that during the mid-1930s some political observers believed he was the real dictator of Germany and Hitler was just a puppet. Schacht's position was not just a reward for the large contributions he had brought to the Nazi party. Hitler recognized that he was one of the most able financiers in Germany. "Hitler never interfered with my work," Schacht later said. "He never attempted to give me any instructions but let me carry out my own ideas."[11]

Schacht proved his financial genius by financing rearmament in part by the so-called mefo bills, a cover name for IOUs that were paid to the industrialists for rearmament work. No mention of these notes ever appeared on the records of the central bank, so they helped keep government spending on rearmament secret while at the same time limiting the inflationary impact.[12] Schacht also succeeded in obtaining the raw materials Germany needed for rearmament, in spite of a lack of currency. He accomplished this by arranging a number of barter deals with countries in Eastern Europe: their raw materials for Germany's manufactured goods. On Schacht's sixtieth birthday, in 1937, the army hailed him as "the man who made the rebuilding of the German Army economically possible."[13]

By July of 1934, Germany's rearmament was well under way,

93

and Hitler began dreaming of foreign conquests. For some time, he had been financing the underground Nazi party in Austria.[14] On July 25, 1934, the Austrian Nazis attempted to overthrow the conservative Catholic government of Chancellor Dollfuss. Nazis dressed in Austrian Army uniforms succeeded in seizing several government buildings. They captured Dollfuss and in a scuffle, he was shot in the neck at close range. As Dollfuss lay in his office dying in a pool of blood, the Nazis announced the overthrow of the Austrian government on the radio.[15]

When Hitler heard the news, he was at first thrilled. However, as the hours passed, he received further reports that loyal Austrian Army units were gradually retaking the government buildings and capturing the Nazi revolutionaries. Mussolini, who saw himself as Austria's protector, was furious and immediately sent four divisions to the Brenner Pass with orders to stop Hitler if he tried to intervene in Austria with German troops. Knowing Germany was not yet strong enough to confront Italy, Hitler hastened to dissociate himself from the coup and dispatched his old ally and vice-chancellor, von Papen, to Vienna to try to smooth over the matter.[16]

After the fiasco of the Nazis' Austrian coup, Hitler had to face reality—Germany was not yet strong enough for foreign adventures. Aside from the fact that the coup had been hastily and haphazardly planned and poorly organized, the German Army was not yet strong enough to face any foreign foe.[17] The rearmament program would take time. Germany was diplomatically isolated without even one ally. France, Britain, Italy, and Russia were all united against her, not to mention the small countries of Eastern Europe. These countries, Poland, Czechoslovakia, Romania, and Yugoslavia, all had military alliances with France; together they encircled Germany with a ring of steel. Hitler knew he would have to lie low and wait for some weakness to appear in the united front of his enemies.

Hitler immersed himself in the details of rearmament, although he did not directly interfere with the work of the industrialists or the army. He studied the specifications, range, and armament of every new weapon being produced. For hours each day, he pored over the technical drawings of new tanks, ships, and planes, comparing their strengths and weaknesses with weapons of foreign powers. Field Marshal von Manstein, who was a General Staff officer in the 1930s, later said: "Hitler possessed an astoundingly retentive memory and an imagination that made him quick to grasp all technical matters and problems of armaments. He was amazingly familiar with the effect of the very latest enemy weapons and could reel off whole columns of figures on both our own and the enemy's war production. There can be no question that his insight and unusual energy were responsible for many achievements in the sphere of armaments."[18] During this period of rearmament in the mid-1930s, Hitler also read voraciously on military tactics and strategy. It was, in effect, his graduate education in military science.

Hitler was cautious not to interfere with the day-to-day business of the conservative foreign office. Nevertheless, he became increasingly involved in foreign affairs because it related directly to the next stage of Germany's rearmament effort. A well-read student of history, Hitler knew that one of the primary foreign policy objectives of Britain had always been to keep a balance of power on the Continent. Britain, he correctly assumed, was now worried more about France than about Germany. The French threatened to dominate the Continent, both militarily and economically. France's army of 540,000 men was the largest in Europe (with the exception of Russia). The German 100,000-man army was hardly any threat. In fact, Britain was worried that if France invaded Germany, the British would be faced with the threat they had fought World War I to avoid: one superpower dominating Europe.

This was the division between the Allies for which Hitler had been waiting. He began an attempt to lure the British into bilateral disarmament talks. If the British even sat down to talk with the Germans about disarmament, which had been firmly fixed by the Versailles Treaty, it would in effect nullify the treaty. It would also damage British-French relations. Both the British and Hitler realized this. Hitler's first offer to Britain was to set limits on air armaments. When this didn't work, he offered the British something he thought they couldn't refuse—a naval treaty that would limit the German Navy to 35 percent of the British Navy.

At this time, Hitler was receiving considerable encouragement from a number of highly placed people in Britain. Montagu Norman, the president of the Bank of England, was known to be very pro-German and anti-Semitic. He was a close friend of Hjalmar Schacht, Hitler's minister of economics. Norman and Schacht had met secretly a number of times to work out the details of a proposed British loan to Germany.

Another pro-Nazi Englishman was Lord Rothermere, the owner of a chain of British newspapers. Rothermere had been running a number of pro-Hitler articles. In December of 1934, Rothermere visited Hitler in Germany and came away more an admirer of the Fuehrer than ever. He had particular praise for Hitler's tough anticommunism. There were a large number of other prominent and powerful people in Britain who saw Hitler as a stabilizing force on the Continent and a bulwark against communism.

But of all the sympathizers and friends of Germany in Britain, Hitler and the German Foreign Office were most interested in the opinion of the Prince of Wales, the heir to the throne. On a number of occasions the prince had expressed pro-German sympathies. In a conversation with the German ambassador, von Hoesch, the prince "showed his complete understanding of the German position and aspirations."[19]

On January 13, 1935, the population of the Saar, a small coal-rich region of western Germany bordering France, went to the polls to decide the territory's future. Although the people of the Saar were German speaking, they had been split from Germany by the Versailles Treaty. Hitler waged a strong campaign for the return of the Saar. The election was a big victory for the Nazis; 477,000 people voted to return to Germany and only 21,000 voted to join France.

On the evening of February 28, 1935, thousands of Saarlanders waited in cafés and at home for midnight. On March 1, the Saar would officially be German again. When the clocks chimed midnight, church bells began to ring. In the cafés, people leaped to their feet, raising their beer steins, roaring "Heil! Heil! Heil!" On the street corners loudspeakers began to play the German national anthem, "Deutschland Über Alles" ("Germany Above All"). People danced, sang, shouted, and greeted each other with "Heil Hitler!"

Three hundred thousand Nazis streamed into the Saar the

next morning to celebrate. Hitler arrived in the afternoon. He rode slowly through the streets of Saarbrucken in his open Mercedes, bareheaded in the rain. Wet swastika flags hung from every lamppost and window. Thousands cheered hysterically as the Fuehrer drove by. The speech Hitler delivered in Saarbruecken that day was a combination of a plea for reconciliation between France and Germany, and an ominous warning. After speaking of his hope to "improve relations between France and Germany," Hitler threatened the system of the Versailles Treaty. "In the final analysis," he said, "blood is stronger than all paper documents. The day will come when the writing of the ink will be erased through blood. Woe betide him who does not learn this fact."

The overwhelming support Hitler received from the people of the Saar and his war-threatening speech were viewed with alarm by some of the more perceptive men in the British government and Foreign Office. On March 4, the British government published a white paper that condemned German rearmament as a breach of the Versailles Treaty.

The white paper confused the Germans. Just when Hitler thought the pro-German faction in Britain had the upper hand, the British had suddenly changed course and were once again defending the Versailles system. German agents in Britain assured the German Foreign Office that the white paper did not represent the view of the powers that be in Britain. Nevertheless, Hitler was cautious after the Dollfuss fiasco and decided to play it carefully.

Sir John Simon, the British foreign secretary, was scheduled to visit Berlin on March 5 for disarmament talks. Hitler suddenly announced that he had a cold and would have to postpone Simon's visit. It was rumored in Britain that Hitler's "cold" was due to his anger at the British publication of the white paper. The Nazi leader, however, was actually attempting a much more subtle ploy.

It was time for Germany to progress to the next stage of rearmament. The increasing magnitude of military activities and weapons production could no longer be kept secret. Hitler was now ready for a larger army and conscription, which obviously could not be done in secret. But he was not yet prepared to risk war or sanctions against Germany. He had to be sure he would have British support for his moves. If Britain did nothing to stop Germany's actions, France would not likely act alone.

Hitler decided the current crisis over the white paper and the timing of Sir John Simon's visit would be a perfect opportunity to test British opinion. In spite of assurances from German friends in Britain, Hitler floated a trial balloon to gauge the real sentiments of the British government. In an exclusive interview with Ward Price, of Lord Rothermere's paper, *The Daily Mail*, Goering acknowledged for the first time that Germany had an air force.[20]

As Hitler had anticipated, there was no official condemnation from the British for this clear violation of the Versailles Treaty. Instead, Sir John Simon told Parliament he still intended to go to Berlin when Hitler recovered from his cold. This was a clear diplomatic signal that Britain approved of Germany's rearmament. Hitler now had the green light to proceed.

The French, naturally, condemned Germany's building an air force as a treaty violation. In response France extended the period of military service for draftees. Recognizing they would not have British cooperation, the French government did not even consider sanctions or military action. Nevertheless, France's feeble response of extending military service was enough to provide Hitler with an excuse for his next move.

On Saturday, March 16, Hitler announced the reintroduction of conscription and said the army's strength would be built up to thirty-six divisions, or approximately 500,000 men.[21] He assured the world that Germany had no aggressive intentions. He said he was reluctant to take this step but had no choice. Germany had trusted the assurances of President Wilson's fourteen Points and disarmed, believing that the other nations would disarm as well. But now, said Hitler, Germany found that not only were the other powers not disarming but they were also increasing their armament.[22] Germany had to be able to defend itself.

The following day, March 17, Heroes Memorial Day, the Nazis put on a spectacular military celebration. There was a huge parade of army, navy, and Luftwaffe units. Hitler walked alongside General von Blomberg and Field Marshal von Mackensen, the only living field marshal of the old Imperial Army. Thousands cheered as they watched the parade. There was also a solemn service at the Berlin State Opera House. William

Shirer, then a reporter in Berlin, attended the ceremony: "The entire lower floor," he said, "was a sea of military uniforms, the faded grey uniforms and spiked helmets of the Old Imperial Army mingled with the attire of the New Army, including the sky-blue uniforms of the Luftwaffe, which few had seen before. . . . The Generals, one could see by their faces, were immensely pleased."[23]

The spirit of Prussian militarism was reborn. Hitler had accomplished what the generals had been trying to do for years. Germany was now free to rebuild her army to a size befitting a world power. Although there was considerable Nazi propaganda about Hitler having broken the "shackles of Versailles" and freed Germany from her "enslavement," the Versailles Treaty had been weakened but not destroyed completely. One major obstacle remained in Hitler's path before Germany could be considered fully rearmed—the Germans would have to reoccupy the demilitarized Rhineland.[24]

Despite Hitler's open flounting of the Versailles Treaty by reintroducing conscription, Sir John Simon and Anthony Eden (who would soon be Simon's successor as foreign secretary) arrived in Berlin on March 28 to discuss arms limitations. By simply meeting publicly with Hitler to talk about disarmament, England was sanctioning the possibility of Germany's rearmament. The talks were held in the Chancellery in Berlin and went well, although Eden later wrote that he was "most unfavorably impressed" by Hitler's personality and found him "rather shifty." Hitler dismissed Simon's reproach for breaking the Versailles Treaty simply by saying that he had never signed it.

With an unusual hint of humor, the Fuehrer said Germany was not accustomed to violating treaties, except when the Prussian Army had helped the British at Waterloo: "Did Wellington, when Blücher came to his assistance at Waterloo, first ask the legal experts of the foreign office whether the strength of the Prussian forces exceeded the limits fixed by treaty?"[25] Hitler's implication was clear; he wanted to let the British know that he thought they were not permitting German rearmament out of feelings of charity or guilt. A number of important people in Britain wanted a rearmed Germany to counterbalance France and her allies.

Although nothing significant was resolved by the talks, the

fact that they were held increased Hitler's prestige both at home and abroad. It was agreed that Hitler would later send a delegation to London to discuss an Anglo-German naval treaty. At the conclusion of the talks, Hitler held a dinner for the British in the Chancellery. He wore formal white tie and tails and seemed completely at ease among his guests. Late that night, after the British diplomats had departed, Hitler sat and talked to some of his close followers about his hopes for an Anglo-German alliance.[26]

In June, Hitler sent Joachim von Ribbentrop, a loyal Nazi who was being groomed to become foreign minister, to London to negotiate the naval treaty. In spite of Ribbentrop's lack of tact in conducting the negotiations, an agreement was reached. The treaty permitted Germany to build a navy that was 35 percent as large as Britain's. However, there was also a clause allowing Germany an increased number of submarines. With revealing symbolism, the treaty was signed on June 18, the 120th anniversary of the British and Prussian victory over Napoleon at Waterloo. Hitler was overjoyed and said it was "the happiest day of his life."

The French felt betrayed and sent an angry protest to London. Even the Italians, who were also a naval power, were upset that they had been ignored. Public opinion in Britain, however, was largely in favor of the treaty. In response to French criticism, an article in a prestigious British magazine stated: "England has no permanent friends, but only permanent interests." At a luncheon at Ascot, the Prince of Wales told Ambassador von Hoesch from Germany that he was very pleased with the Anglo-German naval treaty.

The Prince of Wales's first public expression of his pro-German sympathies was during a speech he made at the annual conference of the British Legion: "I feel," he said, "that there could be no more suitable . . . organization of men to stretch forth the hand of friendship to the Germans than we ex-servicemen."[27] The next day his father, King George V, sent for him and reprimanded him for the speech. "How often have I told you, my dear boy, never to mix in politics, especially where foreign affairs are concerned. The views you expressed yesterday, however sensible, are, I happen to know, contrary to those of the Foreign Office."[28]

Although the prince's speech was given limited coverage in the English press, the Germans hailed it as a real breakthrough. It made the headlines of Dr. Goebbel's Berlin paper, *Der Angriff*. A British correspondent in Berlin reported, "The declaration by the Prince of Wales is regarded by Germany as being the seal to the friendship agreement between the two countries [the naval treaty]. . . . The fact that the Prince of Wales is accustomed to exercise extreme reserve in his public utterance, it is pointed out, gives stronger effect to his pronouncement yesterday."[29] Hitler was delighted to hear of the prince's remarks and felt it would mean more concessions from the British.

The prince was opinionated and vain. His charm and verbal skill gave him the mistaken impression that he could overcome any obstacle. Many people considered him too outspoken for a future constitutional monarch, especially on foreign policy issues. He was strongly opposed to communism and had little tolerance for socialism.

Like many men of his generation who had seen the horrors of war firsthand, the prince was seriously committed to international peace. Modern war, he believed, was so destructive that it was no longer possible to speak in terms of victors and vanquished. There would be nothing left on either side but a heap of ruins. However, the prince was not a pacifist. He firmly believed in a militarily strong British Empire.

The prince especially wanted to prevent another war between England and Germany. He was sympathetic to Germany in part because his mother was a German princess and he had happy memories of childhood visits to Germany. On a strategic level, he believed in the traditional British policy of trying to maintain a balance of power on the Continent, and like many other Englishmen, thought France was getting too strong. The Versailles Treaty, he felt, was entirely too harsh, unfair, and needed to be gotten rid of. As far as Hitler was concerned, the prince admired the way he had suppressed communism and was solving the unemployment problem in Germany.

The prince was even more outspoken in private than in public. His pro-German opinions were something he had given considerable thought to, and he could expound on them at length among his close circle of friends. Instead of seeing Hitler and Mussolini as threats to Britain, the prince made no secret of his admiration for the fascist dictators. There is no doubt that the prince was anti-Semitic; however, many historians have dismissed this as just the normal social prejudice of his class. But it was much more than that. The prince believed many of the same pseudoscientific racial theories as Hitler, which was another bond between the two men. He once told Winston Churchill that Negroes were poorly equipped mentally for the intellectual demands of the modern world and he believed "liberal socialistic ideas of freedom and equality, regardless of race . . . [were] dangerous."[30]

The prince could have drawn encouragement from Hitler's statement in *Mein Kampf* that "it is a criminal absurdity to train a born half-ape [Negro] until one believes a lawyer has been made of him."[31] One of the duke's biographers, Philip Ziegler, wrote: "He believed that the black man was inevitably inferior to the white and was wholly unfitted to govern. He was ill at ease with them socially [blacks] and . . . found any sort of physical contact repulsive. In this attitude he was abetted by his [future] wife."[32]

In October of 1935, Mussolini invaded Ethiopia. The League of Nations led by Britain and France voted for sanctions against Italy. At first, Germany was officially neutral but later in the war began selling arms to Italy. Hitler was delighted with the conflict. Regardless of the outcome of the African War, he was bound to come out ahead. If Mussolini won, it would weaken the international prestige of Germany's principal enemies, France and Britain, and prove that the League of Nations and its sanctions were powerless. On the other hand, if Italy lost, Mussolini's role as protector of Austria and his ambitions in the Danube region (to create an Italian sphere of influence along the Danube) would be weakened.

The war in Ethiopia also turned the world's attention away from Germany. This provided Hitler with a tempting opportunity. The last major step in rearmament would be the reoccupation of the demilitarized zone of the Rhineland. As long as Germany could not have any fortifications or troops in the Rhineland, the French could invade at will and immediately capture Germany's most valuable industrial region. However, Hitler realized, sending German troops into the Rhineland was a dangerous step. For such a flagrant breach of the Versailles Treaty, France and Britain might go to war or at least call for sanctions and blockade

Germany. If the French did attack they could easily overwhelm the Germans, especially if they were assisted by their allies in the east, Poland and Czechoslovakia. Hitler was originally planning to reoccupy the Rhineland in 1937, after Germany's conscripts were thoroughly trained. However, in January of 1936 something happened that caused him to move up his timetable.

On the evening of January 20, King George V, of England, died and was succeeded by Edward VIII (formerly the Prince of Wales). Hitler was encouraged. If King Edward VIII was willing to use his influence in favor of Germany, Britain might refuse to support France when German troops marched into the Rhineland. So it was vital for Hitler to know exactly where the king stood on the Rhineland issue. German agents in Britain were given immediate orders of the highest priority to get whatever information they could about the new king's willingness to actively use his influence to prevent a war over the Rhineland.

One of the most important Nazis in London at the time was the duke of Coburg, who was a German cousin of the British king and had been educated at Eton. The duke reported to Hitler several of his conversations with the king, who seemed sincere in his resolve to establish better relations between Germany and England. The king was also worried about the spread of communism. The duke said the king "complained during the second conversation about Russia and Litvinov, with whom he had, 'unfortunately,' just had to shake hands." Litvinov was a Communist and was Jewish, but since he was the Soviet minister of foreign affairs, the king had to shake hands with him. The duke of Coburg further reported: "To my question whether a discussion between Baldwin [the prime minister] and Hitler would be desireable, he replied . . . 'Who is king here? Baldwin or I? I myself wish to talk to Hitler, and will do so, here or in Germany. Tell him that, please.' "[33]

Hitler was also trying to get information from a secret source very close to the king. In 1933, King Edward, then Prince of Wales, began a romance with Mrs. Wallis Simpson, an American by birth. Mrs. Simpson seemed to hold some special fascination for the prince, who could have had his choice of any number of beautiful Englishwomen. Before long, Wallis Simpson divorced her husband and became the prince's constant companion. When the prince became king, several top men in the Foreign Office and British intelligence became alarmed at Wallis Simpson's relationship with him because some considered her a security risk. She was put under surveillance by British security.

The Prince of Wales and Mrs. Simpson were both friends of the German ambassador in London, Leopold von Hoesch, a cultured professional diplomat. Hoesch was known for giving some of the best parties in London. No expense was spared; the food was excellent, and renowned orchestras were hired to entertain the guests as they dined. Ambassador von Hoesch introduced the prince and Mrs. Simpson to Ribbentrop, Hitler's ambassador-at-large. At a German embassy party, Ribbentrop sat next to Mrs. Simpson. The two seemed to get along very well. The next day, Mrs. Simpson received seventeen roses with a note from Ribbentrop attached. Every morning for the next few days, until Ribbentrop returned to Berlin, Mrs. Simpson received seventeen roses. There was considerable gossip about the seventeen roses in both England and Germany. When Ribbentrop returned to Berlin, the first thing Hitler asked him was: "Why seventeen roses?"

Mrs. Simpson later denied giving any intelligence information to Ribbentrop and said she met him only on two occasions, both of them in public. This was probably true, because a man of Ribbentrop's rank and self-importance would not have been involved in espionage activities. His attentions to Mrs. Simpson were simply a signal to the Prince of Wales that the Germans would be willing to communicate through her.

Why did the Germans think Mrs. Simpson might be willing to help them? She wanted more than anything else to marry the prince. Aware of how strongly he felt about peace between Britain and Germany, she thought that if she embraced his cause, it would bind him to her ever more closely. Quickly becoming a dominant influence over him, she urged him to speak his mind on foreign affairs and not be restrained by the petty politicians and government bureaucrats. She also resented the British establishment, which had rejected her.

The Germans apparently picked up useful information from overhearing Mrs. Simpson's conversations about the king's true feelings. Having had no experience at diplomacy or espionage, she may carelessly have revealed things to people who were German agents. Robert W. Bingham, the American ambassador in England, reported to President Roosevelt that the king was "surrounded by a pro-German cabal." "Many people here," the ambassador went on, "suspected that Mrs. Simpson was actually in German pay." The ambassador added that he thought this was unlikely, but he believed she was a "strong pro-German."[34] The suspicions that Wallis Simpson might be receiving money from the Germans were caused by her lavish expenditures. True, the king was giving her jewels and extravagant presents, but she was spending on a scale that shocked all her friends, even her very wealthy friends. She was continually purchasing new jewels and clothes. On one occasion, she bought eighteen pairs of shoes at one time.

According to some informed observers, Mrs. Simpson had a strong influence on the king's thinking. The worst thing about Mrs. Simpson, according to the Danish ambassador, was that she "tried to mix herself up in politics. She endeavored in every way to single out the German embassy and to have everything German preferred at Court. . . . Under the influence of these surroundings, the king, at times, made statements which tended to show that his sympathies were colored by Nazism and Fascism."[35]

When Prime Minister Stanley Baldwin discovered that vital government documents were left on the king's desk at Fort Belvedere, his private residence, when Wallis Simpson and her friends were visiting, he was highly alarmed. For the first time in British history, the prime minister restricted the documents given to the king to those requiring the royal signature.

Hitler took a personal interest in Wallis Simpson's affairs because she not only knew what the king was thinking, but she could, and did, influence his decisions. At this time, it was vitally important for Hitler to know how the king of England would respond if Germany sent troops into the demilitarized zone of the Rhineland. After carefully weighing the intelligence information on the attitude of the king, Hitler decided the time was right to reoccupy the Rhineland. He ordered the General Staff to draw up the plan and keep the operation top secret. The generals were alarmed. If France and her allies decided to fight, the French, Polish, and Czech armies could immediately mobilize almost a hundred divisions with another hundred divisions in reserve. Against them, Germany had less than forty divisions, and many of these consisted of first-year conscripts who had only a few months of training.

The generals pointed out to Hitler the risks involved. But Hitler insisted France and England would not fight. Although General von Blomberg was not convinced by Hitler's argument, he went ahead and issued orders to prepare for the operation. If the French decided to fight, he reserved "the right to decide on any military countermeasures." Hitler agreed. These "countermeasures" were simply to withdraw back across the Rhine as quickly as possible. Thus, at the outset of the operation the generals did not fully trust Hitler's judgment. However, they did not know about the intelligence information he was getting from London.

All Hitler needed now was some excuse to act that would make it look as if France was forcing him to take a purely defensive measure. When the French Chamber of Deputies ratified the Franco-Soviet Treaty, Hitler had his excuse. He contended that the Franco-Soviet alliance upset the balance of power in Europe. Secret orders went out to waiting German Army units to march into the Rhineland on the first Saturday in March.[36]

In the early morning hours of Saturday, March 7, 1936, on a windy country road east of Frankfurt, a company of gray-clad steel-helmeted soldiers shivered in the darkness. Their commander looked at his watch. Then the officers shouted, *"Achtung!"* The men snapped to attention. The order was given, and they marched. From other jump-off points east of the Rhine, twenty-five thousand other German soldiers like them headed for Frankfurt, Essen, Düsseldorf, Cologne, Mainz, and Saarbruecken.

Sometime after dawn, a squadron of nine Luftwaffe planes came roaring over Cologne from the direction of Berlin. They circled the spire of the Cologne Cathedral and then flew off into the blue eastern sky and disappeared. Nazi officials in the Rhineland refused to confirm reports that the German Army was on its way, but since 5 A.M., grapevine rumors had been spreading through Cologne. Thousands of people spontaneously began to gather in the square opposite the cathedral. A brass band appeared and struck up "The Watch on the Rhine" as the crowd sang: *"Zum Rhein, Zum Rhein, Zum Deutschen Rhein! Wer will des Stromer's Heuter Sein?"* ("The Rhine, the Rhine, the German Rhine! Who guards tonight our Stream Divine?")

It was not long before the new guard for the Rhine came marching over the steel, triple-arched Hohenzollern bridge. Three motorcyclists with regimental flags came first, then an infantry regiment marching three abreast, then a company of horse-drawn machine guns and an antiaircraft unit. Heavy boots thudded against the pavement. Belt buckles and rifle barrels flashed in the sunlight. Yet the red and white carnations that female onlookers gave to the soldiers and put on the horses and vehicles gave this march a festive air. This, however, was not a weekend parade to be taken lightly. It was an open violation of Articles 42 and 43 of the Versailles Treaty, which forbade Germany to have any armed forces beyond a line fifty kilometers (thirty-one miles) east of the Rhine. It was also a violation of the Locarno Treaty, which Germany had signed agreeing to a demilitarized Rhineland.

At noon, Hitler addressed the Reichstag in Berlin. "Men of the German Reichstag . . . ," thundered Hitler, "the German government has reestablished, as of today, absolute and unrestricted sovereignty in the demilitarized zone!" The members of the Reichstag went wild. They stood up shouting, cheering, arms outstretched in heils. Finally, quiet was restored and Hitler continued. "In this historic hour, in the Reich's western provinces German troops are at this minute marching into their future peacetime garrisons."[37] The Reichstag again erupted in hysterical delirium. The thought that the German Army was on the march appealed to the militaristic passions of the Nazi Reichstag deputies. Hitler's speech was also broadcast to the nation over the radio; everywhere Germans responded with wild enthusiasm.

All day, new silver Luftwaffe fighters, with their black-and-white swastika insignias on their wings, flew over the castle-dotted hills and valleys of the Rhineland. They circled over the smoke-blackened industrial cities of the Ruhr, home to one-fourth of Germany's population. From their aircraft, the Nazi pilots could see the green forest-covered hills of Alsace and Lorraine, beyond the border.

In Paris, crowds gathered around the newsstands. The headlines of extras read: "German Troops Invade Rhineland!" Members of the cabinet were demanding military action. Railroad platforms were crowded with soldiers and reservists kissing their wives and sweethearts good-bye before boarding eastbound trains on their way to the Maginot Line.

The news from Paris worried the German General Staff. Actually, the German forces were not nearly as strong as everyone believed. Only three battalions actually crossed the Rhine. The generals suddenly lost their nerve and were afraid the French would fight. They urged the immediate withdrawal of the three battalions back across the Rhine. General Beck, the chief of staff (the highest strategic planning staff of the army), pleaded with Hitler to at least promise the French that Germany would not build any fortifications west of the Rhine. Hitler bluntly turned down both proposals and was disgusted with what he saw as the cowardice of the generals.

In spite of his outward confidence, Hitler was very anxious during the first twenty-four hours. Albert Speer, Hitler's young architect, who was traveling with him on his private train to Munich that night, remembered the "tense atmosphere that evening." "At one station," recalled Speer, "a message was handed into the [train] car. Hitler sighed with relief: 'At last! The King of England will not intervene. He is keeping his promise. That means it can all go well!'"[38] Hitler's statement would seem to indicate he had made some kind of secret agreement with King Edward VIII in which the king promised not to interfere if Germany moved troops into the Rhineland. "Even later," said Speer, "when he was waging war against almost the entire world he always termed the remilitarization of the Rhineland as the most daring of all his undertakings."

After Edward VIII was forced to abdicate and became the Duke of Windsor, Hitler frequently referred to his friendly attitude toward Nazi Germany. "I am certain," said Hitler, "that through him, permanent friendly relations with England could have been achieved. If he had stayed, everything would have been different. His abdication was a severe loss for us."[39]

Even with the English king being sympathetic toward Germany, there was still a danger France or Poland might attack. It was a weekend of tension throughout Europe.

Recalling years later the events of March 1936, Hitler said: "What would have happened . . . if anybody other than myself had been head of the Reich? Anyone you care to mention would have lost his nerve. I was obliged to lie, and what saved us was my unshakable obstinacy and my amazing aplomb. I threatened, unless the situation eased in twenty-four hours, to send six extra divisions into the Rhineland. The fact was, I only had four brigades. Next day, the English newspapers wrote that there had been easing of the international situation."[40]

In London, Ambassador von Hoesch used his intimate friendship with the king to get an immediate meeting. He appealed to the king to preserve the peace and gave him a proposal from Hitler to replace the old Locarno Treaty with a new one. Later, Hoesch received a telephone call from the king: "I sent for the prime minister," said the king, "and gave him a piece of my mind. I told the old so-and-so that I would abdicate if he made war. There was a frightful scene. But you needn't worry. There won't be a war." Putting down the receiver, Hoesch jumped up and down with glee; "I've done it, I've outwitted them all, there won't be a war! . . . It's magnificent, I must inform Berlin immediately."[41]

After his telephone conversation with the king, Hoesch sent a telegram to the Foreign Ministry in Berlin: "Today I got into indirect touch with the court. . . . There is understanding for the German point of view. The directive given to the Government from there [the court or king] is to the effect that no matter how the details of the affair are dealt with, complications of a serious nature are in no circumstances to be allowed to develop."[42]

Reaction in London to Hitler's reoccupation of the Rhineland developed in two clearly distinct stages. At first there were calls for supporting France and taking whatever necessary action against Germany that would force her to back down. However, it seems that once the king got involved and used his influence in the right places, the tone began to change. *The Observer* wrote: "There is no more reason why German territory should be demilitarized than French, Belgian, or British."

Dr. Von Stutterheim, a foreign correspondent for the *Berliner Tageblatt* and an informed observer of events behind the scenes in London, told his editor:

The King is taking an extraordinarily active part in the whole affair, he has caused a number of important people in the government to come and see him and has said to them: "This is a nice way to start my reign." The King won't hear of there being a war. He is absolutely convinced that what must now be done is to get over the "breach of law" [Versailles and Locarno Treaties] as quickly as possible and get on to the practical discussion of the Fuehrer's . . . proposals. In view of the tremendous influence possessed by the King and his immense energy, due importance must be attached to this.[43]

Hitler's "proposals" were a mere sham, but they had served their purpose of defusing the Allied reaction.

Once the British government decided not to become involved, Hitler was safe. The French soon decided against military action without Britain's support. This was a mistake. France alone could easily have defeated Germany. It would have been an opportunity to stop Hitler with little loss of life. "The forty-eight hours after the march into the Rhineland," Hitler later admitted, "were the most nerve-racking of my life. If the French had marched into the Rhineland, we would have had to withdraw with our tails between our legs, for the military resources at our disposal would have been inadequate for even a moderate resistance."

To make the most of his victory, Hitler dissolved the Reichstag and called for new elections as a referendum on his move into the Rhineland. The vote turned out to be a tremendous victory for him, with almost 98 percent approval. According to most neutral observers, the election was a relatively free one with only some irregularities in the vote count. Even considering that fear of the Gestapo made many people vote for the Nazis, the fact remains that the overwhelming majority of Germans freely voted for Hitler's candidates. It was not, however, to the credit of the average German voter that they let Hitler's foreign policy triumph blind them to the tyranny, suppressions of basic free-dom, and persecution of the Jews that were going on around them.

Hitler was at the height of his popularity. He probably enjoyed more support among the people than any other German ruler in modern times. The reason was rather obvious. His string of recent victories in foreign policy was impressive. One by one, he had broken the shackles of the Versailles Treaty, ended reparations,* left the League of Nations, started conscription, and finally ended demilitarization of the Rhineland.[44] And all without causing a war and without the loss of a single life.

The reoccupation of the Rhineland by German troops finally gave Germany full sovereignty over her own territory, marked the successful completion of the first and most important phase of rearmament, and decisively shifted the balance of power in Europe. France's complete military dominance of the Continent was ended. As long as the Germans had been forbidden to build any defenses on either bank of the Rhine, the French Army could have walked into Germany at the time. Now that Germany could build defensive fortifications west of the Rhine, the Reich's borders were secure. The French alliance system with the small states of Central and Eastern Europe—Poland, Czechoslovakia, Romania, and Yugoslavia—was in jeopardy. With German fortifications on the western borders, the German Army could attack in the east and the French could no longer easily march to the aid of their allies.

The Germans fully realized their new position of strength. William Bullitt, U.S. ambassador to France, recounts a conversa-tion with Foreign Minister von Neurath:

Neurath said it was the policy of the German government to do nothing active in foreign affairs until "the Rhineland had been digested." He explained that he meant that until the

---

*Although Hitler claimed he ended reparations, the credit should go to Chancellor Bruening, whose policy of patient negotiations with the Allies finally paid off after he left office. With the beginning of the depression, the Allies realized the Germans could no longer pay reparations and further attempts to force them to do so would only add to the disruption of world trade.

German fortifications had been constructed on the French and Belgian frontiers, the German government would do everything possible to prevent rather than encourage an outbreak by the Nazis in Austria. "As soon as our fortifications are constructed and the countries of central Europe realize that France cannot enter German territory at will, all those countries will begin to feel very differently about their foreign policies."[45]

The reoccupation of the Rhineland also marked an important shift in power in the Nazi coalition government. Hitler now held a much stronger hand in his power struggle with his generals. He had been proven right; France and Britain did not fight over the Rhineland. For wanting to withdraw at the moment of crisis, the generals appeared to be not only pessimists but cowards as well. Even the members of the Officers Corps themselves felt a loss of confidence in their commanders and at the same time an increased respect for Hitler's judgment on both foreign policy and military matters.

Hitler was not yet ready to openly challenge the generals, but he was fed up with the overcautious way General von Fritsch, the commander in chief of the army, was directing rearmament. Fritsch, a traditional, old-fashioned officer, did not share Hitler's confidence in new weapons like tanks and aircraft. He was uneasy with expanding the army's size too rapidly. For most of General von Fritsch's career, he had served in an army with an extremely limited budget; consequently, he was very economical and conservative in his requests for new equipment. Hitler, however, had given the army an unlimited budget, and he was somewhat dismayed that the generals didn't seem to appreciate it or know how to take advantage of it.

Hitler vigorously protested against what he called the "homeopathic-like quantities" of army procurement. "The industrialists were always complaining to me about this niggardly procedure—today an order for ten howitzers, tomorrow for two mortars, and so on. And when one knows that production lines require four to eight months before they can set to work!"[46]

In line with the generals' desire to slow the rearmament process was their idea of avoiding any possibility of war before 1943 or 1944. Consequently, they viewed with alarm Hitler's confrontational foreign policy and brinkmanship. But after his victory in the Rhineland, Hitler was determined to permit the generals to dictate foreign policy no longer. A new power struggle between Hitler and the generals was brewing. But first Hitler would turn his fury on helpless and innocent victims— the Jews.

Chapter 5

Who Got the Confiscated Jewish Property?

After the failure of the Nazi boycott of Jewish stores in April of 1933, and the extremely negative foreign response to it, Hitler realized he had to rethink his anti-Semitic policy. He needed time to get the Nazi regime on a firm foundation; any hostility from abroad would threaten to undermine his rearmament plans. He certainly could not afford to have a new wave of atrocity stories upset the delicate negotiations with Britain. Although he never considered giving up his anti-Semitic views, he was willing to hold back temporarily on any large-scale violence against the Jews. However, even this would not be easy. As soon as the Hitler-Papen government took office, Nazi thugs considered it their right to physically abuse Jews and were looking forward to the looting of Jewish property.

The failure of the April 1933 boycott of Jewish businesses raised a number of questions for the Nazis. First of all, the boycott hurt the German economy as much as it hurt the Jews. Needed foreign investment in Germany was put in jeopardy. After all, this was still the depression. A new wave of bankruptcies of large firms, even if they were Jewish, could put the entire economy in a tailspin. Several of Hitler's financiers complained to him in person. They made it clear they didn't care what happened to the Jews, but their own survival was threatened by any massive economic dislocation at such a delicate time.

Another problem arose in the course of the April 1933 boycott. The Nazis knew they wanted to target "Jewish business," but precisely what was a "Jewish business?" In the case of a large corporation, the question could be very complex. Was a business "Jewish" if the management and employees were predominantly Aryan but the owners were Jewish? And what if a German or foreign bank had loaned a Jewish company a large amount of money? The bank's solvency could be threatened by any Nazi action against the "Jewish" company.[1]

In June of 1933, Hitler was confronted by a very embarrassing situation. The Tietz department store chain, Germany's second largest retail business, was on the verge of bankruptcy. The company had borrowed over a hundred million marks from the German government in 1932 and now needed an additional loan to remain solvent. The fourteen thousand employees of the Tietz chain, who were predominantly non-Jewish, appealed to Hitler to save their jobs. But Hitler hated Jewish-owned department stores. Kurt Schmitt, the minister of economics, argued with Hitler for several hours about extending additional credit to the Tietz company. Schmitt contended that the collapse of such a large company represented a danger to the German economy as a whole, not to mention the problems that would be created by fourteen thousand additional unemployed workers. Hitler refused to give in until Schmitt pointed out that the financial interests of some of Hitler's financiers could be threatened by the chain's bankruptcy.[2]

The persecution of Jews had actually begun the day Hitler took office as chancellor. Eastern European Jews and Jews living in rural areas were the most vulnerable. The Jews from Eastern Europe and Poland were easily recognizable by their beards, black caftans, and black hats or yarmulkes. To nationalistic Germans, their appearance was foreign and alien. Most of the eastern Jews were very poor and worked as peddlers or small shopkeepers. German merchants resented them and accused them of undercutting prices.

Other Jews living in rural areas stood out almost as much as the eastern Jews, even though they dressed like the rest of the population, spoke perfect German, and may have been living in a town for generations. In a small country town everyone knew who was Jewish. In the big cities like Berlin and Munich an individual could blend into the melting pot, which provided some protection for a member of an oppressed minority. Jews in rural areas were continually the victims of spontaneous local boycotts, intimidation of their Aryan customers, and beatings by local Nazi bullies.[3] Polish and eastern Jews were treated even worse; they were often forced to drink castor oil, or had their beards and hair clipped in the shape of steps.

Historian Avraham Barkai recounted:

In Dortmund members of the S.A. and S.S. dragged the butcher, Julius Rosenfeld, and his son from the Dortmund stockyards through the streets of the city to a brickyard at the Voss pit. Rosenfeld and his son were lined up against the wall several times and threatened with pistols. They were forced to sing the "Horst Wessel Song," and were greeted by a rain of blows when they arrived at the brickyard. The young Rosenfeld was forced to set fire to his father's beard with a burning newspaper. After this, father and son were compelled to jump into a clay pit. After five hours, the elder Rosenfeld was released and sent home under the condition that within two hours he bring a slaughtered ox to his tormenters as a ransom for the release of his son.[4]

In some small towns, Jews were actually murdered. In 1934, a group of S.A. men gathered outside a tavern owned by a Jewish couple and threw stones at the windows. When one of the patrons came out, he was beaten and forced to walk through the town with a sign around his neck: I DRINK MY BEER AT A JEW'S PLACE. Soon the same S.A. hooligans returned; this time they entered the tavern and beat up the customers. When the tavern owner's son tried to intervene, they beat him up and arrested him. A few weeks later, the same S.A. men returned to the tavern to start another fight, but this time, they shot and killed the Jewish owner and his son. After some delay the police arrested a few of the S.A. men, but they were released on probation.[5]

Not all Nazi persecution of Jews was motivated simply by

hatred; often the Nazis had some financial reward in mind. There was a typical procedure that occurred in many small German towns in 1934 and 1935. The local party headquarters would send out notices to all Jews in the town who owned automobiles telling them all to report to a particular place at a certain time to register their cars. When the Jews assembled, the Nazis politely asked them to fill out forms stating the model, year, type of car, and proof of ownership. Once the forms were collected and the Nazis were sure the Jews actually owned their cars (automobile finance was rare in Germany in those days), the tone of the Nazis changed completely. They became threatening bullies. The Jews were told that they had to sign over their ownership of their cars for a fraction of their worth. They were pushed and beaten and threatened with being sent to a concentration camp. Everyone had heard stories about the terrible things that happened in the camps, especially to Jews. Those who signed over their cars were allowed to leave, without their cars, of course. The Nazis' intimidation usually worked, and within a few hours a room full of people would have signed over their automobiles.[6]

The Nazi government in Berlin passed laws to eliminate Jews from the professions, the civil service, law, medicine, and the media. Jewish businesses were to be "taken care of" by harassment and "spontaneous" boycotts on the local level. Often the local Nazis would go too far. By 1934 signs began to appear outside many German towns and villages: JEWS NOT WANTED HERE, or JEWS MAY NOT ENTER. Similar signs were put up in taverns and restaurants: JEWS NOT SERVED HERE. There was no law that allowed the discrimination against Jews; it was simply done by local Nazis. Before long the signs outside some towns were worded in more threatening terms: JEWS ENTER THIS TOWN AT YOUR OWN RISK. At this point the Nazi government in Berlin reluctantly intervened.[7] Signs that incited violence would be an embarrassment if seen by foreign reporters or tourists. Although Berlin ordered all threatening signs removed, most of them stayed up.

Local Nazi leaders in small towns throughout Germany were quick to realize that the bullying tactics of the storm troopers could be used for the practical purpose of frightening Jewish owners of small- and medium-size businesses to sell out for a fraction of their true worth. There was as yet no law authorizing the confiscation of Jewish businesses, but that did not stop local Nazi bosses. In Nuremberg, the notorious gauleiter and vicious anti-Semite Julius Streicher targeted a Jewish office equipment firm, the Hartman company, for boycott. Streicher threatened Hartman's customers and suppliers. Most people were too afraid to defy Streicher. The anti-Semitic publicity and periodic picketing of the company by S.A. men was enough to force Hartman into bankruptcy by the end of 1934.[8]

Admittedly not all attacks against Jews were caused by the Brownshirts. By 1934, the German people had been bombarded by so much anti-Semitic propaganda that some of it was bound to be believed. In Bavaria, in the summer of 1935, a group of about twenty young bathers gathered outside a swimming pool to demand the removal of Jews from the pool. They became noisy and began chanting: "This is a German pool, Jews are not allowed," and "Out with the Jews!" A large number of other swimmers joined in the chanting. The pool was in an uproar. The next day, a notice was posted at the entrance of the pool: ENTRY FORBIDDEN TO JEWS.[9]

Even Jewish children became the targets of vicious harassment.[10] A young Jewish boy reported being hit and punched frequently by his classmates. One day the word *Jew* was carved in his desk, and on another occasion, the word *Jew* and a Star of David were painted on the back of his jacket. Many of these petty acts of discrimination were the work of individual members of the Nazi party or the Hitler Youth, undertaken on their own initiative.[11]

The anti-Semitic radicals were a strong force in the Nazi party, but the failure of the April 1933 boycott of Jewish businesses somewhat discredited them. Most of the old guard of the Nazi party were hard-core anti-Semites. Ever since the early 1920s, Hitler had been preaching hatred of the Jews. He had promised his followers that once he was in power, they would "deal with" the Jews. After so many years of blaming every wrong on the Jewish scapegoat, millions of radical Nazi anti-Semites were seething for action. There was also the matter of economically motivated anti-Semitism, which was prevalent among the petty local Nazi leaders, many of whom were small shopkeepers hoping either to put their Jewish competition out of business or take it over at a bargain price.

The leader of radical anti-Semitism in the Nazi party was unquestionably Julius Streicher, the gauleiter of Franconia and a longtime friend of Hitler. When Hitler became chancellor, he felt he had to moderate the anti-Semitic tone of his speeches temporarily. Hence, Streicher was given the role of the party's number one "Jew-baiter." Streicher was untiring in his denunciation of the Jews. His newspaper, *Der Stürmer*, was full of anti-Semitic articles and cartoons. Editorials ranged in topic from the discovery that Christ was not a Jew, to stories about Jewish ritual murder.[12]

There was an underlying pornographic tone to many of the articles, such as reports of Jews who had seduced teenage German girls.[13] Streicher urged his young readers to write in and reveal the names of girls who danced with Jews.

In August 1935, Streicher traveled from his Nuremberg stronghold to bring his anti-Semitic crusade to Berlin. Jew-haters in the capital waited with anticipation while Jewish residents stayed prudently at home. At the Berlin Sportpalast, a capacity audience waited to hear Streicher. His closely shaven head gleamed as he strode up to the platform, with his riding whip in hand. He was wearing a white suit with his black Iron Cross pinned on the left pocket and black army boots. Waving his whip at the audience, he shouted: "The world is about to break Jewish domination. . . . They [the Jews] were never the chosen people. I wouldn't want a god who chose them." The audience, which included Hitler and the kaiser's son Prince August Wilhelm, roared its approval.

Along with his usual anti-Semitic jokes and accusations of a Jewish world conspiracy, Streicher injected an unexpected moderate tone in his speech; he condemned individual acts of violence. So the riot expected after the speech failed to materialize. It was rumored that Hitler had ordered Streicher to moderate his speech and condemn random violence in order to prevent a riot. Although restrained on this occasion, Streicher's followers were still full of hatred. Brownshirts leaving the meeting were seen carrying hook-nosed Jewish puppets on a tiny gallows.

Hitler's partners in the business community and the army sometimes urged him to exercise more control over the anti-Semitic Nazi radicals like Streicher. They completely failed, however, to understand that Hitler himself was Germany's most radical anti-Semite. The Brownshirt hooligans who beat up Jews and smashed up windows were his best followers; his sympathies were with them, but they would temporarily have to contain their fury. They wanted to crush the Jews immediately, whereas he was willing to wait for a more advantageous time.

Hitler's belief in anti-Semitism was unalterable. He had hated Jews since his unpleasant experiences with them as a teenager in Vienna, Austria. In *Mein Kampf*, Hitler wrote that until his arrival in Vienna, he had seen few Jews. He said there were not many Jews in Linz, Austria, where he grew up: "I do not remember having heard the word [Jew] at home during my father's lifetime." He admitted that at first he had been repelled by the anti-Semitic press in Austria. The beginning of his conversion to anti-Semitism, he claimed, was the sight of an Eastern European Jew.

At first, when young Hitler arrived in Vienna, he had eyes only for the magnificent architecture and the splendid buildings. Then, one day, as he was walking through the inner city, he suddenly encountered "an apparition clad in a long black caftan and black hairlocks." "Is this a Jew?" was his first thought. "At Linz, they certainly did not look like that," he recounted in *Mein Kampf*. "Secretly and cautiously, I watched the man, but the longer I stared at this strange face and scrutinized one feature after another, the more another question came to mind: Is this a German?"

To find the answer, Hitler said he turned as usual to books. "For the first time in my life, I bought some anti-Semitic pamphlets." At first he was unconvinced because the arguments in the pamphlet were "extremely unscientific." For weeks, he was uncertain. "However . . . ," he said, "I could no longer actually doubt that they [the Jews] were not Germans of a special religion, but an entirely different race."

Hitler carefully studied the activities of the two most powerful anti-Semitic parties in Austria: the Pan-Germans and the Christian Social party. Initially, Hitler's sympathies were with the Pan-German party, but he was disappointed by its failure to win any followers among the working class. The Pan-German party, said Hitler, was right about one very important thing: their anti-Semitism "was based on a correct understanding of the importance of the racial problem, and not on religious ideas."

Hitler gradually came to admire Karl Lueger, the mayor of Vienna and leader of the Christian Social party. Perhaps because he was a great orator, Lueger was able to win the support of the common people. His style undoubtedly served as a model for Hitler years later. But as much as Hitler admired Lueger as a leader, he believed Lueger did not fully understand the "Jewish danger" and saw his anti-Semitism as a "sham anti-Semitism," because it was based on religion rather than race. "If worse comes to worse, a splash of baptismal water could always save the business and the Jew at the same time."

The greatest "lie," according to Hitler, was that the Jews are "a religious community, while actually they are a race." Thus, there was to be no escape from Hitler's racial anti-Semitism, because it was a matter of birth. There was nothing an individual could do to change it. There was a long and brutal history of Christian anti-Semitism, but at least theoretically, the Jews could escape persecution by converting.[14] Of his experiences in Vienna, Hitler concluded, "This was the time of the greatest spiritual upheaval I have ever had to go through. I had ceased to be a weak-kneed cosmopolitan and became a fanatical anti-Semite."

By Hitler's own testimony, he never changed the anti-Semitic political views he developed in Vienna as a teenager. In 1919, when he was thirty years old, Hitler wrote a letter explaining his views on anti-Semitism; in less than thirteen years, he was to begin to put it all into practice. The letter was written at the request of his military superior, Captain Mayr, in reply to a man named Adolf Gemlich, who asked for an explanation of the "Jewish question." Responding at length, Hitler began by criticizing what he called "emotional anti-Semitism," which was based on personal impressions. "Anti-Semitism as a political movement," he said, "must be based on an understanding of the facts."

"And the facts are: first, the Jews are without question a race and not a religious group . . . thus . . . among us a non-German alien race lives, not willing and not able to give up its racial peculiarities and yet possessing all the political rights we do." He then went on to accuse the Jews of using socialism and democracy as tools to satisfy their lust for money and power.

Hitler concluded: "Anti-Semitism based on emotional grounds will result in pogroms. The anti-Semitism of reason, however, must lead to planned legal restriction against the Jews, and elimination of their privileges. . . . Its ultimate goal, however, must absolutely be the removal of the Jews altogether."[15]

Exactly what Hitler meant at this time (1919) by the phrase "the removal of the Jews altogether" is uncertain. He may simply have been thinking in terms of the expulsion of the Jews from Germany. On the other hand, the phrase may have been an ominous warning of the Holocaust.

Neither his attainment of power and wealth, nor his years of association with well-educated, sophisticated people did anything to change the vicious anti-Semitic ideas Hitler had picked up in Vienna as a penniless youth. As soon as he became chancellor, Hitler was eager to put his anti-Semitic ideas into practice, but he had to wait because of the fragile conditions of the German economy.

In the summer of 1935, a new outbreak of anti-Semitic boycotts and riots occurred in Germany. Even though they were later referred to as the Kurfurstendamm Riots, because the worst incident took place on the Berlin street of that name, the savagery was certainly not limited to the German capital. Nazi Brownshirts painted slogans and Stars of David on the windows of Jewish stores. Sometimes the S.A. hooligans got carried away and smashed in the shop windows. One witness recalled how, as a child, he watched an S.A. man put a sign in front of his grandfather's store that read DON'T BUY FROM JEWS. The S.A. man then knocked at the door. When the shopkeeper opened the door, the Nazi bully beat up the sixty-year-old man and left him lying on the ground.[16]

In some towns, the Nazis targeted the customers of Jewish businesses as well as the stores themselves. Without their uniforms, Hitler Youth boys would hang around outside Jewish-owned businesses. Then they would "accidentally" bump into customers coming out of the stores and paste a sticker to their backs that read: "I am a traitor to the German people, I just shopped in a Jewish store."[17]

By the mid-1930s, almost one-third of the Jewish businesses in Germany had been forced to close.[18] In some instances, local merchants who were members of the Nazi party would help finance the boycott and harassment of their Jewish competitors. Jewish stores would usually be forced out of business simply because their customers were frightened away.

Seizing Jewish-owned real estate proved to be a slightly more difficult problem; threats and physical violence had to be applied directly to the Jewish owners. They would be arrested on some trumped up charge, brought to the local party headquarters or jail, where they were threatened with violence and imprisonment in a concentration camp if they did not sign over their property for about one tenth of its value. Those who refused to sign were usually beaten. Considering that most owners of real estate were older people, a few punches and kicks from a two-hundred-pound Nazi bully could badly injure them.

Those who continued to refuse to give up their property were usually taken to a makeshift Nazi prison in an abandoned warehouse or cellar. There they would be forced to perform exhausting exercises for hours until they collapsed. Then they would be beaten. A favorite Nazi torture was to make a prisoner lie across a stool with his pants down while the guards whipped him until they drew blood. Another sadistic Nazi "exercise" applied to Jewish property owners was to make them stand at attention and then fall forward with their arms and hands outstretched and stiff. Since this was usually done on a stone or brick floor, it did not take long for their fingers to be bruised, bloodied, and broken. Then the documents to sign over their property were placed in front of them. Those who signed were immediately allowed to go home. Only a very courageous and strong individual could resist this type of torture very long. But for those who did, the Nazis had something even worse in store—the concentration camp.[19]

The only good thing that could be said for the early concentration camps was that they were not as bad as the death camps like Auschwitz, which would come later. Most of the concentration camps in the mid-1930s were in old prisons or abandoned warehouses. There were, however, three major camps: Dachau, near Munich; Sachsenhausen, near Berlin; and Buchenwald, in central Germany. These camps would serve as models for the new ones soon to be built. The majority of the prisoners were not Jews but Communists, socialists, or anyone opposed to the Nazi regime.[20] Life in the camps was hard, and the Jews were treated worse than anyone else. At most camps there was a special "Jewish Company" assigned to do all the filthiest chores, like cleaning the latrines. Sadistic guards often forced the Jewish prisoners to perform miserable tasks such as kneeling in the blazing sun pulling out the tufts of grass from between the courtyard and stones with their teeth while the Nazi guards shouted and sneered at them and kicked anyone who did not move fast enough.

Up to the summer of 1933, a number of Jews had been killed in Nazi concentration camps, but after the international protests at the Nazis' April 1933 anti-Semitic boycott, orders came down from the Gestapo not to kill any more Jews. For a while, the treatment of the Jews slightly improved. Of course, Jews were still beaten to death and tortured but as individuals rather than as a group, so Hitler wouldn't be embarrassed by having so many deaths at any one camp at the same time.

The daily routine in a concentration camp was designed to punish the prisoners rather than keep them occupied at useful activities. The day began before dawn with bed making. The straw beds had to be level and smooth enough to suit the strictest Prussian drill sergeant. After bed making, the prisoners had to stand shivering in the winter cold in the courtyard for roll call. Then the men were subjected to morning drill; this would have been rough on new eighteen-year-old army recruits, but it was torture for middle-aged men. Every day, men collapsed, exhausted from the endless deep knee bends and hours of running in formation. The S.S. or S.A. guards were mostly bullies who loved to bark out orders and beat prisoners.

Although the prisoners weren't actually starved, the food was miserable at best. There were three meals a day, which consisted of thick sour rye bread and cabbage or potato soup. Once a week, there was bean or lentil soup, which most prisoners considered their best meal of the week. Occasionally there were a few pieces of fat or leathery meat in the soup.

Since the camps were not regular prisons, there was usually no heat in the winter and of course no warm baths. The prisoners were lucky if there was any running water in the camp at all, or if they got to bathe once a week in cold water. Overcrowding was common; sometimes over a hundred men would have to sleep in a fetid room that should have held no more than twenty.

The worst thing about life in the living hell of the concentration camp was the beatings. At any hour of the day or night, people who lived near the camp could hear the fearful cries and screams of men being tortured and beaten. Naturally, the Jewish prisoners got more than their share of beatings. Erich Muehsam, the well-known Jewish anarchist and writer who fought in the Communist uprising in Munich in 1919, had been arrested by the Nazis as soon as Hitler came to power. Those who saw him at Brandenburg concentration camp said his battered face was always black and blue. At any time of the night or day the S.S. guards would come to "have a look at the dirty Jewish revolutionary." Although Muehsam's wasted limbs were a tragic sight, the S.S. guards would hustle him to his feet and force him to exhibit his circumcised penis for the hundredth time. Then they would hit or kick his genitals and walk away laughing as he collapsed to the floor.[21]

The purpose of the early concentration camps was twofold: first, they were to imprison the major opponents of the regime; second, they were to terrorize the significant percentage of the population that did not support Hitler. The specter of the camps cowered millions of people into silence and submission. This is exactly what Hitler intended. When a local Nazi leader told him many people objected to what was going on in the camps, he exploded. "We must be ruthless!" he shouted. "We must regain our clear conscience as to ruthlessness. Only then can we purge our people of their softness. . . . And their degenerate delight in beer swilling. We have no time for gentle sentiments. . . . Terror is the most effective instrument. I shall not permit myself to be robbed of it simply because a lot of stupid, bourgeois mollycoddlers choose to be offended by it." As the number of anti-Nazis and Jews being arrested mounted, Hitler ordered the construction of new concentration camps at Belsen, Gross-Rosen, Papenburg, and Ravensbruck.

Dr. Hjalmar Schacht, the minister of economics, was the only man in the German government who spoke out against the persecution of the Jews. In a speech that Schacht delivered at Königsberg in East Prussia on August 18, 1935, he denounced the violence and terrorism being used against Jewish businesses. Schacht chastised "the people who, during the night, 'heroically' smeared windowpanes, who call every German buying from a Jewish store a traitor to the nation. I shall make them responsible," said Schacht, "if their actions hurt the German economy." He went on to stress the importance to the economy of allowing Jews to freely conduct their business. However, there was also an anti-Semitic note in Schacht's speech. The Jews, he said, would have to resign themselves to the fact that their influence in Germany was at an end.

Schacht had the courage to confront the anti-Semitic radicals in the Nazi party because he knew the industrialists, and ultimately the army, would stand behind him. He probably also thought he had come to an understanding with Hitler about the importance of leaving Jewish businesses alone. Before becoming minister of economics, he had said to Hitler: "Before I take office, I should like to know how you wish me to deal with the Jewish question?" "In economic matters," responded Hitler, "the Jews can carry on exactly as they have done up to now."[22] Schacht was concerned not because he objected to anti-Semitism, but because he was afraid the violence directed against the Jewish businesses would hurt the economy. A number of Jewish-owned banks in Germany still possessed a large amount of capital, and Schacht cleverly intended to use this money to help finance Hitler's rearmament program.

At the 1935 Nazi party rally in Nuremberg, Hitler launched a new attack against the Jews. He wanted further legal restrictions against them, especially to regulate any social relations between Jews and Germans. From the speakers' platform, before the thousands of hysterical party faithful, Hitler announced the "Law for the Protection of German Blood."[23] The law forbade all marriages and extramarital sexual relations between Jews and Aryans. It also restricted the employment of Aryan female servants under forty-five years of age in Jewish households. The law also forbade Jews to fly the national flag and provided for the exclusion of Jewish children from German schools, beginning March 1, 1936.[24]

Sexual relations between Aryans and Jews had always been a very sensitive issue for anti-Semites, including Hitler. In the early days of the Nazi party, Hitler frequently told lurid tales of "dark Jewish seducers" lying in wait for innocent blonde Aryan girls. Anti-Semitism, especially on the matter of sexual relations between Jews and Aryans, was so widespread among the German population by 1933 that there were a number of violent incidents long before Hitler enacted his "Law for the Protection of German Blood." In many cases, Jews were pursued by mobs through the streets.[25]

Anyone courageous enough to date someone Jewish and go out with them in public risked being assailed by Nazi busybodies. Women who were seen with Jewish men were chastised for their "scandalous, un-German behavior." If they told the Nazi cranks to mind their own business, they were often slapped in the face.

Hitler's "Law for the Protection of German Blood" was supplemented by two further decrees, a few days later. One, dealing with citizenship, changed the terms "Aryan" and "non-Aryan" to Germans and Jews because the Japanese had objected. The law went on to clarify exactly who was a Jew and hence not eligible for German citizenship.[26] Anyone with only one Jewish grandparent was eligible for German citizenship, but those with three or more Jewish grandparents were automatically ineligible. People with two Jewish grandparents "might" become German citizens, unless they were members of a Jewish religious group or were married to a Jew. The second decree outlawed marriages between Germans and Jews. Those who were half-Jewish could marry Germans only with government permission, which would obviously be almost impossible to get. Extramarital relations between Germans and Jews were to be severely penalized.

Although Hitler's new race laws seemed to concern the social degradation of the Jews, they also had an economic effect on the Jewish community. Obviously the law defining citizenship on racial grounds would strip the Jews of their few remaining economic and property rights. (Since the citizenship law was retroactive, Jews who had been German citizens all their lives, would automatically lose their citizenship.) The laws forbidding sexual relations between Jews and Aryans made Germany a blackmailer's paradise. A number of wealthy Jewish men, including Jewish foreigners visiting Germany, were blackmailed for large sums.[27]

The new racial laws not only isolated Jews in Germany, but also further isolated Germany from the international business community. Many foreign businessmen and tourists were disgusted with what they saw in Germany. Martha Dodd, the daughter of the American ambassador, recalled with horror a scene she witnessed in Nuremberg:

> As we were coming out of the hotel, we saw a crowd gathering and gesticulating in the middle of the street. We stopped to find out what it was all about. There was a streetcar in the center of the road from which a young girl was being brutally pushed and shoved. We moved closer and saw the tragic and tortured face, the color of diluted absinthe. She looked ghastly. Her head had been shaved clean of hair and she was wearing a placard across her breast. We followed her for a moment, watching the crowd insult and jibe and drive her. . . . My brother asked several people around us, what was the matter. We understood from their German that she was a gentile who had been consorting with a Jew. The placard said: "I Have Offered Myself to a Jew."[28]

By 1937, Hitler was discouraged. He had not had a significant victory since his great triumph in the reoccupation of the Rhineland in 1936. The masses, Hitler felt, would lose their enthusiasm for anti-Semitism if they weren't continually stirred up. Some of Hitler's most important financiers and Germany's largest industrialists were also restive. They had watched with some disdain as greedy, petty Nazis loudly advocated the Aryanization of small Jewish shops and then grabbed them up at bargain prices. A few years earlier, the great industrialists were just recovering from the depression and had no money for expansion; but by 1937, they had plenty of cash. Why shouldn't they gain by Aryanization just as the small Nazi shopkeepers had? Furthermore, they now had to actually compete with Jewish businesses for scarce raw materials. The Nazi industrialists urged Hitler that the time for the Aryanization of large Jewish firms had come. As a signal to the Nazi big business interests that a new phase in the war against the Jews was about to begin, Hitler launched a new attack on the Jews at the 1937 Nuremberg party rally.

Generally the takeover of large Jewish businesses happened quietly, without violence or a great deal of political propaganda. The Nazis called it "voluntary" Aryanization. Of course, this did not mean that the Jewish owners had any choice in the matter, but simply that some compensation was paid for the business and the takeover was accomplished in a "civilized" manner. The proper legal documents were drawn up, and the Jewish owners were spared a beating or a stay in a concentration camp. Just as the little Nazi shopkeepers profited from the takeover of the small Jewish store across the street, Hitler's big financiers profited proportionately from the Aryanization of large Jewish-owned companies. Thus Hitler was able to pay back his patrons, in Jewish property, at least double the amount they had given him originally.

Once Hitler became chancellor the first category of business the Nazis wanted to seize was Jewish-owned newspapers and publishing houses, all of which had been anti-Nazi. For years Dr. Goebbels, Hitler's minister of propaganda, had waged a fierce war of words with newspapers belonging to the Jewish-owned Ullstein publishing house, Germany's largest publisher. Using threats of confiscation, Dr. Goebbels began negotiating with the Ullstein family to purchase their entire chain. Although all the newspapers and book publishing companies owned by the Ullsteins were worth at least seventy million marks, Goebbels offered them less than five million marks.

Just as Goebbels was about to close the deal with Ullstein, on behalf of the ministry of propaganda, another bidder appeared on the scene, Max Amann, the director of the Nazi publishing house, Eher Verlag. But both Goebbels and Amann lacked the necessary cash to purchase Ullstein. Each of them needed a loan to close the deal, and rather than looking for private financing, they turned to the government. Hitler decided the case in favor of Eher Verlag. Historians have generally believed he did so to prevent Goebbels from becoming too powerful.[29] This is probably true, but he also had another motive. Evidence seems to indicate that Hitler was the major shareholder of Eher Verlag.[30] Thus, when the Ullstein brothers were forced to sell a company worth at least seventy million, for only six million marks, to Max Amann, Hitler's personal fortune was greatly increased.[31]

Four of Germany's largest department stores were Jewish owned. They shared the same fate as the Jewish-owned newspapers. By 1935, both the Tietz and Wertheim chains had been Aryanized. The Schocken department stores, which had some large British shareholders, were able to hold out until 1938. However, these department stores were all taken over by large German business interests instead of being split up among small shopkeepers, as the Nazis had promised.[32]

Large manufacturing companies owned by Jews managed to survive longer than Jewish-owned newspapers or department stores, but by the mid-1930s their turn was about to come. Many of the Jewish-owned companies in heavy industry were worth over fifty million marks. These companies were to be given as choice rewards to Hitler's big contributors for the money they had given to the Nazis.

Even when Jewish owners received some small compensation for their property, they had difficulty getting the money out of Germany.[33] Long before Hitler became chancellor, Germany had an excessive "flight tax on capital." Authoritarian Germans had little respect for the sanctity of private property. It was easy for Hitler to play on this tendency and to completely confiscate the wealth of Jewish individuals. In April of 1938, Goering, as director of the Four-Year [Economic] Plan, issued a decree for the registration of Jewish property.[34] Jews had to register all property they owned in Germany and abroad that was worth more than five thousand marks. Registration was a warning that complete confiscation would soon follow. It became a crime punishable by death for a Jew to have a secret foreign bank account. The Gestapo even sent agents to Switzerland to try to find out which German Jews had Swiss bank accounts. The Swiss banks refused all Nazi demands for information on depositors. The Gestapo agents even attempted to deposit money in the name of suspected Jews; if the money was accepted, the Nazis knew the individual had a Swiss account and he was shipped off to a concentration camp.

Most German Jews were too patriotic or too naive to get their money out of the country in time. They kept hoping things would get better, or at least not get any worse. When they were finally forced to emigrate, they faced the indignity and terrorism of having the last of their money and personal possessions confiscated by brutal Nazi customs officials.[35]

One Jewish woman, Bella Fromm, the former diplomatic correspondent for the Ullstein newspaper chain, related the story of her flight from Nazi Germany. Although she was from a wealthy family, she had to leave most of her money behind in a "blocked account," which the Nazis eventually confiscated completely. She left Germany on a train for France. At 2:00 A.M., she was rudely awakened by two surly Nazi customs officers pounding on her sleeping compartment door. They searched through her suitcases and asked to see her passport. "Emigrant's passport!" said one, with contempt. "Jewish bitch! Trying to smuggle out her valuables, I suppose."

Frau Fromm wisely remained silent rather than risk antagonizing the Nazi customs men even further. They renewed their search, squeezing toothpaste out of the tube and looking in shoes and slippers.

"You Jewish whore!" one of them shouted at her. "Trying to smuggle out all that jewelry." He pointed to a small pile of jewelry that had been emptied on the bed.

"I am not trying to smuggle anything out," Fromm responded. "All that has been the property of my family for generations. Here is the permit issued by the foreign exchange office."

"We'll have to check on that with Berlin," the customs man said. "We reach the frontier in half an hour. You'll have to get off the train."

Frau Fromm begged the men not to make her get off the train, explaining that she would miss her boat for America.

"Then take the next one," one of the Nazis snarled.

The two customs men stood in the train corridor whispering for a few minutes. They had undoubtedly gone through this procedure many times before. Then they returned and gave Frau Fromm a statement to sign: "I am a Jewish thief and have tried to rob Germany by taking German wealth out of Germany. I hereby confess that the jewels found on me do not belong to me and that in trying to take them out, I was eager to inflict injury on Germany. Furthermore, I promise never to try to reenter Germany."

Frau Fromm was allowed to cross the border to France just as long as she signed and left her jewels behind with the real thieves, the Nazis.[36]

On the night of November 9, 1938, the worst pogrom in modern German history took place. This orgy of violence and destruction was set off by the death in Paris, that afternoon, of Ernst vom Rath, the third secretary at the German Embassy. Rath was shot by Herschel Grynszpan, a seventeen-year-old Polish Jew who was enraged because his parents had been expelled from Germany along with thousands of other Polish Jews. They were living miserably in a boxcar at the border because the Poles would not admit them. Grynszpan told the French police he went to the embassy intending to kill the German ambassador, but Rath was sent out to speak with him instead. "Being a Jew is not a crime," sobbed Grynszpan. "I hoped President Roosevelt would take pity on us refugees. . . . I am not a dog."

Hitler was furious that a Jew had dared to shoot a German diplomat. He immediately sent his personal physician to Paris, but Rath died in a coma. The Nazi newspapers urged retribution. Goebbels's paper, Der Angriff, called for "immediate action against the Jews." The Völkischer Beobachter said the Germans "could no longer tolerate" hundreds of thousands of Jews who owned entire streets of shops and grew rich off the wealth of Germany.

On the evening of November 9, Hitler was in Munich to celebrate the anniversary of the 1923 beer hall putsch. At about 9 o'clock, while the Fuehrer was having dinner in the Munich town hall with the party old guard, a messenger brought him the news of Rath's death. Obviously upset, Hitler put down his knife and fork, and summoned Goebbels. The two spoke quietly. Hitler told Goebbels that although the party should not "appear" to be organizing anti-Semitic demonstrations, it should do nothing to stop them if they occurred "spontaneously." As Hitler rose to leave, he whispered to Goebbels, "The S.A. should be allowed to have its fling." Then he left the dinner without delivering his usual speech, much to the surprise of the audience.[37]

After Hitler had left, and consequently would not appear to be responsible for what was about to take place, Goebbels gave a rabble-rousing speech in which he informed the assembled Nazi leaders of vom Rath's death. As he waved the message from Paris in the air, he said, "Do I need to tell you the race of the dirty swine who perpetrated this foul deed? A Jew! . . . We cannot allow this attack by international Jewry to go unchallenged. . . . Our people must be told and their answer must be ruthless."

Goebbels gave further orders on how the pogrom was to be carried out after the meeting broke up. He told Adolf Wagner, the gauleiter of Bavaria, and some local storm trooper leaders: "The hunting season on Jews is officially open. Go out and see how much game you can bag!" Deputy Chief of the S.S., Reinhard Heydrich, sent out a telegram with more precise orders:

> Measures are to be limited to those that will not endanger German lives or property (e.g., synagogues are to be burned only if there is no danger of the fire spreading to the surrounding area).
>
> Jewish stores and homes may be destroyed, but not looted. The police are responsible for preventing looting and arresting looters. Non-Jewish businesses must be protected from any damage.
>
> The police are not to prevent the demonstrations, but should see that they do not exceed the above directives. As soon as the events of the night permit, the police are to arrest as many Jews (especially wealthy ones) as can be held in available detention areas. After their arrest, they are to be transferred as quickly as possible to concentration camps.[38]

Beginning at about 2 A.M., on November 10, in Berlin, Nazi gangs went from one Jewish shop to the next with crowbars and axes, smashing in windows and doors. Their work was made easier by Nazis who had painted Stars of David and racist slogans on all Jewish-owned shops a few days before. Most of the vandals were in civilian clothes and were wearing heavy gloves to protect themselves from flying glass, but the boots they were wearing were the kind usually issued with S.A. uniforms. By dawn, crowds gathered outside some of the stores being ransacked. The Nazis threw merchandise out of the broken store windows to the crowd, laughing and shouting, "Here are some cheap Jewish Christmas presents. Get yours early!"

Although the police were supposed to prevent looting, they did nothing to stop it. A young boy on his way home from school recalled what he saw happening at a Jewish-owned shoe store in Berlin: an eight-year-old boy was crawling through the broken display window. A woman was waiting for him on the street. " 'Look, Mom!' he said. 'Look at these great shoes I just stole!' The mother said, 'Silly, you have shoes for two left feet. Now go right back in there and get the right shoe.' A policeman was standing next to the woman."[39]

Some of the worst destruction took place at Berlin's synagogues, seven of which were either seriously damaged or destroyed. Torah rolls and prayer books were desecrated and burned in the streets. In one Berlin synagogue, a fire was started under the Ark of the Covenant. The huge synagogue on the Fasanenstrasse was a special target for the Nazis. S.A. and S.S. men broke down the heavy wooden doors to get into the sanctuary. The organ was thrown over the balcony. The scrolls of the Law were torn and broken. Rabbinical garments were ripped to shreds. Then the Nazi vandals soaked the wooden benches with gasoline and set the building ablaze. Within a few moments, huge flames and clouds of smoke engulfed the synagogue. Out on the street, firemen with hoses and equipment stood by watching the spectacle. They had been ordered to protect only the neighboring buildings. By morning the synagogue was a smoking heap of rubble.[40]

While the violence and destruction were engulfing the capital of Germany, Chancellor Hitler was safely away from any blame at his mountain retreat in Berchtesgaden. No one knew that he had given Goebbels and the S.S. their instructions. Otto Dietrich, one of Hitler's close associates, admitted years later that Hitler had ordered the pogrom and given Goebbels specific instructions on how to carry it out.

All over Germany, Jews were spat upon, kicked, and beaten by

Nazi mobs. The American consul in Leipzig, David Buffum, reported that what was going on there was at least as bad as what was happening in Berlin.

> Jewish dwellings were smashed into and the contents demolished or looted. In one of the Jewish sections, an eighteen-year-old boy was hurled from a third-story window to land with both legs broken, on a street littered with . . . household furniture. Reported losses from looting of cash, silver, jewelry and otherwise easily convertible articles have been frequent. . . . Jewish shop windows, by the hundreds, were systematically and wantonly smashed. . . . Substantial losses have been sustained. . . . Many of the shop windows at the time of the demolition were filled with costly furs that were seized. . . .
> Three synagogues in Leipzig were fired simultaneously by incendiary bombs and all sacred objects and records desecrated or destroyed. . . . One of the largest clothing stores in the heart of the city was destroyed by flames from incendiary bombs, only the charred walls and gutted roof having been left standing. . . . It is extremely difficult to believe, but the owners of the clothing store were actually charged with setting the fire and on that basis were dragged from their beds at 6 A.M. and clapped into prison.[41]

In Munich, squads of storm troopers were on the move all night, pillaging and smashing windows. Every few hours, they would return to headquarters, brushing glass splinters off their clothes and bandaging cut fingers. Their pockets were full of rings, bracelets, and other loot. Several Jewish-owned shops were set on fire; the entire Munich fire department was out all night to keep the flames from spreading. Many of the S.A. vandals in Munich were wearing their brown uniforms for all to see.[42]

While the common storm trooper thugs were having their orgy of looting and destruction, other Nazis were beginning the more serious work of confiscating valuable Jewish property. A group of Nazi officials along with men from the Gestapo drove through the city in a large black car followed by moving vans.

They forced their way into wealthy Jewish homes and inspected the furnishings. All valuable paintings, silverware, and jewelry were confiscated on the spot and loaded into the moving vans.[43]

Throughout Germany the November 9 pogrom, thereafter called the Crystal Night, had taken a grim and costly toll. At least 267 synagogues had been burned or destroyed; approximately 7,500 Jewish-owned stores were damaged, destroyed, or looted; at least ninety-one Jews were murdered; thousands of shop windows were broken with an estimated cost in glass damage at six million marks (about half the annual production of the Belgian glass industry, which supplied Germany with most of its glass). Total damages for property destroyed on November 9 and 10 was estimated at one billion marks. Over thirty thousand Jewish men were arrested as a result of Crystal Night and sent to concentration camps.[44]

A few days after the Crystal Night pogrom, when the cost of the property damage became known, both Walther Funk, the new minister of economics, and Goering were furious at Goebbels, whom they blamed. "Have you lost your head?" Funk asked Goebbels in indignation. "I knock myself out day and night to preserve the economic stability of the nation and you throw millions out of windows. If you don't put a stop to this immediately, I will resign."[45]

On November 12, Goering, acting on his authority as director of the Four-Year Plan (a program to make Germany economically self-sufficient in four years), called a conference to decide how to deal with the financial repercussions of the pogrom. Attending the conference were Goering, Goebbels, Heydrich, representatives of the justice, interior, and finance ministers, and a Herr Hilgard, representing the German insurance companies.

The extent of the damages threatened to economically undermine the rearmament for which Goering was responsible. The field marshal (Goering was supreme commander of the German Air Force) was very upset after being informed that the replacement of all the damaged glass would have to be purchased abroad and would threaten Germany's already critical lack of foreign exchange. He said Hitler would hold him personally responsible if Germany now lacked the funds to buy vital war materials because of the destruction of November 9. Turning to

Heydrich, he shouted, "I wish you had killed two hundred Jews instead of destroying so much of value." Goebbels was not willing to admit that he was responsible for ordering the pogrom or reveal that the orders had ultimately come from Hitler.[46]

The main problem Goering and the other members of the conference faced was how to deal with the insurance on the damaged property. A number of major insurance companies faced bankruptcy if they paid claims on all the damaged property. Many Jewish shops had been in buildings owned by Aryans. Naturally these people would have to be paid. Jewish-owned property, however, was a different matter. At first, some Nazis suggested the insurance companies simply not pay the Jews. However the representatives of the insurance industry argued that they were afraid such action would damage international customer confidence in their claims-paying ability, even if the Nazi government passed a special law allowing the companies to refuse to pay Jewish claims.

Finally, Goering came up with an idea as ingenious as it was criminal. The insurance companies would pay Jewish claims in full, but the government would immediately confiscate the money from the Jews and then reimburse the insurance companies for part of their losses.* The conference lasted for almost four hours, and the corpulent field marshal was beginning to get hungry and irritated. At last he closed the meeting saying: "German Jewry as punishment for their abominable crimes, etc., etc., will have to make a contribution of one billion marks. That should do it! The swine won't commit another murder. By the way, I would like to say that I would not like to be a Jew in Germany, now."[47] The Nazis had again turned any normal idea of justice on its head and made the victim responsible for the crime.

Hitler ordered an elaborate state funeral for Rath in the

---

*From the record of the conference it is clear that Hilgard, the representative of the insurance companies, objected to Goering's corrupt deal. The German insurance companies did not profit from the situation. In fact, Hilgard had the courage to tell Goering that all the insurance companies would be losers in such a deal. The German insurance companies were forced by the Nazis to go along, even though they objected.

diplomat's hometown of Düsseldorf. He attended the funeral himself. Sitting with a stern expression next to Rath's mother, he did not make a speech but left it to lesser Nazi speakers to denounce the "Jewish-Bolshevik" murderers who were part of an international Jewish conspiracy to destroy Germany. Naturally, there was no mention of the innocent Jews who were murdered in the aftermath of Rath's death.

The November 9 pogrom marked the beginning of the end for the Jews in Germany. Additional decrees from Goering completely drove the Jews out of economic life.[48] After January 1, 1939, Jews were to be forbidden to operate retail shops or mail-order houses or to sell any independently created handicrafts. In part, the harsh measures against the Jews were designed to force them to emigrate. To that end, they were successful, as hundreds of thousands of Jews fled Germany.

The murder of Rath had provided Hitler with just the excuse he needed. For some time he had been planning a major repression of the Jews, but because of international public opinion, it could not appear as if the action was ordered by the government. If it happened "spontaneously," however, that was all right. For this reason, Hitler remained out of sight during the pogrom and pretended to have nothing to do with it. However, he was quick to take advantage of Rath's murder when it occurred. He had two principal motives: to drive the Jews out of Germany and to confiscate their wealth. By November 1938, Germany desperately needed more money for rearmament. Hitler thought he could expropriate the property of the Jews the same way he had seized the property of the trade unions in 1933. However, the financial losses caused by the senseless looting and destruction partly offset the profits. The violence of the pogrom and the unlawful plundering of Jewish wealth was a warning of how ruthless Hitler could be. Few were able to imagine that he would soon be doing far worse.

Chapter 6

Hitler's Extravagance and Corruption

To convince an audience of industrial workers in the Ruhr that he had more sympathy for their needs than those of the upper class, Hitler once said that he was the only major statesman in Europe who did not have a bank account or own any stock. Technically, it was true; Hitler did not have an ordinary bank account or own any stock in his own name. He never carried a wallet and claimed not to be interested in money. In spite of all of his crimes and misdeeds, historians have generally accepted the view that he was not personally greedy for money like most other Nazi leaders.

This chapter will prove, however, that the ascetic Hitler, who seemed to have taken a monkish vow of poverty for the sake of Germany, was a myth created by Nazi propaganda. Far from living a life of simplicity, Hitler actually surrounded himself with luxuries and led the life of a wealthy gentleman of leisure. Although he began his political career as a penniless ordinary soldier, there is now evidence to prove that by the 1930s, Hitler had become one of the richest men in Europe.

Hitler's asceticism played an important part in the image he was trying to project to the German people. According to the Nazi press, he was a vegetarian who neither smoked nor drank, nor had any affairs with women. Supposedly, he led a life of all work and no play. Nothing could have been further from the truth. Although Hitler was a vegetarian and a teetotaler, he led a life of self-indulgence in almost every other respect. His cook, the fat Kannenberg, produced a wide variety of elegant vegetarian dishes for him. A connoisseur of chocolate and sweets, he consumed large quantities of them. Because he occasionally wanted to drink beer, but also sought to avoid alcohol, he had a special dark beer with less than 2 percent alcohol brewed especially for him, at a brewery in Bavaria. Like most dictators, he had a mistress, Eva Braun, and had a number of discreet affairs with women.

Hitler enjoyed all the benefits of great wealth. He was surrounded by servants who catered to his every need. He had several private chauffeurs, his own pilot, a fleet of custom-made Mercedes automobiles, and several personal airplanes. His private railroad cars were equipped with all the luxuries fit for a king. Fine antiques and handcrafted furniture filled his three homes. All his clothes were tailor-made. The china on his dinner table was the finest Meissen, with each piece engraved in gold with an *A.H.* and a swastika. All three of his homes contained libraries filled with rare books, which together made up one of the best rare book collections in Germany. One researcher who collected records of Hitler's personal expenses established that during the years he was in power (1933–1945), Hitler spent over 305 million marks. This sum included only those expenses that could be documented, so the real figure was probably two or three times as much.[1]

Hitler's greatest extravagance was the millions of marks he spent on his personal collection of fine paintings. He began purchasing paintings even before he became chancellor, as soon as his royalties from *Mein Kampf* provided him with some discretionary income. Having been an artist himself, he had long dreamed of the day when he could own fine paintings. In the 1920s, just as he was becoming prominent in politics, he saw a painting by Grützner in the home of his friend and photographer, Heinrich Hoffmann. "As a young man in Vienna, I once saw a Grützner in the window of an art dealer—a picture rather like that one," Hitler said to Hoffmann as he pointed to the painting of an old monk. "Rather timidly, I went in and asked the price. It was quite beyond my reach. Oh dear, I thought to myself, I wonder if I shall ever succeed in life enough to be able to afford to buy myself a Grützner!"[2] Hitler's collection eventually included over thirty Grützner masterpieces.

As soon as Hitler acquired more money from wealthy contributors like Fritz Thyssen, he asked his friend Hoffmann, who had numerous contacts in the art world and was himself a dedicated art collector, to act as his agent in purchasing paintings. Naturally, Hoffmann cut himself in for a fat commission. Albert Speer recalled one afternoon at Hoffmann's home when the photographer showed Hitler a Grützner painting for sale for five thousand marks. Speer, who was himself knowledgeable about art, estimated the painting's market value at about two thousand marks. But not Hitler; he thought it was a good deal. "Do you know, Hoffmann, that's a steal!" said Hitler. "Look at these details. Grützner is greatly underrated. It's simply that he hasn't been discovered yet. Rembrandt also counted for nothing for many decades after his death. His pictures were practically given away. Believe me, this Grützner will someday be worth as much as a Rembrandt. Rembrandt himself couldn't have painted it better."[3] Many of the subjects of Grützner's paintings were inebriated monks. Both the anticlerical theme of the paintings and the artist's skill in painting the smallest details appealed to Hitler.

In his Munich residence, Hitler had a number of paintings, most of which he acquired through Hoffmann. He had several well-known paintings: *Bismarck in Cuirassier Uniform*, by Lenbach, *The Sin*, by Franz Von Stuck, *A Park Scene*, by Feuerbach, and a number of Grützners and paintings by Zugel and Spitzweg.[4] Because a close business and personal friendship developed between Hitler and Hoffmann, the two men sometimes exchanged paintings as gifts. One painting by Loewith that Hoffmann gave Hitler almost got the photographer in trouble. While Dr. Goebbels was visiting Hitler one day, he noticed the painting by Loewith, which Hitler explained had been a present from Hoffmann. Goebbels walked up and examined the picture carefully. "A fine painting, my Fuehrer," he said, and then with a malicious glance at Hoffmann, added, "and I don't wonder, for Loewith . . . was one of the best Jewish painters!"

"Quite!" Hitler responded, with a laugh. "That's why I've hung him!"[5] But Hitler was not as willing to compromise his anti-Semitic ideology as his remark might have indicated. Later, the conflict between what he knew to be a good painting and his anti-Semitism troubled him. He never got rid of the painting but consoled himself by saying: "People talk a lot. Maybe Loewith wasn't a Jew in the first place."

Hitler had very rigid tastes in art. Nineteenth-century paintings were his favorite. His art dealers were instructed to always be on the lookout for works by nineteenth-century painters, including Marées, Piloty, von Schwind, Makart, Overbeck, and, of course, Grützner. He had mixed feelings about Impressionism, but definitely considered all "modern art" from Expressionism on to be "degenerate." "I can't stand slovenly painting," said Hitler, "paintings in which you can't tell whether they're upside down or inside out, and on which the unfortunate frame-maker has to put hooks on all four sides because he can't tell, either!"[6]

As Hitler's wealth increased, he began to collect paintings of the Italian Renaissance and the Baroque period. One of his favorite Baroque paintings was a nude by Bordone that hung in his elaborate mountain villa above the town of Berchtesgaden, in southern Baveria. Another one of Hitler's favorite paintings was Correggio's *Leda*, which he sometimes "borrowed" from the Berlin State Museum. It was said that he was less interested in the painting's artistic qualities than in the erotic feelings inspired by Leda and the swan. In fact, this mythological theme intrigued Hitler so much that he purchased several paintings that showed the naked Leda submitting to the swan.

By the later 1930s, Hitler had acquired a huge collection of fine paintings worth millions of marks. Most of these paintings had been purchased, but some were gifts from industrialists and foreign statesmen like Mussolini. Hitler had so much money to spend on his private art collection by 1938 that he employed two major art dealers, in addition to Hoffmann, to purchase paintings for him. One was Karl Haberstock, a sixty-year-old Berlin dealer. He sold Hitler the sixteenth-century Italian painting *Venus and Amor* by Bordone, *Jupiter and Antiope* by Van Dyck, *Santa Maria della Salute* by Canaletto, and *St. Peter in the Boat* by Rubens. It is not known exactly how much Hitler paid for these paintings, but since they were well-known masterpieces by major artists, the price could not have been cheap.[7] Haberstock later sold Hitler *La Danse* by Watteau for 900,000 marks and *Italian Villa* by Boecklin for 675,000 marks.[8] Hitler was fascinated with Boecklin's romantic exhibitionism—full of mysterious and shadowy heroes.

The number of major artworks in Hitler's collection continued to multiply. A few paintings were gifts, such as *The Plague in Florence* by Makart, which was given to him by Mussolini. Most of Hitler's new artworks, however, were purchased on the open market by his several agents.[9] He now owned Leonardo da Vinci's *Leda and the Swan, A Self-Portrait* by Rembrandt, *The Dancing Children* by Watteau, *The Honey Thief* by Cranach the Elder. He had also acquired Rubens's *Madonna with Child* from the Crown Prince and a famous statue, *The Discus Thrower* by Myron, which was purchased from a family of Italian princes. Thus, even before the war, Hitler had one of the most valuable private art collections in Europe, easily worth hundreds of millions of dollars by today's standards.[10] Where did the money come from to purchase all these masterpieces? Up to now, no one has ever known, but later in this chapter, the question will finally be answered. But first, we must examine another one of Hitler's major expenditures, his villa on the Obersalzberg.

In 1928, Hitler rented a rustic cottage in the mountains above the village of Berchtesgaden. It consisted of only five rooms, furnished with simple wooden Bavarian peasant furniture. The first floor was built of stone and the second floor was wood. Directly behind the house rose the majestic Kehlstein peak. From his yard, Hitler could watch eagles circling the summit of the mountain. In the other direction, the view was equally magnificent. On a clear day, he could see as far as the distant Salzburg plain in his native Austria, beyond the border. Hitler liked the house and view so much that he purchased it a year later, when he did some minor remodeling to add several rooms and a stone patio.

As soon as Hitler became chancellor, he decided his modest residence needed to be upgraded to suit his new status. The house, now renamed the Berghof, was remodeled and enlarged; however, money was still tight for Hitler in 1933, so the renovations were not extensive. By 1936, Hitler's financial picture had improved considerably, so he began the project of totally rebuilding the Berghof. What had been a small mountain chalet was turned into a palatial villa.

Hitler drew up the plans for the new Berghof himself. Only the finest materials were used in the construction. The best woods and the most expensive marble were transported hundreds of miles, and all the windows were lined with lead. The work took about six months to complete. On the main floor, there were a series of huge rooms from which there were magnificent views of the surrounding mountains and the valley below. Most impressive was the great reception and living room, which was sixty feet long and fifty feet wide. On one side of the living room was a huge picture window that could be electronically lowered into the floor if the Fuehrer wanted fresh air and an unhindered view of the mountains; on the other side of the room was a large fireplace.

Italian masterpieces and large Gobelin tapestries covered the walls. Near the entrance to the living room were two nudes: one by Titian and one by Bordone. Some visitors said there were so many paintings in the Berghof that it gave them the impression of being in a museum, rather than a private home. The dining room was also very large, sixty feet long and forty feet wide. A long, massive oak table dominated the room. Etchings by Dürer hung on the wall. Upstairs were smaller rooms, bedrooms, and offices off a long corridor. Hitler's private bedroom suite consisted of a sitting room, study and bedroom and bathroom. The bathroom was made of fine Italian marble, and the fixtures were gold plated. There was a door connecting Hitler's suite to Eva Braun's bedroom.

When Hitler originally purchased the property on the Obersalzberg, it consisted of three acres. To assure his privacy, he had his agents gradually buy up all the surrounding properties until he owned over two hundred acres, the entire mountain slope up to the Kehlstein peak. Farms and cottages that once dotted the landscape were torn down so they would not spoil Hitler's view; in most cases, the owners were paid more than their property was worth to encourage them to sell quickly.[11]

Hitler put Rudolf Hess assistant, Martin Bormann, in charge of the construction and improvements of the Berghof complex. Bormann was a short, heavy, barrel-chested man with a thick neck and the look of a bull. He was subservient to Hitler, but brutal and domineering to his subordinates. Sometimes sleeping only four hours a night, he energetically tackled the construction work as a way of demonstrating his organizational ability to Hitler.

A number of buildings had to be constructed for guards' quarters and housing for the many people attached to Hitler's staff. The roads leading to the Berghof had to be widened and improved. A working farm was set up as part of the Berghof complex, but it was never profitable. The farm was of very little interest to Hitler. On one occasion, when Bormann was showing him around and pointed out the cleanliness of the pig's tiled sty, Hitler commented sarcastically, "I hope that every morning the pigs are washed with soap and then rubbed with eau de cologne." Realizing that the farm was a financial loss, Hitler asked Bormann to show him the account books. After studying the figures for a considerable time, he looked up saying: "Excellent! Not nearly as expensive as I thought—a liter of milk costs me only five marks at the most." (This was about twenty times the usual cost of milk.) But Hitler did nothing to restrain Bormann's spending on the farm and other projects.[12]

Bormann's most extravagant spending on the Berghof complex began when Hitler casually commented on how much he enjoyed the magnificent view, and wondered aloud how spectacular the view must be from the peak of the Kehlstein itself. To please Hitler, Bormann proposed tunneling into the Kehlstein and building an elevator that would take people up to a teahouse that would be constructed on the very summit of the mountain. Never considering costs, Hitler gave his approval. To carve a passage into the heart of the mountain and then build a vertical shaft to the summit, the workmen labored for three years at a cost of over thirty million marks.[13] When it was finished, the Eagle's Nest, as it was called, seemed like something out of a fantasy.

To get to the Eagle's Nest from the Berghof cars had to travel up a winding mountain road for five miles. At the end of the road there were huge double bronze doors large enough for a car to enter, leading to a long tunnel into the heart of the mountain. From there a large elevator with copper walls, cushioned seats, and a carpeted floor went up to the teahouse itself.

In the fall of 1938, the former French ambassador to Germany, André François-Poncet, was invited to the Eagle's Nest by Hitler. After traveling up the mountain road and entering through the huge double bronze doors, François-Poncet proceeded through the tunnel into the heart of the mountain and then took the elevator up to the Eagle's Nest. When he got out of the elevator, he saw before him "a gallery of Roman pillars" and an immense round glass room. "Giant logs were blazing in a huge fireplace, and there was a long table with some thirty chairs around it." There were also several well-furnished side rooms.

To look out in any direction over the endless panorama of mountains was like looking down from an airplane. In the distance lay Salzburg and the surrounding villages. As far as the eye could see, there were mountain peaks with green meadows and woods clinging to their slopes. The Eagle's Nest gave the impression of being suspended in space. The whole view, bathed in the orange-pink glow of autumn dusk, was fantastic.

It all seemed like an hallucination. "Was this the Castle of Monsalvat [of] the Knights of the Grail?" Was it a "billionaire's folly" or "just a hideout of a brigand?" François-Poncet asked himself.

In a friendly mood, Hitler took François-Poncet over to one of the bay windows to point out the scenery. He was obviously pleased to hear the French ambassador's admiration for the view and the great feat of engineering in constructing such a place. But as spectacular as the Eagle's Nest was, the ambassador could not help wondering: "Was this edifice the work of a normal mind or of one tormented by megalomania and haunted by visions of domination and solitude?"[14]

Altogether, Hitler spent well over a hundred million marks on the Berghof complex and the Eagle's Nest, not including the artworks in the Berghof, which were worth at least another hundred million marks. Many other tyrants and kings in history had spent as much or more on their palaces, but usually they built in good times, when the land was prosperous. Germany, in the later 1930s, was anything but prosperous. True, the six million unemployed had been put back to work and the economy had recovered somewhat. Wages, however, were still low, food was rationed, and luxuries were almost unobtainable. The minister of economics was at his wits end to find enough foreign currency to pay for essential imports. In such circum-stances, Hitler's squandering money on personal pleasures like the Eagle's Nest seems all the more disreputable, especially for a man who claimed to be a simple man of the people.

In 1938, Hitler also purchased the luxury apartment building in Munich on the Prinzregenten Platz, where he had rented a nine-room apartment for years. His apartment took up the entire second floor. It was decorated with Oriental carpets, deep cushioned sofas, and heavy velvet curtains. The walls were covered with oil paintings from Hitler's collection. There was a small library for his rare books that he also used as an office. The apartment was cared for by Hitler's butler, Winter, who had once been General von Epp's valet, and his wife, Annie Winter, who served as a maid. The entire ground floor of the building was occupied by Hitler's S.S. bodyguard.

A few years earlier, in 1936, Hitler had secretly purchased another house in Munich, a small suburban villa that he had given to his mistress, Eva Braun. The house was not deeded to her but to Heinrich Hoffmann, Hitler's photographer, who acted as trustee. Eva was a simple, self-effacing woman who had no interest in politics. She was very athletic and, in contrast to Hitler, loved to ski, swim, and dance. When he was busy Hitler often ignored her for weeks or months at a time. In the early years of their relationship, he would regularly give her an envelope of cash, containing a few thousand marks for her spending money. He frequently gave her presents, but they were usually the kind of gifts any upper-middle-class businessman might give his girlfriend, nothing extravagant. Sometimes he took her to a little jewelry store in Munich, owned by an old party comrade, where she would pick out an inexpensive ring or bracelet, rarely costing over one thousand marks. The most expensive gift he gave her was a Mercedes roadster.

When Hitler was in Berlin, Eva had to depend on Martin Bormann, who was now handling most of Hitler's personal funds, for her spending money. At first, Eva and Bormann did not get along because Eva thought it was wrong for a married man to be having affairs with young secretaries and maids. But the ambitious Bormann decided it would be to his advantage to be in the good graces of the dictator's mistress. So, with Hitler's permission, he took her to the fine jewelry shops of Munich and let her choose what she wanted, without considering price. However, due to her own modest nature, Eva's spending on jewelry remained rather limited. Unlike other dictators' mistresses, she never purchased, nor was given, a priceless diamond necklace or rare rubies or emeralds. Eva did, however, spend considerable money on fashionable clothes. Whenever she wanted something for her wardrobe, Bormann would always write out the check without question. Eva continued occasionally to make fun of Bormann behind his back, but they had both come to recognize that they could be useful to each other.[15]

Hitler had another love upon which he spent far more money than he did on his mistress: the love of opera. From 1935 on, he lavished money, both from his own funds and from the government budget, on opera productions in Germany. He had a passionate love of opera since his youth; as a teenager, he had even written an opera.

Deciding that some cultural amenities should be a part of the Nuremberg Nazi party rallies, Hitler arranged for the Berlin State Opera to give a gala performance of *Die Meistersinger* on the first night of the 1933 rally. The Nuremberg rallies, first held in 1923, were an annual spectacle of parades and pageantry intended to impress the German public and foreigners of the strength of Hitler's regime. Over one thousand opera tickets were given to the party bosses, but most of them preferred the Nuremberg beer. When Hitler entered his box, the opera house was almost empty. He was furious and immediately sent out patrols to round up the Nazi officials from the beer halls and bring them to the opera house. But, in spite of his effort and the money he, or rather, the government spent, half the seats remained empty.[16]

The managers of many theaters throughout Germany benefited from Hitler's generosity. In turn, he enjoyed going to the theater whenever he had time to relax. Contrary to popular belief, he often preferred going to operettas like *The Merry Widow* and *Die Fledermaus*, rather than Wagner's operas, which had so fascinated him in his youth.[17]

Hitler usually found time to attend performances more often when he was in Munich than in Berlin. For security reasons,

Hitler never entered a theater until the lights were dimmed and the curtain was about to go up. Then the gold-embroidered swastika Fuehrer standard would appear over the rail of the center box. Dressed in his best white uniform jacket and black trousers, Hitler would quietly slip into his box, with his guests, usually Gauleiter Adolf Wagner. A murmur would go through the audience, then a hushed silence. With high-powered opera glasses, Hitler would watch the female performers and dancers. When one would appear in a scanty costume, he would nudge his crony, Gauleiter Wagner, and smile.

As soon as the performance was over, the director would accompany Hitler to his Mercedes. At the stage entrance, buses would be waiting to take selected female members of the cast to the Kunsterhaus (Artist House), where Hitler would treat them to a party. Considerable public money had been spent on the construction of the Kunsterhaus, so it would be splendid enough to please Hitler. Sitting in an ornate hall, carpeted with Oriental rugs, surrounded by pretty girls, Hitler seemed to be having fun. While Hitler's guests enjoyed expensive food and champagne, the average German couldn't get decent butter, even with a ration card. Hitler wouldn't leave the party until about 3 A.M.

Where did Hitler get the money for his extravagant lifestyle? The answers are not easy to find. He went to great lengths to keep the sources of his funds and his personal finances secret, even from his closest associates. The secrecy about Hitler's money was maintained long after his death. Up until now, historians have never been able to determine the exact sources of his personal wealth. Hitler wanted everyone to believe that he was a penniless idealist. Yet, he had considerable income. Even in 1933, he earned 1,232,335 marks, not counting the 60,000 marks chancellor's salary, which he refused at first but later accepted.[18]

Hitler realized when he became chancellor that at last he would be able to acquire vast wealth. But he also had sense enough to recognize that he had no talent for business or managing money; this, coupled with his desire for secrecy about his finances led him to an ingenious idea. His money would be held for him in the name of trustees,* who would be old comrades with business ability who could be absolutely counted on to obey and say nothing. This would enable him to declare, as we have seen, that he had no bank account and owned no stock. The men who acted as his trustees were all colorless individuals who hid in Hitler's shadow. It is now possible to identify at least two of the men who were trustees for Hitler: Max Amann, the director of Eher Verlag, the Nazi party publishing house, and Martin Bormann, the administrator of the Adolf Hitler Fund. The money these trustees administered came from several different sources: Hitler's royalties from *Mein Kampf*, the Adolf Hitler Fund, the profits of the Eher Publishing Company, and the income from Hitler's stock in major German companies.

Hitler's first and most legitimate source of personal income was from his book, *Mein Kampf*. It had sold reasonably well when it was initially published, averaging approximately five to ten thousand copies a year during the 1920s. In the early 1930s, the sales rose with Hitler's political success, averaging about fifty thousand copies per year. When Hitler became chancellor in 1933, sales of *Mein Kampf* reached a total of one million copies, making Adolf Hitler a millionaire for the first time. He had at first received 10 percent royalties, but with the increased sales, the rate was raised to 15 percent. With the Nazis in power, *Mein Kampf* became compulsory reading in schools and was given, at government expense, to all newlyweds at their wedding, so continuous sales were guaranteed. By 1940, *Mein Kampf* had sold over six million copies.

Hitler also earned royalties on his articles and reprints of his speeches. He also got royalties on all postage stamps bearing his picture. However, before the beginning of the war, Hitler's profile was used on only a few commemorative issues, so this income did not amount to much until after 1941. Hitler's earnings from royalties were the only income he did not try to keep secret.

In 1935, when Hitler saw the staggering bills for the construction of his palatial Obersalzberg home, the Berghof, he seemed somewhat embarrassed and remarked to Albert Speer: "I've

---

*It is not known if any formal trust agreements were made between Hitler and his "trustees." It is possible that nothing was ever put on paper, and all Hitler's instructions were verbal.

completely used up the income from my book, although Amann's given me a further advance of several hundred thousand. Even so, there's not enough money."[19] At the time, Speer evidently believed Hitler, but it was all a lie. Hitler obviously didn't want even a close collaborator like Speer to know the real source of his money. The Berghof and the Obersalzberg complex could never have been financed on the royalties from *Mein Kampf* alone. In fact, it appears that hardly any money from *Mein Kampf* was spent on the Berghof; most of the costs apparently were paid for out of the Adolf Hitler Fund.

As will be recalled from Chapter 1, in 1933 Hjalmar Schacht, the banker, and Goering, then the president (speaker) of the Reichstag, asked the most prominent industrialists in Germany to contribute to a fund to finance the coming elections. Gustav Krupp, the munitions tycoon, volunteered to serve as chairman of the fund. During 1933 and 1934, the contributions to the fund were spent on political projects.[20] But after all opposition in Germany was crushed, the fund became Hitler's personal trust fund, administered by Martin Bormann. Thus, over a hundred million marks a year were put at Hitler's disposal. Hitler's personal use of this fund was kept secret from the German people, indeed few of them knew the fund existed. Even the Nazi party treasurer, Franz Schwarz, complained that he had no idea how large the Adolf Hitler Fund was, and his auditors were firmly refused whenever they tried to question Bormann.

Whenever Hitler wanted money for anything, Bormann paid. Bormann never asked any questions nor tried to restrain Hitler's spending. He wrote out checks for paintings and covert projects with equal ease. Although the stated purpose of the fund was to "help support the political organizations of the Nazi party," the top Nazi industrialists must have had some idea that Hitler was diverting the money for his personal spending. In one respect, some industrialists considered the fund "protection money," but at the same time, others who were more politically minded, realized it made Hitler dependent on them. Gustav Krupp apparently had no objections if Hitler used the fund money for personal spending. In a letter he wrote to Hjalmar Schacht, Krupp said the purpose of the fund was "to represent a token of gratitude to the leader of the nation."[21]

Hitler had, at one time, informed the industrialists who contributed to the fund that he would use some of the money to finance "cultural projects" and to help Nazi party members who were "in need." True enough, Hitler did use some of the money to support his favorite opera companies and to purchase paintings for his art collection. It was also true that each year he gave large sums of money to party members, although it is very questionable if they were ever "in need." Actually, Hitler gave the money to Nazi party bosses to insure their personal loyalty to him. He also took money from the fund to purchase artworks that he gave as presents to Nazi officials; to Goering, who was a hunter, he gave *The Falconer*, by Hans Makart; to Goebbels, for his wedding anniversary, Spitzweg's *The Eternal Honeymoon*; to Grand Admiral Raeder, *A Naval Battle* by van der Velde; and to Ohnesorge, the postmaster general, *The Old Post Coach*, by Paul Hey.[22]

One of the best kept secrets of Hitler's personal finances is that he was one of the world's greatest press tycoons, with personal holdings comparable to, and probably exceeding, Hearst or Beaverbrook. Hitler was chairman of the board and controlling stockholder of the Eher Publishing Company, which owned over a hundred large newspapers and book publishing houses. In 1938, Eher Publishing controlled over 50 percent of the major newspapers in Germany. By 1944, it controlled 90 percent of German newspapers. There are no exact figures for the total value of assets of the Eher and its subsidiaries, but an estimate would be in the neighborhood of ten billion marks (approximately two billion 1940 U.S. dollars or twenty billion 1990 U.S. dollars). We know that when Eher Publishing was seized by the Allies at the end of the war, its liquid assets alone, in bank accounts, government bonds, and stocks, came to almost 600 million marks. It is reasonable to conclude that 75 to 90 percent of Eher Publishing stock was owned by Adolf Hitler.

The man who built up Hitler's publishing empire for him was Max Amann, a short, tough little Bavarian who had been the sergeant major of Hitler's regiment during World War I.[23] Amann had lost an arm in a hunting accident, but he still had a reputation for being able to outshout and out-cuss anyone.

In the early 1920s, Hitler asked Amann to become the business manager of the Nazi newspaper, the *Völkischer Beobachter*. He recognized that Amann, who had once been a bank clerk, was a shrewd businessman. Amann soon proved worthy of the confidence Hitler had in him. He turned the *Völkischer Beobachter* and the company that owned it, Eher Publishing, into a profitable enterprise. He was a genius when it came to securing advertising for the Nazi paper from companies selling cigarettes, cosmetics, and over-the-counter medicines.

After Hitler became chancellor, the growth of the Eher Publishing empire mushroomed. Amann worked quickly and ruthlessly taking over Communist, socialist, and trade union newspapers. Hitler always remained in the background, but intervened in favor of Amann whenever other Nazi bosses like Goebbels tried to compete with Eher Publishing. Amann and Hitler further expanded their publishing empire by "purchasing" the great Jewish-owned newspapers and publishing houses for a fraction of their true worth.

"Aryan" newspaper owners and publishers were sometimes paid a price closer to the true value of their property, depending on their political allegiance. Those who had opposed the Nazis before 1933 were often treated as badly as the Jews. With the power to virtually confiscate newspapers and publishing houses, it did not take Amann and Hitler long to build Eher Publishing into a business with over a hundred million marks profit per year and a newspaper circulation of twenty million papers daily.

In addition to his job as manager of Eher Publishing, Amann also acted as Hitler's "trustee." Dr. Otto Dietrich, the Nazi press chief, called Amann "Hitler's banker." It was widely known in Nazi circles that Hitler could get money from Amann whenever he wanted it. It was assumed this money came from the royalties Hitler earned on *Mein Kampf* or was an advance against future royalties. A few perceptive individuals, however, noticed that Amann was providing Hitler with far larger sums than would have been justified by the royalties from *Mein Kampf*. Hitler completely trusted Amann and even gave him his power of attorney in 1938.[24] To preserve secrecy, he also exempted Amann from any financial supervision by the Nazi party treasurer, Franz Schwarz.

Hitler and Amann went to great lengths to keep their true business relationship secret. Just before Germany surrendered in 1945, Amann saw to it that the records pertaining to the ownership of Eher Publishing were destroyed. In the early days of the Nazi party, however, they were not so careful, and there remains considerable evidence to indicate that Hitler was the major shareholder in Eher Publishing. The Eher Publishing house had originally been owned by a group of shareholders, the majority of whom were members of the shadowy Thule Society, a secret racist, occult group that financed Hitler in the early 1920s. In 1920, General von Epp, one of the first high-ranking officers to support the Nazis, loaned Hitler's friend Dietrich Eckart sixty thousand marks from Free Corps funds to purchase the majority of shares in Eher Publishing.[25] By 1921, however, an entry in the court register of corporations lists Adolf Hitler as chairman of the board and states that "he claims to have all the shares of the Eher Firm in his possession."[26]

Many years later, during the war, Hitler revealed to some close associates how he had obtained the shares. He said that a supporter had given him shares worth five thousand marks, and he had bought more shares. He did not say where he got the money to purchase the other shares. Some investigations in the 1930s were able to establish that Eher Publishing was "the personal property of Hitler and Amann," although they did not know exactly how many shares were owned by each.[27] Kurt Lüdecke, who was a personal friend of Hitler and worked for Eher Publishing, said "Eher Verlag [Publishing] had mush-roomed out to a million dollar concern, and was now one of the largest publishing houses in the Reich. Amann was its manager, Hitler the principal owner."[28]

Another indication that Hitler was a majority shareholder in Eher Publishing was the fact that, like Hitler personally, the Eher Publishing Company was exempt from taxation. This special tax-exempt status, not given to any other German companies, also explains how Eher grew so rapidly. Whenever Hitler asked for money, Amann withdrew it directly from the Eher Publishing account at the Reichsbank. "Amann," said Lüdecke, "was Hitler's banker and close friend; to my knowledge, he and Roehm were the only Nazis to whom the Fuehrer ever said *du*. (The *du* form of address was used only for very close personal friends.) Amann was in on Hitler's personal financial affairs as well as his secrets.[29] Hitler, in turn, saw to it that the diligent Amann was amply rewarded with a salary of 120,000 marks and a 5 percent share in the Eher Publishing Company. With his newly acquired wealth, Amann purchased a country villa on the Tegernsee Lake that cost half a million marks.

Hitler had other secret holdings about which very little is known, even today. The directors of some major German companies sometimes made gifts of sizable blocks of their company stock to Hitler. Often this was done to obtain a lucrative military contract or some other special favor from the government. Usually, one of the firm's directors, who was a Nazi party member and personally known to Hitler, was appointed as Hitler's trustee so that Hitler's ownership would remain secret.

Although the exact amount of Hitler's stock holdings may never be known, it is almost certain that a huge fortune that would be conservatively valued at several hundred million dollars today, was involved. The reason the directors of the companies involved made such a gift in the first place was to give Hitler a significant stake in the company so he would have a vested interest in the firm's welfare. To achieve such a purpose the gift would have to have been a large sum; anything less would almost have been an insult.

At the same time that Hitler was hoarding his own secret fortune, he was squandering billions of marks in public money on his megalomaniacal architectural fantasies. Hitler's personal extravagance and greed were merely evidence of his corruption and duplicity; on the other hand, his waste of public funds was so extensive that it seriously damaged the German economy.

Since his youth, Hitler had dreamed of being an artist or an architect. As a teenager, he had gone to Vienna to study at the Academy of Fine Arts. He was crushed when he failed to pass the entrance examination. But, in spite of a hand-to-mouth existence, he continued to paint pictures of great buildings, refusing to abandon his dream. Once he became chancellor, he was determined to realize his youthful ambitions, regardless of the cost to the public. "How I wish I had become an architect," he often said to associates in the 1930s.

Hitler could talk for hours about the great neo-baroque buildings that inspired him. "The Vienna Opera House is the most magnificent opera house in the world!" he would say. He also admired the Paris Opera House and the Palace of Justice in Brussels. He had memorized every detail and measurement of these buildings. With ease, he would pick up a pencil and sketch their heavy cornices or the perspective from an angle. He was determined to build buildings like these in Germany.

Hitler's building program began moderately enough in 1933 with the construction of the neoclassical House of German Art in Munich. It replaced an earlier museum that had burned in 1931. The first signs of Hitler's architectural megalomania soon appeared when he decided the Chancellery in Berlin was not grand enough for the Fuehrer of Germany. He said it was "impossible" for him to work in the chancellor's office. It was "much too small. Six hundred and fifty square feet—it might do for one of my assistants. Where would I sit with a state visitor? In this little corner here? And this desk is just about the right size for my office manager."[30]

The whole purpose of the new Chancellery was to glorify Hitler and intimidate visitors with his power. Everything was on a huge scale. The visitor would enter the Chancellery through double doors seventeen feet high and then walk down a gallery 480 feet long. Hitler particularly liked the long gallery because it was twice as long as the Hall of Mirrors at Versailles. "On the long walk from the entrance to the reception hall," he said, "they'll get a taste of the power and grandeur of the German Reich."[31]

Up until 1937, Hitler restrained his ambition to begin a number of massive construction projects. The simple fact was he had no choice because there was no money. Every spare cent was being spent on rearmament. But once the first stage of the rearmament program was completed, Hitler ordered the construction of thousands of monuments and government buildings throughout Germany. Grandiose was the only word that adequately describes Hitler's plans to rebuild Germany. In Munich, there were massive new government and Nazi party buildings: the House of German Art, the House of German Law, the Monuments to Martyrs of the 1923 Putsch. To accommodate the hundreds of thousands who attended the Nazi party rallies in Nuremberg, huge stadiums and meeting halls were constructed. Every city in Germany had at least several of Hitler's new buildings under construction, and everywhere the emphasis was the same—on size, which intended to impress and intimidate. Hitler was always promising his favorite local party bosses he would build a new opera house or monument for their town.

It was in Berlin, however, that the most ambitious building projects were undertaken. Whole blocks of buildings around the Chancellery were razed to make way for Hitler's new government offices. Hitler designed many of the buildings himself and worked closely with the architects during the construction. No architectural detail was too small for his attention. He would frequently visit construction sites to watch a new window or staircase being installed. Paces ahead of his staff, he would step carefully over construction debris, completely at home on a building site.

Hitler was trying to show the world through architecture the new military and political power of the Third Reich.* The ruins of Greece and Rome, he thought, were the best testament to the greatness of their civilizations. Likewise, future generations would understand the glory of the Third Reich by its monumental buildings. "Why always the biggest?" said Hitler. "I do this to restore every German's self-respect. In a hundred ways I want to say to the people—'We are not inferior; on the contrary, we are the complete equal of every nation.'" Actually, Hitler was trying his best to impress upon the Germans by his architecture that they were superior to all other nations.

The massive size of Hitler's new buildings and the total number of all his building projects taken together put a great strain on the German economy. Up until 1936, there were still many unemployed in Germany, and Hitler's building campaign put people to work. "I believe," he said, "the most efficient way to create work for the German people is to revive the German economy by initiating large-scale monumental building projects." By 1937, however, the number of skilled workers required

*Hitler used the term Third Reich because he regarded his government as the successor of the two previous German empires, or Reichs. The First Reich was the Holy Roman Empire, founded in A.D. 962, which ruled most of central Europe. The Second Reich began in 1871, with the unification of Germany under the Hohenzollern dynasty.

to construct Hitler's huge buildings was creating a labor shortage. Most of Hitler's buildings were useless from the economic point of view, since they were either monuments to glorify the Nazi state or government buildings that encouraged the expansion of a costly bureaucracy. If the same amount of money had been spent on building homes and factories for the private sector, it would have added to the national wealth. Only the construction of the autobahn, bridges, and railway stations was truly useful.

Hitler's rigid view of architecture rejected "modern" construction with glass and steel, in favor of more expensive, traditional building materials, such as granite, marble, and wood. So much quarried stone was required for Hitler's projects that quarries in Germany could not keep up with the demand by 1937. Large amounts of granite and marble had to be imported at great expense from Italy, Scandinavia, and France. Germany quickly ran out of foreign exchange to pay for such imports. The minister of finance, Count von Schwerin von Krosigk, was aghast at Hitler's "squandering" of public funds and repeatedly protested. Hitler could come up with only the weakest arguments to justify his spending. "If the minister of finance," he said, "could realize what a source of income to the state my buildings will be in fifty years! Remember what happened with Ludwig II. Everyone said he was mad because of the cost of his palaces. But today? Most tourists go to Upper Bavaria solely to see them. The entrance fees alone have long since paid for the building costs."

Hitler had elaborate wooden models constructed to perfect scale of the new buildings. He would sit for hours playing with the models like a child; tilting his head down, he would try to imagine the perspective of a certain building from street level. On one occasion, he was playing with his building models when he received one of his financial experts, who reported that there was no more money to pay for such projects. Like a child, Hitler threw a tantrum and then almost with tears in his eyes, said: "But can't you see how much my buildings mean to me. You can't deny me this!" If the Ministry of Finance could not supply Hitler with enough money to pay for the expensive building materials he wanted, there was a more reprehensible way to get the material for almost nothing. Himmler, the commander of the S.S., was more than willing to oblige the Fuehrer and set up new quarries at concentration camps. That thousands of prisoners would die to provide the stone for his new buildings meant nothing to Hitler.

Hitler's corruption and extravagance set a perfect example for his henchmen to follow. Some of them, particularly Goering and Ley, the head of the Nazi Labor Front, probably looted more and lived even higher than Hitler, but the whole Nazi regime was based on the idea that power entitled its holders to loot. Almost all Nazi leaders were financially corrupt. But perhaps a corrupt Nazi who would sell passports to wealthy Jews at exorbitant prices was better than a "correct" Nazi like Himmler, who wouldn't let a Jew escape, regardless of the bribe.

Chapter 7

Easy Prey—Big Profits

n the fall of 1937, a joke was making the rounds in Europe. "Have you heard the latest about Hitler? You know he has gone to Berchtesgaden and refuses to be disturbed. He has a street map of Vienna on the wall and sits all day, at a draftsman's table, designing architectural monstrosities he is going to build to replace some of the historic buildings of Vienna." As the joke indicated, everyone thought it was only a matter of time before Hitler marched on Austria. In fact, he was busy drawing plans, but they were military ones rather than architectural.[1]

Hitler summoned the commanders of the German armed forces to a top secret conference on November 5, at the Chancellery. The meeting, which began at four o'clock in the afternoon, lasted until eight in the evening. During that time, Hitler outlined his strategic objectives for the next few years and left no doubt about his intention to go to war. Present at the conference, in addition to Hitler, were Field Marshal von Blomberg, commander in chief of the armed forces; General von Fritsch, commander in chief of the army; Admiral Raeder, commander in chief of the navy; Goering, commander in chief of the Luftwaffe; Baron von Neurath, the foreign minister; and Hitler's military adjutant, Colonel Hossbach.[2]

Hitler began by discussing Germany's desperate economic

position, particularly in regard to her lack of vital raw materials. The problem of the nation's food supply was even worse. Germany simply did not produce enough food to feed her population. Thus, the aim of German policy, said Hitler, must be to secure the necessary living space for the German people.* The only remaining questions were when and where Germany would attack. There were three possible scenarios that would be favorable to Germany. First, if Germany completed her rearmament program by 1943, she would have military superiority over France and England combined. However, after 1943, if the French and English began rearmament programs of their own, they would rapidly catch up with Germany. Second, an opportunity to strike might come if France became paralyzed by internal strife. Third, if France became involved in a war with a third power, Germany might also have a favorable opportunity to attack. The situation Hitler had in mind for the third scenario was France and Italy becoming directly involved in the Spanish Civil War.

In any event, said Hitler, Germany would have to secure her rear by eliminating the threat from Austria and Czechoslovakia. Hence, the "invasion and subjection of Czechoslovakia and Austria would be Germany's first aim." The conquest of these two states would considerably improve Germany's strategic position. Hitler said that he thought the risks involved in such military operations were acceptable, because it was "highly likely" that Britain had already written off Czechoslovakia. In any case, Britain did not want to become involved in a general European war, and Britain's attitude would certainly have an effect on France. Italy, Hitler assured his listeners, was not concerned about Czechoslovakia, but the Italian attitude on the Austrian question was not certain. To a large extent, said Hitler, it depended on whether or not the Duce would still be alive at the time. Hitler set the date for his aggression to be by 1943 to 1945, at the latest, but then added that, because of the current tension in the Mediterranean, an opportunity for Germany could come as early as next summer (1938).

---

*Hitler's listeners understood that this meant the conquest of other countries into which the German people would then move.

The military commanders never questioned the immorality of Hitler's plans to attack small neighboring states. They did, however, raise practical objections. They did not think Germany would be ready for war by 1943, and cautious Field Marshal von Blomberg believed the Czech fortifications would be more of a problem than Hitler thought. At the conclusion of the meeting, Hitler did not order his generals to draw up any specific plan of attack on Austria, Czechoslovakia, or France. Some historians have incorrectly assumed that Hitler had decided on a definite timetable for war at the meeting. Actually, he knew he would have to fight eventually if Germany was to expand in the east, but he intended to wait and see how the international situation developed over the next few years.[3]

Since Hitler was planning to go to war in the near future, the German economy would have to be prepared for further increases in military production. By 1936, however, spending on rearmament was already straining the economy to the breaking point. Hitler and the war party among the industrialists (this was not an organized group, but a loose-knit faction that believed war would improve their economic position) wanted to go over to complete economic autarchy—i.e., national self-sufficiency. But reasonable economists, like the banker Schacht, who was minister of economics, warned that autarchy would be so expensive it would bankrupt the country.

War preparation that might bankrupt the country could, however, be very profitable for certain individual companies. If Germany was to wage war in the near future, she needed to become self-sufficient in two important areas, oil and rubber. Naturally, any program to develop synthetic oil and rubber would greatly benefit companies like I.G. Farben, which were already established in the field of synthetics.

At the urging of some of the more aggressive Nazi financial experts and with Hitler's approval, a four-year economic plan was prepared. This plan was a significant turning point on Germany's march toward war.

At the annual Nazi Nuremberg rally on September 9, 1936, Hitler proclaimed the Four-Year Plan: "In four years," he said, "Germany must be wholly independent of foreign imports if the same materials can be produced in Germany." Privately, Hitler admitted that the real objective of the Four-Year Plan was to have the armed forces ready for combat and German industry ready to support a major war effort in four years. "Just as we produce 700,000 to 800,000 tons of gasoline at the present time, we could be producing three million tons. Just as we produce several thousand tons of rubber, we could already be producing 70,000 to 80,000 tons per year," Hitler stated in a secret memorandum.

Seventy-five percent of the money spent on the Four-Year Plan was to go to I.G. Farben for the development of synthetic gasoline and rubber. Naturally, a number of business interests were opposed to the Four-Year Plan. The Army Ordnance Department also stubbornly resisted. Army economic experts pointed out it was much cheaper to import and stockpile oil and rubber than try to produce it synthetically in Germany.

Hitler was willing to disregard the short-term costs because synthetics were the only way Germany could become independent in natural resources in the long run. Moreover, it would not be safe for Germany to go to war depending on stockpiles of oil and rubber. If the war lasted longer than expected, and the stockpiles ran out, Germany would have to surrender. Nevertheless, because of the great expense involved in developing synthetic oil and rubber, Hitler realized there would be stubborn resistance, so he appointed Goering to be director of the Four-Year Plan. Goering's power and ruthlessness would be needed to smash all opposition. Thus in 1937, it was obvious that a great confrontation between the Nazis and their conservative allies was about to occur.

By 1938, Field Marshal von Blomberg, the minister of war, and General von Fritsch, commander in chief of the army, were seen as the major obstructions to Hitler's aggressive foreign policy, the Four-Year Plan, and the modernization of the military. Both Blomberg and Fritsch were cautious commanders who believed Germany needed many years to prepare properly for war. These two generals were too powerful for Hitler to confront them directly, so covert means would have to be found to isolate them from the rest of the army and destroy them by personal attack. To this end, the Gestapo put a watch on both generals and tapped their phone conversations.

Nazis like Goering and some of his financial backers stood to make fortunes on the Four-Year Plan, from profits on lucrative government defense contracts to develope synthetic fuel and rubber. To get these contracts, companies would pay big "commissions" to high-ranking Nazis like Goering. Consequently, both the companies and other Nazis like Goering were willing to go to any lengths to eliminate all opponents of the massive government spending and economic restrictions the Four-Year Plan required. When the opponents of the plan were people in high places, the easiest way to get rid of them was by sex scandals.

When Field Marshal von Blomberg, who was a widower, remarried in 1938, Goering and Himmler saw their chance. Although Blomberg's new wife was young and beautiful, she was from a very humble background. This fact alone caused gossip. However, a serious sex scandal soon erupted in which she was accused, falsely, of having been a prostitute. The Gestapo supplied the "evidence." Hitler was shocked. After seeing the police dossier on her, he muttered: "If a German field marshal marries a whore, then anything in the world is possible."

The plot against Blomberg and his wife was hatched by Goering, the S.S., and their shadowy financial backers. Hitler seems to have been completely taken by surprise. Goering wanted to take over Blomberg's position as minister of war. However, the logical successor to Blomberg would have been the conservative General von Fritsch, the commander in chief of the army. To forestall this possibility, the Gestapo produced more trumped-up "evidence" to discredit General von Fritsch. Since he was a bachelor and rarely seen in the company of women, he was accused of having committed homosexual "offenses."

Hitler was in a predicament. He didn't want to replace Blomberg with Goering because he was afraid Goering would then be too powerful and a rival to his [Hitler's] own position as Fuehrer. Furthermore, Blomberg was very pro-Nazi, so it wouldn't be easy to replace him with a general who was as politically reliable.

When the news spread in Berlin that Field Marshal von Blomberg and General von Fritsch had been dismissed, a crisis atmosphere developed. There were rumors that the army might oust the Nazis. However, Hitler once again demonstrated his ability as a political manipulator. He saw through the plans of

Goering and Himmler and turned the situation to his own advantage. On the night of February 4, 1938, German radio announced that Hitler named himself supreme commander of the armed forces to replace Blomberg, and directly under him was General Keitel, who was appointed chief of the high command of the armed forces. Hitler also took over Blomberg's job as minister of war, but he did not use the title, and the Ministry's work was delegated to the high command. To appease Goering for not getting Blomberg's job, Hitler promoted him to the rank of field marshal. General von Brauchitsch was appointed commander in chief of the army to replace Fritsch.

It was also announced that sixteen senior generals were relieved of their commands, and forty-four others were transferred. Moreover, the shake-up extended to the Foreign Office, where the conservative foreign minister, von Neurath, was replaced by the Nazi Ribbentrop. Three important ambassadors were also dismissed: Hassell in Rome, Dirksen in Tokyo, and Papen, who had been Hitler's vice-chancellor in 1933, in Vienna. Finally, the report concluded with the statement that Walther Funk had been appointed as Schacht's successor as minister of economics.

The next day, the headlines of the *Völkischer Beobachter* read: "Strongest Concentration of All Powers in Fuehrer's Hands!" It was true that Hitler had increased his power considerably by the dismissal of so many senior generals; however, the Blomberg-Fritsch crisis should not be viewed solely as a personal triumph for Hitler. It was instead a victory for the German war party, including the pro-Nazi industrialists supporting the Four-Year Plan, the more aggressive generals, like General von Reichenau, who had played a key role in the Roehm purge, Nazis like Goering and Ribbentrop, and of course Hitler himself. Germany was now ready to go to war with a new expansion-minded leadership. Her first victim, as Hitler explained at his military conference on November 5, would be innocent Austria.

After the fiasco of the Nazi putsch in Austria in 1934, during which Chancellor Dollfuss had been murdered, Hitler followed a more careful policy of trying to subvert Austria gradually. Toward this end, Hitler had sent his old ally and arch intriguer, Franz von Papen, to Vienna to soften up the Austrians. In spite of Papen's attempts to work quietly, the political conflicts that had been simmering in Austria for four years were about to boil over again in 1938. Of course, the Nazis were to blame for most of the trouble, because the illegal Austrian Nazi party, which was financed primarily by Hitler, was carrying out a reign of terror against the government. The whole province of Styria was in a virtual state of civil war as the Nazis battled the Austrian patriots of the semi-Fascist Fatherland front. Austrian Chancellor von Schuschnigg ordered the police to crack down on the more radical Nazis after plans for an uprising and reign of terror were found by police in a raid on a Nazi hideout.[4]

Against this background, Hitler invited Chancellor von Schuschnigg to come to Berchtesgaden for a private discussion to try to improve Austro-German relations. Schuschnigg, a Jesuit-educated intellectual and a devout Catholic, was skeptical of Hitler's intentions but decided to meet with him anyway to try to buy time for Austria. At the insistence of Papen, who made the arrangements for Hitler, Schuschnigg agreed to keep the meeting secret from the press. Thus, on the evening of February 11, accompanied only by his foreign secretary, Guido Schmidt, Schuschnigg quietly left Vienna by the night train for Salzburg. In the morning at Salzburg, Schuschnigg and Schmidt got off the train and drove through the snow-covered mountainous countryside to the German border. There they were met by Papen who, in a jovial mood, casually remarked that he hoped Schuschnigg would not mind the presence of a few German generals who happened to be visiting Hitler. It was a warning of what was to come.

Near Berchtesgaden they had to change from a car to a military half-track to take them up the steep, icy mountain road to the Berghof. Hitler, wearing black pants and a brown jacket with a bright red swastika armband, came out on the terrace to greet his guests when they arrived. He immediately led Schuschnigg upstairs to the huge living room of the Berghof with its immense picture window. Schuschnigg started to make some polite conversation about the beauty of the view when Hitler rudely cut him short: "We haven't come here to talk about the lovely view or the weather!" All the resentments and hatreds Hitler had felt as a penniless youth in Vienna suddenly came boiling up in him. Schuschnigg, a sophisticated intellectual from an upper-class Austrian family, was just the sort of man Hitler hated. He was just like the directors of the Vienna Art Academy who had rejected him so many years before.

"You have done everything to avoid a friendly policy toward Germany!" Hitler exclaimed. "The whole history of Austria is just one uninterrupted act of high treason . . . and I can tell you, Herr Schuschnigg, that I am absolutely determined to put an end to this business. The German Reich is a great power and no one will interfere if it restores order in a nation on its border."

Stunned, Schuschnigg tried to reply calmly and not excite Hitler any further. But the Austrian chancellor's quiet reasonableness seemed in itself to enrage Hitler. He became very insulting and said that Austria's contribution to German history was "absolute zero." When Schuschnigg tried to contradict him, Hitler began to shout, "I am telling you once more that things can't continue this way. I have a historic mission to fulfill. . . . Providence has selected me to do so. . . . I have achieved more in history than any other German."

After this extremely conceited statement, Hitler became more threatening. "I am telling you that I intend to clean up the whole so-called Austrian question—one way or another. Do you think I don't know that you are fortifying Austria's border with the Reich? . . . I have only to give an order and all this comic stuff on the border will be blown to pieces, overnight. You don't seriously think you could hold me up even for half an hour, do you? Who knows—perhaps you will find me one morning in Vienna, like a spring storm! . . . I'd like to spare the Austrians that. . . . The S.A. and the [Nazi] Austrian Legion would come in after the troops and nobody—not even I—could stop them from wreaking vengeance. Do you want to turn Austria into a second Spain? I would like to avoid all that—if possible."[5]

Schuschnigg was an intelligent but soft-spoken man. Trained as a lawyer, he could hold his own in any debate based on rational logic. But Hitler overwhelmed him with insults and wild gesticulations. He never gave Schuschnigg time to think, continually barking one threat after another at him. While shouting, Hitler was watching for a sign of his opponent's weakness. Before their meeting, Nazi intelligence had, at Hitler's orders, supplied him with a detailed study of Schuschnigg's personality and vulnerabilities.

Soon Schuschnigg only sought escape from Hitler's harsh loud voice. He became almost nauseated at the sight of the ranting madman in front of him. Hitler knew he had Schuschnigg just where he wanted him. Although the Austrian chancellor was certainly not a coward, he was about to break or walk out. At this point, Hitler temporarily backed off and suggested they break for lunch.

After a brief lunch, during which Hitler calmed down and behaved normally, the "talks" resumed. Hitler presented Schuschnigg with a written ultimatum. When the Austrian chancellor tried to protest, Hitler ranted and raved so much that he seemed out of his mind. Finally, he regained some self-control, raced to the door, and called for General Keitel. Schuschnigg was afraid this madman was summoning General Keitel to order the German Army to march into Austria. When Keitel appeared and asked Hitler what he wanted, Schuschnigg was shown out of the room. Then Hitler smiled at the general and said he didn't really want anything other than the general's presence.

The bluff worked. Schuschnigg was so intimidated, he agreed to sign Hitler's ultimatum. In it, he promised to legalize the Austrian Nazi party, release Nazis who were then in jail, allow close collaboration between the German and Austrian armies and, most significantly, agree to appoint three pro-Nazis to his cabinet, as ministers of the interior, defense, and finance. The key position of minister of the interior, which controlled the police, was to be given to a pro-Hitler, pan-German,* Artur Seyss-Inquart.

Why had Hitler suddenly decided to step up the pressure against Austria? In his secret military conference at the Chancellery on November 5, 1937, Hitler had said he would not attack Austria until 1943 unless France became involved in a war in the Mediterranean with Italy. But France and Italy were not at war. True, there was unrest in Austria, but that had been going on for years. Historians have been unable to determine exactly why Hitler decided to move against Austria in early 1938.

---

*The pan-Germans favored a union between Germany and Austria.

New evidence now shows that the reason for Hitler's sudden action against Austria was Germany's desperate economic position. The simple fact was Germany did not have enough raw materials to continue rearmament. There were serious shortages of strategic metals, oil, rubber, cotton, and fats. From 1933 to 1937, Germany had been able to purchase some of the needed raw materials on world markets, but by 1938, she had run out of money to buy imports.

In his diary, on February 4, 1937, General Jodl, one of the most able strategists of the high command, wrote: "Decisive conference about the scarcity of raw materials by the Commissioner of the Four-Year Plan [Goering]. Only 50% of steel and iron needed, is available, therefore, rationing necessary. . . . Armed Forces and constructions for Four-Year Plan must be cut down by about 40%. . . . Until further notice, no more orders to be placed with industry so they will have a chance to fill the many orders previously placed with them.

"Bad harvest, especially of bread grains, demanded considerable use of foreign currency for feeding the people."[6]

Since Germany had to unexpectedly use all available money to import food after the poor harvest in 1936, there was little cash left to pay for imports of metal ores. This created an especially critical situation in the steel industry. There were shortages of nickel, manganese, tungsten, and molybdenum, which were all needed to produce high-grade steel. Some steel factories doing rearmament work had to cut back production to 75 percent of capacity.[7]

A number of industrialists complained angrily to Goering, who was head of the Four-Year Plan. They convinced him that disaster lay ahead unless something was done quickly. Without foreign exchange to pay for imports of fats and other agricultural products, Germany faced possible food shortages in the near future. Hitler and Goering both remembered the effect of the British naval blockade during World War I, which had cut Germany off from world food supplies and resulted in hunger riots and the eventual downfall of the monarchy. In 1938, however, Britain and France didn't need a naval blockade; they could limit German rearmament by simply doing nothing because they controlled a large percentage of the world's raw materials. Without foreign loans or credits to buy these raw materials, Hitler was trapped. He had spent Germany into insolvency.

There was only one way out—march into central Europe, where there were some of the natural resources Germany needed, including an adequate food supply. The first step would be to move into Austria. Once Austria was taken, Czechoslovakia would be at a strategic disadvantage because it would be surrounded on three sides. Nazi financial experts pointed out that the annexation of Austria would temporarily solve many of Germany's economic problems and particularly provide enough foreign exchange and gold to keep Germany financially afloat for at least a year.

Rumors about Schuschnigg's secret meeting with Hitler spread through Vienna the next day, causing considerable worry.[8] Fearing the worst, people began to take money out of the country, and Austrian stocks plummeted in value. In desperation, Schuschnigg tried to get foreign support for Austria. But neither Britain nor France were willing to make any commitment of military support.[9]

The situation in Austria was deteriorating rapidly. Schuschnigg's concessions to the Nazis only made them bolder. There were large demonstrations that turned into pitched battles between Schuschnigg supporters and the Nazis. The new minister of the interior, Seyss-Inquart, ordered the police not to intervene. Nazi mobs invaded the Lepoldstadt section of the city, where many Jews lived, shouting "Heil Hitler" and "Hang the Jews." Fearing a complete breakdown of law and order, Schuschnigg decided to make a last stand. On March 9, to prove to the world that a majority of Austrians were against a union with Nazi Germany, he called for a plebiscite to decide once and for all if Austria was to remain independent.

Schuschnigg's calling for a plebiscite infuriated Hitler. Furthermore, it was a serious threat to his plans of acquiring *lebensraum* (living space) in the east. If a majority of Austrians voted against union with Germany, then Hitler's best justification for taking over the little country would be lost, as far as international opinion was concerned. Without such a justification, a German invasion might result in a war with Britain, France, or Italy. Moreover, Hitler intended for Austria to be his first step on the road to the conquest and domination of Eastern Europe. If Austria remained free and independent, it would make a German attack on Czechoslovakia much more difficult, if not impossible.

With his life's ambition for conquest threatened, Hitler moved quickly. He summoned Goering and General Keitel to an emergency meeting at the Chancellery. They decided Germany had to march into Austria before Schuschnigg's plebiscite was held. But as Keitel pointed out, there were no plans drawn up for an invasion of Austria. When General Beck, the conservative chief of the General Staff, was asked what plans the General Staff had made for an operation against Austria he replied: "We have prepared nothing, nothing has been done, nothing at all." Clearly, Hitler had not been planning to invade Austria as early as 1938. Germany's desperate economic position and Goering's intrigues had forced him to move faster than he had originally intended. He now had no choice but to order the generals to draw up makeshift plans for the attack on Austria as best they could in the little time available.[10]

What worried Hitler most now was how Italy would respond to a German invasion of Austria. When the Nazis had tried to take over Austria in 1934, Mussolini immediately massed his troops on the Brenner Pass to let the Germans know Italy was ready to fight to preserve Austrian independence. But much had changed since 1934; Italy had become involved in the Ethiopian adventure and was now tied down in the Spanish Civil War. Immediately, Hitler sent a message to Mussolini, begging him not to intervene if German troops marched into Austria.

On March 11, Goering, realizing the economic urgency of the annexation of Austria even more than Hitler, got on the phone to Seyss-Inquart in Vienna, and told him to demand Schuschnigg's immediate resignation and the appointment of a pro-Nazi cabinet, under a threat of war.[11] Goering was acting on his own authority because he knew rich spoils were to be obtained in Austria. Hitler, meanwhile, was afraid to do anything before hearing from Mussolini. Nevertheless, a few hours later, Goering was on the phone again to Vienna, this time ordering Seyss-Inquart to send a fake telegram to Berlin, requesting German troops to intervene "to restore order." At 7:45 that evening, the music program on Radio Vienna was suddenly interrupted for an announcement. Chancellor von Schuschnigg spoke. He said he was resigning under the threat of the German ultimatum. "We have yielded only to brute force," he told the Austrian people. By midnight, Seyss-Inquart had formed a Nazi cabinet that included Goering's brother-in-law.

The next day, March 12, the sixty-five thousand German troops that were massed on the Austro-German border invaded Austria before sunrise. There was no resistance. By midmorning, the Austrian roads were crowded for miles with German tanks, trucks, and military cars. Villagers draped their houses in red swastika flags and Austrian police saluted German troops as they went by.

That afternoon, Hitler arrived in Linz, the city where he lived as a youth. When he appeared on the balcony of the baroque city hall, the crowd roared its approval with shouts of "Sieg Heil." He raised his arm to silence the crowd. "I believed in this divine mission. I have lived and fought for it," he said, choking with emotion. "Now I have fulfilled it." By nightfall, the Germans were in control of most of Austria.

Hitler remained in Linz on Sunday, March 13, only leaving to place a wreath on his parents' grave in the nearby village of Leonding. It was a brisk sunny spring day on Monday morning as Hitler's thirty-five-car motorcade set out on the hundred-mile journey to Vienna. At 5 P.M., the bells of hundreds of Vienna's churches began to ring as Hitler drove into the city. A half million Viennese lined the streets to cheer him and roar "Sieg Heil." It's not surprising that there was no opposition in sight; for three days the Austrian Nazis and newly arrived Gestapo agents had been arresting all the leading anti-Nazis.[12]

That night, Hitler stayed at the palatial Imperial Hotel. Talking with his staff after midnight, he told how as an impoverished young man he had often passed this splendid hotel with its glittering chandeliers, red carpets, and spectacular ballrooms. One winter night, he was hired to shovel snow off the hotel sidewalks for a few pennies. As he worked, he watched the aristocrats dressed in their uniforms and the ladies in their ballgowns arrive and leave. He said he could still remember the smell of ladies' perfume that night. The sound of the cheerful waltzes being played inside made him angry at the injustice in his life. "I resolved that night," he said, "that someday I would come back to the Imperial Hotel and walk over the red carpet in that glittering interior where the Hapsburgs danced. I didn't know how or when, but I have waited for this day and tonight, I am here."[13]

On Tuesday, Hitler rose early, had a small breakfast of prunes, a roll, and some chocolate and then reviewed the largest military parade held in Vienna since 1918. His large black Mercedes slowly drove up the Ringstrasse to the Burg Gate, where 200,000 people cheered him. From a platform on the steps of the Hapsburgs' palace, he saluted the Austrian Nazis and German troops. Later, he spoke to the crowd: "In this hour, I report to the German people the greatest achievement of my life! I declare to history the entrance of my native land into the German Reich!" After his speech, the parade of goose-stepping troops and tanks continued.

Although Hitler had not been in Vienna for years, he stayed only four hours after his speech. Then he boarded a plane for Berlin. Perhaps his memories of Vienna, when he was a penniless youth living among the homeless, were too painful for him to bear, or perhaps he still hated cheerful cosmopolitan Vienna. In *Mein Kampf*, he said, "To me the giant city [Vienna] seemed the embodiment of racial desecration. . . . I was repelled by the conglomeration of races . . . the Czechs, Poles, Hungarians . . . and everywhere the eternal fungus of humanity—Jews and more Jews."

The fact that Hitler did not linger in Vienna did not mean he was not interested in revenge. Before he departed, he left orders with his subordinates to deal with all his old enemies. In *Mein Kampf*, Hitler described with considerable frankness his hatred for the Hapsburgs, the Communists, and the Jews. True, his ideological beliefs were opposed to theirs, but these people were more than just his political opponents. All his frustration, racial and class resentment, anger and humiliation, were focused on them. He blamed the Hapsburgs and the Austrian upper class for his failure to become a great artist. He hated the Communists because they had beaten him up when he refused to join a union. He was resentful and humiliated that the Jews and Slavs, whom he saw as inferior, were more successful than he was. But now, the tables were turned. He was the conqueror, and all his old enemies would pay.

The Nazis wasted no time in embarking on what they jokingly called "the great spring cleaning," a wholesale purge of the Jews, monarchists, Schuschnigg supporters, Communists, and socialists. Naturally, the Jews suffered the worst. In the Jewish quarter of Vienna, teenage boys were flogged on the street with a cat-o'-nine-tails; old men were brought to tears as Nazi thugs jerked their beards; and everywhere Hitler's followers were spitting in the faces of Jewish women. Throughout the city, Jews were grabbed by storm troopers and forced to get down on their hands and knees and scrub pro-Schuschnigg slogans off the sidewalks. As the victims scrubbed, crowds would gather and chant: "Who found work for the Jews? Adolf Hitler!"

In Germany, the Nuremberg racial laws evolved over three years of gradual escalating persecution of the Jews, but in Austria the same laws were put into effect in three days. Jewish lawyers were immediately disbarred and Jewish doctors were expelled from the hospitals. The largest department store in Vienna, which was Jewish owned, was expropriated. Five major newspapers owned by Jews were quickly taken over by the Nazis. The harsh enforcement of the Nuremberg laws were bad, but the unofficial looting was even worse.[14] Nazis would simply back trucks up to Jewish delicatessens and load up with huge wursts and armloads of long bread rolls. Employees who were Nazis would sometimes physically throw out the Jewish owners of stores and restaurants and then put up a sign, REOPENED UNDER AYRAN MANAGEMENT, and perch themselves behind the cash register.

William Shirer, then a correspondent in Vienna, watched S.S. men "carting off silver, tapestries, paintings, and other loot from the Rothschild palace."[15] Baron Louis de Rothschild, who was Jewish, was arrested by the Gestapo and only able to buy his freedom after turning his Austrian steel mills over to the Hermann Goering Works, a giant government-run steel company controlled by Goering. Hundreds of German businessmen flocked like vultures to Vienna to buy up Jewish businesses at bargain prices.[16] Hitler's bloodless conquest of Austria was his greatest triumph yet. His popularity in Germany and his prestige with the generals was greatly increased. Most important, the looting of Austria would enable the German economy to keep going for another year. Although Austria was a small country, its gold reserve of $38 million was larger than the meager gold reserve Germany had left. When Dr. Schacht, the president of the Reichsbank, arrived in Vienna to take over the Austrian National Bank, he claimed the entire gold reserve for Germany, along with Austria's foreign exchange reserves, which amounted to almost $500 million.[17]

The strategic position of Germany was much stronger after the annexation of Austria. Germany now surrounded Czechoslovakia on three sides. The Czechs now had no chance of repelling a German invasion but could only hope to hold out until a French attack was able to draw off German troops in the west. The new German borders with Hungary and Yugoslavia gave the Nazis direct access to some of the raw materials they needed from the Balkans. Hitler's Germany had suddenly become the major power on the Danube, with a population larger than the German Empire's in 1914. All the nations of Central Europe and the Balkans began to reevaluate their trade with Germany and the alternative of accepting Nazi "protection" or taking the consequences.[18]

The day after Hitler's victory over Austria, he returned to Berlin to a triumphant welcome. Two million people lined the four-mile route from Tempelhof airport to the Chancellery. Hitler stood in his big black Mercedes alongside the driver, like a conquering Caesar standing in a chariot. As he stepped onto the Chancellery balcony to speak, a large white banner that said "Fuehrer! Your Sudetenland is also waiting for you!" was unfurled in the center of the surging crowd. The Sudetenland was the western portion of Czechoslovakia inhabited by a large German minority.

Emboldened by his easy conquest of Austria, Hitler now set his sights on Czechoslovakia. He had been planning the attack since his secret military conference at the Chancellery on November 5, 1937; only the timing was still open to question. The conquest of the Czech state could provide Hitler with rich plunder in terms of arms, industries, and gold reserves. Even more significant was Czechoslovakia's strategic position. From a military standpoint, it was the key to the French alliance system in Eastern Europe. Czechoslovakia's central geographic position linked France's ally, Poland, in the north with the French-supported "Little Entant" (a defensive alliance of Czechoslovakia, Yugoslavia, and Romania) in the south. Furthermore, the Czechs had the best-trained and most modern army in Central Europe, and Czech airfields were only two hundred miles from Berlin. From Hitler's point of view, Czechoslovakia was a dagger pointed at the heart of Germany that had to be eliminated. The possession of Czechoslovakia would also put Germany one step closer to the desperately needed Romanian oil fields, and the mineral resources of the Balkans, and outflank Poland, which Hitler was planning to attack in the near future.

Rather than a direct attack against his enemies, Hitler's method was first to weaken them by sowing internal dissension.[19] In the case of Czechoslovakia, this was easy to do. The mountainous western region of the country bordering Germany, called the Sudetenland, was inhabited by over three million Germans. Since the early 1930s there had been a strong and restive Nazi movement among the Sudeten Germans, led by Konrad Henlein, who was financed by Berlin.[20] On instructions from Hitler, the Sudeten Nazis embarked on a campaign of terror and riot against their Czech rulers. At the same time, Henlein made impossible demands for more autonomy that he knew the Czech state could not grant. By May, there was a virtual state of civil war in some Sudeten towns. Afraid that Germany was massing troops on her border for an imminent attack, the Czechs ordered a partial mobilization of their army on May 20.

The Czech mobilization made Hitler furious. He had hated the Czechs ever since his days as a schoolboy in Austria. Furthermore, the Czechs were Slavs, and Slavs, according to his racial theory, were inferior to Germans. On May 28, he summoned his top generals to a military conference in the Chancellery. As the officers stood around a large map table in the pleasant winter garden room, with its green potted plants, Hitler explained his plan of attack on Czechoslovakia with sweeping gestures.[21] Two days later he issued a written draft of what he had discussed at the conference. It read: "It is my unalterable decision to smash Czechoslovakia by military action in the near future." An additional note stated "the execution of this directive must be assured by 1 October 1938, at the latest."[22]

Why was Hitler in such a rush to attack Czechoslovakia? The

German economy was still in difficulty because of the heavy spending on rearmament. Goering, as director of the Four-Year Plan and economic czar, had informed Hitler that the rearmament program would soon have to be cut back by approximately 30 percent, for lack of funds.[23]

The conquest of Austria and the seizure of Austrian gold and assets had provided such a boost for the German economy and rearmament, why not do the same thing in Czechoslovakia? According to the calculations of the Nazis, however, something would have to be done fast, because money for rearmament purchases would start to run out by the fall of that year (1938). Thus, to keep his regime financially afloat, Hitler embarked on a foreign policy that required continual new conquests in rapid succession.[24] This is not to say that he did not want to attack these nations anyway, but the timetable was forced on him by economic circumstances.

The senior generals were alarmed by Hitler's rash plan to attack Czechoslovakia so soon. They were afraid it would immediately lead to another world war, with Britain, France, and possibly Russia intervening on Czechoslovakia's side. German defensive fortifications in the Rhineland were not yet completed, and there would be only about thirty divisions available for defense in the west. Against them, the French could mobilize a hundred divisions that would have little trouble marching straight into Germany. There were even doubts in the minds of the generals about the chance of the German attack on Czechoslovakia itself. Germany had only fifty-five divisions to attack the Czechs, who had forty-five divisions entrenched behind a heavily fortified line. To be assured of victory, an attacking army traditionally wanted a superiority of three to one when attacking a fortified position.

The general leading the opposition to Hitler's planned attack on Czechoslovakia was General Ludwig Beck, the chief of the General Staff. He wrote up several memoranda explaining in detail Germany's inadequate preparations for war. The probable outcome of such a conflict, he thought, would be a German defeat. He tried to get his superior, General von Brauchitsch, the commander in chief of the army, to make a stand against Hitler. There were several stormy meetings between Hitler and the generals. Hitler even appealed to the younger generals behind the backs of the senior commanders. The younger generals were sympathetic to Hitler. They were also ambitious and willing to take more risks than their superiors. Thus, for the first time, Hitler made some headway in splitting the powerful Officer Corps. Still, many of the top commanders agreed with General Beck, but when he resigned in protest in August, none of the other generals had the courage to follow his example.

At that point, General Beck and several other generals including General von Witzleben, commander of the Berlin military district, began conspiring to overthrow Hitler. Their plan was very simple—at the moment Hitler gave the order to attack Czechoslovakia, they would arrest him and the other leading Nazis. The army would seal off Berlin so the S.S. could not intervene. The generals had not decided whether to put Hitler on trial or declare him insane. Nevertheless, they informed the British of their plans and urged Britain and France not to yield to Hitler's demands on Czechoslovakia.

This was the most serious rift between Hitler and the army since the Roehm purge in 1934. It must be remembered, however, that only a small number of generals were actually involved in the plot against Hitler and most of the top commanders remained loyal. As far as the industrialists were concerned, they were also divided, with some of the munitions manufacturers pressing for an aggressive foreign policy, while other business leaders were becoming frightened and dissatisfied. A clear indication of the dissatisfaction in the business community was that both Dr. Hjalmar Schacht, the president of the Reichsbank, and Johannes Popitz, the Prussian minister of finance, both former collaborators of Hitler, were in on the conspiracy.

During the tense summer of 1938, rioting and civil unrest were widespread in the Sudetenland. The Nazi propaganda machine churned out numerous atrocity stories alleging the Czechs had attacked "defenseless" Sudeten Germans. Hitler actually believed some of these stories himself. Surprisingly, many of the fake atrocity stories had not been invented by the Nazi Propaganda Ministry but had originated from Sudeten Nazi newspapers.

At the Nazi party rally in September, both Hitler and Goering made bellicose speeches against the Czechs. Goering's speech was the more violent of the two. He called the Czechs "a vile race of dwarfs" and said that Moscow and the Jews stood behind them. Clearly, Goering was trying to force Hitler into taking action against Czechoslovakia.

The day after the Nuremberg speeches by Hitler and Goering, new rioting broke out in the Sudetenland. Thousands of protesters carrying swastika flags jammed the streets of the Sudeten towns shouting, "We want self-determination!" The Czech police opened fire on the crowd. As the conflict escalated, the Czech government declared martial law in the Sudetenland.[25]

Throughout Europe, there were rumors of war. In the midst of the crisis, Neville Chamberlain, the prime minister of Britain, sent a telegram to Hitler suggesting that they meet immediately in an effort to find a peaceful solution to the Sudeten problem. Hitler was pleased the leader of the British Empire was coming to him.

Chamberlain was neither a fool nor a coward. He wanted to avoid another world war, if possible. His foreign policy was at the time called appeasement. He was trying to satisfy reasonable German demands but would not tolerate German domination of the Continent. Being from a business background, Chamberlain distrusted professional diplomats, believing more could be accomplished by honest discussions between heads of state. In Chamberlain's mind, the Nazis, when compared to the Communists, were the lesser of two evils. Saying little about Nazi domestic policy, Chamberlain neglected to vigorously criticize Hitler's anti-Semitism. From all indications, Chamberlain really believed he could convince Hitler to follow a "reasonable" foreign policy. Furthermore, it is probable that he had a secret agenda, known to only a few top officials in the British government, which he intended to advance by going to Germany.

After flying to Munich, Chamberlain traveled by train and car to meet Hitler at Berchtesgaden. As the prime minister arrived at Hitler's villa, low dark clouds obscured the mountain peaks, and it was beginning to rain. Hitler stood at the top of the long flight of steps in front of the Berghof to greet his guest. After tea, the two men, accompanied only by an interpreter, retired to Hitler's study. In a quiet tone, Hitler began the discussion by listing his grievances with the Czechs. His voice rose as he gave examples of the Czech "injustices" against the Sudeten Germans. This could not continue, Hitler said. He was prepared to risk war and was determined "to settle the situation one way or another."[26]

At this point, Chamberlain, who had been listening quietly, became irritated: "If you are determined to settle the matter by force," he said, "why did you let me come here? I have wasted my time."

Outside, it had become dark, the mountain wind was howling, and a heavy rain was beating against the windowpane. The fate of the world hung in the balance as these two men talked.

Hitler clearly saw that unlike Schuschnigg, Chamberlain could be pushed no further, so he backed down. A peaceful solution was still possible, Hitler said, if the Sudetenland was separated from Czechoslovakia. Chamberlain replied that for his part he was willing to detach the Sudetenland, but he would have to get the approval of the government for such a step. Hitler promised not to take any military action against Czechoslovakia until Chamberlain had a chance to consult with his government in London and return to Germany.

With hindsight it is easy to see what a folly Chamberlain's policy was. At the time, however, France and her allies outnumbered the German Army at least two to one, and if the Russians joined the French, Germany would easily be outnumbered three or four to one. Although Chamberlain has long been criticized for giving in to Hitler, a less emotional strategic assessment would seem to indicate that this was really not the case at all. It is more likely that Chamberlain came to Munich intending to help Germany acquire the Sudetenland without war. That was his secret agenda. The policy of appeasement was window dressing for the public. Chamberlain's real foreign policy was based on the same principle on which British foreign policy had been based for over a hundred years: maintaining a balance of power on the Continent.

Since the Versailles Treaty, France was so strong, she dominated Europe. This was the reason Britain did not take a hard line against Germany during the Rhineland crisis. But recently Britain had two new reasons to fear France: the Franco-Soviet Pact; and the danger of a leftist popular-front government in Paris that might be controlled by Communists. Ever since the French Revolution, the British had been afraid of radical politics in France. An alliance between a Communist France and Red

Russia would easily have been able to crush Nazi Germany in 1938. Then Britain's worst fear would have been realized— Europe dominated by one great hostile power block.

Chamberlain saw Hitler as a bulwark against communism. He was afraid that if Hitler was so rash as to go to war over Czechoslovakia, Germany would lose to France and her allies. This was what Chamberlain had really come to Munich to prevent. He was trying to talk Hitler out of war and show that Britain would help him get what he wanted by peaceful means. Chamberlain believed that taking the Sudetenland and its defensive fortresses away from Czechoslovakia would improve the balance of power between France and Germany.[27]

Hitler knew what Chamberlain was trying to do. He knew the first objective of British foreign policy was to maintain a balance of power in Europe and said so in *Mein Kampf*. Hitler was playing a subtle psychological game with Chamberlain, trying to get as many concessions out of him as possible. His histrionic ranting against the Czechs was intended partly to make Chamberlain wonder if he was actually mentally unbalanced. In which case, there would be a danger that he might actually go too far and cause a war and Germany's defeat. Consequently, Chamberlain went out of his way to accommodate Hitler, giving up more than he would have to a more "reasonable" German leader.

Although maintaining the European balance of power was Chamberlain's primary foreign policy objective, it was not something that could be openly disclosed to the public. Since most of the British people still resented Germany for World War I, Chamberlain could gain support for his foreign policy only on the grounds that it was necessary to maintain the peace. In this way, the prime minister succeeded in selling his policy of "appeasement" to the cabinet.[28]

How did Chamberlain get the French to go along with giving the Sudetenland to Hitler? The prime minister probably indicated that if the French insisted on backing an uncompromising stand by the Czechs, then Britain "might" not aid France if she was attacked by Hitler. On the other hand, if France agreed to sacrifice the Sudetenland then Chamberlain pledged an Anglo-French defense pact and British troops to help defend France against Nazi Germany.

The politically divided French government was so eager to

avoid war that they went along with Chamberlain, selling out their Czech ally. Abandoned by their friends, the Czechs had no choice but to accept Chamberlain's giving the Sudetenland to Hitler.

On September 22, Chamberlain returned to Germany to meet with Hitler again. This time, they met at Godesberg on the Rhine. Chamberlain was angered to find that Hitler refused to accept the terms he had agreed to at their last meeting. Hitler now demanded immediate occupation of the Sudetenland by German troops without any plebiscites. Chamberlain complained that Hitler's demand amounted to an "ultimatum." At this point, the talks broke off, and Chamberlain returned to England. For the sake of his own political career, he could not appear to be giving in to Hitler too easily, nor, on a personal level was he willing to let an upstart German dictator bully him so openly.

Meanwhile, Czechoslovakia ordered a mobilization of its army. Everyone believed Europe would be at war in a matter of days. In London and Paris, the atmosphere was extremely tense, with people trying on gas masks in fear of a surprise German air attack using mustard gas bombs. Children were being sent to the countryside to stay with relatives. The French Army began to mobilize a hundred divisions, and trainloads of troops left Paris for the Maginot Line.

Not willing to give up so easily, Chamberlain requested Mussolini to intercede with Hitler as a mediator. Hitler quickly accepted Mussolini's proposal for a conference of the four major powers, Britain, France, Germany, and Italy, in Munich to resolve the Czech crisis. On September 29, the leaders of the four powers, Chamberlain, Daladier, Hitler, and Mussolini, met in Munich. The Russians and the Czechs were not asked to attend. Nevertheless, as the conference opened, Mussolini presented a list of "compromise Italian proposals," which was really a list of German demands given to him a few hours before. Chamberlain won a few minor concessions but was willing to go along with handing the Sudetenland over to Germany immediately. The only dispute concerned compensation for the Czech government property in the Sudetenland that was to be turned over to the Germans. Hitler insisted there would be no compensation. Chamberlain gave in on that point, but he then objected to the German proposal that the Czechs leaving the Sudetenland could not take their livestock with them. "Does this mean that the farmers will be expelled but that their cattle will be retained?" asked the prime minister.

"Our time is too valuable to be wasted on such trivialities!" Hitler snapped back. But the matter of livestock was, in truth, not a triviality to Germany, where fats were in short supply and had to be imported at great expense. Nevertheless, Chamberlain agreed to pass over the point, although it seemed like out-and-out theft to him. Daladier had little to say and seemed like a tired old man. He must have realized that handing over the Sudetenland would seriously weaken France's allies in Eastern Europe.

The conference lasted from about noon until nine in the evening. In the end, Hitler got just what he wanted; the Sudetenland with its fortifications undamaged would be handed over to the Germans in ten days. Britain and France promised to guarantee the new Czech borders. As the four leaders left the conference, it was obvious from their appearances how their nations fared from the settlement. Hitler and Mussolini, both in uniform, looked like conquerors in excellent spirits as they left on their way to a late-night banquet. Chamberlain was yawning and sleepy as he returned to his hotel. Daladier, appearing to be a completely broken man, was too tired even to respond to reporters' questions as he stumbled to his car.[29]

Hitler had done it again. Another bloodless triumph. His popularity with the German people rose to new heights. They were overjoyed, not only at the acquisition of the Sudetenland, but also by the fact that there would be no war. Even among the generals, there was a new respect for Hitler. The generals who were planning to overthrow Hitler called off the coup as soon as the news that Chamberlain was coming to Munich was announced. If there was to be no war over Czechoslovakia, the reason for the coup had suddenly evaporated. One of the conspirators, Hans Gisevius, later wrote: "The impossible had happened, Chamberlain and Daladier were flying to Munich. . . . the troops would never revolt against the victorious Fuehrer. . . . Chamberlain saved Hitler."[30]

After the Czechs were deserted by Britain and France, who had been their protectors, they had little choice but to agree to the Munich settlement and yield the Sudetenland to the Germans. On September 30, 1938, grumbling Czech soldiers left their fortifications and bunkers and began their sad retreat out of the Sudetenland. The next morning, October 1, German troops marched in. They were welcomed by cheering civilians just as they had been in Austria. A few days later, Hitler made his triumphant entry into the Sudetenland. In spite of the dark clouds and a drizzling rain, hysterical crowds of Sudeten Germans shouted themselves hoarse welcoming their "deliverer." Women in Sudeten peasant costumes showered him with flowers.

Germany's annexation of the Sudetenland was a great strategic victory for Hitler. It changed the whole balance of power in Central Europe in Germany's favor. Czechoslovakia was stripped of 75 percent of its defensive strength when its Sudeten fortifications were lost. Although the Czech Army remained intact, the flat Bohemian Plain was almost indefensible against an enemy surrounding it on three sides. The loss of the Sudetenland was a critical defeat for France. The Czechs' Sudeten fortified line was the key to France's whole system of alliances in Eastern Europe. What confidence could Poland, Yugoslavia, or Romania have in a French guarantee after the betrayal of the Czechs? Militarily, it looked as if the fall of Czechoslovakia was only a matter of time, so the neighboring states, Poland and Hungary, were eager to get their share if a partition took place. The Slovaks, a majority of the population in the eastern half of the country, began agitating for independence. Thus, what was left of Czechoslovakia was besieged from without and within and ripe for Hitler's next conquest.

Surprisingly, the victor, Hitler, was tormented by mixed feelings about the results of the Munich conference and his peaceful acquisition of the Sudetenland. After seeing how easily the western Allies caved in to all his demands, he wondered if he would have been able to get away with overrunning all of Czechoslovakia at once, without Britain or France going to war in the Czechs' defense. After his return to Berlin, he was overheard saying of Chamberlain, "That fellow has spoiled my entry into Prague."[31]

On the other hand, when Hitler toured the Czech Sudeten bunkers and fortifications, he saw just how lucky he had been that the crisis had not resulted in war. He was amazed at the strength of the Czech defenses. At last he saw for himself what the generals had been telling him about Germany's unpreparedness. After the Munich Conference, General Keitel, chief of the high command, said: "We [the generals] were extraordinarily happy that it had not come to a military operation because . . . our means of attack against the frontier fortifications of Czechoslovakia were insufficient. From a purely military point of view, we lacked the means for an attack which involved the piercing of the frontier fortifications."[32]

Nevertheless, Hitler had not gotten everything he wanted or needed out of the Munich Conference. The Sudetenland was rich in neither natural resources nor industries. There was some iron ore and lignite, and the Sudeten region contained extensive textile, glass, and porcelain industries. But the major Czech industrial centers of Prague, Brno, Pilsen, and Bratislava escaped the German grasp. The Nazis were anxious to get their hands on Czech industries like the famous Skoda Munitions Works. Another primary concern for Hitler was that the Czechs still had one of the best-equipped armies in Europe. If he could capture all their weapons intact, German rearmament would make a quantum leap forward. The Czech arsenal would provide him with enough weapons for a major war.

By the fall of 1938, Germany was near bankruptcy again. The Austrian gold and foreign exchange had run out. The German economy desperately needed another shot in the arm just to keep it going. The Czech gold reserves, foreign exchange, and other wealth would be enough to tide Germany over for another year. Not surprisingly, Hitler soon turned his attention to undermining the rest of Czechoslovakia.

The results of Munich were not obvious at first in Britain and France. Chamberlain and Daladier were hailed as heroes who saved the peace. Trusting Hitler, Chamberlain believed he had made a favorable change in the European balance of power. Germany's new strength would make Hitler content, or so he thought. Chamberlain was aware of Germany's economic difficulties, but he thought this would cause Hitler to cut back on rearmament spending, not motivate him to make further conquests. Only Winston Churchill recognized Munich for what it really was: "total and unmitigated defeat."

The loss of the Sudeten territory disrupted the entire Czech communication system and economy. Within a few months, the country started falling apart. The large Slovak minority was agitating for their own independent republic in the eastern half of the country, where they were a majority. Nazi agents were active in trying to stir up conflicts between the different minority groups, including Slovaks, Hungarians, Poles, Germans, and Ruthenians, and the Czech government. The Polish and Hungarian governments were also trying to fan discontent among the Polish and Hungarian minorities. By the beginning of 1939, Hitler had the Czechs where he wanted them. If they cracked down on the Slovaks and other separatists, German troops could move in to "preserve order." Of course the Germans had no legal authority to move in, but they would do so under the excuse of a great power acting in its sphere of influence to protect the interest of its citizens. If the Czech government did nothing, the country would break apart. In March, the crisis escalated. There were riots in Prague, and the Slovak parliament was on the verge of declaring independence. The aged president of Czechoslovakia, Hacha, declared martial law. There were rumors German troops were about to march in. At this point, President Hacha made a fatal mistake and requested an appointment to see Hitler.

In a shameless scene, even worse than the treatment of Austrian Chancellor von Schuschnigg a year earlier, Hitler, Goering, and Ribbentrop, who was the German foreign minister, intimidated and threatened the old Czech president. Hitler's performance was a masterpiece of merciless bullying. Shouting and raging, he threatened to invade Czechoslovakia by 6 A.M. the next morning unless Hacha ordered the Czech Army not to resist the German troops. In other words, if the Czechs resisted, there would be bloodshed; if they yielded, the Nazis would call it a "peaceful occupation" not an "invasion," but either way the Czechs would loose their freedom. Goering threatened to bomb Prague to ashes within hours. However, if the Czechs would cooperate peacefully with the Nazis, Hitler would generously grant them autonomy. Like many other Nazi promises that were just lies, Hitler had no intention of giving the Czechs true autonomy but rather a sort of benevolent occupation, as long as they produced goods for the Germans. Goering and Ribbentrop literally pursued old Hacha around the table thrusting pens and the surrender papers at him to sign. Poor President Hacha even passed out under the pressure, but in the end, he yielded to Hitler and ordered the Czech Army not to resist the Germans.[33]

At 6 A.M. on the morning of Wednesday, March 15, four great German armies invaded Czechoslovakia. Although there was no armed resistance, Nazi tanks, trucks, and artillery had rough going against an early spring snowstorm that left the roads covered with ice.[34] By nine the first German motorized units were driving into the suburbs of Prague. The Czechs gathered along the sidewalks to boo the Nazi invaders. Thousands of people jammed Wenceslas Square in the center of the city. Both men and women in the crowd were crying. A few people started to sing the Czech national anthem, "Where Is My Native Land?" Then a thousand voices joined into a great chorus until German tanks came clattering into the square. The Germans maintained perfect discipline, even when a few Czech teenagers started to throw snowballs at the tanks.

Hitler took the train from Berlin to the Czech border that morning. There he transferred into a convoy of automobiles accompanied by armored cars. Hitler sat in his usual place in the front seat of the first car, next to his driver, Kempka. As they started off, they encountered a blizzard. Before long, they were passing columns of German troops struggling through the ice and snow. It was almost dusk by the time Hitler's car drove unnoticed through the gates of Hradschin Castle, overlooking Prague. With the swastika flag flying from the castle's towers, Hitler slept well that night in the residence of the kings of ancient Bohemia. In the morning, as he looked down on the beautiful old city of his new "protectorate" from the windows of the castle, the Gestapo was already going to work arresting Jews and prominent anti-Nazis.[35]

In some respects, Hitler's conquest of Czechoslovakia was even more successful than his takeover of Austria a year earlier. The value of the spoils Germany took in Czechoslovakia far exceeded that which was obtained in Austria, particularly in the area of captured military weapons. Months before the invasion of Czechoslovakia, Hitler and army economics experts were drawing up lists of the quantities of arms and heavy weapons that could be seized from the Czechs. The modern equipment of the Czech Army would be equal to about two years of Germany's arms production. At a time when Hitler was being forced to cut back on rearmament for economic reasons, the Czech arsenal was an especially tempting target. There were also several major munitions factories in Czechoslovakia, which the Nazis wanted to take over.[36]

When the German troops invaded Czechoslovakia, officers from the army's economic section traveled with the advance units. Their mission was to seize all Czech weapons, equipment, and ammunition and to ship them back to Germany as rapidly as possible. The Czechs did not have time to hide any significant amount of weapons. The best evidence of the success of the Nazi pillage of Czechoslovakia was given by Hitler himself in a speech he made to the Reichstag boasting of his recent triumph. He carefully listed the numbers of weapons seized: 1,582 airplanes; 2,175 pieces of field artillery; 469 tanks; 500 antiaircraft guns; 43,000 machine guns; 1,090,000 rifles; 114,000 revolvers; a billion rounds of ammunition and 3 million artillery shells.[37] These weapons were enough to equip thirty divisions— almost equivalent to 50 percent of the strength of the German Army at the time. The captured artillery was especially significant because the Czechs possessed some of Europe's most modern heavy artillery weapons; the Germans were particularly deficient in this critical area. To Hitler, the captured weapons were the most important booty from the invasion of Czechoslovakia.[38]

The gold and foreign exchange looted in Czechoslovakia was of considerable help to the bankrupt German economy. German agents seized over a hundred million dollars' worth of gold from the Czechoslovakian National Bank and almost three hundred million dollars' worth of foreign exchange from Czech businesses and investors. The Nazis also pillaged almost one billion dollars' worth of raw materials and industrial goods. Especially important were the Czech metal stockpiles of copper, aluminum, and tin, along with ore supplies for the steel industry.[39] Dr. Benes, the former Czech president, wrote:

In the months following the occupation, vast numbers of German trains and trucks came every day into the Czech lands and returned by night filled with booty. Nothing you can read in the history of antiquity, or of the Middle Ages

about the robber expeditions of barbarous nations, sur-
passes this Nazi military expedition into the Czechoslovak
Republic. The Nazis took away all raw material, the enormous reserve supplies of grain, industrial and agricultural
products, practically everything they could lay their hands
on. Furthermore, vast "purchases" were made by both the
German authorities and by German individuals who
flooded the country. The exchange rate of the crown [the
Czech currency] was manipulated in favor of all such
German purchasers.[40]

Aside from all the booty Hitler acquired in Czechoslovakia,
the German military position was considerably strengthened by
the control of Czechoslovakian territory. Germany now out-
flanked Poland, Hitler's next intended victim. But as impressive
as this bloodless victory was, there was also a very negative side
to Hitler's conquest of Czechoslovakia (from the German point
of view) that he didn't even seem to recognize at the time. When
Hitler stood looking out over Prague from Hradschin Castle
reveling in his victory, one of his adjutants brought him the
good news that France and Britain were not mobilizing their
armies. "I knew it," he said arrogantly. "In fourteen days, no
one will talk about it [the invasion of Czechoslovakia] anymore!"[41]

Chamberlain was offended that Hitler had broken his word,
and the prime minister suffered a serious loss of prestige in
Britain. But more significantly, from the British point of view,
there had been a change in the European balance of power. By
crushing Czechoslovakia, Germany had tipped the scale of
power and now was as strong as France and her allies. Britain
would not tolerate any further aggressive moves by Germany.
Incredibly, Hitler did not seem to realize this.

Part II

Part II

Chapter 8

Victory and Looting in Poland and the West

On the night of August 31, 1939, tanks, artillery, and several hundred thousand German soldiers quietly moved up to the Polish border. At dawn on September 1, the attack began. There was a thick ground mist, which quieted the rumble of the tanks and muffled the first sounds of battle. Just after the first light, the German cruiser *Schleswig-Holstein*, lying off Danzig, fired a direct hit on the Polish ammunition dump at Westerplatte. It was a gray morning with a gentle rain.

Later that day, as the skies cleared, waves of Nazi bombers came roaring out of the western sky. They bombed Polish air bases, troops, fortifications, bridges, railroads, and all major cities. The Polish Air Force was caught on the ground and virtually destroyed on the first day. On paper, the two armies were almost equal, but the German Army was the most modern in Europe, while the Polish troops were equipped to fight World War I over again. Although the Polish Army had over a million men, the German air attacks caused such confusion that the Poles were only able to mobilize less than half of their forces. From five different directions, German armies led by hundreds of panzer tanks smashed through the Polish defenses.

Hitler had been planning his attack on Poland for a long time. At his military conference of November 5, 1937, before he attacked Austria and Czechoslovakia, he had already mentioned Poland as his third victim. On April 3, 1939, he had issued his first specific orders for the attack on Poland, code named Case White. A few weeks later he summoned his military chiefs to his study at the Chancellery for more specific instructions. He began by telling the officers that the only solution to Germany's economic problem was to obtain more living space (lebensraum) in Europe. But he warned them that unlike Austria and Czechoslovakia, "further success cannot be obtained without the shedding of blood." He said war was inevitable. He had decided "to attack Poland at the first suitable opportunity." "It is a question of expanding our living space in the east, of securing our food supplies." Naturally he was worried about Britain and France going to war, but he said he would try to "isolate Poland" and thus limit the war.[1]

Hitler addressed the Reichstag at ten in the morning on September 1. He told the deputies that Germany had been at war with Poland since dawn and falsely accused the Poles of firing the first shots. Now that it had come to war, he said: "I am asking no more of any German man than I myself did during the four years of World War I. The German people will suffer no hardships which I do not suffer. . . . From now on, I am nothing more than the first soldier of the Reich. I have once more put on the coat that was most sacred and dear to me. I will not take it off again until victory is assured, or I will not survive the outcome."

On this small point at least Hitler was telling the truth. Henceforth, he wore a gray military jacket instead of his brown Nazi party uniform. When he returned to the Chancellery from the Reichstag, the streets were noticeably empty. There were no cheering crowds as there had been in 1914 at the declaration of war.

The early days of the war went very well for Germany. Their first objective was to recapture German lands lost in 1918: Danzig, the Corridor, and Upper Silesia. German tanks cut through the Polish infantry and cavalry and broke out into the flat open plains of Poland. Although the Poles fought bravely, there was no way they could stop the advancing Germans. Hitler was pleased not only with the progress of his armies but also with the fact that Britain and France had not declared war on Germany, as their guarantee to Poland had promised. But on

Hitler the Conqueror, relaxing aboard his private train, on which he traveled across Europe in great luxury during the war.

This photo of Hitler and his cabinet was taken soon after he was appointed chancellor on January 30, 1933. His new partners, the conservative Nationalists, held a large majority of the posts.

Hitler with his two most important early collaborators, Vice Chancellor von Papen (with white handkerchief in coat pocket) and General Blomberg (to Hitler's right), the minister of defense. In the mid-1930s, Blomberg was actually more powerful than Hitler.

Nazi brown shirts blocking the entrance to a Jewish-owned department store during the boycott of Jewish businesses. Anyone who attempted to walk past these bullies risked a severe beating.

Although Nazi goons had no trouble frightening customers away from Jewish-owned businesses, the boycott was soon called off because Hitler's financiers were afraid the bankruptcy of Jewish firms would cause the collapse of German banks, damaging the entire economy.

Hitler in his glory at the symphony with Emmy Goering. Hermann Goering is in the background.

Hitler with Frau Wagner, the daughter-in-law of the famous composer, who had been one of the first society ladies to support him. Once he was in power, she became one of the most prominent women in Germany.

Hitler at the Berlin auto show. He was a strong supporter of the German automobile industry, and it was said that he secretly owned a large block of stock in one of the country's major automobile firms.

Prince August Wilhelm, the son of Kaiser Wilhelm, speaking at a Nazi meeting. The prince was Hitler's most important supporter among the nobility. His endorsement of the Nazis helped bring in large contributions from a number of prominent aristocrats.

Prince August Wilhelm in a Nazi storm trooper uniform (marked with an "X"), marching in support of Hitler. He made it "acceptable" for upper-class people to join the Nazis.

Hitler's popularity with German women was a key underpinning of his power base. One side of his multifaceted personality was the charmer who loved to flatter an attractive woman and kiss her hand in the old Viennese manner.

"Give me your children." Another side of Hitler's personality was the hypnotic spellbinder who held the youth of Germany in thrall and led them to their doom, like the Pied Piper of Hamlin.

Hitler in white tie, greeting the French ambassador. Photos like this were censored by Hitler himself if they showed him to be less than perfect. In this case, he was straightening his cuff.

The tension is obvious on Hitler's face as he sits waiting to get up and announce his declaration of war on Poland. Everyone realized this might cause another world war with Britain and France. Several of his financiers, including Thyssen and Schacht, broke with him over this issue.

Goering, Keitel, Hitler, and Ribbentrop plan their campaign of conquest in the East. Hitler's objectives—Poland, Russia, the Ukraine, and the Caucasus—were the same as Kaiser Wilhelm's objectives in World War I.

When Hitler invaded Russia, most German military transportation was horse-drawn. This contrasts with the popular image of a fully-motorized German army.

In 1939, Germany did not produce
enough grain to feed her own
people. Hence capturing the
agriculturally rich "black earth"
area of the Ukraine was one of
Hitler's major goals in the war.

The iron ore mine at Krivoy Rog in the Ukraine was one of the richest in the world and an important prize for the Nazis.

Hitler with his two most important partners in the army, Field Marshal Keitel (right) and Field Marshal Reichenau (with monocle, left), as they inspect the front in the east.

Slave laborers building the Krupp factory at Auschwitz. Several other major German companies also had factories inside the Auschwitz concentration camp to take advantage of the cheap labor. The SS rented prisoners to German businesses for a few cents per day. *Main Commission for the Investigation of Nazi Crimes and National Museum of Auschwitz-Birkenau*

Slave laborers working in the quarry at Sachsenhausen concentration camp. Several concentration camps were built near quarries to provide the vast quantities of stone and marble needed to fulfill Hitler's architectural fantasies for monumental government buildings.

Alfried Krupp and some of his executives on trial at Nuremberg for the use of slave labor and other crimes during the war.

Executives and directors of I.G. Farben, Germany's largest company, on trial at Nuremberg. Carl Krauch, chairman of the board, and eleven others were convicted and sentenced to prison.

September 3, the British ambassador in Berlin delivered an ultimatum to the Germans: if German troops did not begin withdrawing from Poland by eleven o'clock, Britain and Germany would be at war.

Hitler was sitting at his large desk in his Chancellery office when a translation of the British ultimatum was read to him. Ribbentrop was standing a few yards away looking out the window. Hitler sat immobile, staring straight ahead. He said nothing. After the translator had finished there was a long pause and awkward silence. Scowling, Hitler turned to Ribbentrop and asked: "What now?" The foreign minister had obviously misled him about the probable intentions of the British.[2]

A few hours after the British and French declaration of war (the French had delivered their ultimatum shortly after the British), Hitler left Berlin in his special headquarters train for the front in Poland. Before he departed from the German capital, he issued a proclamation stating that the British balance of power policy and the encirclement of Germany were the basic causes of the war.

By the fifth day of the war, Hitler and his generals were sure of victory. They had captured the corridor the night before. The Polish cavalry had tried to stop the German tanks, but courage alone could not stop armored might. Everywhere, the Poles were either surrounded or in disorganized retreat. Hitler followed his armies in his private train, which was equipped with radio transmitters to serve as field headquarters. On board there were offices, kitchens, small bedrooms, and a lounge with comfortable armchairs and sofas. There were antiaircraft guns to protect the train from air attack, but in spite of this, the train was usually stopped near a tunnel at night, in case of an enemy air attack.

Every morning, Hitler rose early, received the military news from his adjutants, and then set out for the front lines in an open car so he could be seen by the soldiers. He wore a pistol and carried a leather whip. All aspects of the war interested him, from the welfare of the troops and inspecting field kitchens to the details of the attack plans.

Near Plevno, Hitler met General Heinz Guderian, the commander of the panzer forces, and the two rode together in a car behind the advancing army. They stopped to look at the blown bridges over the Vistula River. Seeing a destroyed Polish artillery regiment, Hitler asked: "Our dive bombers did that?" When Guderian replied, "No, our panzers!" Hitler was astonished. He asked Guderian about the casualties and was surprised they were so low compared to the losses his own regiment had suffered in the first days of World War I. "I was able to show him," said Guderian, "that our small number of casualties . . . were due to the effectiveness of our tanks." Hitler was fascinated. The conversation then turned to technical matters. Hitler asked Guderian what the strong points of the tanks were and what still needed improvement.[3]

By the afternoon of September 8, the Fourth Panzer Division reached the outskirts of Warsaw. The Poles still heroically resisted, so Hitler ordered his armies to lay siege to the Polish capital. Day after day, the Poles held out until they were finally stabbed in the back by the Soviets, who invaded Poland from the east. This was the final fruit of Hitler's great diplomatic coup—a so-called nonaggression pact with Stalin that was really a secret deal to partition Poland. Overestimating Germany's strength, the French and British were unwilling to attack in the west, so there was little else they could do to help Poland. On September 27 Warsaw fell, and the Poles surrendered to the Germans.

Observers had predicted that the war in Poland would last at least several months, but it was all over in a matter of weeks. As the world watched in horror, Hitler had unleashed a new terrifying kind of warfare on Poland, the blitzkrieg. At first, the blitzkrieg was seen simply as a new type of military tactic that emphasized mobility, surprise air assault, and breakthroughs by concentrations of tanks. Actually, the blitzkrieg was much more. It was one of Hitler's most innovative ideas. Brilliant and terrible at the same time, it was a new strategy of total war especially adapted to Germany's unique combination of economic weakness, lack of natural resources, and military expertise.

By the mid-1930s, Hitler and the German leadership thought they would probably have to wage a war to break out of economic encirclement. But how? Hitler realized that for economic reasons, primarily lack of raw materials, Germany would be unable to wage a major war against the Allies that would last longer than a few months. (As was later seen, the Germans used up half of their total ammunition supply in the brief Polish campaign.) As Hitler saw it, the only alternative for Germany was a strategy of taking on opponents one at a time and crushing them quickly with a swift strike of all of Germany's might. Thus, Germany could gradually enlarge the foundation of her economy and raw materials by adding the captured resources of each successive victory to her arsenal. Finally, Germany would have under her control the necessary resources to wage a world war.

Lacking the humanity to be a magnanimous conqueror, Hitler showed no mercy to the defeated Poles. Before the war started, he had told his officers: "The destruction of Poland is our primary task. . . . Be merciless! Be brutal. . . . The war is to be a war of annihilation." Hitler's plan was clear: the Polish people were to be a source of slave labor for Germany, and the Polish leaders were to be "eliminated." Although Hitler had not previously hated Poles the way he hated Jews, he had no shame about "liquidating" them. "It is only in this manner," he told a Nazi audience, "that we can acquire the vital territory which we need. After all who, today, remembers the extermination of the Armenians!"[4]

The half of Poland captured by German troops was further divided into two territories. Those areas that had been part of Germany before 1914 once again became a part of Germany. The rump of what was left of Poland became a German colony called the General Government. The Nazis followed a different economic policy in each territory.[5] In the areas that were to become part of Germany, the policy was called "Germanization." This meant that a million Poles and Jews were to be expelled from Posen, Danzig, and Upper Silesia at the rate of ten thousand per day and sent to the General Government. Ethnic Germans from the Baltic would be settled in their places.[6] This also meant that the "expelled" people would lose their homes and farms. The Germans paid no compensation.

A total of over 700,000 homes and farms were seized from Poles and Jews in the lands incorporated into Germany.[7] Naturally, non-German businesses in this area were also confiscated. In the district around Lodz, which became part of Germany, the Nazis took over 70 banks, 3,500 textile factories and shops, 800 large firms, 500 wholesale companies, and 8,500 retail businesses. Not a cent was paid to the Polish or Jewish owners.[8] The factories and large businesses were usually taken over by German companies that had helped finance Hitler. The small businesses and shops were given to "deserving" Nazi party members.

In occupied Poland, the General Government, the Nazi policy was plunder and exploitation. Hitler appointed his lawyer, Hans Frank, as chief administrator and later governor general of occupied Poland with instructions to "mercilessly squeeze everything he could out of the Poles." On October 3, 1939, Frank described the policy for Poland that Hitler had ordered:

> Poland can only be administered by utilizing the country through means of ruthlessness, exploitation, deportation of all supplies, raw materials, machines, factory installations, etc., which are important for the German war economy, availability of all workers for work within Germany, reduction of the entire Polish economy to absolute minimum necessary for bare existence of the population. . . . Poland shall be treated as a colony; the Poles shall be the slaves of the Greater German World Empire. . . . By destroying Polish industry . . . Poland will be reduced to its proper position as an agrarian country which will have to depend on Germany for importation of industrial products.[9]

In the early days of the occupation, the Nazis immediately began the plundering of Poland. Robbery was conducted under the pretense of searching for arms. Said one observer, "Watches, money, and other valuables were taken at the same time. In Warsaw and other large cities, whole blocks of houses were surrounded by troops while a general search was carried out under the direction of Gestapo officers. Searches in Jewish quarters usually resulted in the expropriation of every kind of portable property—food was often taken as well as money."[10]

The Nazis also confiscated thousands of private businesses, from large industries to small hotels and shops. German businessmen who were members of the Nazi party naturally got the best Polish companies. I.G. Farben executives rushed in to try to take over the Boruta, Wola, and Winnica chemical companies, which were among the most valuable firms in Poland.[11]

The Germans often simply plundered Polish factories for valuable machines and shipped them back to Germany. For example, the equipment of one large machinery factory was given to a German munitions firm that sent engineers to Poland to confiscate all the machines, equipment, and even office furniture and then transport it back to Germany.[12]

After the Germans had carted off all their booty, little was left for the people of Poland to live on; this was just how Hitler wanted it. He believed Imperial Germany had not been harsh enough with the Poles. The Poles, he said were "idle, stupid and vain."[13] Most German nationalists shared Hitler's belief that the Poles were racial and cultural inferiors. When Poland was given German territory at the end of World War I, it only deepened the hatred and contempt the Germans had for the Poles.

Hitler thought the Poles could be forced to work only if they were hungry. The Polish peasants who were lucky enough to be allowed to keep their farms had to give over 50 percent of their grains to the Germans. There was hardly enough left to feed their families. The average daily food ration assigned by the Nazis to people living in occupied Poland was 2,600 calories for Germans, 670 calories for Poles, and 184 calories for Jews. From the first, Nazi tyranny in Poland was applied with a vengeance to the Jews. Both Jews and Poles would have starved quickly if it had not been for the black market. Clothing was as scarce as food, and shoes were simply unavailable. Since the Germans seized all the leather, Poles had nothing to wear but wooden clogs.

The richest prize Hitler won in Poland was the Province of Upper Silesia, which was abundant in natural resources, especially coal, iron, and zinc. It produced almost as much iron as the Ruhr, 90 percent of Germany's zinc needs, and eighty million tons of coal a year. Upper Silesia had been German territory before 1918 and would be essential to the German war economy. With his rapid victory over Poland, Hitler faced a difficult choice. Should he try to make peace with Britain and France or would the captured Polish resources strengthen Germany enough to enable him to attack in the west?

Did Hitler's partners, the German militarists and the Nazi financiers, want war, or was Hitler alone responsible for World War II? To answer this question it must first be recognized that World War II was really a continuation of World War I.[14] Naturally, politicians on both sides tried to obscure this fact. Neither the Germans nor the French and British people wanted to face the prospect of the terrible slaughter of World War I again. Nevertheless, on several occasions, Hitler revealed that the war he started in Poland in 1939 was simply taking up where the fighting left off in 1918. Referring to World War I in a speech he gave after the attack on Poland, he said: "Today the second act in this drama is being written."[15]

To recognize that World War II was a continuation of World War I, it is only necessary to examine the German war aims, since Germany was the initial aggressor in both cases. Contrary to popular myths, Germany's war objectives in World War II were not the result of Hitler's megalomaniacal ambitions; they were the very same war aims Germany had in World War I. Hitler, the loyal soldier of the old Imperial Army, was just championing these objectives anew. In World War I, Germany wanted the annexation of the French Lorraine, Belgium, Luxembourg, the permanent weakening of France, the isolation of Britain, and recognition of Germany's hegemony on the Continent. In the east, Germany sought the annexation of much of Poland and the Baltic States, to make economic satellite states of Romania, the Ukraine, the Crimea, and a permanently weakened Russia.[16]

The old elite of Imperial Germany, the generals, the industrialists, the Junkers, and the bureaucracy, all had a voice in determining German war aims in World War I. In the case of the nationalistic-minded industrialists and Junkers, their political representatives in the Reichstag had, on numerous occasions, endorsed these annexationist war aims and even pressured the government to pursue such objectives aggressively.*

Germany's expansionist goals in World War I were caused in part by arrogant nationalism, greed, and militarism, but they

---

*Even prior to 1918 not all German industrialists or even all Junkers supported an expansionist foreign policy. The moderates, however, were probably in a minority.

were also the result of a justifiable fear of encirclement. Since the time of Bismarck, Prussia, and later Germany, faced enemies on all sides but primarily France in the west, Russia in the east, and Britain in the Atlantic. This encirclement was not only political and military but economic as well. The German steel cartel had to break into the closed market systems of the British, French, and Russian empires and America. In January 1914, German Chancellor Bethmann Hollweg expressed Germany's frustration with encirclement to the French ambassador. "Each day Germany sees her population growing immeasurably. Her navy, her industry, her commerce are developing incomparably. She needs 'expansion,' she has a claim to a 'place in the sun'. . . . If you [French] deny her this, which is the legitimate claim of every living creature, you still cannot impede her growth!"[17]

Because of the Versailles Treaty Germany's problem of economic encirclement was much worse in 1939 than it had been in 1914. Many Ruhr industrialists realized that the gains and profits they had made from cartelization (the combination of companies to fix prices) and rearmament were only temporary. Without new markets and sources of raw materials, the Ruhr faced another economic depression in a year or two. Sales would begin to decline, unemployment would rise, bankruptcies would increase, and there would be food shortages and civil unrest. There were those who argued that only another expansionist war to break out of encirclement and then the economic reorganization of the Continent under German hegemony could enable Germany to survive and prosper.

Although some industrialists and some generals may have seen war as a solution to their problems, did they want a war with Poland? Ever since the formation of the Polish state in 1919, even the more moderate German generals like General von Seeckt, the commander of the German Army from 1920 to 1926, were anxious to crush Poland: "Poland's existence is intolerable, incompatible with the essential conditions of Germany's life. Poland must go and will go," said von Seeckt. "Its obliteration must be one of the fundamental drives of German policy."[18] A number of pro-Nazi industrialists worked side by side with Hitler planning the attack on Poland. Even Hitler's vicious propaganda against the Poles as an "inferior race" was nothing new. The Imperial government had used similar propaganda during World War I about the "eternal" struggle of the Teuton against the "incompetent" Slavs.

After World War II, the German generals made a major issue of their opposition to Hitler's going to war with France and Britain. But really, many of them were only opposed to his timing. They wanted another two years to prepare for war. For years, the German Army had regarded France as the "hereditary enemy," the major power standing in the way of German hegemony in Europe. Even before the turn of the century, some industrialists in the Ruhr had wanted a war of conquest to annex the iron ore region of French Lorraine. Italian minister of commerce Nitti recalled a conversation with a group of German industrialists in 1913: "They spoke unashamedly of the need to get their hands on the iron ore basin of French Lorraine; war appeared to them as a business proposition."[19]

The economic conditions underlying the rivalry between France and Germany had grown worse since 1914. Not only had the Germans failed to acquire the iron of French Lorraine, but in 1918, they also lost the iron ore mines of the German half of Lorraine to France. The great German steel cartel had to have a secure source of iron ore. Without it, they could not plan for the future and could not export on long-term orders, since they did not control the price of the raw materials.

The French steel cartel, the *Comite de Forges*, was in direct competition with the German steel cartel. Individual firms like the French arms manufacturer Schneider-Creuzot vied with Krupp for the same markets and raw materials. Some French companies were not content to play a passive game throughout the 1920s and 1930s. They tried to weaken the German steel cartel by continuously raising the price of iron ore the Germans needed to manufacture steel. A few French iron magnates went even further by trying to make a deal with some Swedish iron executives to raise prices. Swedish ore was Germany's only alternative source. This led the pro-Nazi members of the steel cartel to urge Hitler to do something quickly, before German industry was strangled by French pressure.

On October 6, after his victory in Poland, Hitler made a public appeal to Britain and France for peace in a speech to the Reichstag. As the speech clearly indicated, he was already thinking about attacking in the west. "Why," he asked, "should this war in the west be fought? For the restoration of Poland? Poland of the Versailles Treaty will never rise again." He said he recognized that there were problems between Germany and the Allies but suggested that they could better be solved at a peace conference before "millions of human lives are sacrificed in vain." "Let those who consider war to be a better solution reject my outstretched hand."[20]

Although he was talking peace, Hitler was already planning to continue the war. He had discussed the attack in the west with a few of his military commanders. Most of them thought Germany was not ready. Even Goering was shocked. Nevertheless, Hitler persisted. He said he did not intend to use the Schlieffen plan (which called for the main weight of the German attack to be on the right flank along the Belgian coast) as in 1914, but to attack directly through Belgium and Luxembourg to the west, to capture the channel ports.

On October 10, he further clarified these plans in a secret conference at the Chancellery with the top commanders of the three military services. He read to them a memorandum he had written on the military situation—Directive No. 6 for the Conduct of the War.[21] It began with an historical analysis of France's hostility to Germany going back as far as the Peace of Westphalia in 1648. He admitted there was a risk in attacking France so soon, but he said that the Allies had time on their side. Although he believed Germany was militarily stronger than France and Britain at present, they would soon catch up and surpass the Reich because they had the command of natural resources throughout the world. On the other hand, Germany's limited resources of food and raw materials made a long war impossible.

Thus for both economic and military reasons, Germany would have to avoid trench warfare. Panzers would have to achieve a quick breakthrough, as they had done in Poland. Germany, Hitler went on, had an historic opportunity to fight a one-front war while the treaty with the Soviets protected the rear. But this situation might not last long. Germany's basic "war aim," he said, is "the destruction of the power and ability of the Western powers to ever again be able to oppose the state consolidation and further development of the German people in Europe."

There was nothing particularly Nazi about Hitler's war aim. Hitler's partners—the Nazi business tycoons and the militarists—all endorsed his aim. In fact, Hitler himself could be seen as an agent of the traditional forces of German expansion and imperialism. War was the way to break out of the Allied encirclement and to establish a German empire in Central and Eastern Europe. Behind all of Hitler's rhetoric, Germany's war aims also reflected the need of Europe's largest industrial power to gain new markets and sources of raw materials.

Before Hitler had an opportunity to attack France, his attention was distracted by a British threat in Scandinavia. Almost half of Germany's iron ore came from Sweden by way of Norway. In February, German intelligence reported to Hitler that the British were planning to mine Norwegian waters to cut the traffic of ore ships down the coast of Norway. The British and French also intended to land troops in Norway to cut completely the flow of Swedish ore to Germany. Hitler had to act fast. On March 1, 1940, he issued orders for the occupation of Norway and Denmark.[22] Hitler felt it necessary to occupy Denmark to secure shipping lanes to Norway and the North Atlantic.

On April 9, German ambassadors presented ultimatums to the Danish and Norwegian governments, demanding that they accept "German protection" to prevent being occupied by the British and French. German troops immediately marched into Denmark, which was too weak to defend itself against the overwhelming Nazi odds. The Danes put up a token resistance and then surrendered.

The German occupation of Norway was not as easy. In a daring move, the German Navy outwitted the British and sailed into Norwegian waters. Within a few days, the Germans had captured all the major Norwegian cities and ports, including Narvik, the transshipment point for the vital Swedish iron ore. Although in some places the Norwegians tried to resist for a while, the cause was hopeless. German losses were minimal. The king of Norway, however, courageously refused to surrender and retreated to the mountainous interior. British and French troops finally landed in Norway but were too late to drive the Germans out. All they accomplished was to aid the Norwegian king and government to escape by ship to London. Hitler had won another significant victory. He now had guaranteed access to the iron ore and other vital resources of Scandinavia. He also had gained easy access to the North Atlantic for his submarines and air bases for the Luftwaffe to attack England.

Once Hitler and the German leadership had decided to attack in the west, the only thing they could not agree on was the timing of the attack. As was the case prior to the invasions of Czechoslovakia and Poland, the generals did not think the army was ready to attack France. There were heated arguments between Hitler and the senior generals. But, in the end, Hitler waited through the winter of 1939 to 1940, as the generals had insisted. The Germans might even have waited longer if it had not been for the effect of the British naval blockade. Because of the blockade, German foreign trade and the import of vital raw materials fell by almost 50 percent. The fuel shortage was especially critical and hampered military preparation for the attack on France. Hitler and the industrialists could see the handwriting on the wall; if Germany did not attack soon, she would slowly be strangled by the blockade.

At the time, however, it seemed the German generals had good reason to want to delay the attack. The strength of the French Army was formidable. The French had 800,000 combat troops and a trained reserve of almost five million men. Military experts still considered the French Army to be the strongest in Europe. Although the French poilu, the foot soldier, may have looked sloppy, he was known to be a tough fighter. Admittedly, the equipment of the French Army was old, and they lacked planes and tanks, but they had the Maginot Line, the world's most elaborate fortification system. All along the eastern border of France, there was a giant chain of giant pillboxes, fortifications, and underground defensive systems that made up the Maginot Line. In a word, the Maginot Line was said to be "impregnable."

Hitler was famous for his military "intuition." This "intuition" was really just a good understanding of human psychology and the psychology of his opponents in particular. He correctly recognized that after their experiences in World War I, the French would be obsessed with defense. A large part of a generation of young Frenchmen had been killed in the futile offensives of 1917. The French were not about to let this happen again. So they had spent billions of francs on defensive fortifications. "I have studied the Maginot Line," Hitler told a British journalist, "and learned much from it." Hitler learned that the line ended at the Belgium border; there was little need to study any more than that.

The German high command's original plan for the attack on France was basically the old Schlieffen plan of 1914. The main force would be the right wing advancing through Holland and Belgium and the Ardennes. The left wing would attack the Maginot Line. The problem with this plan was that it lacked any surprises; it was exactly what the French expected the Germans to do. The French would respond by sending their army north into Belgium, and trench warfare would develop. Furthermore, the German tanks with the main right-wing attacking force would be hampered by the numerous canals and rivers in western Belgium and Holland.

Hitler had pondered on this problem, trying to come up with something that would inject an element of surprise into the German plans. He was thinking of shifting the main emphasis of the attack from the right wing to the center. At about the same time, General von Manstein, an armored warfare strategist, proposed a plan that also called for the main attack to go through the Ardennes. The high command had rejected Manstein's plan as too risky, but Hitler embraced it. Believing that the thickly wooded Ardennes was impassable for tanks, the French had stationed only a few weak units in that sector. The Maginot Line only went as far north as the Belgian border, so there were no elaborate defenses in the Ardennes region of Belgium. According to Manstein's plan, once the tanks were out of the Ardennes, they would be in the open countryside with little opposition. From there, they could dash to the coast and trap the Allied armies in Belgium. Only after considerable argument did Hitler persuade the conservative high command to adopt Manstein's plan.[23]

On May 9, Hitler boarded his private train at midday and quietly departed from a small station outside Berlin. Throughout the afternoon, the train traveled north toward Hamburg. After dark, however, it changed direction and headed to the west. At three in the morning, it arrived at a small station outside Aachen, where cars were waiting to take Hitler and his staff to a secret new headquarters called Felsennest. Felsennest was located in a heavily wooded area. Hitler's bunker had been blasted out of solid rock and was surrounded with barbed wire and concealed fortifications. From here, Hitler intended to direct the war against France.

Before dawn, on May 10, 1940, the German attack on Belgium, Holland, and Luxembourg began. Parachute troops were dropped at strategic locations behind the front lines. This was Hitler's own idea. Another small force of troops in gliders landed on top of the key Belgium fort of Eben Emael and quickly captured it. Holland fell in five days, and the Belgium defense system was on the point of collapse. During the first few days of the invasion, Hitler spent all his time, day and night, in the map room at his secret headquarters, following the advance of his troops. He slept little, alternating between a state of wild excitement and exhaustion.

In Germany, Alfried Krupp was listening to the radio broadcast of German victories with several other industrialists. On a map spread out on the table they pointed to the captured towns. They were interested in whether or not their Dutch competitors' factories had fallen into German hands. An observer overheard them speaking excitedly: "Here is a village. . . . There is Muller; he is yours [and] there is Herr Schmidt or Huber. . . . He has two plants, we will have him arrested." Then Alfried Krupp turned to one of the other men and said: "This factory is yours."[24] They were like hungry vultures swooping down on a helpless prey.

Meanwhile, the main center attack group, forty-four divisions strong and led by a column of panzers over one hundred miles long, crossed the Ardennes and the French border. The panzers got through the hilly Ardennes forest with no difficulty. They encountered little resistance and quickly overran the few divisions of second-rate French troops in their path. By May 13, they crossed the Meuse River. Hitler could hardly believe how well things were going. The speed of the advance was so unlike anything he had known in World War I. He was afraid the French must be holding a powerful force in reserve to attack from the south. "The Fuehrer is terribly nervous," said General Halder, the chief of the General Staff. "He is frightened by his own success, is unwilling to take any chances and is trying to hold us back." By May 16, the panzers were moving forward again at a rate of forty miles a day. On May 20, Amiens fell; that night, the leading panzers reached the Channel coast.

The Allied armies in Belgium were cut off and trapped. The Germans began to close in from the north and south. The Allies were in complete confusion. The British began to fall back toward the coast and the port of Dunkirk. On May 24, as the Allied forces were pressed into a pocket around Dunkirk, the German panzers suddenly came to a halt a few miles south of Dunkirk. This allowed the British time to organize one of the most daring rescue missions in history. Hundreds of ships, large and small, crossed the Channel under attack from the Luftwaffe to evacuate 338,226 British and French soldiers. By June 4, when the panzers began moving again and entered Dunkirk, most of the British army had escaped.

Why were the German panzers ordered to halt just as they were about to crush the British at Dunkirk? For years controversy has surrounded this question. Did Hitler want to spare the British the humiliation of a complete defeat in the hope of soon concluding a peace settlement with them? There is little evidence to support this theory. In contrast, Hitler had two other, obvious reasons to halt his panzers which can be supported by abundant evidence. The first reason was purely a military one. With hindsight, it is clear that the French and British armies were beaten by May 24, but it was not so obvious to Hitler at the time. The panzer units were overextended because they had outrun their supply line. Furthermore, even if the French Army in Belgium was destroyed, the battle for France and the capture of Paris remained. Hitler had no way of knowing that the demoralized French would put up little resistance, so he was saving his panzers for the battle ahead.

The second reason Hitler halted his forces involved a political decision caused by the nature of the coalition of forces that made up the Nazi government. The army had performed so well in the first weeks of the war in the west that Hitler was afraid their power would become a threat to his position. Consequently, when Goering suggested that the Luftwaffe be allowed to finish the British off at Dunkirk, Hitler jumped at the idea. The destructive power of bombing at the time was untested and far overrated, but naturally, neither Goering nor Hitler knew this. Hitler never intended to let the British escape.

On June 5, the Germans turned south and launched their attack on Paris. The French had lost one-third of their army in Belgium. But, what was worse, the remaining troops were demoralized and disorganized. The roads were clogged with refugees, making troop movement difficult. General Waygand, the new commander in chief of the Allied armies, who had just replaced General Gamelin, tried to hold the Germans on the Somme, but within little more than a week, the battle was over. The Germans took Paris on June 14. Premier Reynaud resigned on June 16, and Marshal Petain formed a new government to negotiate the armistice.

With a touch of drama, Hitler ordered that the armistice should be signed in the same railroad car in which Germany had surrendered in 1918. On the afternoon of June 21, Hitler arrived in the Compiègne Forest in a big black Mercedes. It was a lovely warm summer day. Journalist William Shirer, who was present, observed that "Hitler's face was . . . brimming with revenge. There was also in it, as in his springy step, a note of the triumphant conqueror, the defier of the world. There was also something else . . . a sort of scornful, inner joy at being present at this great reversal of fate—a reversal he himself had wrought."[25]

The armistice was to go into effect at 1:35 A.M. on June 25, 1940. At the time, Hitler's temporary headquarters were located in the small French village of Bruly le Peche, near Sedan. The inhabitants of the village had been evacuated and the small peasant houses were taken over as quarters for Hitler's staff. That night, shortly before the hour of the armistice, Hitler and his staff were sitting around a table in the living room of one of the village houses. Hitler gave orders to turn out the lights and open the windows. A bugle sounded outside to signal the end of the fighting. Occasional flashes of lightning from a distant thunderstorm illuminated the room. Some of the men around the table were overcome with emotion. Hitler broke the silence to say only two words: "This responsibility . . ." Then his voice trailed off.[26] A few moments later, he ordered the lights to be turned on again. This was the high point of Hitler's life.

For four years, Hitler had served as an ordinary soldier during some of the bloodiest fighting of World War I. Even more than most men, his war experiences had made a profound and lasting impression on his character and life. In his own mind, he never laid down his arms in 1918 but continued fighting with political rather than military weapons. Now he had accomplished in a little more than a month what the proud German Imperial Army had not been able to do in four years. Ludendorff and the other great strategists of the German General Staff had not been able to achieve the breakthrough in the west and the destruction of France he had accomplished. He alone had sensed the weakness of France and Britain. Against all the advice of the military professionals he had forced through a bold plan of attack that had yielded an historic victory comparable to any of Frederick the Great's or Napoleon's.

Hitler's prestige with his partners, who had formed the coalition government with him in 1933, was never greater. The triumph over France would give Germany the hegemony on the Continent that the German power elite had been seeking since the turn of the century. The steel and chemical cartels now could control all the natural resources and markets of Europe. The German Army had avenged its honor and been proven the strongest fighting force in the world. Even the generals who, a few months ago, had been contemptuous of Hitler's common origins now regarded him with awe—a kind of natural military genius. Almost unnoticed in the light of his great military victory, Hitler suffered only one setback, but it would ultimately be his undoing. Chamberlain had resigned and Winston Churchill had replaced him as British prime minister. In Winston Churchill, Hitler would meet his nemesis.

Now that Hitler had conquered France, what did he intend to do with it? Basically, he wanted to loot France of all the raw materials Germany needed, annex the French provinces of Alsace and Lorraine, and put French industry to work for the German war effort. About 50 percent of French agricultural and industrial production would go to Germany. Of all the occupied countries, France was to become the most important supplier of goods to Germany. In spite of promises made by Nazi propaganda in France, Hitler never seriously considered making France an equal partner in the so-called New Order. France was simply to be exploited for Germany's benefit.

As director of the Four-Year Plan, Goering outlined the policy of economic exploitation to be followed in France, Belgium, and Holland:

> The aim is the strengthening of German war potential. For this purpose, all mines, iron works, rolling mills, firms producing primary materials, and also important manufacturing firms such as machine-tool factories, locomotive and wagon works, and so on, should be used at their full capacity and firms unimportant for war shall have their production reduced or be closed. Raw materials important for war which will not be used, as well as machine tools, especially such as came from works which have been closed . . . will be transported to the homeland. The consumption of the population is to be shrunk to the lowest possible level.[27]

In France, the total amount of goods requisitioned by the Nazis was staggering. Hitler used several methods to extract wealth from France. First, there was the occupation cost that France had agreed to pay as part of the armistice. The clause was similar to the one France had imposed on Germany in 1918. France had to pay 400 million francs a day, which amounted to about 60 percent of the French government income.

Then, there was the requisition of agricultural products by the Germans. The French were forced to deliver 3 million tons of wheat, 2 million tons of oats, 700,000 tons of potatoes, 75,000 tons of butter, 50,000 tons of cheese, half of the wine production, and 87 million bottles of champagne. The Nazis also took enormous amounts of raw materials, including 73 percent of the French iron production, approximately 80 percent of the copper and nickel output, and 55 percent of the aluminum output. The French were allowed to keep only 30 percent of their wool production, 16 percent of their cotton, and 13 percent of their linen production.[28]

During the Nazi occupation, Paris was unnaturally quiet. On many city streets a car would go by only once every five minutes. The Germans had looted and requisitioned all the petroleum reserves and over 80 percent of the production of French oil. In addition, over 85 percent of the new vehicles produced in French automobile and truck factories went to the German army.

The situation was almost as bad in other sectors of the French transportation industry. The Germans removed almost one-third of the French train cars, including over four thousand locomotives.

One of the most brutal acts committed by the Nazis after the conquest of France was the annexation of Alsace-Lorraine to Germany and the expulsion of all French citizens from the area. This action created a hundred thousand refugees and deprived France of her valuable iron ore and steel industry. After the fall of France, the Germans decreed that any French-speaking resident of Alsace-Lorraine who wanted to retain their French citizenship would be immediately expelled. These people lost homes, farms, businesses, virtually everything but the clothes on their backs.

Hitler made no effort to conceal his attitude about the looting of French industry. "The French have lost the war," he said, "and consequently they must pay for the damages."[29] He wanted to be sure the French people were burdened at least as heavily by the war effort, as the Germans had been by the Versailles reparations. Some German steel barons were more than willing to take advantage of Hitler's attitude to further enrich themselves. With the Nazis' cooperation, they took over factories and real estate in France. In addition, the Germans seized valuable machinery from French plants like the massive steel metal bending machine, worth 700,000 francs, taken from the Alsthom factory in Belfort.[30]

The defeat of France was a windfall for I.G. Farben. One major firm dominated the chemical industry in France, the Kuhlmann Company. Kuhlmann was second only to Farben itself in the European market. Because of their past partnership in various cartel agreements, the Kuhlmann directors hoped for lenient treatment from Farben. But the Germans reacted angrily to the Kuhlmann suggestion that their business relationship remain basically unchanged. One Farben executive pounded the table shouting that the 1927 cartel agreement was no longer valid after the German victory.

The directors of Kuhlmann were given an ultimatum: either surrender 51 percent control to Farben, or Kuhlmann would be classified as a "Jewish" company because it had had a few Jewish executives and directors. Once classified as a "Jewish" company, it could be confiscated without compensation under the Aryanization Laws. Farben could make such threats because they could count on Hitler and Goering to give them complete backing on anything they wanted as far as business was concerned. In the end, the French gave in. The French chemical industry was now dominated by Farben and was no longer a competitor in foreign markets.

Hitler's pillage of France was restrained compared to the looting of Poland. With the exception of the brutal treatment of the French in Lorraine, French owners were in most cases given some compensation when private property was seized. However, the French certainly suffered as a result of Hitler's expropriations. During the Nazi occupation, shortages of fuel, raw materials, food, and labor made life difficult for the French people.

The fuel shortage was probably the most difficult to endure; for this meant not only no gasoline for automobile transportation but no heat as well, because there was also a shortage of coal. In the damp old brick and stone buildings of Paris, the children cried in pain from the cold. Day after day, there was no heat, and the cold inside homes grew worse and worse. Because food, particularly fats, was scarce and what was available was lower in calories, people felt the cold more.

In addition to the material hardships, the French had to contend with the loss of freedom, the humiliation of occupation, and the compulsory labor of French workers in Germany. However, as in the other Nazi-occupied countries, the people who always suffered most were the Jews. Jewish refugees from Germany, Austria, and other Nazi-occupied countries who were in France were immediate targets for deportation to concentration camps. The Vichy government openly helped the Germans round up and deport all Jews who were not French citizens. Jewish private property was also the target for unrestrained Nazi looting. Two days after the fall of Paris, when many Jews had not returned to open their businesses as the Nazis demanded, their shops were broken into with crowbars and axes and the merchandise simply carted away. The most notable victims of such thefts were Jewish art dealers. A few days after the beginning of the occupation, large moving vans with Cologne license plates were seen parked in front of several Jewish-owned art galleries in Paris. Paintings and valuable art objects were loaded into the vans, which drove off for an unknown destination.

In celebration of his victory over France, Hitler decided to allow himself a little time for a few pleasures. He had always wanted to see Paris. For years, he had studied and admired the architecture of its great buildings. So on the morning of June 23, before dawn, he landed at Le Bourget Airport on the outskirts of Paris, accompanied by his architects—Speer and Giessler—his photographer, Hoffmann, and numerous bodyguards. Hitler and his party drove through Paris in three large black open Mercedes. Their first stop was the Opéra. Hitler considered this one of the most beautiful buildings in the world. From his studies he knew his way around the Opéra as well as the French guide.

He also visited the Madeleine, Arc de Triomphe, the Eiffel Tower, and the Panthéon. The highlight of his visit, however, was Les Invalides, where he stood for a long time in silence, looking down on the tomb of Napoleon. Finally, he turned and said to Hoffmann: "That was the greatest and finest moment of my life."[31] A few Parisians on their way to work early were stunned to see the Nazi dictator riding through their streets. But by nine in the morning, Hitler went back to the airport and left Paris. He never returned.

Hitler spent the last days of June touring the battlefields of World War I with his old army comrade Max Amann, now the publisher of the Nazi party newspaper. He was relaxed and enjoying himself. He was in no rush to do anything. Germany was still at war with England, but Hitler was sure the British would soon ask for an armistice. After a few weeks he sent secret peace feelers to the British and indicated in his speech to the Reichstag that he would be willing to negotiate. The Germans were also in contact with political circles in Britain that favored a negotiated peace. But Churchill was determined to see the war through to a victorious conclusion. When the British opposition failed to unseat Churchill, Hitler began to think about invading England to put his old admirer, the Duke of Windsor, back on the British throne.

Hitler ordered his generals to draw up plans for the invasion of England, code named operation Sea Lion. The German Army could have easily defeated the British forces, which had not yet been reequipped after their escape from Dunkirk. The only problem Hitler faced was getting his troops across the Channel. The British Navy so outnumbered the German Navy that a cross-channel invasion was out of the question, unless the Luftwaffe had absolute air superiority. With air superiority, the Luftwaffe could have possibly kept British ships out of the Channel long enough for the German Army to get across. Thus, Hitler concluded that before Britain could be invaded, the R.A.F. would have to be wiped out. Goering assured Hitler the Luftwaffe could do the job. The Battle of Britain followed. But after a month of intense fighting in the air, the Luftwaffe failed to defeat the R.A.F. Quietly, Hitler abandoned his plans to invade England and turned his attention to the east. He was about to attempt to conquer Russia, the prize that had eluded even Napoleon.

Chapter 9

Foreign Friends: Kennedy, Lindbergh, and the Windsors

There were four non-Germans whose opinions and sentiments had a profound effect on Hitler in the late 1930s and early 1940s. Two of them were American, Ambassador Joseph Kennedy and Charles Lindbergh, the famous aviator, and two of them were British, the Duke and Duchess of Windsor. At that time Hitler was very unsure just how fast he could proceed with his aggressive foreign policy. In other words, how far could he push the Western democracies? Correctly gauging the strength of appeasement sentiment in Britain and isolationist sentiment in America was of vital importance to him.

Opinions expressed publicly and privately to Nazi emissaries by Kennedy, Lindbergh, and the Windsors led Hitler to believe that there was a large body of opinion in America and Britain that was sympathetic to nazism and had no objection to anti-Semitism. The effect of this on Hitler turned out to be disastrous. Not only did it lead him to believe he could get away with military aggression and persecution of the Jews but it also helped him convince his German partners, the pro-Nazi generals and the pro-Nazi industrialists, that a powerful segment of opinion in the United States and Britain had no objection to Nazi goals.

In 1938 with war brewing in Europe, President Roosevelt

appointed a new United States ambassador in London who turned out to be a great help to Hitler. The new ambassador was Joe Kennedy. Originally Kennedy's appointment had been suggested as a joke. The idea of an Irishman representing the United States at the Court of St. James made the president laugh so hard he almost fell out of his wheelchair. But as he thought about it he realized the Irish Catholic Kennedy might be able to defuse some traditionally anti-British feelings, particularly among Irish Americans. Roosevelt was already thinking of giving aid to Britain in the confrontation with Hitler, and the anti-British sentiments among the Irish in big cities like Boston and New York was a problem for him.

Although intelligent and perceptive, Joe Kennedy was anything but a diplomat. Nevertheless, he quickly settled into his new job as ambassador, and much to everyone's surprise became a close friend of the prime minister, Neville Chamberlain.[1] Kennedy and Chamberlain had two things in common—their desire to maintain peace and their business background. Chamberlain, the former chancellor of the exchequer, and Kennedy, the former stock market trader, both understood the tremendous economic cost of war. When Kennedy first arrived in Europe, he didn't realize how close the world was to war. It didn't take him long to decide to commit himself to the advocacy of peace at almost any price.

Kennedy supported Chamberlain's policy of appeasement without reservations. He realized a war would disrupt trade and commerce and destroy capital investments. Personally Kennedy was a cautious conservative man who had already made his fortune and wanted to keep it. In support of Chamberlain, the draft of one of his speeches included the line: "I can't for the life of me understand why anybody would want to go to war to save the Czechs."[2] He was forced to cut the line by the State Department.

President Roosevelt soon became irritated by Kennedy's vocal proappeasement views and his support of Chamberlain. As a father with four sons, two of them of military age, Kennedy was afraid of what a war would do to his family. In one speech he gave in England in the summer of 1938, Kennedy said, "I should like to ask you if you know of any dispute or controversy existing in the world which is worth the life of your son, or anyone else's son?" When Roosevelt heard about this he was so angered he said: "This young man needs his wrists slapped rather hard."[3] What irritated and worried Roosevelt was that Kennedy was making his own foreign policy rather than carrying out the foreign policy of the United States government.

According to the British press, Ambassador Kennedy was a frequent visitor at Cliveden, the great country estate of Nancy Astor. The "Cliveden Set" was a group of wealthy and socially prominent people who supported Chamberlain's policy of appeasement. It was at Cliveden that Kennedy first met and talked to Charles Lindbergh, who had nothing but praise for Hitler.

Lindbergh made several trips to Germany from 1936 to 1938. He was wined and dined by the Nazi elite. What Lindbergh saw of the Luftwaffe greatly impressed him. He admired German efficiency and order. The political views of Kennedy and Lindbergh were much alike. Both favored appeasement for Britain and isolationism for the United States. Both were sympathetic to Nazi Germany and admired Hitler for getting rid of the Communists. In his diary Lindbergh wrote: "Kennedy interested me greatly. He is not the usual type of politician or diplomat. His views on the European situation seem intelligent and interesting. I hope to see more of him."[4]

Kennedy's support of Franco and the fascists in the Spanish Civil War caused an open break with other New Deal Democrats, most of whom supported the loyalists or Communists. As an Irish Catholic, Kennedy stood in defense of the church and against communism.[5] He thought the Communist economic system was a fraud that would produce nothing but misery. Although perceptive on financial matters, Kennedy had other views on the Spanish situation that betrayed an extreme ignorance of reality. He privately told some of his friends in the Cliveden set that the United States policy on Spain was "a Jewish production."[6]

Kennedy was willing to go further in trying to appease Hitler than even Chamberlain. Recognizing Hitler's economic predicament and Germany's need of natural resources, Kennedy proposed giving southeastern Europe to Germany as a sphere of influence.[7] Although such a concession would have been extremely generous, it was no longer enough to satisfy Hitler. Furthermore, Britain and France would not even agree to share these markets and resources with Germany, let alone cede them to German dominance.

As the Sudeten conflict and the Czech crisis came to a head in the fall of 1938, there were rumors in London that the German Army was planning to overthrow Hitler. Kennedy was opposed to encouraging a military coup in Germany because he was afraid the only winner in a conflict between Hitler and the army would ultimately be the Communists. On September 19, Kennedy sent a telegram to Lindbergh, who was in France, urging him to come to London at once. Two days later the Lindberghs returned to London. The fall air was thick with mist and fog as they arrived at the American embassy for lunch. In his diary Lindbergh wrote: "Talked with Ambassador Kennedy for an hour after lunch. We discussed the crisis and the aviation and general military situation in Europe. Everyone in the embassy is extremely worried."[8]

In Lindbergh's opinion the Luftwaffe was the strongest air force in the world. He believed Nazi bombers could easily flatten Paris and even London without any serious opposition. Kennedy was so alarmed that he asked Lindbergh to summarize everything he had said in a written report. The next day Lindbergh had the report ready for Kennedy. Chamberlain was just getting ready to leave for Germany to meet Hitler for the second time.[9] Kennedy slipped a copy of Lindbergh's report to the prime minister before he departed. This was just what Chamberlain needed to justify to the British government his appeasement of Hitler. Lindbergh's report was also useful to Chamberlain to help him frighten the French into abandoning the Czechs at Munich. Chamberlain, Kennedy, and Lindbergh were making conquest easy for Hitler.[10]

Far from being ashamed of the role he played in delivering the Czechs into the hands of Hitler at Munich, Kennedy later bragged about it to reporters. He also used his influence in the movie industry to have any criticism of Chamberlain or the Munich Agreement, which abandoned the Czechs to Hitler, cut from the newsreels. It is alleged that Kennedy accomplished more than just his political objectives during the Munich crisis. Jan Masaryk, the Czech representative in London, later claimed that Kennedy sold Czech securities short just before the dismemberment of his country and made a killing.[11]

Kennedy vigorously defended Chamberlain's deal with Hitler at Munich.[12] Speaking at the British Naval League Annual Trafalgar Day dinner, he said the Munich Agreement should serve as an example for further compromises with Germany. The settlement of the Czech crisis, he said, proved it was possible to "get along" with Hitler. In America the speech was widely criticized. The White House and State Department received numerous inquiries asking if American policy toward Hitler had changed. President Roosevelt thought Kennedy's speech was so dangerous that a week later he made a radio broadcast to dispel any misconception the ambassador may have created about United States foreign policy. Roosevelt left no doubt that it was his intention to isolate Hitler not "get along" with him.[13]

In an effort to establish better relations between the United States and Germany, Kennedy met with Germany's ambassador to London, Herbert von Dirksen. Assuring von Dirksen of his sympathy for Germany, Kennedy said President Roosevelt misunderstood the German situation because he was misinformed by people under the influence of the Jews. Kennedy said he was pleased with the economic progress Germany had made under Hitler. On the other hand he was worried about what was going on in Soviet Russia. He also assured the German ambassador that Chamberlain was anxious for a permanent settlement with Hitler. Kennedy "repeatedly expressed his conviction that in economic matters Germany had to have a free hand in the East as well as in the Southeast [the Balkans]."

In his report to Berlin regarding Kennedy, von Dirksen said:

The Ambassador then touched upon the Jewish question and stated that it was naturally of great importance to German-American relations. In this connection it was not so much the fact that we wanted to get rid of the Jews that was so harmful to us, but rather the loud clamor with which we accompanied this purpose. He himself understood our

Jewish policy completely; he was from Boston and there, in one golf club, and in other clubs, no Jews had been admitted for the past 50 years. . . . Such pronounced attitudes were quite common [in the United States], but people avoided making so much outward fuss about it.[14]

The implication of Kennedy's statement to von Dirksen that Germany could "get rid of" the Jews if they just did it quietly was extremely harmful. This coupled with the Roosevelt administration's restrictions against Jewish immigrants led Hitler to believe America didn't care about the fate of the Jews. When Kennedy used the words "get rid of" he must have meant discrimination against Jews in certain professions or the expulsion of Jews from Germany. It is impossible to believe that he would have meant killing or genocide.* When von Dirksen's reports were published by the State Department after the war, Kennedy denied ever having made such a statement. These denials were made at a time when such evidence might have damaged the political career of his son John F. Kennedy.

There is overwhelming evidence that von Dirksen not Kennedy was telling the truth. Numerous contemporaries of Joe Kennedy have stated that he was anti-Semitic and sympathetic to Hitler. Kennedy frequently complained of Jewish influence over the American press. He was openly contemptuous of the Jews who worked in Hollywood and bragged of having beat "these pants pressers" at their own game. Kennedy complained that while he was ambassador in London, Eleanor Roosevelt was always asking him to invite "some little Susie Glotz" to tea at the embassy.[15] Kennedy agreed with the mistaken view of his friend Chamberlain that "the world's Jews had forced England into war."[16]

---

*Kennedy's advocates might make two points in his defense. First of all, he wanted to appease Hitler because he wanted to preserve peace and he had no way of knowing Hitler's plans for war. Second, many other American politicians in the 1930s were just as anti-Semitic as he was, or more so. Although there may be some truth in these points, neither is a valid excuse for his behavior.

When Nazi barbarism on Crystal Night forced the world's attention on the plight of Jewish refugees, Kennedy reluctantly became involved. He gave some halfhearted assistance to George Rublee, a seventy-year-old Washington attorney who was trying to arrange for the emigration of Jews from Nazi Germany.[17] With considerable political grandstanding, Kennedy proposed a plan to rescue the German Jews that he had worked out with Chamberlain. This plan called for the relocation of German Jews to sparsely settled parts of Africa and other uninhabited places in the British Empire.

This Kennedy-Chamberlain plan, although hailed by the press, was in some respects little better than Himmler's Madagascar plan, which proposed settling Germany's Jews on the remote island of Madagascar off the African coast. Nevertheless, there was a catch; the world Jewish community would have to raise over $600 million to pay the costs of transporting and settling the refugees. Like Hitler, Kennedy was trying to put the responsibility of relocating the refugees onto the Jewish community.[18] Naturally the "Kennedy Plan" fell through. Rublee, who was working tirelessly to find a solution for the refugees, said Kennedy "did not seem very interested and never gave me any real support or assistance."[19]

In the spring of 1939 just a few months before the outbreak of the war, Joe Kennedy made a bold private initiative to seek a rapprochement with Hitler. On April 29, Kennedy met with James D. Mooney, the head of General Motors in Germany, at the American embassy in London. Together they concocted a plan for a massive American and British gold loan for Hitler. Kennedy was to meet Goering's economic representative, Dr. Helmuth Wohlthat, to iron out the details of the deal over dinner in Paris at Mooney's suite in the Ritz. Informed by British intelligence of Kennedy's plan, the State Department refused to give him permission to go to France.[20]

But Kennedy and Mooney were not about to give up. Mooney finally persuaded Dr. Wohlthat to come to London and meet with Kennedy secretly. On May 9, Dr. Wohlthat, who represented not just Goering but several powerful pro-Nazi industrialists as well secretly arrived in London. He met Kennedy just before noon in the Berkeley Hotel. The ambassador and Wohlthat talked for about two hours. The two men were in complete agreement on everything. The deal called for a one-billion-dollar gold loan to Germany, return of her colonies, primarily in Africa, and the removal of any restrictions on German trade. For his part Hitler would agree to limitations on armaments, nonaggression agreements with neighboring countries, and free trade. Kennedy and Mooney already had commitments from major international financiers to provide the necessary money for the loan.[21]

Before Kennedy and Wohlthat could meet for a second time, the British blew the Nazi's cover. Headlines of the London papers read "Goering's Mystery Man Is Here." Wohlthat returned to Germany immediately, but all the details of the deal had been agreed to. Mooney then traveled back to Germany to meet privately with both Hitler and Goering. Hitler seemed to be pleased with the deal. Would he have kept his side of the bargain once he received the loan? Would he have given up aggression in return for economic progress? Most probably he would have only put off his attack on Poland for a year or two while secretly using most of the money from the loan to build new weapons. The answer will always remain a mystery because the American and British governments found out about the Kennedy-Mooney deal and raised such vociferous objections that the financiers backed out.[22]

At about 4 A.M. on September 3 the phone at President Roosevelt's bedside rang. It was Joe Kennedy calling from London. His voice choked with emotion as he told the president that Chamberlain had just declared war. In complete despair Kennedy said a new Dark Age would descend on Europe, and the end result of the war would be chaos and ruin no matter who won. Roosevelt tried to calm and reassure Kennedy, but he just kept repeating, "It's the end of the world . . . the end of everything."[23]

Kennedy immediately turned his attention from trying to prevent war, to trying to keep America out of the war.[24] Kennedy did not believe a European war was a threat to any of America's vital interests. When he returned home for Christmas in December, he was promoting isolationism. At a speech he delivered in an Irish Catholic church in Boston he said, "Don't let anything . . . make you believe you can make the situation [in Europe] one whit better by getting into the war. There is no place in this fight for us. It's going to be bad enough as it is." There was, Kennedy continued, "no reason—economic, financial, or social—to justify the United States entering the war. This is not our fight."[25]

Kennedy returned to his post in London, but when the blitz started after the fall of France, he wished he was back home in the States. He had no desire to die in Britain's war; so every night just before dark and before the German bombers came over, he went out to his house in the country. The British mocked him as "Jittery Joe." However, this mockery was probably more for Kennedy's "defeatist" attitude than his personal behavior. Kennedy was in contact with the secret group in the cabinet that was trying to work out an armistice with Hitler. Churchill decided to nip such efforts in the bud with a harsh crackdown on all defeatists. A code clerk at the American embassy was arrested on vague charges that he was giving official secrets to people suspected of pro-Nazi activities. The arrest may have been deliberately engineered by Churchill to embarrass Kennedy.[26]

Kennedy soon resigned as United States ambassador to Britain. He was accused of still being involved in efforts to reach a negotiated peace between Britain and Germany, and even of contributing money to Hitler. In his book *Trading with the Enemy* author Charles Higham states that J. Edgar Hoover sent an incriminating report on Kennedy to the White House. "Information has been received at this Bureau from a source that is socially prominent and known to be in touch with some of the people involved, but for whom we cannot vouch, to the effect that Joseph P. Kennedy, the former Ambassador to England, and Ben Smith, the Wall Street operator, some time in the past had a meeting with Goering in Vichy, France, and that thereafter Kennedy and Smith had donated a considerable amount of money to the German cause. They are both described as being very anti-British and pro-German."[27]

With the war on in Europe Kennedy gradually began to withdraw from European politics; at the same time Charles Lindbergh became more active.

* * *

By 1941 Lindbergh was the leading figure in the America First Committee, an isolationist group organized to keep America out of the war. President Roosevelt wanted to fight Hitler sooner rather than later. Polls, however, showed that the majority of the American people were against becoming involved in a European war. Lindbergh capitalized on these isolationist feelings. He spoke to enthusiastic crowds at America First rallies across the country. Up to the fall of 1941 Lindbergh was careful to keep his anti-Semitic sentiments in check.

On the evening of September 11 in Des Moines, however, Lindbergh made his first blatantly anti-Semitic speech. He said there were three groups trying to drag America into the war: "the British, the Jews, and the Roosevelt administration." "No person of honesty and vision," said Lindbergh, "can look on their [the Jews'] pro-war policy . . . without seeing the dangers involved . . . both for us—and for them. Instead of agitating for war, the Jewish groups in this country should be opposing it in every possible way, for they will be among the first to feel its consequences. . . . Their [the Jews'] greatest danger to this country," Lindbergh continued, "lies in their large ownership and influence in our motion pictures, our press, our radio and our Government."[28]

The charges that the Jews controlled the press, the radio, and the movies were the same as Henry Ford had made in the *International Jew* more than twenty years earlier. In fact Lindbergh and Henry Ford had been close friends for years. In addition to their mutual interest in engines, automobiles, and airplanes, both were puritanical Protestant moralists who felt American culture was being corrupted by sinister forces. From the content of the Des Moines speech apparently Ford's anti-Semitism had rubbed off on Lindbergh.

However, the Des Moines speech was not well received by the press or the American people, who saw it for what it was—a Nazi racist attack. It was the beginning of the end for the America First Committee. In spite of his prejudice, Lindbergh was an intelligent man and must have known anti-Semitism would not be popular in America. In fact before the speech he scribbled a note in the margin of the text: "I realize that in speaking this frankly I am entering in where angels fear to tread."[29] Why then did he do it? Lindbergh learned the rhetoric of Jew baiting from Henry Ford, but his hatred of Jews may have had more complex personal psychological motives. In 1932 the Lindberghs' first child was kidnapped and murdered. An unemployed carpenter and German immigrant, Bruno Hauptmann, was arrested and convicted of the crime. Hauptmann's trial, however, raised more questions than it answered. Many people including Charles Lindbergh believed others must have been involved in the kidnapping. An American Nazi paper printed an article in 1935 by Julius Streicher, the rabid anti-Semite who was the gauleiter in Nuremberg, that suggested a Jewish conspiracy was responsible for the murder of the Lindbergh baby.[30]

It seems the Nazis were trying to influence him with lurid stories about "Jewish ritual murder."[31] Supposedly, Jews kidnapped Christian children and used their blood for ritual sacrifice. This vicious anti-Semitic lie originated in the twelfth century and has been a part of the lore of anti-Jewish hate propaganda ever since.[32] Whether or not Lindbergh believed such idiocy is not known. Because of his suspicions of Jews and his highly traumatized condition after the kidnapping, he might have been vulnerable to such conspiracy theories. Certainly he believed there was an international Jewish political conspiracy and said as much in his Des Moines speech.

After the Japanese attack on Pearl Harbor, both Kennedy and Lindbergh prudently ceased their involvement in foreign affairs. Both of them were intelligent men and realized that the mood of the American people was clearly against them.

Long before Kennedy or Lindbergh became involved in efforts to appease Hitler, King Edward VIII of England was an admirer of the Nazi dictator. When the king tried to force the British people to accept Mrs. Simpson, a twice divorced American, as queen, the British government took the opportunity to oust him, in 1936. The real reason the government was so anxious to get rid of the king seems to have been a justified fear of his pro-Hitler sympathies.

As soon as the furor over the abdication quieted somewhat, the former king, now the Duke of Windsor, thought it was time to reestablish his public image and political influence. He decided to visit Germany to "study labor conditions"; the duke knew he would receive a warm welcome from the German public and the Nazi leaders.

Hitler also had a political reason for wanting the duke to visit Germany. The duke was apparently toying with the idea of becoming the popular idol of the British fascist movement led by Sir Oswald Mosley. Mosley had always been a staunch supporter of the Duke of Windsor.[33] The British fascist movement was still relatively small in 1937 but had a growing appeal to the unemployed. Hitler believed that if the duke joined with Mosley they could gather a large popular following and influence British foreign policy in Germany's favor.

The duke's brother King George tried to persuade him not to go to Germany. Lord Beaverbrook, the press tycoon, even traveled to France in a last-minute effort to discourage the duke from visiting Hitler. But the duchess exerted the greatest influence on the duke, and she was enthusiastically in favor of the trip. Very pleased about the Windsors' visit, Hitler ordered Dr. Ley, the leader of the Nazi Labor Front, to personally accompany the duke on his tour. Hitler immediately began to think about schemes to put the duke back on the British throne.

When the duke and duchess arrived in Berlin by train on October 11, they were greeted on the platform by the third secretary of the British embassy, who informed them that the British ambassador, Sir Neville Henderson, was not in Berlin. In contrast to this deliberate snub by the British government, an official German delegation, headed by Dr. Ley, was also waiting for the Windsors at the station. With a military brass band they gave them a warm welcome befitting a king and queen.

The Windsors traveled all over Germany visiting workers, homes, factories, and Hitler Youth camps. They met with most of the prominent Nazi leaders, including Hess, Goebbels, and even Himmler. In Nuremberg, the duke of Coburg gave a formal dinner in the Duke of Windsor's honor. Most of the guests wore Nazi dress uniforms, including swastika armbands. The duke and duchess didn't seem to mind a bit. Everywhere the Windsors went they were greeted by cheering crowds of Germans.

The only problem on the trip was that Dr. Ley, the Windsors' escort, was an alcoholic, and he frightened the duchess to death when he drove at breakneck speeds. "Ley had a powerful black

Mercedes-Benz," recalled Hans Sopple, one of Ley's aides. "The more he drank the faster he would drive. . . . Let him get a few drinks and he wanted to grab the wheel. I was with him when he decided the Duke and Duchess of Windsor would definitely visit the workers' barracks at a factory on the outskirts of Munich. He was drunk, of course. He drove the car through locked gates and then raced up and down at full speed between the barracks, scaring the hell out of the workers and nearly running over several."[34]

After the incident at the Munich factory, Hitler instructed Goering to replace Ley as the duke's official host. Goering immediately invited the duke and duchess to visit him at Karinhall. Before the Windsors arrived, Goering and his wife, Emmy, had a discussion about the duke's abdication: "I don't understand this woman [the duchess] not giving up her marriage in view of everything that was involved," said Emmy Goering to her husband. Goering, however, said he was "firmly convinced that the marriage was simply a pretext to get rid of the king."[35]

When the Windsors arrived at Karinhall, one of the first things Goering showed the duke was his electric train set. The duke seemed as interested in it as Goering, and the two men played with it for over an hour. Things did not go as well when Goering attempted to demonstrate one of his fat-reducing machines to the duchess, who was renowned for her slim figure. Forgetting that he was in his military uniform with medals instead of his workout suit, Goering mounted the machine, his clothes got caught in its vibrating rollers, and he was almost strangled.

Revealing his true sympathies, the duke inspected the Death's Head Division of Hitler's elite S.S. guards at a military training school in Pomerania. When the honor guard marched past, the duke raised his right arm in a "Heil Hitler" salute that brought a roar of approval from the crowd. The high point in the Windsors' visit came when at the conclusion of their trip they met Hitler at Berchtesgaden.

As Hitler's interpreter, Schmidt, recalled:

The Duke expressed his admiration for the industrial welfare arrangements he had seen, especially at the Krupp works in Essen. Social progress in Germany was the principal subject of conversation between Hitler and the Windsors during the afternoon. Hitler was evidently making an effort to be as amiable as possible toward the Duke, whom he regarded as Germany's friend. He [the duke] was frank and friendly with Hitler, and displayed the social charm for which he is known throughout the world. The Duchess . . . was simply and appropriately dressed and made a lasting impression on Hitler. "She would have made a good Queen," he said when they had gone.[36]

The duke and duchess were both enthusiastic about what they had seen in Germany. Undoubtedly, they were flattered by the friendly reception they received from Hitler and the German people. Although few people at the time realized just how pro-Nazi the duke actually was, the *New York Times* showed considerable insight in an article on October 23, 1937, at the conclusion of the Windsors' visit to Germany.

The Duke's decision to see for himself the Third Reich's industries and social institutions and his gestures and remarks during the last two weeks have demonstrated adequately that the abdication did rob Germany of a firm friend, if not indeed a devoted admirer, on the British throne. He has lent himself, perhaps unconsciously but easily, to National Socialist propaganda. The Duke is reported to have become very critical of English politics as he sees them and is reported as declaring that the British ministers of today and their possible successors are no match for the German or Italian dictators.[37]

Once the war broke out in Europe, the Duke of Windsor became an officer in the British Army, attached to the British military mission in France. He worked in liaison with the French Army. He inspected various sections of the front including the Maginot Line. He recognized the weakness in the Allies' anti-tank defenses in several key sectors of the front.

The duke spent much of his time during the first months of the war in Paris, where the duchess was staying. Their circle of associates included hundreds of people. So it was easy for pro-

Nazis like their friend Charles Bedaux to meet with them inconspicuously at social gatherings. Allied intelligence discovered that military secrets were being passed to the Germans from a high-level source. The duke was suspect. But the duke was not a Nazi agent. His weakness was that he couldn't keep a secret from the duchess. Being the dominant person in the relationship, she persistently questioned him about his military activities and always got results.

According to biographer Charles Higham, General Ironside, the chief of the Imperial General Staff, determined that the duchess was carelessly chatting about classified Allied defense information with people thought to be Nazi sympathizers at parties in Paris.[38] Is it possible that the Duchess of Windsor was a German agent? There is no evidence that she was being paid by the Germans or was actually working for them. However, she was hoping that the war party in the British government would be thrown out and that King George, who was an anti-Nazi, would be forced to abdicate. This she reasoned would be followed by the return of the Duke of Windsor to the throne. So she would have had a motive for aiding the Nazis. Nevertheless, there is no way to determine whether she was deliberately revealing Allied defense information or if she was just extremely careless.

If Nazi agents in Paris relayed that the source of their information was the Duchess of Windsor, it would have been brought directly to Hitler's attention. He was fully aware of her influence over the duke and concluded that she knew everything the duke knew. Information about the Allied defenses that Nazi agents gleaned or overheard from her conversations may have been a factor in Hitler's sudden decision to change the German plan of attack against France.[39]

German intelligence and Hitler were aware of the secret past of the Duchess of Windsor, which was unknown to the public. The duchess had gone to great lengths to cover up the facts about the period of her life when she lived in China. Her husband at the time was Earl Winfield Spencer, a bisexual U.S. Navy officer. According to author Charles Higham, Spencer introduced her to Chinese brothels, where she was said to have engaged in "perverse sexual practices."[40]

British intelligence was also aware of the duchess's scandalous background and had probably used this information to force Edward VIII (the Duke of Windsor) to abdicate. Of more interest to Hitler and the Nazis was the duchess's sympathy for fascism and her romantic involvement with two Fascists. In his very revealing biography of the duchess, Higham states that while in China the duchess, then Wallis Spencer, had two passionate romances with handsome Italian Fascists. In 1924 Wallis met Alberto Da Zara, the naval attaché to the Italian embassy in Peking. Da Zara was a good-looking, blond officer with charming manners. He was a poet, a fine horseman, and a devoted follower of Mussolini.[41]

Sometime after her romance with Da Zara, Wallis fell in love with another Italian, Count Galeazzo Ciano, who was only twenty-one years old at the time. The dark, handsome Ciano was studying to be a diplomat. They spent much of one summer together at a beautiful resort on the China coast. According to Higham, Wallis became pregnant by Ciano. There were rumors she decided to have an abortion. Count Ciano later married Mussolini's daughter and in 1940 was Italian foreign minister. Da Zara and Ciano had, it seems, converted Wallis to fascism. There was even information to suggest that for a time in China she acted as a spy for Italy or Japan by getting information out of British naval officers she seduced.[42] This was the kind of woman Hitler considered reliable.

For some unknown reason Hitler was fascinated by the duchess. He had his intelligence agents bring him all German and foreign press clippings and news stories about her. He even had several films made from newsreel items about her and frequently viewed them, apparently to try to get a better understanding of her personality.

There is some evidence that Hitler's interest in the duchess may have been justified. She made several statements that express an open contempt of the war effort and a hostility against Britain and the British people. While American journalist Clare Boothe Luce was in Paris in 1940 the duchess complained to her about the royal family saying they were "jealous" of the duke's popularity. When Mrs. Luce asked why the duke didn't spend more time at the front to help raise morale, the duchess replied: "What? And get himself killed in this silly war?"

One evening when Mrs. Luce was playing cards with the

Windsors, a BBC news broadcast came over the radio stating that the Luftwaffe was strafing the coastal villages of England.

"That upset me," said Mrs. Luce. "I mentioned that I had driven through many of these same villages, and I hated to think of those decent, kindly people being so wantonly attacked. The duchess glanced up from her cards: 'After what they did to me, I can't say I feel sorry for them—a whole nation against a lone woman!'"

Amazingly the duke was silent and said nothing to rebuke his wife.

After the evacuation of the British from Dunkirk and the defeat of the French armies, the Duke and Duchess of Windsor fled Paris before the French surrendered. Unlike other British soldiers, the duke did not try to return to England but instead went to neutral Spain. He and the duchess stayed in Madrid for about a week, where they expressed "defeatist" sentiments to anyone who would listen.

U.S. Ambassador Weddell said in a report sent to Washington:

> In a conversation last night with one of the Embassy staff the Duke of Windsor declared that the most important thing now to be done was to end the war before thousands more were killed or maimed to save the faces of a few politicians.
>
> With regard to the defeat of France he stated that stories that the French troops would not fight were not true. They had fought magnificently, but the organization behind them was totally inadequate. In the past 10 years Germany had totally reorganized the order of its society in preparation for this war. Countries which were unwilling to accept such a reorganization of society and its concomitant sacrifices should direct their policies accordingly and thereby avoid dangerous adventures. He stated that this applied not merely to Europe, but to the United States also. The Duchess put the same thing somewhat more directly by declaring that France had lost because it was internally diseased and that a country which was not in condition to fight a war should never have declared war. . . . These observations have their value in reflecting the views of an element in England, possibly a growing one who find in Windsor and his circle a group who are realists in world

politics and who hope to come into their own in event of peace.[43]

After their stay in Madrid, the duke and duchess traveled to Lisbon, where they stayed with a wealthy banker. At dinner parties they gave and attended, the Windsors were both very outspoken in their opposition to the current government in Britain.[44] The British ambassador called on the duke and told him there was a British airplane standing by ready to take him to England the next day. But the duke refused to leave Lisbon. He said he would not return to Britain until his wife received proper recognition from the royal family.

The real reason the duke was remaining in Lisbon was because he expected a negotiated peace soon to be concluded between Britain and Germany. At the time such expectations were not unrealistic. Poland and France had been defeated by Hitler, and Britain was fighting alone with what seemed like little chance of victory. Hitler had already publicly offered a peace proposal. There were rumors that secret negotiations were going on in Sweden between the Nazis and some members of the British peace party. There were many people in Britain who wanted peace, even members of the government like Lord Halifax, the foreign secretary.[45]

The duke evidently thought that if the British government wasn't ready to negotiate peace immediately, the Luftwaffe bombing of London would soon make them "see reason." He was expecting Churchill to be thrown out and King George to be forced to abdicate. He apparently then planned to return to England and become king again. All of this was very possible. If Churchill had not moved swiftly to threaten the peace plotters with charges of treason, he might have been ousted by Parliament. As part of any negotiated peace settlement, Hitler would have insisted that the Duke of Windsor be returned to the throne.[46]

On the German side, Hitler was trying to give the Duke and Duchess of Windsor all the encouragement he could. As soon as Hitler learned the Windsors had fled to Spain, he ordered Ribbentrop, the German foreign minister, to send an agent to get in contact with them immediately and protect them from British agents. The man Ribbentrop entrusted with this mission was Walter Schellenberg, an officer of the S.D., the intelligence service of the S.S.[47]

Ribbentrop explained to Schellenberg the nature of his mission:

> Since his abdication, the Duke has been under strict surveillance by the British Secret Service. We know what his feelings are: it's almost as if he were their prisoner. Every attempt that he's made to free himself, however discreet he may have been, has failed. And we know from our reports that he still entertains the same sympathetic feelings toward Germany, and that given the right circumstances he wouldn't be averse to escaping from his present environment—the whole thing's getting on his nerves. We've had word that he has even spoken about living in Spain and that if he did go there he'd be ready to be friends with Germany again as he was before.

"The Fuehrer," Ribbentrop continued, "feels that if the atmosphere seemed propitious you might perhaps make the Duke some material offer. Now, we should be prepared to deposit in Switzerland for his own use a sum of fifty million Swiss francs." Ribbentrop later added that the fifty million Swiss francs was not the absolute maximum. If the duke needed more money, Hitler was ready to go higher.

In an ominous tone, Ribbentrop warned Schellenberg that if the British Secret Service should try to interfere with the duke, he was to risk his life if necessary to stop them. "Whatever happens, the Duke of Windsor must be brought safely to the country of his choice. Hitler attaches the greatest importance to this operation." Ribbentrop concluded the briefing by saying that Hitler wanted to receive daily reports on the progress of the mission.

Before dismissing Schellenberg, Ribbentrop telephoned Hitler to ask if there were any last-minute orders before Schellenberg departed. "Schellenberg," said Hitler, "should particularly bear in mind the importance of the Duchess's attitude and try as hard as possible to get her support. She has great influence over the Duke."[48]

When Schellenberg arrived in Madrid, he reported that the

duke had recently told an important Spanish fascist that he was considering dissociating himself from the present British government and publicly breaking with his brother, the king. The duke described the king as "completely stupid" and the queen as "shrewd." He was hostile to Churchill and said he was thinking of returning to Spain.[49]

Winston Churchill was worried. He knew the Windsors were in contact with Nazi sympathizers and agents in Lisbon. Furthermore Churchill was well aware of the duke and duchess's admiration for Hitler and their anger over the way they had been treated by the royal family. Churchill also knew the peace plotters like Halifax and Lloyd George were planning to rally around the former monarch.

King George was also worried about his brother's ambitions. He was afraid the Duke of Windsor was now sorry he had abdicated and wanted the throne back. The troubled king confided to one of his ministers that all of his ancestors had succeeded to the throne after their predecessors had died. "Mine is not only alive," said the king, "but very much so."

Knowing the situation would only grow worse with time, Churchill decided to act boldly. He sent the duke a telegram in which he reminded him that as an officer in the British Army he had to obey orders like any other soldier. Churchill implied that if he refused to return to England he faced the threat of court-martial. The duke was deeply insulted by this telegram, but the threat obviously worried him. The duke soon received another telegram from Churchill offering him the appointment of governor general of the Bahamas. To a man who had once ruled the world's greatest empire the prospect of ruling a few small islands reminded him of Napoleon's exile to Saint Helena.

Still the duke tried to delay, hoping for a turn in the political situation. A few days later the duke was warned that there was a plot afoot against his security by certain British interests. It is not clear whether or not the Germans were responsible for this rumor. Possibly the Nazis were trying to frighten the duke into seeking protection in facist Spain.[50]

With no decisive turn in the war or the political situation in sight, the duke and duchess finally decided to give up and yield to Churchill's demands. The duke decided he would accept the post in the Bahamas and wait there for the situation to ripen. On the day of the Windsors' departure for the Bahamas there was a rumor that a bomb had been planted on their ship.[51] It is not known who started this rumor. The Portuguese police searched the ship several times. There was feverish activity when the duke and duchess arrived at the dock. A few miles away in the tower room of the German embassy, Schellenberg was watching through binoculars. He watched the duke and duchess go on board. Finally the ship cast off and slowly moved down the broad mouth of the Tagus River toward the sea.

Both the British and Hitler thought the chapter on the Duke of Windsor was finally closed once the duke was safely in the Bahamas. But the duke had other ideas. During an interview in Nassau with the well-known American journalist Fulton Oursler, the duke expressed strong pro-Nazi sympathies. According to a revealing article recently written by Oursler's son, when Oursler suggested that the German people might overthrow Hitler, the duke said he didn't think so. He frankly stated that he thought it would be a "tragic thing" if Hitler was overthrown. He believed Hitler was "the right and logical" leader of Germany.[52]

The duke knew that Oursler was a friend of President Roosevelt. This was not just an ordinary interview but had been carefully set up by the duke. Suddenly, he looked around to see that no one else was in the room. Then leaning close to the reporter he said, "Do you suppose that your President would consider intervening as a mediator."[53] Oursler was speechless. After two hours the duke terminated the interview and said he would be in contact with Oursler again the next day.

On Oursler's return to the United States he dutifully reported to President Roosevelt. The duke had made a big mistake in asking Roosevelt to be an intermediary for a peace settlement between Britain and Germany. Obviously he didn't know that Roosevelt bitterly opposed any compromise with Hitler. When Oursler related what the duke had said, the president's hands trembled in anger. Roosevelt didn't even dignify the duke's message with an answer. So ended the Duke of Windsor's attempt to make a compromise peace with Hitler and get himself back on the throne in the process.

In contrast to the efforts of some pro-Nazi foreigners to help Hitler, his formal allies and partners in the Tripartite Pact, Italy and Japan, proved to be of little use to him. Italy was more of a liability than an asset because of her military and economic weaknesses. Although Japan was a great military power, her strategic goals were so different from Germany's that they were never able to coordinate their military policies.

When the news of Japan's attack on Pearl Harbor first reached Hitler's headquarters, he was delighted.[54] At the time the German troops were hard-pressed by the Russian counteroffensive on the Moscow front, and morale was very low. Japan's entry into the war was just the psychological boost Hitler needed. Waving the telegram describing Japan's attack on Pearl Harbor in his hand, he burst into a staff conference looking like a man who had suddenly been freed of all his burdens. To a member of his staff he said enthusiastically, "We cannot lose the war! Now we have a partner who has not been defeated in three thousand years."[55]

Most of Hitler's generals were stunned when on December 11 he declared war on the United States. He acted as if America's entry into the war made no difference at all. Roosevelt was already giving aid to Britain he reasoned, and a war in the Pacific would tie down the bulk of American forces for some time.

When Hitler attacked Russia in the summer of 1941 he had tried to discourage the Japanese from joining the war against the Soviet Union.[56] He thought it would be a short war that he could win easily, and he didn't want to have to divide the spoils with an ally. By December of 1942, however, victory in Russia no longer seemed so certain. Hitler now wanted Japanese help against Stalin but realized he wasn't likely to get it.

Japan's strategic goals were such that her military actions would be of little advantage to Hitler. Japan needed oil, rubber, and other natural resources of Southeast Asia, not the frozen wastes of Siberia. In Manchuria and occupied China, Japan had all the land on the Asian continent she needed for the moment. The only hope Hitler ever had of getting Japan to join him in the war on Russia would have been during the early months of spectacular victories. If he had offered to share the oil of the Caucasus with Japan there would have been a slight chance of the Japanese joining the attack against the Soviet Union. After the attack on Pearl Harbor, Japan was committed to building her empire in Southeast Asia and the Pacific. The only help Japan could give Germany was to keep an army in Manchuria to tie down Russian troops in Siberia. But even on this issue there was less than full cooperation between Hitler and his Asian partner.

Hitler never even tried to fully exploit his partnership with Japan because according to his racial theories the Japanese were inferiors. Although he applauded Japanese victories over the British in Southeast Asia, secretly he was distressed to see British, Dutch, and French colonies falling to the yellow race.[57]

Chapter 10

Wealth to Be Won in Russia

Just after midnight on June 22, 1941, German soldiers crouching in their positions along the bank of the River Niemen watched the last freight train from Russia carrying vital raw materials to Germany across the bridge over the Niemen.[1] After the train passed there was silence. Along a three thousand mile front 3.5 million German and Axis troops waited in darkness for the order to attack. At 3:00 A.M. the western sky suddenly lit up as bright as day from the flashes of six thousand artillery pieces firing at once.[2]

Russian troops in forward positions near the border of German-occupied Poland were stunned. They were cut down by German machine guns as they stumbled out of their barracks half-naked and half-asleep. All around them was smoke, destruction, and the squeaking clatter of German panzers moving forward. When one Russian officer called his unit's headquarters in the rear to say that he was under attack, his commander told him it must just be a German training exercise. "Go back to sleep," the commander said. "A German attack is impossible." Stalin and the Russian generals believed Hitler wouldn't attack Russia because Germany was so dependent on Russian agricultural products and raw materials, particularly oil. But Stalin didn't realize how determined Hitler was to end that dependence and seize the grain and oil for himself.[3]

Ever since he had abandoned the idea of invading England, Hitler had been planning his attack on Russia. On December 18, 1940, he issued Directive 21 to his top military commanders.[4] It was marked TOP SECRET. "The German Armed Forces must be prepared to *crush Soviet Russia in a rapid campaign* even before the end of the war against England. For this the army will have to employ all available units with the reservation that the occupied territories must be protected against surprise attack." The attack on Russia was code named Operation Barbarossa after the Holy Roman (German) Emperor Frederick I known as Barbarossa (Red Beard). "When Barbarossa begins," said Hitler, "the world will hold its breath."

Once Hitler made his decision to attack Russia he was completely consumed by the task. He spent every afternoon and evening bent over war maps with his generals. He felt that destroying communism and winning living space in the east for the German people was his life's true work. The war in the west had just been the preliminary. Hitler had always believed that Germany should direct her expansion primarily to the east in the tradition of the Teutonic knight. Years before he had said in *Mein Kampf:* "We National Socialists . . . take up where we [Germans] left off six hundred years ago. We stop the endless German movement to the south and west, and turn our gaze toward the land in the east. At long last we break off the colonial and commercial policy of the pre-war period and shift to the land policy of the future. And if we speak of land in Europe today, we primarily have in mind Russia and her vassal border states."[5]

Many historians consider Hitler's attack on Russia as his greatest mistake, caused by an uncontrollable megalomania and a Napoleonic complex. Germany had always tried to avoid a two-front war. Why did Hitler now start another war with Russia before he defeated England? Actually if he wanted to survive the war with Britain, Hitler had little choice but to attack Russia. Germany was slowly being strangled by the British naval blockade, but since Hitler had decided an invasion of England was too risky, his only hope was to conquer Russia, where he would get enough natural resources to outlast Britain.

In World War I the British blockade had brought Germany to

her knees by restricting her access to food imports. This time it was both food and oil imports. Germany was able to survive from 1939 to 1941 only by evading the blockade by importing one million tons of oil from neutral Russia.

Germany's attempts to become agriculturally self-sufficient before 1939 were a dismal failure. During the first year of the war, meat, eggs, butter, and most other foods were rationed. However, the Germans knew the food situation was really getting worse, and the British naval blockade was taking its toll when in the summer of 1941 the government decided to issue ration cards for potatoes for the coming winter. (Potato rationing went into effect in September 1941.) Until then potatoes were the only important food product that was not rationed. Whenever a German housewife could not find enough food in the shops she could at least fill up her family on potatoes. Rationing would stretch out Germany's potato supplies, however even with strict rationing the grain and animal fat reserves would last only through 1942.

Hitler had been worried for some time about Germany's inability to feed its own population. At his secret conference with the nation's top military leaders at the Chancellery on November 5, 1937, he had cited Germany's insufficient food production as one of the principal reasons for his plans to go to war. "In the case of foods," said Hitler, "autarchy [self-sufficiency] is definitely impossible." Germany's problem was even worse than before World War I because increased standards of living had led to increased food consumption. "A further increase in production by making greater demands on the soil is not possible because it already shows signs of deterioration due to the use of artificial fertilizers."

"The considerable expenditure of foreign currency to secure food by import, even in periods when the harvests are good, increases catastrophically when the harvest is really poor," said Hitler. "The possibility of this catastrophe increases correspondingly to increases in the population." Realizing that not even a dictatorship could survive for long against the anger of a hungry people Hitler said, "To deal with the problems of food shortages by permanently lowering the standard of living or by rationing is impossible."

Finally Hitler admitted that what was worrying him most was

that the food imports that Germany was dependent on were carried "over sea lanes which are dominated by Britain. . . . This explains the great weakness of our food situation in wartime. The only way out," stressed Hitler, "is to secure greater living space. . . . It is not a case of conquering people, but of conquering agriculturally useful space."[6] Hitler did not need to remind his listeners that he had stated in *Mein Kampf* years before that only Russia had enough land to satisfy Germany's needs. Like the kaiser before him, Hitler wanted the "black earth" grain belt of the Ukraine.

By 1941, in addition to Germany's serious food shortages there was also a critical lack of oil, which presented an immediate military danger. Germany was cut off from oil imports from the United States, South America, and Iran. The only way Hitler could continue the war was by purchasing oil from Russia. Stalin could, however, cut off Germany's oil at any time, so Hitler decided to strike first.

There was only one problem with Hitler's strategy. General Thomas, the chief of the army's Office of War Economy, conducted a study indicating that Germany did not have enough oil to go to war with Russia. Hitler was counting on capturing the great Russian oil fields in the Caucasus; but General Thomas was afraid the German panzers would not have enough petrol to reach the Caucasus.

Not wanting to irritate Hitler unduly, General Thomas tried to word his report as optimistically as possible. He concluded that during the first months of the war Germany would seize enough food supplies and raw materials in Russia to ease the shortages at home. However the long-term success of the war against the Soviets depended on the army rapidly seizing Russian territory and: "A. Preventing the destruction of food stocks. B. Capturing the oil fields of the Caucasus intact. C. Solving the problem of transportation."[7] Accomplishing these three points would be difficult if not impossible. But although the report made Hitler furious it didn't worry him. He dismissed it as the typical overcautious attitude of the General Staff.

In spite of such pessimistic predictions of fuel shortages Hitler decided to go ahead with the planned attack rather than leave Germany forever subject to Stalin's mercy for oil. After the overwhelming success of the blitzkrieg strategy in the west

Hitler and his generals overoptimistically predicted that Russia could be defeated in four to eight weeks.[8] Hitler told General von Rundstedt: "You only have to kick in the door and the whole rotten structure will come crashing down."

Initially Hitler's invasion went very well. The Russians were taken by surprise and were completely disorganized. By the second day of the fighting the Germans had broken through the front in several places. The Luftwaffe caught the Soviet air force on the ground and inflicted heavy damage. Nazi dive bombers disrupted Russian troop concentrations and communications. After one week the panzers had cut through the Russian lines and surrounded large numbers of troops.

Hitler's armies were advancing in three major directions. Army Group North, which was moving up through the Baltic states toward Leningrad, encountered little resistance. Army Group Center was taking Napoleon's road to Moscow. They surrounded and defeated a Russian army of a quarter of a million men at Minsk and then went straight ahead for Smolensk, only two hundred miles from Moscow. Although it encountered the strongest enemy resistance, Army Group South was making steady progress toward Kiev, the capital of the Ukraine.

Shortly after the German army invaded Russia Hitler flew to Rastenburg in East Prussia to take up residence at his new headquarters called Wolf's Lair. From here he would direct the war in Russia. The Wolf's Lair was situated in a gloomy forest where the sun barely penetrated through the thick foliage even on clear days. The countryside around Rastenburg was sparsely populated and dominated by lakes, forests, and marshes. The headquarters compound was surrounded by several rings of electric fence and barbed wire. A visitor had to pass through numerous checkpoints before reaching Hitler's bunker, which was a massive structure half underground with a concrete roof twelve feet thick. There were a few other bunkers and numerous wooden barracks in the compound.

Life at Wolf's Lair was Spartan and depressing. General Jodl, the chief of operations, said the headquarters was "a cross between a cloister and a concentration camp." The forest was so dark lights had to be left on inside the buildings all day. The high humidity from the nearby marshes and lakes caused everyone including Hitler to complain about the swarms of mosquitoes in the summer. To share the privations of his troops, Hitler deliberately gave up all pleasures while at Wolf's Lair. He no longer listened to music or watched movies. His bedroom in the bunker contained nothing but a simple army camp bed, a straight wooden chair, and a dresser. The only exception to the stark military simplicity was Hitler's portrait of Frederick the Great in a blue uniform by Anton Graff. Hitler took this painting with him wherever he lived and looked upon it as a continual source of inspiration.

Hitler's daily schedule at Wolf's Lair revolved around the two military situation conferences held each day, one in the early afternoon and the other at midnight. Each conference would usually begin with General Jodl briefly explaining the most recent military developments. Hitler and his generals would then hunch over the large-scale maps following the troop movements. A discussion of the measures to be taken followed. At this early stage of the Russian campaign Hitler behaved reasonably, listening to different points of view.

After the midday situation conference he would have lunch with his staff officers. There would be lengthy conversations on a wide range of topics. Most of the officers had aristocratic backgrounds. In the past Hitler had been somewhat uncomfortable with such men. But now he was spending his time completely surrounded by them, with the exception of his female secretaries, Bormann, his private secretary, and a few personal adjutants. The former corporal turned warlord now mixed well with the upper-class Officer Corps. As long as things were going so well at the front there was little to argue about.

Hitler didn't just stay safely at his headquarters but frequently flew to the front to confer with his field commanders. He walked through the ruins of the Ukrainian city of Uman while the debris was still smoking. When he saw thousands of prisoners being held in a gravel pit he ordered the Ukrainians be separated from the Russians and released. He also had a Ukrainian doctor who was treating the wounded prisoners brought to him and talked with him for a long time. Hitler soon abandoned any idea of fair treatment for Ukrainians, because like Russians they were Slavs, whom he considered to be racial inferiors. After a day of traveling up and down the front lines, talking to everyone from generals to ordinary soldiers, Hitler would sometimes spend the night at a local base or headquarters. While touring the front near Poltava Hitler spent the night at Field Marshal von Reichenau's headquarters in a crumbling old castle, but because it was infested with bugs he got little sleep.

Throughout July the German armies continued to advance on three broad fronts. Army Group North had captured the Baltic countries and was almost to Leningrad; Army Group Center was near Smolensk; and Army Group South was engaged in heavy fighting outside Kiev. At this point a conflict arose between Hitler and the generals. The generals wanted to push on toward Moscow with Army Group Center. Hitler, however, wanted Army Group Center to halt and send some of their panzer units south to help capture Kiev and the Ukraine. The generals believed Russia would fall if Moscow was captured. Mindful of Napoleon's experience Hitler was less interested in the Russian capital than he was in the wealth of the Ukraine. Here he could capture grain, industries, coal, and even some badly needed oil.[9]

General Guderian left the front and flew to Hitler's headquarters to try to convince him to press the attack on Moscow. Guderian argued the strategic advantages. Hitler listened quietly but then explained why Germany needed the industrial and agricultural resources of the Ukraine, the coal of the Donets Basin, and the oil of the Romny fields. Furthermore he said he wanted Army Group South to capture the Crimea, which had the potential of being "a Soviet aircraft carrier for attacking the Romanian oil fields." After his meeting with General Guderian Hitler commented: "My generals know nothing about the economic aspects of war."[10]

In his desire to capture the Ukraine before he took Moscow, Hitler had the support of the German industrialists. As early as May 1939 top German industrialists and bankers at a board meeting of the Reichsbank had discussed the necessity of "Germanizing" Russia as far as the Urals.[11] Some of the directors of I.G. Farben were anxious to get their hands on Russia's huge chemical and synthetic rubber factories. In fact they were so eager that Otto Ambros, chairman of I.G.'s Synthetic Rubber Commission, asked for official permission to follow the front-line troops into Russia in order to be the first on the scene when the rubber and chemical plants were captured.[12] Directors of the steel cartel like Albert Voegler and Walter Rohland had pointed out to Hitler the value of the Donets Basin, which produced 60 percent of Russian iron ore and 60 percent of her coal, and urged him to move in that direction.

In late July and early August of 1941 Hitler became ill. This was just when the crucial decision had to be made whether to try to capture Moscow or the Ukraine first. He complained of stomach pains, nausea, and diarrhea. Alternately he suffered from chills and fever.[13] Illnesses of this sort were fairly common in the swampy land around Rastenburg. Hitler's doctor, Morell, prescribed more pills, which was probably the last thing Hitler needed, since he was already taking so many different prescription drugs. Although Hitler's bout of "swamp fever" made work almost impossible for him for a few weeks, it was not the most serious threat to his health during this period.

In July, when Ribbentrop was visiting Hitler's headquarters, the two became involved in a heated argument over the Russian campaign. Ribbentrop had been against the war from the beginning. The foreign minister became so infuriated he started to shout back at Hitler. The Fuehrer suddenly stammered, clutching at his chest, and fell backward into his chair. For a moment everyone thought Hitler was having a heart attack. In a few days he recovered, but from then on he worried about his heart condition.

When Hitler's health improved enough for him to take an interest in military matters again, he found that General Halder, the chief of the General Staff, and his superior, Field Marshal von Brauchitsch, the commander in chief of the army, had been deliberately obstructing and delaying his plan to shift the main attack from Moscow to the Ukraine. More arguments and insults between Hitler and the generals followed. Hitler said the General Staff officers were mentally fossilized by out-of-date theories. General Halder in turn found Hitler's "interference" in army affairs "unbearable." He suggested to Field Marshal von Brauchitsch that they resign together. But Brauchitsch realized the Officer Corps could only force Hitler out if they all acted together; unfortunately there were still plenty of generals like Field Marshal Keitel, the chief of the high command of the armed forces, who remained loyal to Hitler.

In the end Hitler and the industrialists had their way, and the generals yielded. Army Group Center halted while its panzer units were sent south to help capture Kiev. On September 19 Kiev fell. It was a great victory for Hitler, with over 600,000 Russian troops being captured in the Kiev pocket. Another victory that excited Hitler was the capture of the Romny oil fields, over a hundred miles east of Kiev. Although the Romny fields were not large, for the Germans their capture marked the start of the most ambitious campaign of all, the drive to the Caucasus. A group of 6,654 German oil technicians were organized as oil commandos to travel with the army to get the Caucasian oil fields back into production as soon as they were captured.[14]

After his great victory in the Ukraine at Kiev, Hitler decided to resume the attack on Moscow. By the time the panzer units returned to Army Group Center and were ready to attack again, it was October and some of the best weeks of fall fighting weather had been lost. The Russians also had six weeks to strengthen their defenses between Smolensk and Moscow. Nevertheless Hitler's attack on Moscow, code named Operation Typhoon, got off to a good start. During the first two weeks of October, two Soviet armies were encircled and destroyed with the loss of over a half million men. In the south the German advances also continued. General von Rundstedt's troops were nearing the strategic city of Rostov, and the Crimea was about to fall.

Then the October rains began; the unpaved Russian roads turned to mud soup. Trucks, cars, and wagons were often stuck up to their axles in mud and had to be pulled out by men and horses. The German advance slowed but could not be stopped. Army Group Center continued to advance toward Moscow.

In mid-October Stalin decided to move Moscow's armament factories east of the Urals. Panic broke out in the capital. There was looting and a number of Communist bosses fled to the east. Women factory workers were sent to the outskirts of the city to dig trenches for a last stand against the Nazis. But the German advance gradually slowed to a halt because supplies, especially petrol, could not keep up with the advancing troops.

Hitler and his generals had planned Operation Typhoon to be a great battle of encirclement. Two German armies would sweep around Moscow to the north and south, cut the city off and crush it. Hitler realized that everything now depended on the weather. Soon it would be winter with subzero temperatures and heavy snow. If he was going to conquer Moscow, Hitler knew he would have to do it in the next few weeks, but his resources were running low. German panzer units were down to approximately one-third of their original strength. The generals urged Hitler to call off the advance for the winter and dig in to defensive positions. So close to victory, Hitler could not be discouraged; he ordered Typhoon to go forward as soon as the panzers had sufficient fuel.

On November 15 the Germans began moving again, sweeping north and south of Moscow. As they fought their way forward they had to cope with a new enemy: snow. The Russian winter had started earlier than expected. Nevertheless the Germans forged ahead through fog and snow. On December 1 Hitler's great pincer moved around Moscow and was about to be closed. The next day advanced units of General von Block's army reached the Moscow suburbs and in the distance could see the golden domes of the Kremlin against the gray winter sky.

But the German advance was suddenly brought to a halt by the weather. The thermometer plunged below zero; then heavy snow began to fall. Icy winds from Siberia began blowing across the open countryside. Supplies could no longer reach the troops. The panzers ran out of fuel. To deliver adequate supplies of fuel, ammunition, and food sixty-five trains a day had to reach the front. After the temperature plunged to forty degrees below zero, only about twenty trains a day got through. German locomotives were not built to withstand such cold temperatures. The pipes on many burst, and water froze in the boilers of others. The German soldiers fighting in summer clothing in subzero weather without enough food faced a grim fate. Lubricating oils hardened in rifles and artillery pieces. Fires had to be built underneath tanks to keep the engines from freezing.

On December 6 to Hitler's surprise, the Russians launched a major counterattack on the front around Moscow. Already exhausted, the German troops gave ground. The generals wanted to retreat, but Hitler refused: "No withdrawal! Not a single yard of retreat!" He was afraid any retreat would cause panic, repeating Napoleon's fateful retreat from Moscow. For a few days it looked as if the Russians might break through the German line. Stalin threw in fresh divisions from Siberia, but the Germans managed to hold on.

There is little doubt that Hitler's refusal to permit a withdrawal averted panic, but the cost was very high in casualties and losses of equipment. After seeing most of his generals terrified by the Russian offensive, Hitler could no longer conceal his contempt for them and openly ridiculed them as cowards. Those commanders who ordered withdrawal in defiance of Hitler's orders were harshly punished and publicly disgraced.

Hitler's determination and willpower had saved the German Army from disaster, yet he had lost his bid to capture Moscow. On December 7 while the fighting was raging around Moscow, Hitler received the news of the Japanese attack on Pearl Harbor. He was thrilled, although he realized Japan had no intention of joining the war against Russia.[15]

Blaming the top generals for the defeat at the gates of Moscow, Hitler sacked Field Marshal Brauchitsch, the commander in chief of the army, for cowardice. To everyone's surprise Hitler took over the job of commander in chief of the army himself. This marked a turning point in his relationship with his most powerful coalition partner, the army. From now on he had constant quarrels with the generals.

After his early victories over France and Poland and after having saved the army from panic during the Russian counterattack at Moscow, Hitler had an inflated opinion of his own military abilities. The generals on the other hand greatly resented his "intrusion" into their professional sphere. Hitler's ambition, however, was to take over the army completely, as he revealed in a contemptuous comment he made shortly after declaring himself commander in chief: "Anyone can do this little job of directing military operations. The task of the commander in chief is to educate the army to be National Socialist. I do not know any general who can do that as I want it done. I therefore decided to take over the command of the army myself."

By February the Russian winter offensive had worn itself out against Hitler's "hedgehog" defensive positions. On the night of February 26 Hitler said to his adjutants, "Sunday will be the first of March. Boys, you can't imagine what that means to me—how much the last three months have worn out my strength and tested my nervous resistance."[16]

When the rains began in March and April both the Russian and German armies were immobilized by the mud. But regardless, Hitler was glad to see the coming of spring. A month before when his headquarters at Rastenburg in East Prussia was still covered in snow, Hitler said to Bormann, his private secretary: "I've always detested snow . . . you know I've always hated it. Now I know why. It was a presentiment."[17] In some places the German line had been pushed back two hundred miles. In spite of this defeat Hitler was enthusiastically looking forward to the spring offensive. He believed the worst was now behind him.

During February of 1942 there had been a significant change in the leadership of the Nazi party. Dr. Fritz Todt, Hitler's minister of armaments and munitions, was killed in a mysterious plane crash. The minister of armaments and munitions was the second most powerful position in the economy. Goering in his role as chief of the Four-Year Plan saw himself as Germany's economic dictator. He and Dr. Todt had been bitter rivals for the control of the economy. The rivalry was not just between individuals but between the cartels and industries each man represented. Goering was the front man for I.G. Farben, while Todt represented the steel cartel of the Ruhr.

On the day that Todt's plane crashed taking off from Rastenburg Airport, Albert Speer, Hitler's architect, "just happened" to be at Hitler's headquarters. A few hours after the crash Hitler summoned Speer to his office. In a formal manner Hitler said, "Herr Speer, I appoint you to be the successor to Minister Todt in all his capacities."

Speer tried to say that he didn't know anything about armaments, but Hitler cut him off: "I have confidence in you. I know you will manage it. Besides I have no one else. Get in touch with the Ministry at once and take over!"[18]

Before Speer could leave the room, Hitler's adjutant came in, announcing that Goering had just arrived and wanted to see Hitler urgently. Goering, upon being informed of Dr. Todt's death, immediately rushed in his private train to Hitler's headquarters from his hunting lodge about sixty miles away. Hitler told the adjutant to show Goering in. Then turning to Speer he said, "Stay here a moment longer."

Blustering in, Goering briefly stated high condolences to Hitler and said: "Best if I take over Dr. Todt's assignments within the framework of the Four-Year Plan. This would avoid frictions and difficulties we had in the past as a result of overlapping responsibilities."

Ignoring Goering's suggestion Hitler told him that he had already appointed Speer as Todt's successor. Goering was stunned; it took him a few seconds to regain his composure. Then he coolly said, "I hope you will understand, Mein Fuehrer, if I do not attend Dr. Todt's funeral. You know what battles I had with him."

Suspicious that "foul play" might have been involved in Dr. Todt's plane crash, Hitler ordered an investigation. The report issued by the investigating commission stated there had been an explosion aboard the plane but ruled out sabotage, saying instead that the plane's self-destruct mechanism had accidentally been set off. Most Nazi insiders regarded the investigation as a cover-up. Apparently Hitler still had his suspicions too, for whenever Dr. Todt's death was mentioned he became nervous and irritable. "I want to hear no more about that. I forbid further discussion of the subject," he would say.[19] Shortly before his death, Dr. Todt had placed a considerable sum of money in a safe for his longtime personal secretary, "in case something should happen to him."

Who murdered Dr. Todt? Goering was considered a prime suspect. Although he was already the most powerful man in the economy, he wanted to increase his power even more by being both chief of the Four-Year Plan and minister of armaments. His patron, I.G. Farben, was also eager to gain additional wealth and plunder at the expense of other business groups, primarily the steel cartel. Goering's Luftwaffe intelligence would have had no difficulty arranging a plane crash. However, Goering ended up gaining nothing from Todt's death, and perhaps a plane crash was a bit too obvious to have been carried out by the Luftwaffe.

The other likely suspects were Albert Speer and intelligence agents acting for the steel cartel. For several years the steel cartel was chafing under Goering's leadership of the economy and his obvious favoritism for I.G. Farben. Todt was too weak to stand up to Goering. It was to the advantage of the steel cartel to get Todt out of the way, replacing him with Albert Speer, who was one of the few people to enjoy Hitler's complete confidence. Speer was one of Hitler's closest friends. The bond between the two men was based on their mutual love of architecture. Speer would use his personal relationship with Hitler to turn his new post as minister of armaments into the most powerful economic post in the Third Reich. Extremely ambitious, Speer eventually planned to be Hitler's successor.

Although after the war Speer tried to pretend he was a "nonpolitical" technocrat, he was in fact one of Hitler's most devoted followers. No one worked harder to impose Hitler's Nazi tyranny on Europe than Albert Speer. After the war Speer also tried to obscure any links he had with the steel cartel, portraying himself as the average, middle-class young architect. His grandfather, however, had been one of the wealthiest industrialists in Germany. As the owner of the largest machine tool firm in the country, he had close personal ties with many prominent industrialists. Once Speer took office as minister of armaments his links to the steel cartel became evident with his selection of three of the cartel's most influential directors, Albert Voegler, Hermann Rochling, and Walter Rohland as his close personal advisers.

Hitler decided the German spring and summer offensives should be concentrated in the south on capturing the Ukraine and then pushing on into the Caucasus to the badly needed oil. In a rare honest appraisal of the war Hitler admitted, "If I do not get the oil of Maikop and Grozny, then I must end this war."[20] But the Germans not only needed oil for themselves they also wanted to deny it to the Soviets. To accomplish this Hitler declared the city of Stalingrad as a second objective of the campaign, because it was a strategic transportation link for the oil being shipped by barge and rail from the Caucasus north up the Volga.[21]

In May the Soviets attacked at Kharkov before Hitler could begin his new offensive. But the Germans easily turned back the attack and inflicted heavy casualties on the Soviets. Once again full of confidence, Hitler launched his great spring offensive. The Germans drove the Russians out of the Crimea and captured

Sevastopol, the major Russian naval base on the Black Sea. Meanwhile other German armies were driving farther east. In July they took Voronezh. The Soviet troops fled in panic when the Germans captured Rostov at the mouth of the Don River. Hitler's troops were at the gateway to the Caucasus with little resistance in front of them. The Germans had, however, outrun their supply lines, and the panzers were consuming gasoline faster than it could be shipped to the front.

With the main offensive taking place in the south, Hitler decided to move his headquarters to the Ukraine, where he would be closer to the front. The new headquarters, code named Werewolf, was located in a woods a few miles northeast of Vinnitsa, a dreary spot on the flat Ukrainian plain. The land baked under the July sun. Hitler complained there was never a breeze but plenty of dust and mosquitoes. Although he now ruled an empire that included most of Europe, Hitler lived in a small wooden cabin, one of more than a dozen that made up the Werewolf compound. Hitler found the heat unbearable, and tempers often flared as he and the generals argued over strategic objectives.

In spite of the difficult living conditions for Hitler in his Ukrainian headquarters, he was in his glory because he believed his dream of a great German Empire from the Atlantic to the Urals was about to become a reality. He was obsessed with the idea of a German empire to rival Britain's. "The basic reason for English pride is India," said Hitler. He believed the vast spaces over which the British ruled gave them a sense of their own superiority. He wanted to do the same for the Germans.

"What India was for England," Hitler said, "the territories of Russia will be for us. If only I could make the German people understand what this space means for our future!"[22] He wanted to encourage German peasants who were overcrowded at home to settle in Russia. The generals were strong supporters of this idea and wanted to reward demobilized soldiers with land in the east.[23] "The German colonists," said Hitler, "ought to live on handsome spacious farms." The German governors would rule from "marvelous palaces," but the Russian natives outside would live in ignorance and misery.

Sitting in his Ukrainian headquarters on those hot sultry nights in the summer of 1942 "Hitler the Conqueror" described to his entourage how he would deal with the Russians and Ukrainians in his empire: "We shan't settle in Russian towns, we'll let them fall to pieces . . . and above all, no remorse on this subject! We're not going to play children's nurses; we're absolutely without obligations as far as these people are concerned." Hitler wanted Russians to live in ignorance in "hovels" infested with fleas. The only thing the Germans should teach them was how to read road signs so they wouldn't get run over by German vehicles.

One hot night in mid-July Bormann came into the tearoom at Hitler's Werewolf headquarters, his clothes covered with dust after a long drive through the Ukrainian countryside. Tired and discouraged, he complained about the number of blond-haired, blue-eyed Ukrainian babies he had seen on his journey. He was afraid that Ukrainians were multiplying so fast German colonization could never keep up with it. Hitler voiced hearty agreement and explained his plan to remedy the situation.

The next morning Hitler's "plan" was put in writing and sent out to the German occupation authorities as "The Fuehrer's Guidelines for the Government of the Eastern Territories": "the Slavs are to work for us. Insofar as we don't need them, they may die. Therefore compulsory vaccination and German health services are superfluous. The fertility of the Slavs is undesirable. They may use contraceptives and practice abortion, the more the better. Education is dangerous. It is sufficient if they can count up to a hundred. At best an education is admissible which produces useful servants for us. Every educated person is a future enemy. Religion we leave to them as a means of diversion. As to food, they are not to get more than necessary. We are the masters, we come first."[24]

Always contemptuous of the Russians, Hitler said: "For them the word 'liberty' means the right to wash only on feast-days. If we arrive bringing soft soap, we'll obtain no sympathy. . . . There's only one duty: to Germanize this country by the immigration of Germans, and to look upon the natives as Redskins."[25] Having been a devoted reader of Karl May's books on the American West as a youth, Hitler frequently referred to the Russians as "Redskins." He saw a parallel between his effort to conquer and colonize land in Russia with the conquest of the American West by the white man and the subjugation of the

Indians or "Redskins." "I don't see why," he said, "a German who eats a piece of bread should torment himself with the idea that the soil that produces this bread has been won by the sword. When we eat wheat from Canada, we don't think about the despoiled Indians."[26]

Believing his new empire to have natural riches that rivaled America's, Hitler said: "Where can you find more nickel, more coal, more manganese or more molybdenum than in the Ukraine? And nowhere is there iron ore richer than the Ukrainian ore." He had extensive plans for the economic exploitation of his empire. Besides being a source of raw materials he saw conquered Russia as a market for cheap German goods particularly textiles and consumer goods.

Such plans were not simply a product of Hitler's megalomania. His goals were also shared by most Nazis. Indeed Hitler's prospective empire consisted of exactly the same territories the Germans wanted to take from Russia during World War I: the Baltic states, the Ukraine, the Crimea, and the Caucasus.[27]

To fully exploit Russia's assets, the Germans set up a number of special "Eastern Monopoly Companies" with joint government and private participation. The Kontinentale Oil Company was set up to take over oil production in Russia; Chemie Ost was given a monopoly of chemical resources; and Osfaser G.M.B.H. was to exploit textile production. There were other monopoly companies set up to control the production of tobacco, furs, hides, and agricultural goods. The most successful monopoly company was the BHO, which was organized to exploit Russian coal, iron, and mining industries.

The cartels and the industrialists close to the Nazi elite were the ones to profit most from the monopoly companies. Hitler's personal friends, the industrialists Alfried Krupp, Wilhelm Keppler, Friedrich Flick, and Paul Pleiger, were given control over properties worth billions. Hermann Goering, the chief of the Four-Year Plan, was not to be left out of the scramble for wealth in Russia. The Hermann Goering Works took over one of Russia's largest steel mills at Zaporozhye and several plants in the Krivoi Rog industrial area.[28]

Alfried Krupp, the head of the Krupp steel firm, probably profited more from Hitler's Russian empire than any other industrialist. As Hitler's armies marched farther into Russia,

Krupp sat in his office on the Ruhr studying a huge map of Russia with red pins marking the factories and mines he was to take over. Technically the German government assigned various Russian plants to German companies for "sponsorship," but it was likely that in many cases the "sponsor" would virtually become the new owner. The best properties Krupp acquired were in the Ukraine. After the fall of Dnepropetrovsk, Krupp's agents took over the huge Molotov Works, one of the largest steel mills in Europe. Krupp also took over two of the most modern machine factories in the world, the Azova Plant and the Ilyitch Works, both located in the Ukraine.

Aware of the German plan to seize Russia's industrial capacity and use it for their own ends, the Soviets tried to move whole factories or at least all the valuable machinery east of the Urals before they fell into Nazi hands. Fortunately for Krupp, steel mills and iron foundries were difficult if not impossible to move. In early July the Russians tried to move the armor plate factory at Mariupol in front of the advancing German troops, but they failed and Krupp agents seized the Mariupol factory almost intact. Some of the Russian factories assigned to Krupp were too old and obsolete to interest him, so he ordered his workers to seize all useful parts, materials, and machines from such factories and ship them back to Germany. In addition to the factories, Krupp was also given numerous mines, which yielded a rich harvest of iron, chromium, and manganese ore. The Krupp engineers were so efficient in putting the mines and factories back to work that within a few months Krupp was not only producing weapons for Hitler but also able to export steel products to Turkey, Romania, and Bulgaria.[29]

Russian factories not needed by the Germans were ruthlessly shut down without a care for the fate of the workers. Goering's Four-Year Plan office sent out secret orders, later known as the notorious "Green file," regarding the "surplus" Russian population: "many tens of millions of people in the industrial areas will become redundant and will either die or will have to emigrate to Siberia. Any attempts to save the population in these parts from death by starvation through the import of surpluses from the Black Earth Zone [the fertile agricultural region of the Ukraine] would be at the expense of supplies to Europe. It would . . . undermine Germany's power to resist the blockade."[30]

Germany was suffering from a shortage of grains and animal fats at the beginning of the war. Hitler and the generals took the food shortage very seriously. All Germans remembered the terrible period of hunger caused by the British blockade during World War I. Hitler believed the revolution of 1918 was at least in part the result of the privations caused by the blockade. With the conquest of the Ukraine, the Germans simply seized most of the agricultural produce for themselves, making even the peasants go hungry.

During their occupation of Russia the Germans pillaged ten million tons of grain, three million tons of potatoes, and 600,000 tons of meat, along with large quantities of vegetables, eggs, butter, and sugar; however, less than 50 percent of this food ever reached Germany.[31] Much (from the Ukraine) of it was consumed by the German army. Even Dr. Goebbels complained: "As regard to food, we are not to expect too much [from the Ukraine] in the immediate future. German troops have devoured everything there. There are no cattle left and there is a dearth of horses and other draft animals, so that the plows must again be drawn by human beings. It is not hard to imagine what the results will be."[32]

To extract as much agricultural produce from the Ukraine and occupied Russia as possible, Hitler set up an occupation government ruled by brutal Nazi governors.[33] Posts in the occupation government in the east were handed out as rewards to small-time Nazi party hacks, and former small-town lawyers, railway clerks, and shopkeepers found themselves ruling vast territories. They lived in the large manor houses of the old Russian aristocrats, had Russian and Ukrainian mistresses, and ample opportunity to fill their pockets with booty.

The worst of these petty tyrants was probably Erich Koch, the governor of the Ukraine. Koch, the gauleiter of East Prussia, was a protégé of Hermann Goering. His associates included a number of corrupt businessmen and an Indian maharajah whom Koch was trying to swindle out of his legendary treasure of gold.[34] Koch had several palatial estates both in East Prussia and in the Ukraine. He sometimes rode in a carriage that had belonged to the czars and was pulled by four magnificent gray horses.

In order to have a place in the Ukraine where his guests could hunt, Koch seized the vast forest of Tsuman, the former estate of the Radziwll family, the great Polish landlords. Before 1914 the Radziwlls had given splendid hunting parties at Tsuman. Koch wanted to do the same, but he had a problem with the workers on the Tsuman estate. After 1918 the Tsuman forest had been producing resin, tar, and timber. Koch didn't want this commercial activity to interfere with his pleasure, so he banned all resin tapping. When some of the workers complained, he had them shot as "partisans." Even other Nazis believed this was going too far, because there were no partisans in this part of the Ukraine. Charges were filed against Koch. Ultimately the matter was decided by Hitler, who always protected his old party cronies and refused to take any action against Koch.

Before the Germans could exploit the wealth of Russia they had to conquer it, and up until the end of July 1942 there was some confusion about exactly what their military priorities would be. The General Staff wanted first to take Stalingrad before moving into the Caucasus. Hitler, on the other hand, wanted the oil of the Caucasus more than Stalingrad, at least at first. He went behind the back of the General Staff and appealed directly to the field commanders, telling General von Kleist that his panzer army would be the instrument by which the Reich would be assured of its oil supply for all time.[35] General Halder, the chief of the General Staff, commented bitterly on Hitler's efforts to persuade the field commanders of the priority of the Caucasus oil region. "Hitler succeeded in winning over the consent of leaders of lower rank by clearly misrepresenting those ideas which the OKH [high command] as the superior organ, had rejected."[36]

At this time it was not clear who was really running the war, Hitler or the high command. The General Staff still planned all military operations; sometimes Hitler would intervene and alter the plan; sometimes he would not. Hitler obviously did not yet feel strong enough to challenge the authority of the high command directly if he took the trouble to persuade lower-ranking field commanders to support his strategy against the senior generals.

As far as the southern front was concerned a compromise was finally reached between Hitler and the high command. On July

23 Directive 45 was issued to the advancing German armies in Southern Russia: Army Group A was to advance southward across the Don, with the aim of taking possession of the Caucasus with its oil resources; Army Group B was to attack Stalingrad.

The German invasion of the Caucasus was hampered by a lack of fuel and extremely long supply lines, but the Russian armies in the region were badly disorganized and put up little resistance. On August 9 the German panzers reached the Mikop oil field in the northwest Caucasus near the Black Sea. At first German officers reported that the Russians had not had time to destroy the wells. Hitler was thrilled when he heard the news. When the German oil experts arrived at Mikop a few days later, however, they found the Soviets had sabotaged the wells by plugging them with cement. It was estimated it would take several months to get the fields back into full production.[37]

Hitler was so angered by the report from the experts at Mikop that their commander was ordered to report back to the Fuehrer's headquarters to explain the problems. The main difficulty was supply. To get oil flowing again the German technicians needed pipe, tools, and equipment that had to be supplied over a thousand miles. The nearest rail line was in Armavir, far to the rear.

The problem of supplying the advancing German troops was also quickly getting worse. Petrol was a particular problem. Trucks carrying gasoline to the panzers had to travel so far that they used up much of their cargo just to get to their destination. General von Kleist sent a desperate message from the Kalmuck Steppe that summed up the situation: "No enemy in front of me and no reserves behind me." In response to General von Kleist's pleas, Hitler ordered the Luftwaffe to airlift petrol to the panzers. Some fuel got through but not enough.[38]

The German armies were now less than one hundred miles from the Caspian Sea and close to their ultimate goal, Russia's largest oil fields—Grozny and Baku. But their advance was slowed to a few miles a day. Fuel was so scarce that the Germans were reduced to using camels to bring up their supplies. The front lines were over 1,200 miles from Hitler's headquarters in the Ukraine. There was an unreal atmosphere to the war in the Caucasus, the almost tropical heat, the dust, the barren desert landscape, and the Oriental dress of the natives. The stars were out at night over the peaks of the Caucasus when German officers' watches set on Berlin time read one o'clock in the afternoon.

If the German troops were able to hold on to the Caucasus territory long enough, a number of Nazis would become very wealthy. The Kontinentale Oil Company had been set up with joint private and government participation to exploit the oil of the Caucasus. Hitler was not at all ashamed of looting Russia's oil. "We are the real profiteers in this war," Hitler told Albert Speer, "and we will come out of it bursting with fat! We will give back nothing and will take everything we can make use of. And if others protest I don't give a damn."

The German company set up to plunder the oil of the Caucasus, Kontinentale, was given a ninety-nine-year monopoly on the extraction, refining, and distribution of Russian petroleum in return for a payment of a 7.5 percent royalty to the government. The executive director of Kontinentale was a Farben man.[39] The other directors included representatives of the major German banks, Goering's representatives, and other Nazi industrialists like Hitler's friend Wilhelm Keppler. One German military officer associated with Kontinentale said in anticipation: "At last we Germans will have a chance to enrich ourselves."[40]

No Germans would be getting rich on oil unless the armies in the Caucasus made faster progress. Hitler was becoming irritated with the situation. On September 9 he dismissed General List and personally took over the command of Army Group A. But even Hitler had little success pushing the offensive in the Caucasus. This was due in part to the fact that a major battle was developing farther to the north at Stalingrad. He began stripping the army in the Caucasus to send units north.

The Germans launched their main attack on Stalingrad in September with over a half million men of the Sixth Army under the command of General Friedrich Paulus. The German artillery bombardment that preceded the fighting flattened almost half of the city. In the first day German troops quickly entered Stalingrad, but just when they had overrun most of it, Russian resistance stiffened. The Sixth Army became bogged down in hand-to-hand fighting in the rubble. Piles of bricks from the damaged buildings made the streets impassable for the panzers, which stalled in the debris and were destroyed by the Russians. Almost every day the Germans would drive the Russians back, but at night the Soviets would ferry reinforcements into Stalingrad from the opposite bank of the Volga and recapture lost ground.

In late September the Germans were making little progress in Stalingrad while the Sixth Army was being bled white. Hitler was obsessed with capturing Stalingrad, not because it was named after his archenemy, as some biographers have contended, but because it controlled the "Russia oil artery," the Volga.[41] In addition to military problems Hitler was angry about the generals suggesting breaking off the attack to retreat and regroup before the Russian winter began. "He trusts none of the generals," wrote General Engle, Hitler's army adjutant, in his diary. "Nothing seems to suit him and he curses himself for having gone to war with such poor generals."[42]

A hostile atmosphere lurked just below the surface at Hitler's headquarters. After bitter disputes with several generals, Hitler refused to shake hands with any staff officer. He ordered a stenographer and an S.S. officer to be present at the daily situation conferences so the generals would not be able to say they had misunderstood his orders. Finally fed up with General Halder's cautious negative attitude, Hitler dismissed him from his post as chief of the General Staff on September 24 saying, "You and I have been suffering from nerves. Half my nervous exhaustion is due to you. It is not worth it to go on. We need National Socialist ardor now, not professional ability. I cannot expect this of an officer of the old school such as you."

But change generals as he might the military situation at Stalingrad did not improve. On November 19 the Russians under the command of General Zhukov launched a counterattack against the Sixth Army from the northeast and the southeast. The Russian plan was to envelop the Sixth Army in a giant pincer move. The German line to the north and south of Stalingrad was thinly held by poorly trained Romanian troops. The generals urged Hitler to let the Sixth Army retreat while there was still time, but he would not hear of it. "Stay and fight!" he ordered. "I am not leaving the Volga." Soon the Russian ring closed around the Sixth Army.

The General Staff suggested that Army Group A be withdrawn from the Caucasus before they too were cut off. This was the last thing Hitler wanted to do. In spite of constant Soviet guerrilla attacks the German engineers were making progress in restoring production at Mikop. Only a few wells were repaired and back in operation by November, but output from Mikop was expected to rise to 1,800 barrels a day by April, and 24,000 a day by 1943.[43] This oil was one of the reasons for which Hitler had invaded Russia in the first place. He was not about to quit now.

Encircled at Stalingrad were 300,000 men of the Sixth Army. The German-held pocket was only twenty-five miles wide and about twelve miles deep. General Paulus's forces were still strong enough to break out of the Russian circle, but it would mean sacrificing all their heavy weapons. On the night of November 23 Hitler was forced to make an important decision. General Paulus wanted to attempt a breakout, but Goering assured Hitler that the Luftwaffe could keep the Sixth Army in Stalingrad supplied by air. In spite of Goering's poor record of keeping military promises, Hitler believed him.

Just as he had done at Dunkirk, Hitler made his choice at least partly for political reasons. He distrusted Paulus and the generals and preferred to believe the politically more reliable but militarily incompetent Goering. Thus Hitler made his worst mistake of the war because he was concerned about the struggle against the generals at a time when he should only have been thinking about the war. If the German leadership had not been so divided, the disaster at Stalingrad would probably never have happened.

In spite of Goering's boasts the Luftwaffe was able to fly in only a fraction of the over seven hundred tons of supplies needed daily by the 300,000 men of the Sixth Army. The heavy fogs around Stalingrad in December further hampered the airlift. In mid-December General Manstein attempted to relieve the Sixth Army by attacking the encircling Russians from the west. He came within thirty miles of success. For a few nights the trapped soldiers on the Sixth Army could see the flares of their rescuers on the horizon. But in the end the Russians beat back Manstein's attack.

The besieged Sixth Army valiantly fought on for another month. Rations were continually reduced. Ammunition was running low. In late January General Paulus reported that his men were starving, freezing, and almost out of ammunition. He requested permission to surrender. Hitler's reply was: "The Sixth Army will do its historic duty at Stalingrad to the last man." A few days later Hitler promoted Paulus to the rank of field marshal because he said: "There is no record in military history of a German field marshal being taken prisoner." But he was quickly disappointed when on the night of January 31 the Russians announced that Paulus and the Sixth Army had surrendered.

Hitler felt personally betrayed by Paulus because he had just promoted him. "The man should have shot himself," Hitler said. "I can't understand . . . what a coward . . . so many men have to die and then a man like him besmirches the heroism of so many others at the last moment."[44] Hitler's already low opinion of the generals fell even further. He said Paulus was the last general he would ever promote to field marshal.

Stalingrad was the worst defeat the German Army had suffered in over a hundred years. Militarily it marked the turning of the tide for Hitler. It also marked the beginning of the end for the Nazi coalition. Up to this time only a minority of conservative or politically enlightened generals were so opposed to Hitler that they wanted to remove him, but after Stalingrad this became the view of the majority of the Officer Corps. Hitler, however, was determined to hang on. He had gone too far to turn back. In a speech he delivered a few months earlier he had accompanied his promise to take Stalingrad with threats against the Jews. If the Jews caused "an international war to exterminate the Aryan peoples it would not be the Aryan peoples that would be annihilated but Jewry itself."[45] More than a few Germans knew that Hitler had already been killing Jews for quite some time.

Chapter 11

Motives for Genocide

On September 29, 1941, ten days after the German capture of Kiev, the Nazis ordered all Jews in the city to report to a central public square with their personal possessions to be "resettled." The unsuspecting people obeyed the order and gathered by the thousands with their children. Convoys of German trucks took them outside the city to the "resettlement" area. The S.S. unit in charge of the operation was commanded by a ferocious-looking red-haired S.S. officer named Hermann Paul Blobel, who was described even by his fellow S.S. officers as a brutal bloodhound without inhibitions. Perhaps for this reason Adolf Eichmann, an S.S. "expert" on Jewish affairs, found him to be one of the most effective executioners Hitler had.

Blobel, who had been an architect and builder before the war, organized the Kiev massacres with precision. As soon as the Jews climbed down from the trucks, they were assembled in groups and marched to a waiting area just out of view of one of the several execution sites. When their turn came the victims were marched forward in groups of fifteen. They were ordered to undress and leave their clothing and belongings in a neat row so they could find them again after they had been deloused. Then the fifteen victims were marched around the side of a high mound of dirt to a large deep ditch where they were ordered to kneel down at the edge of the pit. Thirty S.S. men stood behind them with rifles. At the order from the commander they fired. The victims immediately toppled over into the mass grave. The S.S. execution squad usually worked for about an hour and then was replaced by another thirty men. From dawn to dusk the murders continued without letup. By the end of the second day, 33,771 people had been killed and buried.

Meanwhile other groups of S.S. men worked with typical German thoroughness gathering and cataloging all the victims' personal possessions. Money, valuables, clothing, and even underwear were separated in neat piles. By the time the Kiev killings were over the Nazis had hauled away 137 truckloads of booty. Although the executions usually went smoothly, occasionally there were difficulties. The firing squad was instructed to aim at the victims' heads. If they missed, another S.S. man would come forward with a rifle and shoot the victim in the head from a distance of three to six feet. Of course there was blood and human tissue at the edge of the pit that had to be cleaned up. If the victims failed to fall into the pit, their bodies had to be thrown in on top of the others. It was inevitable that some of these poor people were only wounded and buried alive.

The Nazis hated any complication that would slow down the killing process. They did everything possible to fool the victims until the last minute. Once in a while as the people were being marched up to the side of the mass grave they would see it full of naked bleeding bodies and try to escape or resist, in which case they were immediately shot or beaten to submission.

Blobel had no qualms about killing women and even children. Like Hitler, he considered all Jews as potential partisans, saboteurs, or spies. Nevertheless after the Kiev massacre Blobel was worried that some day the world might find out about his evil deed. He reported back to Berlin and asked Eichmann's permission to dig up the corpses and burn them. When burning proved to be too slow, he experimented with dynamiting the mass graves.

A year later a newly arrived German officer was riding in a car with Blobel on a country road outside Kiev when suddenly a field erupted in an explosion. When the startled officer asked what was going on, Blobel calmly looked at the field and replied:

"My Jews are buried here." On several occasions later in the war, Blobel was invited to Berlin to lecture other S.S. officers on methods of destroying evidence of their crimes. He would graphically describe the problems associated with digging open mass graves full of decaying corpses and burning them. But no matter how hard the S.S. worked to cover up what they had done, there could be no hiding of the unspeakable crimes Hitler and his henchmen committed against the Jewish people.[1]

Although there are a number of excellent books on almost every aspect of the Holocaust, very little research has been done on Hitler's motives for genocide. That will be the subject of this chapter. Contrary to the opinion of most historians, Hitler's plans to exterminate the Jews were not based solely on racial hatred. When Hitler and the Nazis decided to wipe out the Jewish people, they were motivated at least in part by the thought that it would be profitable. Hitler wanted empty lands in the east for German settlers, thus he felt it was necessary to "depopulate" this already overcrowded region.

Up until the beginning of the war Hitler was not exactly sure what he wanted to do with the Jews. For years he had preached racial hatred and called on Germans to "get rid of" the Jews. He had said the Jews must "disappear" from Germany. Indeed, by 1939 the German Jews were disappearing, through emigration. At the conference of Nazi officials called by Goering on November 12, 1938, after the Nazi terror attacks on Jewish synagogues and stores on Crystal Night, Jewish emigration was one of the main topics discussed.

"In spite of the elimination of the Jews from the economy," said S.S. General Reinhard Heydrich, "the essential problem still remains one of forcing the Jews to leave Germany. May I make a few suggestions? We have organized a center for Jewish emigration at Vienna, thanks to which we have been able to evacuate fifty thousand Jews from Austria, while in the Reich only nineteen thousand Jews were expelled during the same period."

"The story has made the world press," Goering replied. "On the first night the Jews were expelled into Czechoslovakia. The next morning the Czechs sent them off to Hungary. From there they went back again to Germany and Czechoslovakia. They went back and forth. Finally they landed on an old barge on the Danube."

"There were barely one hundred Jews involved in that. . . . At least forty-five thousand have been evacuated legally," said Heydrich.

"We did it by demanding that rich Jews who wish to emigrate pay us certain sums, which we collected from the Jewish community," explained Heydrich. "This money has made it possible for us to expel a certain number of poor Jews. The problem was not to make the rich Jews leave, but to evacuate the Jewish mob."

"What are you thinking of, my children?" Goering said, laughing. "It's no use forcing hundreds of thousands of poor Jews to leave if it costs too much."[2]

The Center for Jewish Emigration in Vienna to which Heydrich referred during the November 12 conference was directed by Adolf Eichmann.

Growing up in Austria, Eichmann had been a troubled youth with an unimpressive school record. He had a succession of mediocre jobs, including that of a traveling salesman for an oil company. During this period of his life he was not any more or less anti-Semitic than most other Austrians and even had some Jewish associates who occasionally entertained him in their homes. Eichmann eventually came out of his shell and became a hard-drinking extrovert who was known for racing his red motorcycle along the road from Linz to Vienna. His aimless existence was suddenly given purpose when he heard Hitler speak for the first time.

> After hearing Hitler speak I felt a loathing of myself that I had mixed with those Jews who were the enemies of the German people and who defiled our blood. I felt a certain change in my outlook coming over me. I began to think these foreign-looking people were, indeed, the enemy of us all. They all seemed to be traders and financiers, people willing to take very little part in the real work of the community, people who insisted our ways had nothing to do with them. I wondered about my friendship with Jews and I felt that they had always treated me as someone rather

inferior. I felt that no country, unassisted by others, could have beaten the German army during the war. I believed that Hitler was right when he said that the Jews had intrigued to link as many nations as possible against our country and bring about the terrible times we were then going through.[3]

Eichmann soon joined the Austrian S.S. With dark hair and an average build, Eichmann was hardly the ideal blond S.S. superman; however, he singled himself out by becoming a self-styled "expert" on Jewish affairs. He learned a few words of Hebrew and Yiddish and visited Palestine. He got in touch with some Arab leaders and was trying to set up an international anti-Jewish organization, but the British found out about his activities and threw him out of Palestine. On his way back to Germany he stopped in Cairo to meet with the Grand Mufti of Jerusalem, who later came to Berlin and became one of Hitler's collaborators, recruiting Arabs for the Nazi cause.

Eichmann's main accomplishment as far as his Nazi superiors were concerned was the way he organized Jewish emigration from Austria after the Anschluss (the unification of Austria and Germany). In Nazi terminology "emigration" was really a euphemism for "expulsion." Using a combination of terror and blackmail, Eichmann forced thousands of Jews to leave Austria. The basic procedure was rather simple: a Jew would be arrested on some trumped-up charge and threatened with being sent to a concentration camp, then emigration would be "suggested" by the S.S. as an alternative. If the victim agreed to emigrate, all charges were dropped.

On January 24, 1939, Goering ordered Heydrich to use the methods Eichmann had developed in Austria to increase the emigration of German Jews. The Nazi emigration procedure forced Jews to submit to all sorts of humiliations. People had to stand in line all day. Any Jew caught leaning against the wall risked being beaten by the S.S. The Nazi bureaucrats treated Jews applying for passports worse than criminals. They seemed to take sadistic pleasure in barking orders and brutally shouting insults. Emigrating Jews were robbed of their homes, businesses, and life savings just to get a passport.

However, getting out of Germany was just the first problem facing victims of Hitler's persecutions. Their next ordeal was trying to find some country to accept them. Most nations refused to open their doors to these persecuted people. The United States, once a country of asylum for the oppressed and a haven for political refugees, refused to alter its strict immigration quotas. Although some politicians like President Roosevelt realized the disastrous effect the immigration policy was having, they were afraid to do anything because of the isolationist mood of the public. The admission of Jewish refugees to Palestine was blocked by Britain. To appease the Arabs the British White Paper of 1939 limited the number of Jewish immigrants to Palestine to just fifteen thousand over the next five years.

In order to make it appear that America was trying to help, President Roosevelt convened a conference at Evian, France, in the summer of 1938, at which the need for finding countries to accept the Jewish refugees was discussed. Roosevelt was actually hoping to divert Jewish refugees from the United States to other countries. But the conference was a dismal failure. One after another the countries of the free world offered lame excuses as to why they would not accept any Jewish immigrants. The United States and Britain refused to change their restrictive policies. The United States would not increase its quota of immigrants, and Britain would not let the Jews go to Palestine. Canada and most of the Latin American nations said they wanted only agricultural immigrants. France, Holland, and Denmark had already accepted large numbers of Jewish refugees and said they could take no more. Perhaps the Australians gave one of the most honest but heartless answers when they said: "As we have no real racial problem, we are not desirous of importing one."[4]

Anti-Semitism was the real underlying reason the nations of the world refused to accept the Jews. This was especially true in the United States, where the Quakers lobbied Congress in 1939 to bring twenty-thousand Jewish children to America. The Roosevelt Administration's unwillingness to support the bill caused its failure. However, about a year later the United States was quick to issue visas to ten thousand English children when Britain was threatened with German attack.

The hypocrisy of the American and British refugee policy was not lost on Hitler. Shortly before President Roosevelt's refugee conference took place at Evian, the Vienna Nazi newspaper the *Völkischer Beobachter* said, "We cannot take seriously President Roosevelt's appeal to the nations of the world as long as the United States maintains racial quotas for immigrants." Hitler himself attacked Roosevelt's refugee policy in a speech at Königsberg saying, "I can only hope and expect that the rest of the world, which has such deep sympathy for these criminals [the Jews], will at least be generous enough to convert this sympathy into practical aid. We, on our part, are ready to put these criminals at the disposal of these countries, for all I care, even on luxury ships."[5]

Hitler's ridicule of the democracies for their failure to accept Jewish refugees was more than just good propaganda. It led him to believe that America and Britain really didn't care about the Jews, so it would be acceptable for Germany to "eliminate" them, as long as it was done quietly. More important, Hitler was able to convince his hesitant colleagues, like Goering, Himmler, and some of the pro-Nazi generals, that Britain and America were indifferent to the fate of the Jews and that their protests against German anti-Semitism were only for propaganda purposes. Just how convincing Hitler was with this argument was seen in 1945 when Himmler and Goering, who both played a direct role in killing millions of Jews, believed that America and Britain would appoint them to head a postwar German government. They obviously felt the Western democracies would have no serious objection to the "elimination" of the Jews. Hitler also used the argument of the world's disinterest in the plight of the Jews to convince some of his weaker Axis partners, such as Hungary, Romania, and Italy, to send their Jews to German concentration camps to be killed.[6]

After the failure of the Evian conference one German newspaper said: "We see that people like to pity the Jews as long as they can use this pity as an instrument of agitation against Germany. But no country is prepared . . . to accept a few thousand Jews. Thus the conference serves to justify Germany's policy against Jewry."[7] The German press at Hitler's urging continued to point out the contradiction between America's words and actions. On the one hand, said the Nazis, the United States government was protesting against Hitler's racial laws and at the same time Negroes were openly discriminated against by law in the United States.

Every morning the first item on Hitler's work schedule was to read the press reports that had been prepared for him by his press chief, Dr. Otto Dietrich. These reports included articles from both the German and the foreign press. Stories about the problems Jewish refugees were having trying to find countries that would accept them delighted him. On May 13, 1939, the passenger ship *St. Louis* sailed from Germany with 930 Jewish refugees. Although they all had Cuban admission papers, when they reached Havana the Cubans refused to permit them to land.

Every day Hitler followed the developing tragedy in the press. The American government then refused to let the refugees into the United States, even though they held quota numbers that would have enabled them to enter the United States just three months after their arrival in Cuba. When the *St. Louis* passed within sight of the Florida coastline, the U.S. Coast Guard was ordered not to let anyone come ashore. On reading of the American government's heartless refusal to help the Jews aboard the *St. Louis*, Hitler laughed. The passengers of the *St. Louis* finally found refuge in Holland, Belgium, and France, but unfortunately when Hitler overran these countries a year later, most of them ended up in concentration camps.

Exactly when Hitler first began to think about wiping out the Jews is difficult to determine, however it was probably sometime after the German Communist uprising of 1918 to 1919, which Hitler blamed on the Jews. This so called stab in the back was in Hitler's eyes "the greatest Jewish crime." An interview with journalist Josef Hell in 1922 is one of the first records of Hitler admitting he wanted to kill the Jews.

When Hell asked, "What do you want to do to the Jews?" Hitler hesitated for a moment. His eyes stared into space. He raised his voice, as if addressing an audience: "Once I really am in power, my first and foremost task will be the annihilation of the Jews. As soon as I have the power to do so, I will have gallows built in rows—at the Marienplatz in Munich, for example—as many as traffic allows. Then the Jews will be hanged indiscriminately, and they will remain hanging until they stink. . . . As soon as they have been untied, the next batch will be strung up, and so on down the line, until the last Jew in Munich has been exterminated. Other cities will follow suit . . . until all Germany has been completely cleansed of Jews."[8]

In spite of the scathing hatred in the above quotation, by the time he actually became chancellor in 1933, Hitler's priorities had changed. His primary objective was still to "get rid of the Jews." But if this could be accomplished by expulsions and emigration he would be satisfied. He didn't necessarily feel the need to kill the Jews. To Hitler's surprise, efforts to force the Jews to emigrate were thwarted by the refusal of the Western democracies to admit them. Meanwhile the number of Jews under German rule increased with the occupation of Czechoslovakia. When the war broke out Hitler found himself with almost two million additional Polish Jews under his control. The war and British control of the sea certainly reduced the chances of emigration for the Jews. But Hitler had not yet abandoned the idea completely.

In May of 1940 S.S. chief Himmler wrote a memorandum on a solution to the Jewish question by suggesting a large-scale emigration of Jews to the island of Madagascar off the African coast. Hitler liked the suggestion and wrote "very good and correct" on the memorandum and distributed it to key Nazi leaders involved with the Jewish question. Madagascar was a French colony, but evidently Hitler thought he could get the French to cede the island for Jewish settlement. Hitler was not intending for Madagascar to be an independent Jewish state. On the contrary, it was to be a sort of giant "reservation" ruled by a German governor and police. Once Hitler began to plan his attack on Russia, he showed no further interest in the Madagascar plan. Now he was thinking of more brutal ways to "solve" the Jewish question. He had made up his mind to exterminate the Jews of Russia to make way for German settlers. The only thing still uncertain was exactly how they would be killed.

Hitler did not approach the problem of extermination of the Jews haphazardly. He had carefully studied some of the most prominent examples of mass murder in history. His four principal inspirations were the slaughter of the American Indians, the killing of the Armenians by the Turks, the Red Terror during the Communist revolution in Russia, and the Japanese butchery at Nanking in 1937.

A speech he delivered to his senior military commanders just before the attack on Poland in August of 1939 revealed his thinking. "Close your hearts to pity." He told his generals:

Act brutally. Eighty million people [the Germans] must obtain what is their right. . . . Genghis Khan sent millions of women and children to death knowingly and with a light heart. . . . The goal to be obtained in the war is not reaching certain lines but physically demolishing the opponent. And so in the East I have put my death-head formations in place with the command to relentlessly and without compassion send to death many women and children of Polish origin. Only thus can we gain the living space that we need. Who after all is today speaking about the destruction of the Armenians? . . . Poland will be depopulated and settled with Germans. As for the rest . . . the fate of Russia will be exactly the same.[9]

Hitler aspired to be a modern-day Genghis Khan. He had carefully studied the ancient migrations and destructions of peoples. His morality was that of the Dark Ages combined with a Darwinist survival-of-the-fittest philosophy. "Natural instincts," he once told one of his associates, "bid all living beings not merely to conquer their enemies, but also to destroy them. In ancient times it was the victor's prerogative to destroy entire tribes, entire peoples."

Hitler's cynical reference to no one remembering the Armenians was unfortunately true. In 1915 the Turks in Anatolia had massacred nearly one million Armenian Christians for their alleged treachery. Those Armenians who were lucky enough to survive were deported. The Turks thus had eliminated a religious minority that had lived in Turkey for over a thousand years. Hitler thought he would be able to do the same with the Jews.

Hitler drew another example of mass murder from American

history. Since his youth he had been obsessed with the Wild West stories of Karl May. He viewed the fighting between cowboys and Indians in racial terms. In many of his speeches he referred with admiration to the victory of the white race in settling the American continent and driving out the inferior peoples, the Indians. With great fascination he listened to stories, which some of his associates who had been in America told him about the massacres of the Indians by the U.S. Cavalry.

He was very interested in the way the Indian population had rapidly declined due to epidemics and starvation when the United States government forced them to live on the reservations. He thought the American government's forced migrations of the Indians over great distances to barren reservation land was a deliberate policy of extermination. Just how much Hitler took from the American example of the destruction of the Indian nations for his plans of the Holocaust is hard to say; however, frightening parallels can be drawn. For some time Hitler considered deporting the Jews to a large "reservation" in the Lubin area where their numbers would be reduced through starvation and disease.

The bloody slaughter of the Russian upper and middle class by the Communists during the Russian Revolution made a deep impression on Hitler. It was after hearing stories of the Red Terror from Russian emigrés that Hitler began thinking about the mass murder of civilians. Because a few Jews like Trotsky, Zinoviev, and Kamenev were prominent Communist leaders, Hitler actually believed the Jews were responsible for the Red Terror. Nothing could have been further from the truth. The majority of Jews in Russia were absorbed in their religion and played no part in the Communist revolution. Nevertheless the Communists provided Hitler with abundant examples of mass murder and slaughter.

In 1930 Stalin announced a massive land "collectivization." The government expropriated the land and livestock of the peasants and turned everything over to socialist collective farms. The peasants resisted this government theft, and rather than give up their cattle, they slaughtered them and ate them. Stalin responded with terror and murder. The Red Army and the secret police surrounded resisting villages, shooting all the inhabitants. The kulaks, or so-called rich peasants, who were also the most productive farmers, were either executed or deported to concentration camps. Stalin once admitted to Winston Churchill that ten million peasants had been murdered during the period of forced collectivization.

Admiring Stalin for his brutality, Hitler said: "Stalin is one of the most extraordinary figures in world history." He even compared the Russian dictator to Charlemagne. "Stalin . . . ," said Hitler, "must command our unconditional respect. In his own way he is a hell of a fellow! He knows his models, Genghis Khan and the others, very well."[10]

Historical examples of mass murders were useful to Hitler in many ways, not the least of which was convincing himself that the bloody task of killing millions of human beings could be accomplished. At first he worried how the rest of the world would respond to large-scale exterminations. True, Stalin got away with the slaughter of the kulaks with little more than stern reprimands from the West, but Russia was an isolated self-sufficient country, whereas Germany was dependent on foreign trade. If Hitler wanted a more suitable and current example he did not have to wait long.

In December of 1937 the city of Nanking in China fell to the invading Japanese. What was termed by the world press as "the rape of Nanking" took place in the month that followed. The Japanese army indulged in rape, looting, and murder on an unprecedented scale. Twenty thousand Chinese civilians were herded together and slaughtered with machine guns in a single day. The gutters literally ran red with human blood. The Japanese even used human beings for bayonet practice. Three hundred thousand Chinese men, women, and children were murdered within a month. The Yangtze River, which flowed through Nanking, was full of bloated corpses. Hitler carefully monitored the international response to the Nanking atrocities. There was an outcry of moral indignation in the democratic press, but neither Britain, France, nor the United States took any action against Japan.

In the fall of 1939 after the German armies attacked Poland, and Britain and France declared war, Hitler was finally ready to put his plans for exterminating the Jews into action. Realistically the war cut off any possibility of getting rid of the Jews through emigration. In 1939 a few months before the beginning of the war Hitler gave a warning to the world in a speech before the Reichstag: "Once again," he said, "I will assume the part of a prophet.

"If the international Jewish financiers succeed in plunging the nations of Europe into another world war, then the result will be not the Bolshevisation of the world and thereby the victory of Jewry—but the annihilation of the Jewish race in Europe."[11]

After the defeat of Poland, as a first step toward the "final solution," Hitler ordered the concentration of the Jews into ghettos in occupied Poland. These ghettos were located in the Jewish quarters of the major Polish cities, like Warsaw, Lodz, Lublin, and Cracow. In the summer of 1940 the Germans began building walls across streets to isolate the ghettos. Jews were forbidden to live outside the ghetto. Special permission was required for any ghetto Jew who wanted to leave the ghetto. This was only given for working parties that were taken out under guard to work for the Germans.[12]

Jews were uprooted from their homes in most of the small villages and towns and forced into the ghettos in the cities. During this process of deportation in 1940 the Jews were often mistreated, plundered, and forced to endure numerous hardships, but they were not killed, at least as an official policy. The reason the Jews were spared was because they were needed for work. Shortly after taking office, Hans Frank, the Nazi governor general of Poland, wrote: "Especially urgent is the instituting of forced labor for the Jews. The Jewish population if possible must be extracted from the Jewish cities and be put to work on roads."[13]

A very significant change in Hitler's Jewish policy came with the invasion of Russia. While Operation Barbarossa was still in the planning stage, Hitler began issuing decrees that prepared the way for the mass murder of the Jews. On May 13, 1941, he ordered that Russian civilians who opposed the German Army in the coming invasion should be considered outlaws and shot without trial.[14] At the same time he issued another decree that gave Himmler and the S.S. "special power" to operate behind the front independently of the army. It would be the task of the S.S. to root out and destroy all partisans and civilian opposition to the German forces.

On June 6 Hitler issued his famous "commissar order." He told Field Marshal von Brauchitsch, the commander in chief of the army, to issue instructions to the army to liquidate all captured Soviet commissars, even those with the troops and in uniform, as bearers of an ideology dramatically opposed to National Socialism. Brauchitsch vigorously objected, but Hitler cut him off saying: "I cannot demand that my generals understand my orders but I do demand that they follow them." This would initiate the beginning of the most ruthless phase of the war. It stated: "These commissars are the originators of barbarous, Asiatic methods of warfare, and they must therefore be treated with all possible severity and dispatch. . . . Whether captured during the battle or while offering resistance, they must be shot at once."[15]

None of Hitler's barbaric orders issued in the spring and summer of 1941 actually mentioned the Jews. Certainly these orders laid the groundwork under which the Jews could be labeled as partisans and shot by the S.S. However, the first military orders that actually mentioned action against the Jews were issued by army officers, not Hitler. These orders expose the long-standing lie that no German Army officers had anything to do with the Holocaust. It is true that the vast majority of officers of the regular army had nothing to do with the killing of Jews. Those army officers who were involved were the pro-Nazis like Keitel, chief of the high command of the armed forces, and Reichenau, the commander of the Sixth Army.

On June 4 the high command of the armed forces (OKW) issued a directive entitled "Guidelines for the Conduct of the Troops in Russia."* It stated: "1. Bolshevism is the mortal enemy of the National Socialist German people. Germany's struggle is directed against this destructive ideology and its carriers. 2. This struggle demands ruthless and energetic measures against Bolshevik agitators, guerrillas, saboteurs, Jews, and the complete elimination of every active or passive resistance."[16]

After the attack against Russia was already in progress, Field

---

*Field Marshal Keitel was chief of the high command of the armed forces and hence ultimately responsible for this order. Some sources give May 19, 1941, as the date of this order: see Noaks, pp. 1089–90.

Marshal Keitel issued orders on Jews in occupied eastern territories that singled out Jews alone for "special treatment": "The struggle against Bolshevism demands ruthless and energetic measures, above all against the Jews, the main carriers of Bolshevism."[17]

Later in the campaign, as more Russian territory and millions of Jews were falling into German hands, one of the army commanders at the front, Field Marshal von Reichenau, issued orders that virtually instructed soldiers of the regular army to murder the Jews: "The most essential aim of the war against the Jewish-Bolshevistic system is a complete destruction and elimination of Asiatic influence from European Culture. In this connection the troops are facing tasks which go beyond the normal routine of soldiering. . . . Therefore, the soldier must have full understanding for the necessity of a severe but just revenge on subhuman Jewry. The Army also has to crush any revolts in the rear which, as experience proves, have always been caused by Jews."[18]

Hitler thought Field Marshal von Reichenau's directive on the Jews was "excellent." Reichenau had been a collaborator with Hitler since the early 1930s. He had played a key role in the Officer Corps' support of the Hitler-Papen coalition government. Reichenau was as eager to see the east open to German settlement as the Nazis were. Indeed this was one of the reasons such officers became Hitler's secret partners in the first place. Copies of Reichenau's directive on the Jews were given to other field commanders as an example of the tone to take when dealing with the Jewish question.

Apparently Hitler never actually issued any written order for the killing of the Jews. Sometime in the spring of 1941 he verbally instructed Himmler and Goering to arrange the organizations and procedures necessary to eliminate the Jews. At least several months before the invasion of Russia, Heydrich informed the S.S. Action Commandos that their task would be "liquidation of the Jews."

The S.S. Action Commandos (Einsatzgruppe) had been formed before the invasion of Poland. Their role in the war against Poland had been to kill partisans operating behind the German lines and to herd the Jews into ghettos. For the invasion of Russia Heydrich had four S.S. Action Commandos under his command; each one had a strength of between five hundred to a thousand men. The total strength of all four S.S. Action Commando groups did not exceed three thousand men. All of the men were members of the S.S. and had been given special training and indoctrination on the necessity of exterminating "subhumans," particularly Jews.

As soon as the German armies invaded Russia the S.S. Action Commandos moved in behind them. S.S. General Otto Ohlendorf, the commander of S.S. Action Commando D, later explained how his men operated:

The unit would enter a village or city and order the prominent Jewish citizens to call together all Jews for the purpose of resettlement. They were requested to hand over their valuables to the leaders of the unit and shortly before the execution to surrender their outer clothing. The men, women and children were led to a place of execution which in most cases was located next to a more deeply excavated anti-tank ditch. Then they were shot kneeling or standing, and the corpses thrown into the ditch. I never permitted the shooting by individuals in Group D, but ordered that several men should shoot at the same time to avoid direct personal responsibility.[19]

Ohlendorf was an unlikely mass murderer. He had attended three universities and worked as a research economist. He was a handsome suave man with a compelling personality. At the time he commanded S.S. Action Commando D he was just thirty-four years old. Before he had gone to Russia to begin his killing spree, he had been the research director of the Institute for Applied Economic Science in Kiel. Ohlendorf's character can only be explained by saying he had a Jekyll-and-Hyde personality. He later shocked even the prosecution at Nuremberg when calmly explaining in his well-modulated voice why he had killed Jewish children. "I believe . . . the order [to liquidate Jewish children] was not just intended to achieve temporary security but also permanent security because the children would grow up and surely, being the children of parents who had been killed, would constitute no less a danger than the parents."

When S.S. chief Himmler visited S.S. Action Commando D in

the field on one occasion, Ohlendorf pointed out to him the psychological burden killing was imposing on his men. "I didn't even get an answer," Ohlendorf recalled.

About a month after the invasion began Hitler and Goering were so pleased with the way the S.S. Action Commandos were "cleansing" the area behind the front line that they decided Heydrich, the man in charge of the S.S. killing squads, should be promoted and put in charge of the extermination of all the Jews in Europe, or as expressed in Nazi code language "the final solution to the Jewish question." As was customary Hitler was careful not to sign any such order but left it to Goering to put it in writing.

On July 31, 1941, Goering wrote to Heydrich:

Grueppenfuehrer Heydrich. Supplementing the task assigned to you by the decree of January 24, 1939, to solve the Jewish problem by means of emigration and evacuation . . . I hereby charge you to carry out preparations as regards organizational, financial, and material matters for a total solution of the Jewish question in all the territories of Europe under German occupation. I charge you further to submit to me as soon as possible a general plan of the administrative and financial measures necessary for carrying out the desired final solution [*Endlosung*] of the Jewish question.[20]

Reinhard Heydrich was born in Saxony in 1904. He was the son of Bruno Heydrich, a talented musician and the founder of the Halle Conservatory. Heydrich became a lieutenant in the navy but was dismissed because of a scandal involving a woman. After being cashiered from the navy, Heydrich joined the S.S. He rose rapidly in the ranks of the Nazi organization. To Himmler, the tall, blond, and brilliant Heydrich was the ideal S.S. officer. Himmler soon appointed him chief of the S.D., the intelligence service of the S.S. Heydrich developed the S.D. into a dangerous secret police organization that kept files on everyone, including other prominent Nazis.

Heydrich played an important role in the Roehm purge, on June 30, 1934, gathering some of the evidence that eventually convinced Hitler to take action against the S.A. In 1937 Heydrich sent Stalin the forged document that had led to the great purge of the Russian generals. A year later Heydrich was involved in fabricating the sexual charges brought against the two top generals in the German Army, Blomberg and Fritsch. After Crystal Night, Heydrich began to take a leading role in the persecution of the Jews. He was appointed the administrator of the concentration camps by Himmler.

In Heydrich the Jews had a dangerous enemy. He was cold, sadistic, and greedy for power. Totally amoral, he had no sense of pity or compassion. The key to Heydrich's fanaticism was a secret fear that he might have some Jewish ancestry. Perhaps to compensate for this perceived taint he was all the more brutal with his Jewish victims. One of his colleagues told a story that perfectly illustrated Heydrich's dark self-hatred. As he was returning home drunk one night, Heydrich suddenly saw his own reflection in the mirror. He pulled out his pistol and fired two shots at the image of his head.

Hitler was aware of Heydrich's possible non-Aryan origin but promoted him in spite of this. A flaw of this sort was just the kind he loved to find in his subordinates' characters because it gave him more control over them. Hitler knew Heydrich would blindly obey any order. He was just the kind of man to be assigned the inhuman task of exterminating the Jews.

Why did Hitler suddenly decide to embark on the extermination of the Jews in June of 1941? He realized that the "Germanization" of Russia would require some form of depopulation to make room for German settlers. Because Russia was occupied by his armies, millions of additional people now became available for slave labor. He believed that many of these people, Russians and Ukrainians for example, would make better manual laborers than the Jews. So there was no longer a need for the Jews as workers. They had become in Hitler's eyes a surplus population to be eliminated.

Hitler also believed he would overrun Russia as quickly as he had conquered France. Because it would be difficult to conceal mass murders of the Jews during peacetime, he wanted to kill as many of them as possible before the Russians surrendered.[21]

Now considering the Jews a superfluous population useless even for slave labor, Hitler was ready to begin the program of "depopulation" he had talked about for years. "We shall have to develop a technique of depopulation," he had told one of his followers in the 1920s. "If you ask me what I mean by depopulation, I mean the removal of entire racial units. And that is what I intend to carry out—that, roughly, is my task. Nature is cruel, therefore, we too may be cruel. If I can send the flower of the German nation into the hell of war without the smallest pity for the spilling of precious German blood, then surely I have the right to remove millions of an inferior human race that breeds like vermin!" Of course by now Hitler had found his first "technique of depopulation"—the S.S. killing squads or Action Commandos.

"Depopulation," the wholesale "removal" of surplus and "inferior" peoples, was an idea supported by both pro-Nazis in industry and many of the militarists. Before Hitler came to power it was widely believed among conservatives that Germany was overpopulated, and a surplus population especially with high unemployment was a breeding ground for socialist revolution. The obvious solution to pan-German nationalists was an expansion to the east, where unemployed Germans would be settled on farms. But Poland and Russia were also overpopulated. Where would the Slavs and Jews go to make room for the German settlers? They would have to be "removed." Just what was meant by "removal" depended on who was advocating it, the conservative nationalists, the militarists, or the anti-Semites. "Removal" could mean anything from mass migrations to starvation, or "liquidation."

Several radical nationalist organizations in pre-Nazi Germany had been advocates of depopulation. The same people who financed Hitler had financed some of these groups. In 1906 one rabid nationalist wrote: "Let us bravely organize great forced migrations of the inferior peoples of Europe. Posterity will be grateful to us. Coercion will be necessary. They must be driven into reserves where we shall keep them segregated so that we may obtain the space necessary for our expansion."

Almost as anti-Semitic as the Nazis, the early German racists claimed the Jewish race was the "source of all danger" and deserving of no compassion. It was not too difficult to see what fate they had in mind for the Jews. One retired general who was a racist and an extreme nationalist urged the Germans to take by force the lands in the east they needed. As far as the current Slavic or Jewish inhabitants were concerned he was quite clear: "Our civilization must build its temples on mountains of corpses, oceans of tears, and innumerable dying men. It cannot be otherwise."

While the racist politicians in the pre-1914 era were advocating anti-Semitism and depopulation of the east, some militarists were studying how to reduce the enemy population through starvation, epidemics, and disease. Given the prevailing psychology favoring depopulation among the German racists, it was easy for Hitler to convince them to go one step further and turn actions against partisans into the mass murders by the S.S. death squads.

When Hitler ordered the extermination of the Jews, he expected little resistance from the Germans. In this respect he was correct. Years of his anti-Semitic propaganda had hardened most people to the point where they didn't care about the fate of the Jews. True, many decent German soldiers were shocked by what they saw of the S.S. Action Commandos killing innocent civilians, but only a few protested. However, even among the fanatical Nazis there was some reluctance actually to be involved in the killing process. Most Nazis would have preferred to ship the Jews off to some wasteland in the east and let them starve. That would have been much easier than shooting women and children in the back of the neck.

Hans Frank, the German governor of Poland, told some of his lieutenants in December of 1941 that "many of the measures carried out against the Jews were being criticized." But what are the alternatives, Frank asked his colleagues, "What should be done with the Jews? Do you think they will be settled in the 'Ostland' [the Baltic area], in villages? . . . Why all this bother? We can do nothing with them either in the 'Ostland' or in the Ukraine. So, liquidate them yourself. Gentlemen, I must ask you to rid yourself of all feeling of pity. We must annihilate the Jews."[22]

As Hitler's armies continued their advance into Russia, the S.S. Action Commandos continued their killing. S.S. Action Group A, which operated in the Baltic region, reported exterminating 125,000 Jews by October 15, 1941; Action Groups B and C, working in the central region, claimed to have killed 45,000 and 75,000 respectively. Ohlendorf's Group D, operating in the south, had killed 55,000 Jews by December 12.[23] Hitler personally followed the work of the killing squads with interest. The S.S. units were instructed to type out the reports from the Action Groups on large-print "Fuehrer" typewriters so Hitler could read them without having to wear glasses.

Hitler took a sadistic pleasure in reading the death toll of Jewish men, women, and children killed on his orders. Never once did he express the slightest reluctance about ordering the deaths of millions. Even when he looked at photographs of executions, he showed no visible emotions. Hitler had not the slightest sympathy or empathy for the suffering of the Jews as fellow human beings. This was in strange contrast to his humane attitude toward animals.

His pilot, Hans Baur, remembered him watching films from India sent by a maharaja. Hitler could calmly look at scenes of the bloody bodies of people who had been attacked by tigers. But during scenes of animals being hunted and killed he would sometimes cover his eyes with his hands like a child and ask to be told when it was over. He hated blood sports and sometimes would cry at the sight of a wounded animal.

A few months after the invasion of Russia, Minister of Propaganda Goebbels arrived at Hitler's headquarters with new proposals for increased persecution of the Jews in Germany. Hitler gave Goebbels permission to deport to the east seventy-six thousand Berlin Jews. During their conversation Hitler also spoke of the "prophecy" he had made during his speech to the Reichstag in January of 1939, when he warned that all of European Jewry would be eliminated if there was another world war. Although he was not directly involved in the extermination of the Jews, Goebbels was fully aware of what was going on.

A few months later Dr. Goebbels again visited Hitler's headquarters and wrote in his diary: "We talked about the Jewish question. Here the Fuehrer is as uncompromising as ever. The Jews must be got out of Europe, if necessary by applying most brutal methods. . . . It can be said that about 60 percent of them will have to be liquidated whereas only about 40 percent can be used for forced labor."

All this was being done, Goebbels continued,

with considerable circumspection and according to a method that does not attract too much attention. A judgment is being visited upon the Jews that, while barbaric, is fully deserved by them. The prophecy which the Fuehrer made about them for having brought on a new world war is beginning to come true in a most terrible manner. One must not be sentimental in these matters. If we did not fight the Jews, they would destroy us. It's a life-and-death struggle between the Aryan race and the Jewish bacillus. . . . Here, too, the Fuehrer is the undismayed champion of a radical solution.

Fortunately a whole series of possibilities presents itself for us in wartime that would be denied us in peacetime. . . . The ghettos that will be emptied in the cities of the General Government [Poland] will now be refilled with Jews thrown out of the Reich. This process is to be repeated from time to time. . . . The fact that Jewry's representatives in England and America are today organizing and sponsoring the war against Germany must be paid for dearly by its representatives in Europe—and that's only right.[24]

Although the Jews were the only ethnic group singled out by Hitler at this time for mass extermination they were not the only ones who were dying at Nazi hands.* Hitler was also waging a war of "depopulation" against Russian prisoners of war using slightly different techniques. In the first few months of the war with Russia hundreds of thousands of prisoners were captured. Hitler pointed out to his generals that since the Russians had not signed the Geneva Convention, the German Army need take no responsibility for the prisoners.[25]

Privately Hitler told Field Marshal Keitel that the Russian prisoners were to be treated harshly so they would quickly die and Germany would not be burdened with feeding and caring for them. Furthermore Hitler believed that the prisoners, being healthy young men, represented the biologically vital element of

*Hitler later also ordered the extermination of the Gypsies.

285

the Russian population and eliminating them would help reduce the Russian birth rate, and thus depopulate the territories Germany wanted to settle.

The hapless Russian prisoners were rounded up after they surrendered and were put in "cages," which were simple barbed wire enclosures. They were given almost no food and no shelter from the weather. Hundreds of thousands of them died of starvation. As they were given no medical care by the Germans, hundreds of thousands also died from epidemics that spread through the "cages." During the epidemics the Germans used flamethrowers to burn the bodies of the dead and dying. The Germans captured almost 2 million Russian prisoners and over 1.3 million died of starvation and disease.[26] Goering even told the Italian Foreign Minister Ciano a joke about what was going on in the German POW camps: "After having eaten everything possible, including the soles of their boots, they have begun to eat each other, and what is more serious, have eaten a German sentry."

Hitler used his own vile mistreatment of the Russian prisoners of war as an excuse to commit further brutalities against the Jews. "Why," said Hitler, "should I look at a Jew through other eyes than if he were a Russian prisoner of war? In the POW camps, many are dying. It's not my fault. I didn't want either the war or the POW camps. Why did the Jew provoke this war?" For submitting to Hitler's orders for the mistreatment of Russian prisoners of war a number of German generals became equally responsible and put a stain on the honor of the German Army.

In most accounts of the mass executions done by the S.S. Action Groups there is little mention of any resistance on the part of the victims. Why did the Jews submit so quietly to their fate? The responsibility for this rests with the Soviet Government. First of all, the Jews were taken by surprise. They really believed they were going to be resettled. The Soviet press deliberately reported very few stories of Nazi atrocities committed against Jews. All Soviet press accounts talked about was the sufferings of the Russians. They justified this in their own minds by classifying the Jews as Russian citizens. Nevertheless the result was that the Jews got no warning.

Second, the years of living under a brutal Communist dictatorship made all people, the Jews included, afraid to oppose any governmental authority. The Red Terror had conditioned people to accept their fates without complaint, for protest was useless. Once the Jews had adequate warning of what was happening they put up a heroic resistance with what few weapons they had. The Russian Jews who were able to escape to the woods became very effective guerrilla fighters behind Nazi lines. Had the Jews of Russia been forewarned and armed, as many as a million more might have escaped because Hitler did not have enough available men to crush a population that was actively resisting.

Hitler encountered one unexpected difficulty in murdering unarmed civilians. It was having a demoralizing effect on the S.S. Action Groups, who had been so carefully brainwashed to hate Jews. Many of the men suffered from nervous disorders, some took to drinking, others asked to be transferred. Faced with these problems, Himmler decided to visit Minsk and witness an execution for himself. One hundred prisoners, both men and women, most of them Jews, were selected to be shot. After the firing squad fired the first volley Himmler looked away. There was a second volley but two of the female prisoners were still gasping. "Don't torture these women!" Himmler ordered. "Get on with it, shoot quickly!"

General Bach-Zelewski, who was standing next to Himmler, said to him: "Look at the eyes of the men [in the firing squad], how deeply shaken they are. These men are finished for the rest of their lives. What kind of followers are we training here? Either neurotics or savages." Himmler admitted the work was "repulsive" but said Hitler's orders had to be obeyed.[27] As a result of this incident, however, Himmler ordered that henceforth women and children would not be shot but exterminated in gas vans.

The gas vans produced by two Berlin firms turned out to be a failure for Nazi purposes. They were difficult to operate and did not kill enough people at a time. Although the Nazis tried to disguise their appearance, word soon got around, and the Ukrainian and Russian children would point to one and say: "Here comes the death wagon."[28] Better, more efficient ways of killing people had to be found. To this end Heydrich summoned officials from all branches of the government to attend a conference to discuss "the final solution of the Jewish question."

Fifteen German officials representing the S.S., the Nazi party, and the government bureaucracy met at noon on January 20,

1942, for lunch at Wannsee, a wealthy lakeside suburb of Berlin. The meeting had been postponed several times because some of the participants were busy liquidating Jews. In attendance were representatives of Goering's Four-Year Plan, the Foreign Ministry, Rosenberg's Eastern Ministry, which administered occupied Russia, the Ministry of Justice, and the Nazi administration in Poland. There were also a number of more sinister S.S. types present, who had already been playing a key role in murdering Jews: Heydrich, Gestapo Chief Müller, Adolf Eichmann, the S.S. "expert" on Jewish affairs, and S.S. Major Fritz Lang, police chief in Latvia.[29]

Heydrich opened the meeting by informing his listeners that he had been ordered by Goering to prepare a plan for "a final solution to the Jewish question." He then reviewed the measures Hitler had taken in an attempt to solve the Jewish question up to that time. First there had been emigration, then the plan to deport the Jews to Madagascar; but the war made any such plans of transporting the Jews abroad obsolete.

Pointing to a large wall chart, which indicated the numbers of Jews in various countries to be "evacuated," Heydrich said that instead of emigration the Fuehrer had given his sanction to "the evacuation" of the Jews "to the east."

Heydrich said:

> The Jews should be sent to the east to work as laborers . . . with the sexes being separated. The Jews capable of work will be employed in road building and undoubtedly a large part of them will be eliminated by natural diminution.
>
> The remnant that finally is able to survive all this—since this is undoubtedly the part with the strongest resistance— must be given "special treatment," since these people, representing natural selection, are to be regarded as the germ cell of a new Jewish race, if they are allowed to go free.
>
> In the execution of the final solution, Europe is to be combed from west to east. . . . The evacuated Jews are to be brought group by group to the so-called transit ghettos and from there transported farther to the east.

A discussion then developed over which Jews, if any, would be exempt from the plan. The Foreign Ministry representative was afraid there might be difficulties in some foreign countries under occupation. Several of the government bureaucrats got into a lengthy debate over how individuals who were half-Jewish (*Mischlinges*) would be treated. Heydrich agreed to make a significant exception when State Secretary Neumann, the representative of Goering's Four-Year Plan (the economy), insisted that Jews working in war industries be exempted until they could be replaced by other workers.

In economic terms the Wannsee Conference represented a compromise between Nazi industrialists, who wanted to work Jews to death as slave laborers in the factories, and the S.S., who wanted to work them to death on the roads of Russia. Heydrich had expected stiffer opposition from Neumann and a few of the other more moderate representatives under Goering's influence. Most of Heydrich's suggestions, as Eichmann remembered, were received with "enthusiasm."

Most of the conference was conducted in Nazi double-talk. Long before, Hitler had decided that liquidation of the Jews should remain top secret; code words like "final solution," "evacuation," "deportation to the east" all meant eventual death of the Jews involved. However, there was a certain amount of genuine confusion at the conference. Although Hitler had ordered that the Jews be deported to the east, he had not yet actually made up his mind what would happen to them once they arrived there. Certainly they were to be killed, but how? Would they be exterminated immediately or gradually worked to death? Thus each Nazi official had some leeway in interpreting the "final solution" for himself.

Several of the participants of the Wannsee Conference later argued that they never realized Heydrich was talking about exterminations. Although Heydrich never mentioned gas chambers, he clearly stated that most of the Jews would not survive the hard labor planned for them. One of the purposes of the conference was to involve the government bureaucracy in the final solution. So to some extent it is true that not all the participants at the conference knew as much about liquidation of the Jews as Eichmann, Müller, and Heydrich.

Two of the participants representing Hans Frank, the Nazi governor of Poland, found Heydrich's plan too moderate. State Secretary Buhler, Frank's assistant, said of the several million

Jews in Poland, that most were unfit for work. Since the Polish Jews were already in the "east" and did not have to be transported, he urged the "final solution" be put into operation there at once. Buhler and his boss, Frank, knew about the mass murders the S.S. Action Groups were committing in Russia and wanted to do the same thing in Poland. Shortly before Buhler left to attend the Wannsee Conference Frank had openly called for the annihilation of the Jews.

After the conference was over Heydrich, Gestapo Chief Müller, and Eichmann sat around a cozy fireplace drinking and singing anti-Semitic songs. "After a while," said Eichmann, "we climbed onto the chairs and drank a toast; then onto the table and traipsed round and round—on the chairs and on the table again." Eichmann was greatly relieved. "At that moment," he said, "I sensed a kind of Pontius Pilate feeling, for I was free of all guilt. . . . Who was I to judge?"[30] His superior, Heydrich, was responsible. They were carrying out the direct orders of the Fuehrer.

There can be no real doubt that Hitler was the evil genius behind the Wannsee Conference and the "final solution." On January 23, just three days after the conference, Hitler told Himmler:

One must act radically. When one pulls out a tooth, one does it with a single tug, and the pain quickly goes away. The Jew must clear out of Europe. Otherwise no understanding will be possible between Europeans. It's the Jew who prevents everything. When I think about it, I realize that I'm extraordinarily humane. At the time of the rule of the popes, the Jews were mistreated in Rome. Until 1830, eight Jews mounted on donkeys were led once a year through the streets of Rome. For my part, I restrict myself to telling them they must go away. If they break their pipes on the journey, I can't do anything about it. But if they refuse to go voluntarily, I see no other solution but extermination.[31]

Chapter 12

"Generals Know Nothing About Economics"

itler's defeat at Stalingrad marked the critical turning point in World War II. After the surrender of the Sixth Army a three-day mourning period was declared in Germany during which all places of public entertainment, including movie houses and theaters, were closed. The German people were depressed and worried. Slogans and propaganda about being the "master race" suddenly seemed very hollow. For the first time the average person began to doubt the inevitability of final victory. In cities and towns like Vienna, where local units had been serving with the Sixth Army, there was a public outpouring of grief and despondency.

Along with the grief there was a growing bitterness over what had happened at Stalingrad. People began to whisper and grumble that the defeat was the result of "bad leadership." Wild rumors about Hitler's condition began to circulate. It was said that he was ill or isolated by the generals and had no idea what was happening in Russia.

Hitler himself was never the same after Stalingrad. He clearly recognized the defeat of the Sixth Army as the turning of the tide, but since he believed he could only negotiate peace from a position of strength, he saw no immediate way to end the war. Physically the defeat took a heavy toll on him. His nerves were on the verge of giving out. Previously he had prided himself on his ability to remain calm and rational in moments of crisis. Now he easily flew into a rage and shouted at his officers for even minor mistakes.

People who had not seen him in several months were amazed at how much he had aged in one year. His hair was rapidly graying, and he walked with a stooped posture. Doctor Morell, Hitler's personal physician, was giving him both an antidepressant drug and stimulants. Perhaps as a side effect of the drugs or possibly from the nervous strain, Hitler complained about sensitivity to bright light and disturbances in balance. When he walked he said he had the feeling of tipping to the right.

The Russian Army's advance showed no sign of letting up after Stalingrad. Much to Hitler's regret, he had to order the withdrawal of the German troops from the Caucasus before they were cut off. With their retreat went all his hopes and dreams for German self-sufficiency in oil. By a series of brilliant moves General von Kleist succeeded in extracting the army from the Caucasus. Field Marshal von Manstein was able to stabilize the German line, preventing an all-out Russian breakthrough.

It was now evident that the Russians were attacking with considerably larger forces than Hitler thought they had available. He had previously refused to believe intelligence reports that Stalin had an almost endless supply of fresh divisions from Siberia. To meet this threat Hitler's only alternative was to order a new mobilization in Germany and to draft previously exempt "essential workers" into the army. Dr. Goebbel's new propaganda theme was "Do you want total war?" By such tactics the Germans succeeded in raising 1.5 million men, but they were scraping the bottom of the barrel.

The drafting of more German workers into the army, combined with the realization that it was no longer possible to win a quick blitzkrieg victory in Russia, forced the Nazis to face the problem of a labor shortage. Albert Speer, the new minister of armament, said the labor shortage was the most serious problem he encountered when he took office. Armaments factories in Berlin were not able to use all the machinery in their workshops because they did not have enough workers. Furthermore, there were not enough laborers to man a night shift. For over a year

the munitions manufacturers had been requesting more workers. Goering, one of their spokesmen, had been the first to
suggest the use of Russians, Ukrainians, and Poles as slave
labor.[1]

Hitler appointed a commissioner of foreign labor recruitment,
whose job was to secure the necessary slave labor for German
industry. The position was given to Fritz Sauckel, a ruthless,
short, fat, pig-eyed little Nazi who had risen from a common
seaman to become the gauleiter of Thuringia. Speer and Sauckel
were summoned to Hitler's quarters to get their orders. Germany should not be experiencing a labor shortage, Hitler told them,
because Nazi-occupied Europe contained over 250 million people. All of them should be put to work for the German war
effort. He told Sauckel to gather the required workers by
"whatever means necessary."[2]

Both Speer and Sauckel suggested to Hitler that at least some
of the necessary workers could be obtained by encouraging
German women to work in factories, as was being done in
Britain and America. But Hitler would not hear of it. He was
afraid the women would be "morally corrupted" and their roles
as wives and mothers jeopardized. On several occasions Hitler
expressed similar sentiments that sounded like old-fashioned
middle-class prudishness. He was probably also afraid of wom-
en becoming too independent-minded and self-assertive.
Nevertheless, it was clear that the additional workers would not
be German women but would have to be found in the occupied
territories.

At first many of the foreign workers were volunteers from the
Ukraine. They were attracted by German promises of good jobs,
fair pay, and good food. But when they were packed into freight
cars without food or any sanitary facilities and shipped to
Germany like cattle, their opinions quickly changed.[3] By the
time Sauckel began rounding up workers, Ukrainians had
learned that jobs in Germany meant slave labor, so to avoid
being taken, everyone who was able tried to hide in the woods.

Sauckel, however, was not to be eluded. With the help of the
S.S. and the army he rounded up people on the streets and in the
marketplaces. Russians and Ukrainians were often grabbed as
they came out of theaters or even churches. And the Germans

were not gentle about it. There were scenes of beatings with liberal use of whips and blackjacks. In Kiev the relatives of workers being sent to Germany were not even allowed to hand them food or clothing for the journey. Crying wives and mothers were ruthlessly knocked down in the muddy streets by Nazi rifle butts. The Nazi slave labor program was largely responsible for turning the Ukrainians against Germany. Sauckel never had any hesitation about being too brutal because he was working under direct orders from Hitler.[4] He later testified at Nuremberg that as far as the slave labor program was concerned: "None of the higher [German] authorities, either military or civilian, expressed any misgivings."[5]

One eyewitness account vividly describes the viciousness of the Germans in their efforts to shanghai workers in the occupied eastern territories:

On Oct. 1 a new conscription of labor forces took place. The order came to supply twenty-five workers, but no one reported. All had fled. Then the German militia came to ignite the houses of those who had fled. The fire became very violent, since it had not rained for two months. In addition the grain stacks were in the farmyards. The people were forbidden to extinguish the flames, beaten and arrested, so that seven homesteads burned down. The policemen meanwhile ignited other houses. The people fell on their knees and kissed their hands, but the policemen beat them with rubber truncheons and threatened to burn down the whole village. During the fire the militia went through the adjoining villages, seized the laborers, and brought them in under arrest. Wherever they did not find any laborers, they detained the parents, until the children appeared. That is how the Nazis raged throughout the night in Bielosirka. The workers which had not yet appeared were to be shot. . . .

They are now catching humans like dogcatchers used to catch dogs. They have been hunting for one week and still don't have enough. The imprisoned workers are locked in the schoolhouse. They cannot even go out to perform their natural functions, but have to do it like pigs in the same room. People from many villages went on a pilgrimage to the monastery Potschaew. They were all arrested, locked in, and will be sent to work. Among them there are lame, blind and aged people.[6]

After the war many German industrialists argued that slave labor had been forced on them by Hitler; this was true in many, but not all, cases. Some Nazi businessmen profited from Hitler's slave labor program because it enabled them to lower wages to a few pennies a day, while the price of their products remained unchanged. There were German industrialists with the integrity and courage to refuse to use slave labor. In spite of this there were never enough slaves to satisfy the Nazis' demands. As Albert Speer himself later admitted, many of these workers were forced to work and live under "barbarous conditions," where sanitary facilities were inadequate, disease was rampant, and mortality was high.[7]

When it came to the mistreatment of slave laborers, Alfried Krupp, the steel and munitions manufacturer, was one of the worst violators. When the workers from the east arrived after days in overcrowded trains, they were immediately put to work by Krupp's foreman. The workers were given striped prison uniforms and wooden clogs to wear. They were housed in lice-infested buildings.[8] Some French workers actually had to sleep in dog kennels. In many respects the slave laborers were treated like animals. On the rare occasions when they received meat, it was likely to be horsemeat.

Every morning in Essen thousands of slave laborers were marched to work under the guard of Krupp's policemen wearing smart blue uniforms with a swastika armband. If the workers got out of line on the job, they were savagely beaten with blackjacks. In spite of sending him "entire convoys" of laborers directly from Russia, Speer and Sauckel were unable to supply enough slave laborers to satisfy Alfried Krupp. To get more slaves Krupp decided to organize slave raiding expeditions of his own, with the government's permission. One of Krupp's executives was placed in charge of "labor procurement" and traveled from country to country to round up slave laborers. If they offered any resistance, they were sent back to Essen in leg irons.[9]

With the German Army in retreat in Russia, Hitler ordered that everything of value be taken west with the troops to prevent anything from falling into Soviet hands, hence the Nazis decided to evacuate the entire able-bodied population where retreat was imminent and send them to Germany as slave laborers.[10]

The Nazis even planned to kidnap young boys ages ten to fourteen and send them to Germany to "ease the shortage of apprentices." This they reasoned would also have the added advantage of preventing a reinforcement of the enemy's strength and reducing his "biological potentialities."[11]

The Germans had no sympathy for the people uprooted and kidnapped from their homes. As Himmler said: "Whether ten thousand Russian females fall down from exhaustion when digging an antitank ditch, interests me only insofar as the antitank ditch for Germany is finished."[12] Thus the Nazis freely engaged in the ultimate form of pillage—the trade in human chattel.

By February 1943 the Germans were still retreating and had not yet regained their military equilibrium since the defeat at Stalingrad. On February 15 the S.S. Panzer Corps withdrew from Kharkov in spite of Hitler's orders to hold the city at all costs. Kharkov was the gateway to the Ukrainian industrial area where a number of important factories produced tractors, agricultural machines, and spare parts for tanks. Some of these factories had already been given to Nazi industrialists who were naturally distressed to see them recaptured by the Russians.

Upset by the situation, Hitler flew to the front at Zaporozhye the next day to urge the local army commanders to retake Kharkov. He stayed in Zaporozhye for three days conferring with Field Marshal von Manstein. This was the closest he had ever been to the actual fighting. On the third morning the Russians broke through with a group of tanks and approached the airfield where Hitler's plane was parked. Hitler's pilot, Baur, had to interrupt the conference with General Manstein to urge Hitler to return to the airport at once. Hitler remained calm, finished his discussion with the general, and returned to the airfield just as twenty-two Russian tanks were sighted on the east corner of the field. Curiously, they did not attack but let

Hitler's plane take off unimpeded. It was later learned that the tanks has stopped at the perimeter of the airfield to take up defensive positions because they were out of gas. When Hitler heard this a few days later his only comment was: "Pure luck!"[13]

The Germans managed to retake Kharkov; after that there was a lull in the fighting along the entire front until July. The Germans were planning a new summer offensive at Kursk. In this gamble Hitler was urged on by Field Marshal Keitel, the chief of the General Staff of the army, and Field Marshal von Kluge, the commander of Army Group Center. General Guderian, the inspector of panzer forces, thought the attack was too risky and pleaded with Hitler to call it off.

> After the conference I seized Hitler's hand and asked him if I might be allowed to speak to him. . . . I urged him earnestly to give up the plan for an attack on the Eastern Front. . . . The great commitment would certainly not bring us equivalent gains; our defensive preparations in the west were sure to suffer considerably. I ended with the question: "Why do you want to attack in the east at all this year?" Here Keitel joined in: "We must attack for political reasons." I replied: "How many people do you think even know where Kursk is? It's a matter of profound indifference to the world whether we hold Kursk or not. I repeat my question: "Why do we want to attack in the East at all this year?" Hitler's reply was: "You're quite right. Whenever I think of this attack my stomach turns over."[14]

In the end Hitler decided to go ahead with the attack. On July 5 the Germans struck the Russian salient around Kursk. The Soviets, who had been warned of the attack in advance, were well prepared. Kursk was the greatest tank battle of the war. The German attack was quickly ground to a halt. On one field alone an observer counted over a thousand tanks fighting amid complete confusion. The weather was hot and sultry; the sky was black from burning tanks.

Hitler was very disappointed with the performance of the new German monster tank, the heavier Tiger, on which he was counting to win the battle. They had no machine guns and without light tanks to support them were of little use. Dr. Porsche, one of the industrialists who was a personal friend of Hitler, had sold him on the value of this very heavy tank. When the next tanks failed abysmally, Hitler decided to break off the attack. The Russians remained in possession of the battlefield with its booty of hundreds of disabled but salvageable tanks. The battle of Kursk exhausted Hitler's last reserves. In some respects it was almost as much a disaster as Stalingrad.

One of the men partly responsible for the German defeat at Kursk was Field Marshal Keitel, the chief of the high command of the armed forces and Hitler's closest collaborator in the army. Keitel had the reputation for being a yes-man who rarely opposed Hitler's plans. The advice he gave Hitler to attack at Kursk proved disastrous. But since Keitel was known for his administrative rather than his strategic ability, why did Hitler even listen to him in the first place? "Hitler," said Albert Speer, "gladly sought advice from persons who saw the situation even more optimistically and delusively than he himself. Keitel was often one of those. When the majority of officers would greet Hitler's decisions with marked silence, Keitel would frequently feel called upon to speak up in favor of the measure."[15]

Tall and broad-shouldered with distinguished-looking gray hair and a monocle, the sixty-one-year-old Keitel looked like the perfect field marshal. However, Keitel was often criticized for being Hitler's lackey and nothing but a servile flatterer. On one occasion when Hitler shouted for a pencil, Keitel jumped up to get him one. Other officers thought such behavior undignified for a field marshal. More than once Hitler openly berated Keitel in the presence of others for a minor mistake. This was not just Hitler's temper. He cynically used such tactics to exploit his hold over Keitel. In fact the field marshal was not even an enthusiastic Nazi. Before 1938 he had taken no interest in politics at all.

Field Marshal Keitel had two weaknesses that Hitler was able to exploit. First of all, Keitel was vain and ambitious, and his wife was even more ambitious than he. Secondly, although most people assumed from his appearance and manner that he was a Prussian aristocrat, the truth was he was neither. He was born in Brunswick to a family of modestly well-to-do landowners. Not being a Prussian noble, Keitel would never have been given such a high post in the army if not for Hitler. Even at the peak of his career, Keitel felt insecure as an outsider in the Prussian-dominated Officer Corps.

Ambition alone, however, was not enough to explain Keitel's willingness to obey Hitler's criminal orders. Like a whole generation of German officers who grew up at the turn of the century, Keitel was indoctrinated with extreme German nationalism from childhood on. Such men believed with all sincerity that Germans were superior to all other peoples, who were less than animals. Like the majority of German officers, Keitel didn't need to be a Nazi to agree with Hitler's views on most issues; both shared the common delusion of German superiority and the belief that the state or government was more important than the individual.[16]

Kietel was not a stupid man; he was a hard worker with good organizational and administrative ability. However, his Byzantine flattery of all Hitler's military ideas was helping to lead both of them to disaster. As the number of defeats in Russia mounted, several people tried to urge Hitler to dismiss Keitel. But Hitler refused to part with the field marshal and said he could not do without him because "Keitel is loyal as a dog."

After the German defeat at Kursk the Russians attacked on a broad front toward the Dnieper River. On August 23 they retook Kharkov from the Germans. Farther north the Soviet troops retook Poltavia on September 22 and Smolensk on September 25. The German generals later blamed the defeat in Russia on Hitler's stubborn refusal to permit retreats. After 1943 many generals wanted to pull back to a line along the old Polish-Russian border, which they argued would be easier to defend. Hitler, however, believed if Germany lost its sources of raw materials in Russia, it lost the war. In his adamant refusal to retreat, he was fighting to defend factories and mines.

After the war the generals said they were never allowed to participate in the secret meetings on economic strategy, where the figures on the supply and demand of essential commodities, like oil, wheat, and vital minerals, were presented. This was only partly true. Hitler always emphasized the economic strategy behind his military plans when he argued with the generals.[17]

By November of 1943 the Russian advance threatened Nikopol, the manganese mining center. Extremely worried, Hitler ordered all available troops to defend Nikopol. "Without manganese," he told the generals "the war would be lost in no time." Manganese was one of the principal components of high-strength steels. If Nikopol was lost, Hitler said, armaments production would stop in three months because there were no manganese reserves. General Zeitzler, the chief of the General Staff, tried to convince Hitler that rather than reinforce Nikopol, the time had come to retreat, or else the German troops would be surrounded as they had been at Stalingrad.

Hitler finally agreed to permit retreat from Nikopol but only after Speer conferred with two of the leading steel men, Walter Rohland and Hermann Rochling, who assured him manganese reserves in Germany were sufficient for another year's production. Furthermore, the steel cartel guaranteed Hitler that in case Nikopol was lost the use of other metals as substitutes would enable manganese stocks to be stretched for eighteen months. Fortunately for Hitler the Russian pressure on Nikopol suddenly eased, and the Germans were able to hold it for another four months.[18]

Another situation developed a few months later when economic factors again influenced one of Hitler's military decisions, bringing another conflict with the generals. The advancing Soviets had surrounded the Crimea, and the German forces gradually withdrew to Sevastopol, which Hitler said must be held at all costs. The generals demanded permission to pull out of Sevastopol before they were cut off. Hitler refused on the grounds that the resulting Soviet strength in the Black Sea region might influence Turkey to abandon her neutrality and side with the Allies. Chrome ore from Turkey, Hitler pointed out, was absolutely essential to German armaments production. Furthermore Soviet control of the Crimea would put the Romanian oil fields within range of the Red air force. After the Crimea fell to the Soviets, and a large number of German troops were captured in the process, Hitler's strategic predictions were largely proven correct: the flow of Romanian oil to Germany was disrupted and Turkey was afraid to continue to operate freely as a neutral.[19]

There were many other instances where Hitler refused to let the army retreat because he was trying to hold on to important sources of strategic raw materials. He wanted to wage a major defensive battle to hold the Krivoi Rog mining and industrial region in the Ukraine and was only persuaded by the generals to pull out of the area at the last moment. Later when Finland dropped out of the war and asked German troops to leave Finnish territory, Hitler at first refused. "If the sources of nickel in northern Lapland are lost," he said, "our armaments production will be finished in a few months."[20] Hitler yielded only when Speer assured him that there were sufficient stocks of nickel on hand to continue armament production.

Hitler's stubborn refusal to retreat did not always involve defending sources of raw materials or industrial areas. Several other factors influenced his frequent orders that the troops stand fast. He believed many of his generals were overcautious, if not defeatist, and they usually portrayed the situation at the front as blacker than it really was. Also, from prior examples, he had learned that the enemy often broke its back on a determined hedgehog defense. Finally, he believed retreat undermined the morale of the troops. His attitude was shaped by his experience outside Moscow in the winter of 1941 to 1942 when his order to stand and fight had saved the army from panic. Nevertheless, the generals were correct when they said that Hitler's resistance to allowing limited tactical withdrawals caused many unnecessary losses.

Another factor that influenced Hitler's reluctance to abandon important industrial areas to the Soviets was that many of the factories and mines in these areas had already been given to his financial supporters as rewards. Naturally these Nazi industrialists were not anxious to part with their newly acquired loot.* Their complaints to Hitler, Goering, and Speer had even more weight when they could show that they were producing important war materials in their Russian factories.

---

*Technically Nazi industrialists were usually not given complete ownership of Russian factories, but many were given a sort of trusteeship with a degree of control that was equivalent to temporary ownership. The Nazi government also retained some control over some Russian industries.

If the Germans were forced to retreat at least they would leave nothing behind for the Russians. Hitler ordered a scorched earth policy in all areas lost to the Soviets. As the Red Army advanced on the rich Donets Basin, Himmler said: "Not a human being, not a single head of cattle, not a bushel of crops and not a railway line is to remain behind. Not a house is to remain standing, not a mine is to be available which is not destroyed for years to come and not a well which is not poisoned."[21]

As far as factories were concerned, Nazi industrialists and engineers became experts at dismantling entire plants, machinery and all, and shipping them back to Germany. In agricultural areas German trucks and railroad freight cars lined up outside the grain elevators to take every last stock of wheat with them. The destinations written on the sides of the trains, BERLIN, COLOGNE, FRANKFURT, were an unpleasant reminder to the Russian population who would be left without any food. In one farming region the Germans operated eighty trains a day to transport 400,000 head of cattle out of reach of the approaching Red Army.

On November 6 the Russians recaptured Kiev. Hitler had realized for some time that he could no longer win the war. He knew he could not defeat the Russians, nor drive the Allies out of Italy, nor win the naval conflict in the North Atlantic. His only hope now, as he secretly confided to Field Marshal von Manstein, was to hold on until the Allied coalition broke up. The extreme political differences between communism and capitalism would, he thought, inevitably cause a rift between Russia and the Western powers. Such a grand strategy based on delaying as long as possible made his order to fight for every inch of ground seem more logical.

Sometime after the Soviets recaptured Kiev, Field Marshal von Manstein decided to fly to the Fuehrer's headquarters and urge Hitler to turn over command of the army to a competent general. Only an officer with a military record like Manstein's would have dared to take such action. Having devised the strategic plan that defeated France in 1940 and having captured Sevastopol and the Crimea, Manstein was considered by many to be the most brilliant general in the German Army.

From an old Prussian aristocratic family, Manstein was the descendant of a long line of officers. As a boy he had been schooled in the Prussian Cadet Corps, an institution founded in 1717. There he had been indoctrinated with German national-ism and the principle that an officer's highest duty was to the state. However, Manstein always tried to hold himself above politics. He was never a Nazi, but on the other hand, he refused to join the generals who were involved in the anti-Hitler conspiracy.

Tall and thin, his quiet self-confidence led some people to think Manstein was cold and impersonal, but he was very popular with his troops, who learned to value his discretion and quick grasp of any military situation. Never a desk general, Manstein was always up at the front among his men. Coura-geous on the battlefield, Manstein was not afraid to stand up to Hitler. "At conferences," recalled General Blumentritt, who had been chief of staff of the Fourth Army in Russia, "Manstein often differed from Hitler, in front of others, and would go so far as to declare that some of the ideas which Hitler put forward were nonsense."[22]

On January 4, 1944, Manstein arrived at Hitler's headquarters. He attended the daily situation conference and after it was over asked to see Hitler privately. Reluctantly Hitler gave his consent. As soon as everyone had left the room Manstein asked Hitler if he could speak honestly and openly.

"Please do," Hitler replied, but his voice was icy and distant.

"One thing we must be clear about, Mein Fuehrer," said Manstein, "is that the extremely critical situation we are now in cannot be put down to the enemy's superiority (in numbers) alone, great though it is. It is also due to the way . . . we are led." Manstein recalled:

As I spoke these words, Hitler's expression hardened. He stared at me with the look which made me feel he wished to crush my will to continue. I cannot remember a human gaze ever conveying such willpower. In his otherwise coarse face, the eyes were probably the only attractive and certainly the most expressive feature, and now they were boring into me as if to force me to my knees. At the same moment the notion of an Indian snake charmer flashed through my mind, and I realized that those eyes must have intimidated many a man before me. I still went on talking, however, and told Hitler that things simply could not go on under the present type of leadership.

Manstein then suggested that Hitler appoint a general as commander in chief with full independence within the framework of grand strategy. In practice this amounted to Hitler relinquishing command. As might have been expected he reacted negatively, insisting that only he could decide what forces were available for the different theaters of war and what policies should be pursued on each front.

No other commander would have as much authority as he had, said Hitler. " 'Even I cannot get the Field Marshals to obey me!' he cried. 'Do you imagine, for example, that they would obey you any more readily? If it comes to the worst, I can dismiss them. No one else would have the authority to do that.'

"When I replied that my orders were always carried out," said Manstein, "Hitler made no further comment and brought the meeting to a close."[23] Soon after this meeting Field Marshal von Manstein was relieved of his command.

Hitler's biggest mistake in the Russian campaign was his failure to take advantage of the natural anti-Communist sentiment of the people in the east, particularly in the Ukraine. When the Germans first entered the Ukraine they were welcomed as liberators. If Hitler had abolished the collective farms, permitted private ownership of property, and allowed some measure of national independence, the Ukrainians and even many Russians would have been willing to help fight Stalin. But Hitler was too greedy and narrow-minded. He was afraid that any economic independence would result in fewer goods for the Germans to seize. The fact that economic freedom would have increased productivity and made the subject people good trading partners with the Germans is something he never even considered. His political philosophy did not allow him to regard the Ukrainians or Russians as partners of any kind. He clung obstinately to his quack racial theories in which the Slavs were considered as inferior *Untermenschen* (subhumans) fit only for slave labor.

The military defeats in Russia were responsible for the continued deterioration of Hitler's health. Because he was under constant stress the tremor of his left arm and leg, from which he had suffered after his failed putsch in 1923, now reappeared.

When walking he almost dragged his left foot. His eyes were bloodshot and his face puffy. On March 20, 1943, on his doctor's instruction he took a three-month vacation to Obersalzberg to recover.

Since the beginning of the war in Russia Hitler had been working harder than ever before in his life. In the past he would work hard for short periods of time, such as during an election campaign or a diplomatic crisis like the Munich Conference in 1938, where the fate of Czechoslovakia was decided. As soon as the crisis was over, however, he would lapse back into his Bohemian indolence. A full schedule of hard work day after day was not suited to his temperament.

By the spring of 1943 he was showing all the symptoms of someone burned out from continual stress. He often appeared absentminded and exhausted and had difficulty making decisions. Even when he took a vacation he couldn't get any real rest because the problems of the war followed him wherever he was. When he went to Obersalzberg the entire military staff went with him. When his associates would express concern for his health, Hitler would often say: "It's easy to advise me to take a vacation. But it's impossible. I cannot leave current military decisions to others even for twenty-four hours."[24] In a way there was an ironic justice in this. The man whose evil genius had started the war now could not escape it even for an instant. It dogged his every step.

Hitler's problems were not just limited to the Russian front. In November 1942 American and British troops landed in French North Africa. By May of 1943 the last German and Italian troops in North Africa had surrendered. A month later the Allies landed in Sicily. Within a few weeks Mussolini was overthrown and arrested. A new Italian government was formed under General Badoglio, who was obviously intending to get Italy out of the war.

Hitler was angered by Mussolini's downfall more than he was actually surprised. Responding to this crisis with a decisiveness and energy that he had not shown for months, he immediately ordered German troops in Italy to seize Rome, disarm the Italian army, arrest Badoglio and the king, rescue Mussolini, and reinstall a Fascist government in power. German troops had no difficulty in occupying Rome and disarming most of the Italian

Army, but the king and Badoglio escaped to the Allies. (By this time the Allies had landed in Italy.) No one knew where Mussolini was being held prisoner. There was a strange bond of close personal friendship between Hitler and Mussolini that endured all their reverses. Perhaps because Mussolini helped finance the Nazis in the early days, Hitler never abandoned him despite his obvious weaknesses.

German intelligence finally learned that Mussolini was being held in a resort hotel at Gran Sasso, one of the highest peaks in the Apennines. All approaches to the hotel were heavily guarded by Italian troops and police. Hitler personally chose Colonel Otto Skorzeny, an S.S. commando and paratroop leader, to rescue Mussolini. Going over the plans of the rescue operation, Skorzeny explained to Hitler that his commandos would not be able to use parachutes because of the high altitude and dangerous air currents. The use of gliders seemed to be the only way the S.S. commandos could reach Mussolini.

A few days later on September 11, 1943, twelve tow planes took off from a German-held Italian airfield pulling twelve light wooden gliders behind them swaying in the wind. The gliders carried Skorzeny and 108 crack S.S. commandos. Before long the gliders were over Gran Sasso. The lead plane pulling Skorzeny's glider released the tow rope, and the commandos held to the crossbars as the wind whistled through the frail craft plummeting earthward. The glider pilot tried to slow their descent, but in the high thin mountain air it was difficult. Skorzeny could see the ground rushing up toward them. What had looked like a small landing field from the air turned out to be nothing but a mountainside filled with dangerous boulders. Skorzeny's glider hit the ground then skidded, cracked, and came to a stop badly damaged but with most of the commandos uninjured.

As Skorzeny leaped out of the glider, pistol in hand, he saw the hotel terrace was only fifteen yards away. Mussolini's bald head appeared at a second-floor window. As the German commandos sprinted toward the hotel, Mussolini shouted, "Don't shed blood." Skorzeny shouted back: "Away from the window." The stunned Italian troops put up no resistance as the commandos rushed into the hotel lobby. The guards outside Mussolini's door raised their hands when they saw German commandos with submachine guns coming at them from two directions. Entering the room Skorzeny greeted Mussolini with the Fascist salute and said: "Duce, the Fuehrer sent me! You are free!" Embracing him Mussolini replied, "I knew my friend Adolf Hitler would not leave me in the lurch." After a dangerous takeoff from the mountainside in a small spotter plane, Mussolini and Skorzeny arrived safely in Vienna that night. It had been one of the most daring and dangerous exploits of the war, but henceforth Mussolini would be little more than Hitler's puppet.

Hitler's small triumph in staging the rescue of Mussolini was overshadowed by a disastrous turn in the air war against Germany. On the night of July 25, 1943, the British Air Force began a series of carpet bombing raids on Hamburg using incendiary bombs. A large part of the city was left in ruins. The first raid knocked the city's water pipes out of action so the fire department could not put out the fires in the following raids. A number of large fires burning together at the same time created cyclonelike firestorms. Even the asphalt on the streets started to burn. People were either asphyxiated in their basements or burned alive in the streets. Both residential and industrial areas were gutted.

Even the usually cynical Dr. Goebbels was horror-struck and wrote in his diary:

During the night we had the heaviest raid yet made on Hamburg. The English appeared over the city with 800 to 1,000 bombers.

Kaufmann [the gauleiter of Hamburg] gave me a first hand report on the effect of the British air raid. He spoke of a catastrophe the extent of which simply staggers the imagination. A city of a million inhabitants has been destroyed in a manner unparalleled in history. We are faced with problems that are almost impossible of solution. Food must be found for this population of a million. Shelter must be secured. The people must be evacuated as far as possible. They must be given clothing. In short, we are facing problems there of which we had no conception even a few weeks ago. Kaufmann believes the entire city must be evacuated except for small patches. He spoke of about 800,000 homeless people who are wandering up and down the streets not knowing what to do.[25]

Hitler was furious about the bombing and blamed the British Jews for such tactics. He also cursed Goering and the commanders of the Luftwaffe for failing to prevent such a catastrophe. Speer informed Hitler that a series of air raids of this sort extended to six other major German cities would bring armaments production to a halt. Fortunately for the Germans the British did not continue the Hamburg-type air raids on a systematic basis. Nevertheless, the Hamburg-type air raids marked the beginning of a new phase in the air war. From then on all of Germany's major cities and industries were subjected to regular air raids.

The gauleiters now began sending Hitler hundreds of photographs of bomb-damaged cities and towns in their districts. On one occasion one of Hitler's secretaries had been in Munich during a heavy air raid. When she returned to Obersalzberg she told Hitler: "Mein Fuehrer, all these photos people show you are a long way from reality. You should see the poor people in tears, at the end of their tether, standing in front of their burning houses watching everything they have in the world go up in smoke."

"I know. I know what it's like," he replied, "but it's all going to change. We've got new planes, and there will be an end to this horror very soon."[26]

In fact Hitler was so affected by the night air raids that he was staying up even later than usual, until almost dawn. At about 4:30 A.M. Luftwaffe fighter command would report to him if any enemy planes were still in German air space. He said he simply could not go to sleep knowing enemy bombers were still over Germany.

The massive Allied air raids on German cities damaged Hitler's prestige among the industrialists much in the same way Stalingrad had hurt his prestige in the army. Millions of dollars' worth of damage was being done to factories and industrial plants every night. The average German industrialist now began thinking more about how to get out of the war, rather than how to get more war contracts. Anti-Nazis in the business community were actively looking for ways to overthrow the Nazi government. Even Nazi industrialists began to think about a negotiated peace, at least with the west.

Goering's prestige with Hitler and the public declined every time there was a massive air raid on another German city. A serious drug addiction and an escapist mentality led Goering to partially withdraw from military affairs into an artificial world of his looted art treasures and luxuries. Many of the Nazi industrialists who had formerly been Goering's patrons switched their backing and contributions to Himmler and Speer. In the economic sphere the energetic Speer completely eclipsed Goering to become Germany's economic dictator. Gaining Hitler's complete confidence, Speer worked miracles in increasing Germany's arms production, in spite of the bombings, right up to the end of the war. In April 1943, Field Marshal Milch of the Luftwaffe had made a prophetic remark about the damage the Allied air raids could do if they selected the right targets: "The synthetic oil plants are the worst possible place they could hit us. With them stands or falls our very ability to fight this war. After all, if the synthetic fuel plants are effectively attacked, not only our aircraft but the tanks and submarines will also come to a standstill."[27]

Oil production had always been critical to the German war effort. Hitler had initially believed that he could not continue the war with Britain unless he was able to seize the Russian oil fields. In this he failed. In fact the Germans were consuming tremendous quantities of petrol in the Russian campaign, yet they managed to get by. The reason was the dramatic increase in synthetic gasoline production. In 1941 the Germans got about eighty thousand barrels of oil a day from Romania and produced approximately sixty-five thousand barrels of synthetic fuel a day in Germany. By 1943 Romania was supplying Germany with only sixty thousand barrels a day.[28]

The German synthetic oil plants had been able to increase production to such an extent because they had suffered very little from Allied air raids. It has remained one of the great mysteries of the war why the Allies did not bomb the German synthetic oil factories sooner. The Allied commanders were certainly aware of their locations and their strategic significance. Perhaps the answer to this mystery was given by Heinrich Buetefisch, one of the directors of I.G. Farben, when he said:

"There was a gentlemen's agreement between heavy industry in Germany and abroad that I.G.'s synthetic gasoline plants would not be bombed."[29]

In light of Germany's tremendous increase in synthetic oil production another question naturally arises: could the increase in synthetic production have been predicted in advance thereby eliminating the need for the invasion of Russia? Hitler believed he couldn't continue the war with Britain without Russian oil. However, he also needed grain, meat, and other food crops from Russia to feed the German people. Nevertheless, the people who were supplying him with the figures and projections on oil production were the same people who would have become immensely wealthy from a Nazi monopoly of Russian oil resources. It is possible that some German "oil experts" may have deliberately supplied Hitler with figures that minimized synthetic production in order to encourage him to invade Russia so they could get the oil.

The special exemption from bombing that Farben's synthetic fuel plants enjoyed came to an end on May 12, 1944. On that day two hundred bombers of the U.S. Eighth Air Force bombed Farben's Leuna synthetic fuel plant. The next day Speer and Buetefisch climbed through the pile of rubble and twisted pipes that had once been one of Germany's greatest chemical plants. Even the most optimistic forecasters did not expect a return to production for several weeks. Since other synthetic fuel plants all over Germany had also been bombed on May 12, German production of aircraft fuel dropped from 5,800 metric tons a day to 4,800 metric tons a day.

A few days later Speer flew to Obersalzberg. "The enemy has struck us at one of our weakest points," he told Hitler. "If they persist this time, we will soon not have any fuel production worth mentioning."[30] Goering, Keitel, and four of the most important industrialists of the fuel industry, Krauch, Pleiger, Buetefisch, and Fischer, also were present at the meeting. Although Goering had warned the industrialists before the meeting not to say anything "too pessimistic," they openly agreed with Speer's opinion. They all said that if the bombing continued on the synthetic fuel plants the situation would be hopeless.

Hitler, who was notorious for trying to ignore unpleasant

facts, seemed particularly objective that day. He summed up the meeting saying: "In my view the fuel, Buna [synthetic] rubber, and nitrogen plants represent a particularly sensitive point for the conduct of the war, since vital materials for armaments are being manufactured in a small number of plants." Speer said that although Hitler had seemed "torpid and absentminded" at the beginning of the conference, his evaluation of the situation "left the impression of a sober, intense man of keen insight."[31] But since it would take too long to build new synthetic fuel plants, the only solution Hitler and Speer could find was to pull thousands of skilled workers off other jobs and assign them to repairing the damaged plants and to give the fuel plants better fighter and antiaircraft protection.

The shortage of fuel was already severely affecting the Luft-waffe. New pilots were poorly trained because they had only enough fuel to practice for one hour each week. More important, fighter groups were often grounded for lack of fuel when they should have been in combat. The army was also partially immobilized by the fuel shortage.[32] New tank drivers were receiving little practical training.

The German fuel shortage had a decisive effect on the next major battle of the war. On June 6, 1944, the Allies landed in Normandy. The invasion began about 4 A.M. When the German commander on the scene requested reinforcements, he was told no decision could be made until later in the day when Hitler woke up. Hitler had always said the Allies would probably begin with a feigned landing to draw troops away from the real invasion site. The offices of Hitler's staff were thus hesitant to awaken him if the landing was not the real thing. By the time Hitler got up, had breakfast, and received the news, thousands of American and British troops had already landed on the beaches. Hitler was in good spirits and seemed to welcome the prospect of a decisive battle at last. "So this is it!" he said.

Hitler had originally thought the Allies would land in Normandy, but the generals had argued that the Pas de Calais area, where the English Channel was the narrowest, would be the most likely invasion site. Hitler remained calm and confident throughout the day on June 6, but the confusion as to whether or not this was the real invasion delayed the commitment of the German reserves until it was too late. The biggest problem facing the Germans at Normandy was that the fuel shortage caused the Luftwaffe to be almost completely absent from the sky.[33] With complete air superiority the Americans and British subjected the Germans to relentless bombing. Because of constant air attacks the Germans were unable to bring reinforcements up to the beaches.

Just how much German mobility was impeded by the lack of fuel and the Allied air attacks on the roads was perfectly illustrated in the later phase of the battle of Normandy, when a horse-drawn German supply column was caught on the road north of Avranche carrying ammunition and artillery. Allied fighters swooped down out of the sky to strafe the column. The Germans tried to take cover but weren't fast enough. After the attack the road was jammed for three hundred yards with wrecked wagons, smashed artillery pieces, and dead horses. Not all the horses were killed; the living ones were terrified, struggling in their harnesses, creating further confusion.

In spite of the odds against them the Germans stubbornly held their ground and contained the Allies in the coastal area of Normandy. Refusing to permit any retreats Hitler said: "If the invasion is not repulsed, we will lose the war." As the Allied forces built up within the beachhead area, a breakout became inevitable. To convince Hitler of the seriousness of the situation, Field Marshals Rundstedt and Rommel, the commanders in France, urgently requested that Hitler come to the front to see the situation himself.

On June 17 Hitler met Rundstedt and Rommel in France near Soissons. He sat hunched on a stool in front of a large map table while the two field marshals stood on either side of him explaining the military situation. Looking pale and exhausted from lack of sleep, Hitler nervously played with some colored pencils as Rommel gave examples of the enormous enemy superiority. He said there was only one chance: regroup all armored forces in Normandy and try to draw the Allies into a trap beyond the range of their naval guns. Hitler refused to authorize this plan because it would mean retreating from the coastal area, and he was determined to fight for every inch of ground.

Rommel and Rundstedt then stressed that it was impossible to win on the ground without any support from the air. Seeming to evade the issue of the Luftwaffe's almost complete absence from the battle area, Hitler spoke about the new rockets and jet planes he would soon have to drive the enemy from the skies. Appropriately an Allied air raid interrupted the conference temporarily until everyone could take shelter in an underground concrete bunker.

With Allied planes overhead, Rommel took the opportunity to confront Hitler with the reality of the situation. The front in Normandy would soon collapse, he said, and there was nothing to stop the Allies until they reached Germany. Rommel also predicted that the Russians would soon break through on the eastern front. Hitler listened in silence with compressed lips. Finally Rommel suggested it was necessary to end the war.

Shaking with anger Hitler responded: "Herr Field Marshall it is not your job to worry about the future course of the war. It would be better if you concerned yourself with your invasion front."

Rommel and many of the other generals were openly criticizing Hitler for his suicidal refusal to withdraw in Normandy. However, Hitler sincerely believed that he only had to hold on a little longer and the tide would turn in his favor. He was not just evading the issue when he switched the discussion from the lack of air support to the new rocket weapons. The V-1's were ready to be launched against London. Hitler thought they would be decisive and force the British to sue for peace. They were certainly a revolutionary new technology, so it was logical for Hitler to assume they would be effective. Fortunately for the Allies, when the V-1's were launched against London on June 10, the results were disappointing for the Germans.

While at Soissons, when Hitler dined with Rundstedt and Rommel, he had his food tasted by his S.S. bodyguards, two of whom stood behind his chair throughout the meal. The precautions were not unnecessary, because Rommel was thinking of trying to arrest Hitler. This element of suspicion and hostility that existed between the head of state and the commanding generals was no way to conduct a war. In the Normandy campaign alone the Germans lost many opportunities because of this schism in the leadership.

The Germans would continue to fight well in Normandy, but the Allied breakout was inevitable. Germany's lack of fuel was the decisive factor. If the Luftwaffe had been able to put up even half as many planes as the Allies, D-Day might have ended in disaster. (The ratio of Allied planes to those of the Luftwaffe over Normandy was about twenty to one.) With adequate fuel and at least moderate air cover, the Germans could have brought up their panzer reserves early, hit the Allies before they had enough men ashore, and driven them back into the sea. The prediction Hitler made when he said if he didn't get the oil of Russia he would lose the war turned out to be correct.

If the Germans were to be pushed out of France they certainly would not leave empty-handed. Since 1940 they had been looting the great art treasures of France. The story of the looting of French art is told, not for its impact on the war, which was very little, but for what it reveals about the character or rather the lack of character of Hitler, Goering, and the Nazi leadership. The looting of valuable artworks began as soon as the Germans conquered France.

In 1940 Hitler set up a special organization under Alfred Rosenberg to seize important artworks, especially those belonging to Jews. A few of the usually "proper" officers of the German army even played a prominent part in this pillage. Field Marshal Keitel issued an order to the army in France saying that Rosenberg "is entitled to transport to Germany art works which appear valuable to him and to safeguard them there. The Fuehrer has reserved for himself the decision as to their use."[34]

The first victims of Nazi looting were Jews who had fled at the time of the German invasion. Agents of the Gestapo simply entered "abandoned" Jewish homes and seized any paintings or valuable works of art.[35] The Nazis were aided by a number of French collaborators and shadowy middlemen of the art world who were only too eager to curry favor with the conquerors by providing lists of wealthy Jewish art collectors and their addresses.[36] The paintings stolen from the Jews were stored in the Louvre and the nearby Jeu de Paume museum until Hitler's art dealers and Goering had a chance to inspect them and select what they wanted.

When Hitler's art dealer, Haberstock, came to Paris, he arrived in style and stayed at the Ritz Hotel. He would purchase numerous paintings for Hitler on the Paris art market. These dealings were ostensibly legitimate, but the artificially low exchange rate between the French franc and the German mark made them a steal.

Hitler was also informed in detail, by some of his less reputable agents, about paintings seized from Jews. The ones he was interested in seeing were shipped directly to Munich. Whenever Hitler left his headquarters in East Prussia to vacation at Obersalzberg, one of the first places he would visit was the Fuherbau in Munich, where he would sit in a high-backed red leather chair flanked by his cronies as the recently confiscated and "purchased" paintings were presented to him one by one.

Hitler made some effort to cloak his art acquisitions in legitimacy, usually by paying a token purchase price to the French Vichy government. On one occasion he reluctantly refused the famous portrait of Madame de Pompadour by Boucher that Rosenberg had "given" him as a "present." Aware that the painting had been taken from the Louvre, Hitler had sense enough to realize that it was too well known to simply steal. However, Hitler was not so cautious when it came to lesser known works.

Hitler's agents extended their hunt for paintings into unoccupied France. There they learned of a valuable collection of paintings belonging to the wealthy Jewish Schloss family. Hitler was very interested in the collection, which contained a number of Dutch old master paintings, but instead of purchasing the paintings, he instructed the Gestapo to pressure the Vichy police to find some pretext to arrest the Schloss family and confiscate the paintings. Once this was accomplished it was relatively easy for Hitler to get the collection from the Vichy government for a nominal sum.[37]

In his own mind Hitler justified his theft of Jewish-owned paintings with an elaborate artistic conspiracy theory. He believed a Jewish conspiracy was concocted sometime after the end of World War I to get a monopoly on the great paintings of Europe. Central to this plot, said Hitler, were "phony Jewish art critics" who heaped praise on "worthless" modern art. They encouraged non-Jews to buy "worthless rubbish" with tactics like having one Jew bid against another to drive up the price.

At the same time Jewish art collectors were supposedly quietly buying up old master paintings that were "out of favor" with the art critics. Concluding his explanation of this "conspiracy,"

Hitler announced triumphantly: "We now have proof of it, thanks to the seizure of Jewish property. With the money they fraudulently acquired by selling trash [modern art], the Jews were able to buy at wretched prices the works of value they have so cleverly depreciated. Every time an inventory catches my eye of a requisition carried out on an important Jew, I see that genuine artistic treasures are listed there."[38]

It is amazing that Hitler, who actually had some knowledge of the art world, could believe such a ridiculous theory. To suggest that hundreds of art critics and collectors with diverse interests would join together in a massive intrigue just because they were Jewish is a perfect example of how all-pervasive anti-Semitism becomes in the mind of the true believer.

Less than a year after the beginning of the occupation of France the Nazis began transporting some of their stolen loot back to Germany. Rosenberg reported to Hitler that twenty-five railroad cars loaded with paintings and works of art had arrived in Bavaria. "These confiscations," wrote Rosenberg "are in accordance, my Fuehrer, with your orders of October 1940 from Paris. With the assistance of the . . . Secret Police we have systematically located the hideouts of art objects belonging to Jewish owners."[39] It took several weeks to unload and display the trainloads of artworks, the best of which were divided up between Hitler and Goering.

Actually Goering got almost as many of the looted French paintings as Hitler. For weeks at a time the reich marshall would stay in Paris in a large apartment at the Ritz Hotel that was permanently reserved for him. He also had a splendid office at the Quai d'Orsay with high ceilings, large mirrors, and priceless antique furniture. It had formerly been the office of Premier Poincaré. On Goering's desk was an elaborate inkstand that had belonged to Talleyrand. Goering would sit in this office so rich in French history checking off paintings in the catalogues of French museums that aroused his "collector's passion."

Goering frequently visited the Jeu de Paume museum to view the paintings confiscated from the wealthy French Jewish families like the Rothschilds. He would sip on a glass of champagne as he decided which paintings he was going to take back to Germany with him for his home at Karinhall. However, Goering did not simply sit back and wait for others to steal paintings for him. On the contrary, he exhibited considerable energy in tracking down paintings he wanted to seize. Gradually he pushed Rosenberg aside.[40] The handling and transportation of looted paintings became the job of Luftwaffe personnel.[41] Goering also employed a number of French informers and detectives to find paintings for him that had been hidden by their Jewish owners. Although, like Hitler, Goering tried to maintain the illusion that he paid for all his paintings, this was simply not true. At least seven hundred of the major paintings Goering acquired by famous artists, like Fragonard and Boucher, were from confiscated Jewish collections.[42]

It is difficult to determine the exact value of French art treasures stolen by the Germans. After the first six months of the German occupation Alfred Rosenberg stated that the artworks seized in France were worth about one billion marks.[43] They would be worth several billion dollars today. During the next four years the Nazis confiscated thousands of additional paintings and artworks. By 1944 Rosenberg's special staff for pictorial art reported that the seized art treasures were so valuable they were priceless: "The extraordinary artistic and material value of the seized artworks cannot be expressed in figures. The paintings, period furniture of the 17th and 18th centuries, the Gobelins [tapestries], the antiques and Renaissance jewelry of the Rothschilds are objects of such a unique character that their evaluation is impossible, since no comparable values have ever appeared on the art market. A short report, moreover, can only hint at the artistic worth of the collection."

Among the confiscated paintings, according to the report, were several hundred first quality masterpieces of European art that would be considered the most valuable works in any museum. Included in this category were authenticated works of Rembrandt, Rubens, Hals, Vermeer, Velázquez, and Goya. The report also stated that there were five other priceless collections of artworks among the seized treasures.

There was a collection of works by famous French painters of the eighteenth century including paintings of Boucher, Watteau, Fragonard, and Rigaud. "This collection," stated the report, "can compare with those of the best European museums." A collection of Dutch masterpieces of the seventeenth and eighteenth centuries included works of Van Dyck, Ruisdael, Wouwerman, and de Hooch. There was even a collection of English paintings of the eighteenth and early nineteenth centuries with masterpieces by Reynolds, Romney, and Gainsborough.

The collection of French furniture of the seventeenth and eighteenth centuries, said the report, contained hundreds of the best preserved and signed works of the most famous cabinetmakers of the period between Louis XIV and Louis XVI. The collection of Gobelins and Persian tapestries also contained many pieces that were world famous. The report concluded by mentioning the collection of Renaissance jewelry confiscated from the Rothschild family, which it said was "valuable beyond comparison."[44]

Photographs of all the confiscated artworks were compiled into thirty-nine volumes bound in dark blue leather trimmed with gold leaf. Hitler loved to spend hours looking through these volumes of his newly "acquired" treasures. In addition to all his other titles Hitler truly deserved to be called "the greatest art thief of all time."

In a regime so morally corrupt that the head of state and the number two man in the government were both art thieves it is hardly surprising that some ordinary German officers were also involved in pillaging artworks. Over one thousand lesser paintings, tapestries, and antiques from the confiscated Jewish collections were "sold" to German army and Luftwaffe officers. Some people were surprised Hitler did not steal paintings out of the major French museums. He refrained, but only because he was planning to demand these paintings as part of any permanent peace settlement with the French. But by July of 1944 it looked as if France would soon be liberated. The time and energy Hitler and Goering had spent stealing artworks should have been devoted to preparing for the Allied invasion.

Chapter 13

Who Profited from the Holocaust?

Eight hundred naked people marched along together —young and old, men and women, mothers with young children, the sick and infirm, even a one-legged man whose artificial limb had already been stolen by the Nazis. All marched Hitler's death march. They walked along between high barbed wire fences guarded by about twenty-five Ukrainians with leveled rifles. As they walked, many of the people tried to cover themselves with their hands out of modesty. Others were too weak and exhausted to care. A sign pointed the way to their destination: TO THE BATHS AND INHALANTS. Ahead was a building that looked like a large bathhouse. There were even concrete pots of geraniums and other colorful flowers outside. Above the building was a Star of David. As they approached the entrance a husky S.S. man with the voice of a preacher told the people: "Nothing is going to harm you! Just breathe deeply and it will strengthen your lungs. It will help prevent contagious diseases."

A few of the frightened people asked what was going to happen to them. The S.S. man always answered reassuringly: "The men will have to work building houses and streets. But the women won't have to, they can work in the house and kitchen."[1] Some people sensed what was about to take place, but the majority went quietly. One after another they entered the huge semidark chamber smelling of the foul odor of death. By the time five hundred or so people were inside the chamber it seemed full, but then uniformed S.S. men and their helpers began pushing and shoving more people inside. They were determined to pack in hundreds more. The people were ordered to lift their arms above their heads so there would be room for more. The crush was horrifying but the worst was yet to come. "Fill it up," the S.S. commander shouted to his men. Finally when the last person was squeezed inside, the large heavy doors were closed. This was the gas chamber at Belzec. This was Hitler's "final solution" to the Jewish question.

The marching of naked people to the gas chamber was only one aspect of the Holocaust, the final scene of the tragedy. Some extermination camps had the dual purpose of extermination and slave labor. While extermination meant death, slave labor meant enormous profits. Profits for the Nazis of course, not for the Jewish victims. Nazi businessmen like Alfried Krupp, the steel tycoon, helped Hitler and Himmler carry out the Holocaust. By using Jews as slave labor they reaped triple profits from saving on labor costs. The big Nazi tycoons and Hitler were, however, not the only ones involved; many German companies used Jewish slave labor.

The S.S. was in charge of the Jewish concentration camp slave laborers and treated them worse than animals. Jews were subject to beatings, exposure to the cold, disease, filthy and unsanitary living conditions, and worst of all starvation. The starvation was part of a deliberately planned "extermination through work." The Nazis concluded that the Jewish workers could live on body fat for three months. Once the Jews were too weak to work they would be marched naked to the gas chamber.

Nevertheless, Jews were no longer being shot at the edges of ditches in Russia. They now were transported to extermination camps like Auschwitz, Chelmno, and Belzec. This change in Hitler's method of killing Jews was caused by the fortunes of war.

The failure of Hitler's great attack on Moscow in December 1941 and the Russian counterattack that followed marked the first significant change in the fate of Germany. Up to that time Hitler had won one triumph after another. Germany's defeat was not yet assured in the beginning of 1942, but at least now the war could go either way.

The strategic and economic conditions of the war had suddenly changed. First of all there was the military situation: it would now be a longer war than Hitler had originally anticipated. More troops would be needed for Germany to have any hope of conquering Russia, and the only way the army could get more troops was by drafting workers in essential war industries. Yet at the same time Germany needed to increase war production to replace the heavy losses of tanks, trucks, and guns in Russia. This was the dilemma: how to draft more German workers and at the same time increase production?

The obvious solution to Hitler's mind was to employ more slave labor; however, with no new territories being conquered a steady supply of slave labor would now be more difficult to obtain.

During the first months of the war with Russia, when the Germans thought they would win a quick victory, they had tried to kill as many Jews as possible and let the Russian prisoners of war die like flies. Now this was seen as a wasteful mistake, as even Himmler, the commander of the S.S., admitted. In a speech to S.S. officers he explained how such a mistake occurred: "The Russian Army was herded together in great pockets, ground down, taken prisoner. At that time, we did not value the mass of humanity as we value it today, as raw material, as labor. After all, thinking in terms of generations, this is not to be regretted, but what is now deplorable by reason of loss of labor, is that prisoners died in tens and hundreds of thousands of exhaustion and hunger."[2]

From 1942 on there were to be two aspects of Hitler's "final solution to the Jewish question": slave labor and extermination. The man Hitler put in charge of both was Heinrich Himmler, chief of the S.S. Himmler looked more like a schoolteacher than a butcher and mass murderer. He was a slender, narrow-shouldered man. His pince-nez, thin lips, and receding chin gave an impression of weakness rather than brutality. One woman who met him for the first time said even in his black S.S. uniform he seemed more like a lower middle-class government clerk than a brutal monster.

321

To Albert Speer, Himmler "displayed a friendly courtesy that seemed slightly forced."[3] He was willing to listen to other people's arguments, which was a quality rare among top Nazi leaders. In conversation, however, he gave the impression of being petty, pedantic, and not very intelligent.

Himmler made himself indispensable to Hitler by his thoroughness, absolute obedience, and willingness to undertake any task no matter how unsavory. Unlike the generals and industrialists, who sometimes made things difficult for Hitler, Himmler from the beginning followed the basic principle of never contradicting the Fuehrer. To him no plan proposed by Hitler was too impractical or too difficult. In short he was the ideal yes-man. Hitler did not realize at first that it was often Heydrich, head of the intelligence division of the S.S., not Himmler, the S.S. commander, who achieved the impossible. After Heydrich's death the power of the S.S. had become so great that Himmler's position was secure.

Himmler's anti-Semitism was theoretical rather than emotional. He was never a hothead like Julius Streicher, the gauleiter of Nuremberg.* Himmler thought the Jews were responsible for most of the corruptions of the modern world. He wanted to take Germany back to the medieval era of honest simple peasants and heroic knights. He was also concerned with breeding a "pure" Aryan race, much as if he was trying to develop a new breed of cattle. Because of its mystical and pseudoscientific overtones, Himmler's racism at first seemed more ridiculous than dangerous. But Himmler was a cold, sober fanatic willing to order mass murders in the name of racial purity.

The only unpleasant personal experience Himmler was known to have had with Jews was in 1918 and 1919 during the Communist revolution in Germany. Like Hitler and many other Nazis he blamed the Jews for the loss of the war, saying the "Jewish revolutionaries" had "stabbed Germany in the back." This theme was again brought up by Himmler during the war as an excuse for the "final solution." In 1943 he told an audience of S.S. generals: "We know how difficult we should have made it for ourselves if with the bombing raids, the burdens and

---

*Streicher was dismissed from his post of gauleiter in 1940 for corruption.

deprivations of war, we still had the Jews today in every town as secret saboteurs, agitators, and trouble mongers; we would now probably have reached the 1916 to 1917 stage."[4]

Himmler was responsible for organizing the "final solution," but it was Hitler who gave the orders. During a series of secret private conferences, Hitler ordered Himmler to liquidate the Jews. No record of these conferences has survived. The only other person who was occasionally present was Bormann, Hitler's private secretary. Himmler later referred to the extermination of the Jews as a "Fuehrer order" and said it was the most difficult task ever assigned the S.S.

The idea of profiting from the "final solution" by using the Jews as slave labor did not originate with Himmler either but was proposed by Hitler. He apparently developed the plan of using Jewish slave labor and building factories at the concentration camps in a series of private conversations with top Nazi industrialists. Only later did these Nazi tycoons work out the details of the arrangement with Himmler.

By the spring of 1942 the munitions industrialists were demanding more workers if production was to be increased. Although many German businessmen were reluctant to use slave labor, others saw it as a chance to cut costs dramatically. An obvious source of additional slave labor was the Jews. Many of the top Nazis were aware that Jews were being "liquidated" in Russia. Why not use them as slave labor instead?

Hitler liked the idea; he could thus accomplish two objectives at once: get more slave labor and at the same time continue with his long-range plan of exterminating the Jews. There was a minor problem with Himmler, who wanted to set up his own factories to utilize concentration camp slave labor. But several Nazi tycoons used their influence with Hitler to force Himmler to compromise. The Nazi industrialists agreed to pay the S.S. four marks a day per slave laborer.

Hitler approved of the new plan, although he was still as determined as ever to exterminate the Jews. Actually slave labor would be a temporary reprieve for only 25 percent of the Jews, those fit for hard labor. The other 75 percent, old people, the frail, the sick, many women and children, would be killed immediately.

Hitler needed a more sophisticated process of killing than the mass liquidations the S.S. Action Groups had been performing. Careful selection would have to be made to determine who was fit for slave labor and who would be condemned to death immediately. This selection process could hardly be performed in the field; furthermore, in Western Europe those Jews unfit to work could not simply be shot and pushed in a ditch. The Jews would have to be transported to special killing centers in remote locations in Poland where the selection process could be made. The existing concentration camp system would be inadequate for this immense task and would have to be greatly expanded.

The Nazis decided to set up a vast industrial empire based on the slave labor of concentration camp inmates. Pro-Nazi private industrialists were to set up factories at the concentration camps or just outside the camp gates. Other money-making enterprises were to be operated by the S.S. themselves. The center of the Nazi slave labor empire was to be the concentration camp at Auschwitz.

As soon as the plan was approved by Hitler, Himmler immediately ordered Rudolf Hoess, the commandant of Auschwitz, to prepare for a rapid expansion of the camp, which would also require facilities to exterminate two million people. Hoess, a fanatical S.S. man, was not surprised and asked no questions. Himmler had arrived at the figure of two million because Nazi economic experts had told Hitler that they would need about 500,000 slave laborers for the factories at Auschwitz, and as mentioned earlier only 25 percent of the Jews would be fit for hard labor, so the remaining 75 percent would be exterminated immediately.

Auschwitz became a vast institution as large as a modern city. At the peak of its size in 1944 it imprisoned over 100,000 men and women, not including the approximately 12,000 people killed every day. Auschwitz and its sister camp, Birkenau, occupied over eight square miles all surrounded by electrified barbed wire. Auschwitz was primarily the industrial center with factories of Farben, Krupp, and others. Birkenau was the killing center with gas chambers and ovens. The two halves of the dual camp sat on opposite sides of the railway line. The whole Auschwitz camp complex was surrounded by watchtowers for the S.S. guards; at night searchlights swept continuously back and forth along the barbed wire fence to prevent any escapes.

I.G. Farben was the largest private industry at Auschwitz.* They invested heavily in the two factories they built at the camp. The synthetic gasoline and rubber plants when completed would cost over $250 million and would produce 700,000 tons of oil per month and 30,000 tons of rubber per year. Once Farben's plans were ready Goering ordered an increase in the size of the Auschwitz concentration camp so they would have enough slave laborers to begin construction. Goering wrote Himmler in February 1941 requesting that "the largest possible number of skilled and unskilled construction workers . . . be made available from the adjoining concentration camp for the construction of the Buna [synthetic rubber] plant."[5]

In March of 1942 Himmler visited Auschwitz to inspect the Farben construction site. He promised Farben an additional ten thousand slave laborers immediately. After Himmler's visit, Ambros, the managing director of Farben's Auschwitz rubber factory, wrote: "our new friendship with the S.S. is proving very profitable."[6] Profitable for Farben because they were getting workers for practically nothing. Because of the need for slave labor hundreds of thousands of Jews from Poland, Russia, Germany, and western Europe were shipped to Auschwitz.

If the industrialists had refused to build their factories at Auschwitz millions of Jews probably would not have died there. True, the Nazis would most likely have killed the Jews somewhere else if the factories had not been at Auschwitz. However because Auschwitz became the largest concentration camp with more industry than any other camp, it offered the Nazis incentives for profit from the Holocaust that would not have been as great at another location. With less profit motive the enthusiasm for shipping Jews hundreds of miles to kill them would not have been as great.

Just how the S.S. sold Jewish slaves to German companies

---

*I.G. Farben was one of the largest companies in the world. Only a very few Farben executives were involved in the Auschwitz plant. Those responsible for crimes at Auschwitz were sentenced at Nuremberg. The vast majority of people who worked for Farben were not involved in any war crimes.

with factories at Auschwitz was explained by Rudolf Hoess, the camp commandant. Hoess said:

Until December 1, 1943, one of my official functions was to inspect the use as labor of concentration camp prisoners from the Auschwitz camp and subsequently to inspect the use as labor of prisoners from all German concentration camps. . . . According to my knowledge, the large scale use of concentration camp prisoners in the German private industry began in 1940/41. This utilization increased constantly until the end of the war.

Towards the end of 1944, there were approximately 400,000 concentration camp prisoners used in the private armament industry and in establishments essential for armament purposes. . . . According to my estimate, in enterprises with particularly severe working conditions—for instance, in mines—every month one-fifth died or were, because of inability to work, sent back by the enterprises to the camps in order to be exterminated.

The concentration camps have at no time offered labor to the industry. On the contrary, prisoners were sent to enterprises only after the enterprises had made a request for concentration camp prisoners. In their letters of request the enterprises had to state in detail which measures had been taken by them, even before the arrival of the prisoners, to guard them, to quarter them, etc. I visited officially many such establishments to verify such statements and this was always before the inmates would be sent. The enterprises did not have to submit reports on causes of death, etc. On the basis of reports which we received in the camps from the S.S. guard personnel . . . the number of deaths and of persons unable to work was communicated, and on that basis new prisoners were continuously sent out to the respective enterprises for replenishing.

During my official trips I was constantly told by executives of the enterprises that they want more prisoners. In the beginning of the war the enterprises paid little for this labor, perhaps Mk. 1.–Mk. 1.20. Later on, they paid up to Mk. 5.00 for skilled workers. Among the prisoners sent out to be used as labor, there were

1. non-Jewish prisoners who were selected by reason of their professional training, and
2. Jews who were selected merely because of their ability to work.

The age of the prisoners utilized for labor ranged from approximately 13 years upwards. Prisoners over 50 years were but rarely utilized for labor—when they were particularly strong or were trained along special lines—otherwise they were exterminated at once. Prisoners utilized for labor who every evening returned from the plant to the concentration camp had to work in the concentration camp on the same evening whenever collective or individual punishment to this effect had been imposed. Such additional collective or individual penal labor would be imposed because of minor offenses against the discipline, for instance, not saluting according to regulations. In such cases the prisoners had to work as long as daylight would permit, in the summer for two to three hours. In addition, the other customary punishments were imposed.[7]

However, the work on the great Farben factories at Auschwitz soon fell behind schedule. Because the Farben plants were located almost four miles from the main concentration camp, the slave laborers had to be marched back and forth each day. For security reasons they could only make this journey in daylight. This severely cut down on the workday especially in the winter. After several attempted escapes on foggy mornings, the S.S. decided the prisoners would have to wait at the main camp until the fog cleared before being marched to work.

The S.S. originally intended to work the Jewish slave laborers at least eleven hours a day. The Farben executives in charge of the Auschwitz plants were so disappointed with the situation that they decided to build a concentration camp of their own adjacent to their factories. The Nazis immediately approved the Farben decision, and construction began at once. When completed Farben's camp, called I.G. Monowitz, looked like any other Nazi concentration camp with barbed wire fences, watchtowers, searchlights, and armed S.S. guards.

Almost from the beginning Monowitz was severely overcrowded. Barracks that were intended to house five thousand prisoners regularly held twenty thousand. The prisoners slept in lice-infested three-tiered wooden cubicles or bunks. Each cubicle, barely large enough for one man, often held three. Sanitary facilities were totally inadequate for the number of prisoners.

Like most other Nazi concentration camps, the worst torture inflicted on the prisoners at Monowitz was the starvation diet. By the end of the third month they were hardly recognizable as the same people. The S.S. was responsible for feeding the prisoners. However, Farben did at its own expense provide their slave laborers soup at noon.

In the morning the S.S. labor allocation officer from Auschwitz came to Monowitz and stood outside the gate as the squads of slave laborers left for work. Any prisoner who limped or looked too weak was "selected" and sent directly to the gas chamber.

The very short life span of Jewish slave laborers at Monowitz is clearly illustrated in the account of Kai Feinberg, who arrived at Monowitz with his family on December 24, 1942. Feinberg and his father were immediately put to work unloading iron bars and sacks of cement from wagons. They were not given any food or allowed to rest until three o'clock in the morning. "On January 5, 1943," recalled Feinberg, "my father was so weakened that he collapsed before my eyes while having to haul along a 50-kilo sack of cement at a running pace. I wanted to help him but was hit and beaten back by an S.S. man with a stick. . . . One of my father's brothers injured himself in the arm while at work and was gassed. My father's second brother died from weakness while at work in Buna [the Farben rubber factory] one or two weeks after the death of my father."

Feinberg worked until January 15 when he contracted pneumonia. He managed to survive at the camp working on and off until the end of February. he was then declared "unfit" to work and "selected" to be gassed. Luckily the truck going to the gas chamber did not come to the Monowitz rubber factory that day, and Feinberg was sent back to the Auschwitz regular camp. Somehow he was able to stay alive until the end of the war.[8]

Many slave laborers at Auschwitz and other concentration camps worked in factories owned and operated by the S.S. As early as 1933 Himmler began building an S.S. business empire. He started modestly enough with a publishing house for S.S. propaganda literature. As the concentration camps began to fill Himmler realized he had at his command a great pool of slave labor. The first real concentration camp factory was the porcelain factory at Dachau. Half of the production was sold for profit and half was sold to high-ranking S.S. men at a 40 percent discount.

S.S. business enterprises based on slave labor rapidly expanded. Soon the S.S. controlled one of the largest construction and building materials firms in Germany. The need for gravel, stone, and brick was enormous in wartime Germany. Himmler decided to try to gain a monopoly in the field. The location of many concentration camps was determined by the proximity to suitable quarry sites. At Auschwitz, Oranienburg, Neuengamme, Stutthof, and Treblinka the S.S. operated large brick factories. The work done in the quarries and brick factories was performed mostly by unskilled slave laborers. However, the S.S. also operated an agency as a business that hired out skilled craftsmen to private industry.

As the size of the S.S. business empire mushroomed Himmler realized he needed to find a skilled financial expert to manage it. He chose Oswald Pohl, an S.S. officer who was a former navy paymaster. Pohl expanded the industries at the concentration camps and built up a vast administrative bureaucracy under his own control. At his newly requisitioned offices in a Berlin suburb he had fifteen hundred employees. Pohl had absolute financial control over the concentration camps and thus in effect controlled the camps. He and Himmler were usually listed together as the principal shareholders of most of the companies owned by the S.S. Technically Himmler and Pohl held these shares as representatives of the S.S., an independant organization of the Nazi party. However, considering the open corruption at every level of government in Nazi Germany, they, as private individuals, had extensive access to this wealth.

Although businesses like the S.S. Textile and Leather Society, which employed five thousand women prisoners at Ravensbruck concentration camp, were producing a good profit, Himmler was unsatisfied. He was dreaming of an industrial empire that would dominate the German economy.

In June of 1944 Hitler asked Albert Speer to assist the S.S. in its efforts to build up an economic empire extending from raw materials to manufacturing. Hitler said the S.S. must be strong enough so that under his successors it would be able to oppose a minister of finance who wanted to cut its budget.

Speer met with Himmler, who explained his wide-ranging ecnomic plans. The S.S. had recently taken over the Hungarian Weiss firm, an import armaments company. Himmler explained he wanted to use this firm as the basis to build a vast arms cartel. Speer pretended to be helpful but wanted to avoid strengthening the already powerful S.S.

In spite of the millions it brought in from slave labor the S.S. concentration camp empire would never be as successful as the Nazis had hoped. Bureaucrats and ideological fanatics make poor businessmen. The S.S. was always torn between a desire to brutalize their Jewish slave laborers and a desire to exploit them. For example S.S. guards regularly beat their slave laborers with whips and clubs.[9] Some typical offenses that could lead to a beating were: "slow to obey," "working too slowly," "sitting during work hours," "begging bread from prisoners of war" (POWs were given more food than Jews), "eating bones from a garbage pail," "warming hands," and "talking to a female inmate."[10]

The S.S. also lost a tremendous amount of ill-gotten gains through corruption. Less than 60 percent of the valuables seized in ghetto raids and searches at the concentration camps were ever turned in by S.S. men. Indeed the average S.S. man regarded looting as a bonus he was entitled to for participating in such operations.

Most concentration camps were not as orderly and disciplined as often assumed. The administration was often in chaos and turmoil. This may not have been by accident. Franz Stangl, the commandant of Treblinka, suggested that the disorder was a deliberate way to cover up the corruption.

When Stangl arrived at Treblinka to take over as commandant he found himself walking through piles of money, jewelry, precious stones, furs, and other expensive clothing scattered carelessly all over the reception area. Outside the perimeter of the camp he could see the tents and campfires of the Ukrainian guards. They were drunk and singing and dancing with prostitutes.

Stangl believed the total disorder was deliberate in order to make accurate accounting impossible. There were rumors of suitcases stuffed with cash and jewelry being taken out of the camp. "There were enormous, fantastic sums involved," Stangl said, "and everybody wanted a piece of it." Stangl later said that he believed the primary motive behind the entire extermination program was plunder.

The Jews who worked for the S.S. as slave laborers existed in a living hell, but they were more fortunate than those selected for the gas chamber. What happened to the people chosen to be exterminated immediately was told by Rudolf Hoess, commandant of Auschwitz. Hoess was appointed commandant in May 1940. At first he wasn't sure how to carry out mass executions, so he visited the concentration camp at Treblinka, where eighty thousand Jews from the Warsaw ghetto had already been liquidated.

The commandant of Treblinka used carbon monoxide gas to kill the prisoners, but Hoess did not think this was very efficient because it took the victims so long to die. "So when I set up the extermination building at Auschwitz," Hoess later confessed, "I used Cyklon B, which was a crystallized prussic acid which we dropped into the death chamber from a small opening. It took three to fifteen minutes to kill the people in the death chamber depending upon climatic conditions. We knew when the people were dead because their screaming stopped."[11]

The Jews usually arrived at Auschwitz after a torturous journey confined in closed railroad freight cars for several days. There were no sanitary facilities and no water or food. Many did not even have room to sit down. Older people frequently died on the trip. As soon as the train arrived at Auschwitz, the cars were unlocked and the S.S. men hustled the dazed people out and began shouting orders at them. When the prisoners were lined up they were marched by two S.S. doctors who made a spot decision as to whether they would be sent to work or to the gas chamber. "Children of tender years," said Hoess, "were invariably exterminated since by reason of their youth they were unable to work."[12]

Those selected to be exterminated were taken to gas chambers. Once they were locked inside and the airtight doors closed, the S.S. orderlies prepared to pour the Cyklon B crystals into the vents. As some witnesses recalled, a piglike S.S. sergeant would give the order. He would laugh and bark out, "All right, give 'em something to chew on."[13] The S.S. officer in charge would watch through a double glass porthole as the naked victims began to choke on the poison gas.

After all the people in the gas chamber were dead the Nazis waited about half an hour before opening the doors and sending in the Jewish slave laborers to take out the bodies and check any body cavities for diamonds or gold. The inmate dentists went to work extracting any gold teeth from the corpses. At one camp an S.S. officer in charge of this gruesome process handed an S.S. inspector a can full of gold teeth saying: "See for yourself the weight of the gold! And this is just from yesterday and the day before. You can't imagine what we find every day, dollars, diamonds, gold!"[14]

Hoess concluded his description of the Auschwitz gas chamber by saying that the Nazis tried to carry out the exterminations in secret, but "the foul and nauseating stench from the continuous burning of bodies permeated the entire area and all of the people living in the surrounding communities knew that exterminations were going on at Auschwitz."[15]

What kind of man could supervise such murderous bestiality? Rudolf Hoess, the commandant of Auschwitz, was the son of a middle-class shopkeeper in Baden-Baden. He was raised in a very strict Catholic atmosphere, which left him with many inhibitions and guilt complexes that marked his character. As a teenager he joined the army and served on the Turkish front during World War I. He won the Iron Cross and became one of the youngest officers in the German Army. At the end of the war rather than face internment, he led his cavalry unit back to Germany from the Middle East almost a thousand miles through hostile territory. They had to fight their way through Turkey, Romania, Hungary, and Austria to get home.

After the war Hoess joined the anti-Communist Free Corps and was poisoned by fanatical nationalism. In 1923 he was arrested along with Martin Bormann for murdering a man who was accused of collaborating with the French occupation forces in the Rhineland. When he was released from prison in 1928, he joined the S.S. Although Hoess was slightly below average height his military bearing, straight features, and youthful good looks gave the impression of a perfect young officer. After Himmler noticed him at an S.S. cavalry review, he was made an officer of the guard at Dachau concentration camp. In 1940 he was promoted to captain in the S.S. and appointed commandant at the new concentration camp at Auschwitz.

Hoess was one of those Germans who believed in absolute obedience to authority. Although a devoted family man, he never questioned Hitler or Himmler's orders to kill women and children. He was not a sadist like some S.S. killers and later said he was relieved when the gas chambers were built, because he had found the "bloodbaths" involved in the mass executions of women and children by shooting "very unpleasant." Hoess was anti-Semitic, but no more or less so than most S.S. men. It was hardly a coincidence that he pioneered the use of Cyklon B gas, which was originally intended as an insecticide. Hoess viewed the liquidation of the Jews as a kind of pest control. To him Jews were like lice that had to be eliminated.[16] He approached his murderous job with the spirit of a bureaucrat rather than that of an emotionally charged fanatic.

How could any government, even a totalitarian government like Nazi Germany, order such a foul deed as was committed in the gas chambers of Auschwitz? To understand why, one must attempt to understand Hitler's hatred of the Jews. He viewed the Jews as a disease and frequently called them a cancer or a bacillus. On the evening of February 22, 1942, in a conversation with Himmler and a Danish S.S. officer Hitler said: "The discovery of the Jewish virus is one of the greatest revolutions that have taken place in the world. The battle in which we are engaged today is of the same sort as the battle waged, during the last century, by Pasteur and Koch. How many diseases have their origin in the Jewish virus! We shall regain our health only by eliminating the Jew."[17]

The twisted reasoning that compares human beings with a virus almost defies analysis. After all Hitler was not an ignorant or gullible man simply repeating what he had been told. He was well aware who Pasteur and Koch were and the nature of their scientific work. The only possible conclusion is that his mind was so full of hatred that it perverted his logic. When confronted with a logical argument, Hitler would occasionally admit that not all Jews were "bad." "I'm convinced that there are Jews in Germany who've behaved correctly," he said to Walter Hewel, his diplomatic liaison officer. "Probably many Jews are not aware of the destructive power they represent. Now, he who destroys life is himself risking death. That's the secret of what is happening to the Jews. Whose fault is it when a cat devours a mouse? The fault of the mouse, who has never done any harm to a cat?"[18] There was thus no escape even for a "good" Jew in Hitler's thinking.

Hitler, however, did not have to hate people to exterminate them. In fact his whole program of mass extermination was first developed by experimenting not on Jews but on Germans. In *Mein Kampf* Hitler had advocated social Darwinism through a system of what he called "positive eugenics": the selective breeding of "superior" individuals and laws restricting the propagation of the mentally and physically ill. In 1935 Hitler said that during wartime Germany could speed up the process of natural selection by "mercy killings" of the retarded and incurable. A few weeks before the attack on Poland, he issued top secret orders to begin "mercy killings" in Germany. The two men put in charge of this euthanasia program were Philip Bouhler, the chief of the Fuehrer's personal Chancellery (Hitler's private affairs) and Dr. Karl Brandt, one of Hitler's personal physicians. The choice of these two men who were so close to Hitler really meant that the euthanasia program was directed by the Fuehrer himself.[19]

In the fall of 1939 Himmler received a top secret directive from Bouhler that all incurables in German mental hospitals were to be liquidated. But just how would these "useless" individuals be killed? Bouhler drew up some sketches of a gas chamber that looked like a shower room with shower nozzles that would emit poison gas. Hitler liked the idea and approved it at once. From his own experience in World War I he knew just how deadly gas could be.

By the spring of 1940 the euthanasia gas chambers were actually working. The first victims were German children who were physically deformed or retarded. S.S. doctors then selected their victims from German mental hospitals. The doctor would examine a list of patients and mark a plus sign in red ink alongside the names of those who were to be sent to the euthanasia centers. Those usually chosen were the criminally insane, the retarded, or severe schizophrenics.

In spite of all their precautions the Nazis were not able to keep their program of "mercy killings" secret for long.[20] At least two of the euthanasia centers, the ones in Hadamar and Grafeneck, were known to the local inhabitants. The children in Hadamar soon learned to recognize the S.S. bus bringing victims to the clinic and would say, "There goes the murder box again." After the killings, heavy evil-smelling black smoke would rise from the chimney of the crematory. As soon as the news got out there were a number of protests particularly from the church. Bishop von Galen of Munster attacked the government publicly in a sermon he delivered criticizing "mercy killings."

Hitler was furious. He ranted against the Christians and "the sobbing sentimentalists trying to save the lives of worthless imbeciles." However, he was afraid to become involved in a conflict with the church while the war was going on. Reluctantly he decided to call off the euthanasia program. Yet he never had any second thoughts about the morality of "mercy killing." "He . . . considered the Christian faith a hypocritical institution which corrupted men," recalled his secretary Traudl Junge.

Hitler's religion was the law of nature. He said:

Science hasn't yet established the roots of the human species. The only thing that's certain is that we are the highest stage of development in mammals, having begun as reptiles and ended up as man, passing through a phase as monkeys on the way perhaps. We're a link in the chain of creation; we're children of nature, and the laws that govern all living creatures apply to us too. Anything that's ill-adapted to life, or not strong enough, gets eliminated. It's only man himself, and especially the Church, that have decided artificially to prolong the lives of the weak, the misfits and those who are inferior.[21]

After being forced to retreat on his euthanasia program Hitler was very careful in maintaining secrecy on the "final solution" of the Jewish question. All exterminations were carried out at remote concentration camps in Poland. Hitler himself was never directly associated with the final solution in any written order.[22] He gave all orders regarding the liquidation of the Jews verbally. Even within the Nazi party and the S.S. he ordered his men never to mention exterminations and killings but to use the euphemisms "resettlement," "final solution," and "shipped to the east."

In spite of Hitler's attempts to keep the extermination of the Jews secret, most Germans knew something very unpleasant was going on. They saw their Jewish neighbors being taken away by the Gestapo in the middle of the night. They heard Hitler's threats to "eliminate the Jews." German foremen and workers saw the pitiful condition of Jewish slave laborers who were sent to work in German factories and must have realized that the life span of such slave laborers would be so short that their fate was a virtual death sentence. How much the Germans knew about what was going on at the concentration camps is difficult to say; however, there was an expression used by some Germans during the war years that was very revealing. If anyone expressed dissatisfaction with Hitler or the government his friends would often warn him with the words: "You better watch what you say or you'll go up the chimney."

After Reinhard Heydrich was assassinated in Prague in May of 1942, Hitler took his revenge by giving Himmler orders to "cleanse" occupied Poland of Jews. Actually Heydrich had been killed by members of the Czech resistance who were trained in London and parachuted back into Czechoslovakia by the R.A.F. No Jews had been involved in the assassination, but this made no difference to Hitler. Himmler assigned his deputy in Lublin, S.S. Major General Odilo Globocnik, to be in charge of this task, code named Operation Reinhard, in honor of Heydrich. Globocnik began deporting Jews from the ghettos to the concentration camps. Operation Reinhard, however, also had another objective: the systematic looting of Polish Jewry. With extreme thoroughness the S.S. confiscated and catalogued all the personal possessions of the Jews.

Of primary concern was what the Nazis considered liquid assets: currency, stock and bond certificates, gold, silver, precious stones, and jewelry. All liquid assets taken from Jews were sent to the Reichsbank and placed in a secret account under the name Max Heiliger. The next category of items, watches, flashlights, electric razors, alarm clocks, and fountain pens were to be sold to or given to the German troops. Blankets, mattresses, umbrellas, baby carriages, combs, towels, and leather goods were to be sent to the Welfare Office for Ethnic Germans, a Nazi party organization.

All types of clothing were listed in great detail from shoes and boots to women's underclothing. In the case of Jewish clothing, the S.S. warned that care must be taken to remove the Star of David before any clothing was distributed. The redistribution of pillaged secondhand clothing illustrates just how poor Nazi Germany was in consumer goods.

The total value of all items looted from the Jews of Poland during Operation Reinhard was estimated by the Nazis as between 180 and 350 million marks. Six million marks in currency and jewels valued at over forty million marks were deposited in the Max Heiliger account at the Reichsbank. More than 160,000 watches and 7,000 alarm clocks were taken from the Jews. General Globocnik mentioned with pride that at the conclusion of Operation Reinhard, 1,901 railroad cars filled with clothing and linen had been shipped back to Germany. No one ever bothered to estimate the value of "personal thefts" by the S.S. men of Jewish property. Such corruption was frowned upon by Nazi officials and severely punished.

Alfried Krupp was one Nazi steel tycoon who used and abused Jewish slave laborers. According to author William Manchester, Krupp personally contacted Hitler on at least one occasion, requesting Jewish slave laborers from Auschwitz for one of his factories in Silesia.[23] He also built a factory at Auschwitz to take advantage of the "cheap labor." Jewish slave laborers were also used by Alfried Krupp in many of his other factories throughout Europe. In all, thousands of Jewish concentration camp inmates worked for Krupp.[24]

The inhuman conditions imposed on Jewish slave laborers working for Krupp were testified to by one of the Krupp firm's own doctors. "The conditions at the Krupp labor camps," said Dr. Wilhelm Jaeger, "were extremely bad. The diet was insufficient. The sanitary conditions were terrible. Tuberculosis was particularly widespread; so was spotted fever. Lice, the carrier of the disease [spotted fever], together with the countless fleas, bugs, and other vermin tortured the inhabitants of these camps." Dr. Jaeger further testified:

In my report to my superiors at Krupp's dated September 2, 1944, I stated . . . 600 Jewish females from Buchenwald Concentration were brought in to work at the Krupp factories. Upon my first visit at Camp Humboldstrasse, I found these females suffering from open festering wounds and other diseases. I was the first doctor they had seen for at least a fortnight. There were no doctors in attendance at the camp. There were no medical supplies in the camp. They had no shoes and went about in their bare feet. The sole clothing of each consisted of a sack with holes for their arms and head. Their hair was shorn. The camp was surrounded by barbed wire and closely guarded by the S.S. guards.[25]

There were also German companies that actually profited from the ghoulish work of extermination itself. Two firms in the heating equipment business sold ovens to the concentration camps to burn human bodies. Other companies made mattresses from human hair, fertilizer from bones, and one Danzig company made soap from human fat.

The Allies, the United States, Britain, and Russia, did nothing to stop Hitler from exterminating the Jews. They could have so seriously disrupted the extermination process by bombing the rail lines and bridges leading to the camps that Hitler would have abandoned the "final solution."[26] The failure of the Allies to heavily bomb the camps led the Nazi industrialists to relocate more of their factories at places like Auschwitz, and that in turn increased the demand for slave laborers and more Jewish prisoners.

Commandos could have been dropped near the camps and attacked them. Because there were barely enough S.S. guards to contain the prisoners, an attack by Allied paratroopers from the outside would have enabled thousands to escape. Such an attack on Auschwitz or one of the other major camps would also have created a serious military problem for Germany. It would have necessitated diverting troops from the front to capture escaped inmates, especially if the Allies had air dropped weapons to the Jews. The uprising in the Warsaw ghetto in which a few poorly armed Jews held off the German Army proved that if given half a chance the Jews were capable of heroic resistance.

Numerous times attacks on the concentration camps were proposed to Allied military commanders. Such proposals were rejected every time as "too dangerous" or "not strategically worhwhile."[27] The only possible conclusion to be drawn is that anti-Semitism played an important part in the American and British refusal to attack the camps. Although almost too horrible to contemplate, it is possible that some anti-Semitic politicians in Britain and the United States did not want the Jews to escape, because then they would later have a "problem" with them wanting to immigrate to Palestine or the United States. Just as they had done before the war when they refused admission to Jewish refugees trying to escape Germany, a few prejudiced American and British politicians were again indirectly enabling Hitler to carry out "the final solution."

On April 17, 1943, Hitler and Ribbentrop, the German foreign minister, met the Hungarian chief of state, Admiral Horthy, at Klessheim Castle in Austria. Hitler was fed up with Hungary's halfhearted participation in the war. He was also determined to get at the Jews of Hungary, who constituted the largest remaining Jewish community in Europe. At the beginning of the war there had been 500,000 Jews in Hungary. Hungary's persecution of the Jews was mild in comparison to the rest of Axis-held Europe; so, many Polish, Slovakian, and Romanian Jews had escaped to Hungary, swelling its Jewish population to 800,000 in 1944.

When Admiral Horthy said he had already passed anti-Semitic laws to restrict the Jews from Hungary's economy, Hitler exploded saying:

Where the Jews were left to themselves, as for instance, in Poland, the most terrible misery and decay prevailed. They are just pure parasites. In Poland this state of affairs has been fundamentally cleared up. If the Jews there did not want to work, they were shot. If they could not work, they had to succumb. They had to be treated like tuberculosis bacilli, with which a healthy body may become infected.

This was not cruel, if one remembers that even innocent creatures of nature, such as hares and deer, have to be killed, so that no harm is caused by them. Why should the beasts who wanted to bring us Bolshevism be spared. . . . Nations that did not rid themselves of Jews perished. One of the most famous examples is the downfall of that people who were once so proud, the Persians, who today lead a pitiful existence as do the Armenians.[28]

Nothing happened for a year, but by the spring of 1944, when Hitler again met with Admiral Horthy, Germany was desperate for more slave laborers. Hitler was also afraid the Jews of Hungary might escape him permanently by being saved by the advancing Allies. While Admiral Horthy was conferring with Hitler, the Germans carried out a coup in Budapest. At last the Jews of Hungary were within Hitler's grasp.

Hitler's only hope of winning the war was by the use of his new miracle weapons—one of which was a jet fighter. However, the Nazis realized that the aircraft industry needed more slave laborers if they were to have any hope of producing planes on schedule. On March 9, 1944, Himmler wrote to Goering: "The movement of manufacturing plants of the aviation industry to subterranean locations requires further employment of about 100,000 prisoners."[29]

The Nazis felt Jewish slave laborers were ideally suited to the task. Because the conditions under which the laborers had to work and live in the subterranean factories were so miserable anyone else would have refused such work. Furthermore, the laborers had to sleep in the damp caves, which gave them a high mortality rate. On April 9 after his meeting with Hitler, Speer reported: "The Fuehrer himself will contact the Reichsfuehrer S.S. [Himmler] and will give an order that the required 100,000 men are to be made available by bringing in Jews from Hungary."[30]

Himmler sent Adolf Eichmann, the S.S. "expert on Jewish affairs," and a specially selected team of Jew hunters to Budapest to round up the Hungarian Jews. Sensing the defeat of Germany was near, Eichmann was determined to live it up while his power lasted. He was now traveling in style, staying in a suite in one of Budapest's finest hotels. No longer the gray dull bureacrat, he was smoking expensive cigars and guzzling champagne. Speaking about their possible fate at the end of the war, he told another S.S. officer: "I'll jump into the grave laughing because of the satisfaction I've had killing five million Jews."

As Eichmann prepared to deport the Hungarian Jews, Rudolf Hoess, the commandant of Auschwitz, called on him in Budapest. They discussed the 100,000 Jewish slave laborers needed for the German aircraft industry. Present at the meeting was Dieter Wisliceny, another S.S. officer, who later testified that Eichmann and Hoess "talked specifically about the percentage of Hungarian Jews that would be strong enough for labor. On the basis of . . . the Jews he inspected in the collection center, Hoess stated that only 20 or at most 25 percent of these Hungarian Jews would be used for labor. . . . Both Eichmann and Hoess said that all Jews unfit for labor were to be liquidated."[31]

The mathematics was simple: to yield 100,000 Jewish slave laborers, 400,000 Jews were rounded up by Eichmann and deported. The 300,000 unfit to work for German companies were soon exterminated at Auschwitz. They were the last large group of Jews Hitler would get his hands on, but Jews would continue to work and die as slave laborers for the Nazis up until the last day of the war.

Chapter 14

The "Good Germans" and Hitler's Drug Abuse

While the Allies were fighting in France, a small group of high-ranking German officers decided the time had come to stop Hitler. They hoped that if they could kill the tyrant, Germany could get a fair peace settlement from the Western Allies. The leader of this anti-Hitler conspiracy was Colonel Claus von Stauffenberg, the descendant of an aristocratic Swabian family whose ancestors included the famous Prussian Field Marshal Gneisenau. Stauffenberg was a devout Catholic, excellent horseman, musician, and poet.

The handsome dark-haired young Stauffenberg had a distinguished military career. In April 1943, he was only thirty-six years old when he was seriously wounded in North Africa. His car was attacked on the road by a low-flying Allied plane and strafed with machine gun fire. He lost one eye, his right hand, and several fingers on his left hand. During his convalescence Stauffenberg's longstanding anti-Nazi sentiments intensified. He hated totalitarianism and saw Hitler as the Antichrist. Determined to try to save Germany, Stauffenberg joined the anti-Nazi resistance movement, which was composed of several small underground groups. Stauffenberg became part of a group that was comprised mostly of aristocratic officers including General Beck, the former chief of the army General Staff, and

Field Marshal von Witzleben, the former commander in chief of the army in the west (in France). The most prominent nonmilitary member of the group was Carl Goerdeler, the conservative former mayor of Leipzig who was in close contact with a number of prominent Ruhr industrialists.[1]

The German resistance had tried to assassinate Hitler on several previous occasions and failed.[2] Willing to risk his life if necessary to get rid of the Nazis, Stauffenberg decided he would undertake the next assassination attempt himself. If Hitler was killed Stauffenberg's coconspirators in the army would immediately seize control of Berlin and arrest all leading Nazis.

Stauffenberg's chance came on July 20, 1944, when he was summoned to attend a military conference at Hitler's East Prussian headquarters. Stauffenberg flew to East Prussia, arriving in Rastenburg at about 10 A.M. In his briefcase he carried a British-made bomb. He had no problem getting through the sentries and numerous checkpoints at Hitler's headquarters. The first problem occurred when Stauffenberg learned that the conference would not be held in the usual underground concrete bunker but instead would take place in a single-story frame barracks near the bunker. Stauffenberg knew that in the concrete bunker the explosion of the bomb would kill everyone; but in the frame barracks with open windows the pressure of the blast would not be as concentrated. Nevertheless, after conferring with Field Marshal Keitel, Stauffenberg excused himself to go to the washroom, where with his one partially disabled hand he set the bomb to explode in ten minutes. He and Keitel then walked over to the barracks where the conference had already begun.

When they entered the conference room Keitel introduced Stauffenberg to Hitler, who simply looked up from the map and nodded, saying he would hear Stauffenberg's report later. Hitler had met Stauffenberg before and had apparently never taken any particular notice of him. There were about twenty high-ranking officers standing around a large heavy oak map table in the conference room. Taking a place at the table about six feet away from Hitler, Stauffenberg set his briefcase containing the bomb under the table. Because of the warm weather the windows were open. Stauffenberg realized this would release some of the power of the blast but thought the bomb would still easily do its job.

Looking at his watch and seeing that there were only a few minutes until the bomb went off, Stauffenberg whispered to an officer next to him that he was expecting an important call from Berlin and would immediately return. With this he slipped out of the room. No sooner was he gone than an officer who had been standing near him kicked into Stauffenberg's briefcase, which had been left under the table. The officer reached down and moved the briefcase to the other side of one of the two thick wooden supports on which the table rested. This probably saved Hitler's life because it placed a solid heavy obstacle between Hitler and the explosion.

Safely outside, Stauffenberg inconspicuously looked back at the conference barracks and counted the seconds. Inside General Heusinger was giving his report. Hitler was leaning across the table on his elbow. Field Marshal Keitel had just noticed Stauffenberg's absence and was going to look for him when the bomb went off. There was a blinding flash of flame at the instant of the explosion. The ceiling of the barracks collapsed and the wood paneling was ripped off the walls. The heavy oak map table was hurled up into the air and landed in the corner of the room. Colonel Brandt, the man standing next to the bomb, had both legs blown off.

Stauffenberg heard the blast and saw the smoke and debris flying from the windows of the conference barracks. From the powerful force of the blast he felt sure no one inside could have survived. He immediately left Hitler's headquarters to return to Berlin to set the coup in motion.[3]

Of the approximately twenty men in the conference room one was dead and three were mortally wounded, but Hitler was not among them. As the guards ran to try to rescue those in the explosion the first thing they saw was Field Marshal Keitel supporting a dazed Hitler stumbling through the smoke and debris toward the front door of the barracks. Hitler's right arm was partially paralyzed, his right leg burned and full of splinters, his trousers torn to shreds, his eardrums were damaged, and his hair was singed and standing straight up.[4]

It took Stauffenberg's plane four hours to reach Berlin. When he landed in the capital he was shocked to find that his fellow conspirators had not yet taken over the major government buildings, radio and communication centers, nor arrested the leading Nazis. Energetically Stauffenberg began giving orders for the coup and the troops began to march. Unfortunately before the coup progressed very far, word came from Rastenburg that Hitler was still alive. This news ultimately doomed the plot. The average German soldier was not willing to revolt against the "Fuehrer" because they had been so thoroughly indoctrinated by Nazi propaganda. Once Hitler was dead, however, they would have been willing to arrest Goering, Himmler, and other Nazi leaders.[5]

Late that night officers and troops loyal to Hitler retook the War Ministry building and arrested Stauffenberg and the leaders of the plot. They were immediately taken down to the courtyard and executed by a firing squad under the headlights of an armored car. Shortly after midnight all German radio stations interrupted their programming to broadcast a message from Hitler: "If I speak to you today [he began] it is first in order that you should hear my voice and know that I am unhurt and well, and secondly that you should know of a crime unparalleled in German history. A very small clique of ambitious, irresponsible, and at the same time senseless and stupid officers had formed a plot to eliminate me and the High Command of the Armed Forces. . . . The circle of these conspirators is very small and has nothing in common with the spirit of the German Wehrmacht [army] and, above all, none with the German people."[6]

For a change Hitler was essentially telling the truth; very few people were involved in the plot. After the war some German historians would try to make it seem as if the July 20 plot represented a great national uprising against Hitler or at least a revolt of the German army against Hitler. Neither was true. The plot was later called the Generals' Plot, yet the majority of the generals were not involved. There was very little support among lower-ranking officers or enlisted men.[7]

None of this is to detract from the heroism and noble motives of Stauffenberg and his fellow conspirators. Most of them were not officers who had suddenly turned against Hitler because the war was going badly, but officers who had been against Hitler and everything nazism stood for from the beginning. The three leading officers of the conspiracy, Stauffenberg, General Beck, and Field Marshall von Witzleben had always been known for their anti-Nazi sentiments. The pro-Nazi army officers like Field Marshal Keitel, chief of the high command of the armed forces, General Guderian, inspector general of the armed forces, and General Jodl, chief of the operations staff of the armed forces, remained loyal to the regime.[8]

There were a few generals who had once been supporters of Hitler and who cooperated with the conspirators but did not play a major role in the plot. The involvement of Field Marshal von Kluge, the former commander in chief of the army in France, particularly galled Hitler because he had tried to buy Kluge's loyalty by giving him 250,000 marks as a "supplement" to his pay. This was a typical illustration of the lengths Hitler went to in order to maintain the allegiance of the generals. He was always ready to give large cash bribes to high-ranking officers to ensure their loyalty.

Hitler's vengeance against the conspirators was terrible and swift. Anyone associated with the plot was arrested by the Gestapo. A number of high-ranking officers like Field Marshal von Witzleben were humiliated at show trials before the Nazi People's Court.[9] Sentenced to death, they were strangled with piano wire and their bodies hung on meat hooks like animal carcasses. Hitler had this gruesome spectacle filmed and watched the movie several times. He now hated the aristocratic Officer Corps more than ever, but there was little he could do to get rid of them in the middle of the war.

When Hitler learned that Field Marshal Rommel had been talking with the conspirators, he gave Rommel the choice of suicide or arrest by the Gestapo. Hitler could not afford the adverse publicity of putting one of the genuine war heros of the German public on trial. But there was no reason to worry, for Rommel wisely chose the alternative of suicide.

Leftist Nazis like Dr. Goebbels, the minister of propaganda, and Dr. Ley, the leader of the Nazi Labor Front, lashed out against the Junkers, the Prussian upper class, and aristocrats with bitter denunciations. In an editorial in Goebbel's paper *Der Angriff*, Ley condemned the "degenerate blue-blood, aristocratic clique" and called for the "extermination" of the "entire breed." Although Hitler shared many of these sentiments the military situation was too serious to divert time and resources to an internal purge of the aristocracy, whose members still occupied many positions of leadership in the army and industry.[10]

A number of industrialists were indirectly implicated in the plot through their connections with Goerdeler, the former mayor of Leipzig, and Popitz, the Prussian minister of finance. They included Stinnes, Reusch, and Haniel; these were some of the most important names in the steel and coal industry. At Speer's urging Hitler recognized that to prosecute these men could turn all industrialists against him, so they were let off with a warning.

Hitler did, however, order the arrest of one of his former financiers, Hjalmar Schacht, who had been minister of economics and Reichsbank president. Schacht had been meeting with members of the Resistance. The exact reasons why he turned against Hitler are not clear; but like his patron, the steel tycoon Fritz Thyssen, he resented having been pushed aside in the Nazi economic hierarchy by Gustav Krupp and Goering. Thyssen had turned against the Nazis long before Schacht. After having contributed more money to Hitler than anyone else during the early years, Thyssen broke with the Fuehrer in 1939 and fled to Switzerland. He was captured by the Gestapo in France and sent to a concentration camp.

There were many anti-Nazis in the business community. Even firms with large war contracts like Krupp and Farben had anti-Hitler conspirators among their leading executives.* Ewald Loser, one of the three top executives at Krupp, and Dr. Hans Beusch, the director of Krupp's social welfare program, were both active anti-Nazis. Loser had frequent arguments with Gustav and Alfried Krupp about the use of slave labor. The Gestapo arrested Loser and Dr. Beusch in 1944 for their complicity in the plot against Hitler's life, along with Gustav Krupp's brother-in-law, Baron Thilo von Wilmowsky, who was also a Krupp executive and an anti-Nazi.

---

*Actually both businesses had anti-Nazi as well as pro-Nazi executives and employees. Only a very few of the executives of these firms were found guilty at Nuremberg. Unfortunately the thousands of executives and employees who tried to help the people oppressed by the Nazis, at great personal risk to themselves, largely went unnoticed after the war.

The founder of I.G. Farben, Carl Duisberg, and Carl Bosch, the head of the firm until his death in 1940, were both anti-Nazis. In private Bosch frequently referred to Hitler as "that charlatan." When the Nazis began persecuting the Jews Bosch stubbornly resisted orders to dismiss Jewish scientists from I.G. Farben. Bosch had the courage to go as far as to complain against race discrimination personally to Hitler. The Fuehrer was so angry he got up and walked out without saying a word and left Bosch standing alone in the Chancellery study. Only Bosch's international connections saved him from a concentration camp.

After the Gestapo's purge of all those in any way connected with the July 20 plot, the anti-Nazi resistance was so decimated it in effect ceased to exist. Actually the anti-Nazi resistance groups like the Kreisau Circle, which was composed of officers and professional men, had never been very large. Most groups consisted of less than a hundred members. The student resistance group the White Rose was also very small with a handful of supporters. To be a member of these groups people were literally risking their lives. The Gestapo was very efficient at suppressing even the slightest sign of antigovernment activity.

Surprisingly the monarchists were the strongest and largest anti-Nazi group in Germany. Although many monarchists did nothing but talk, most of the officers involved in the July 20 plot were monarchists. Because some monarchists were Nazi party members and others were high-ranking military officers, they were able to operate much more openly than other resistance groups. A monarchist for example could easily make himself known among a group of people simply by praising the aggressive nationalism of Kaiser Wilhelm, something that, even if the Gestapo was listening, was not illegal. On the other hand a socialist who made a favorable comment about the Weimar Republic or Karl Marx would have quickly found himself in a concentration camp.

Most monarchists were to be found among the upper and middle classes, particularly army officers, landowners, independent businessmen, professional men, and civil servants. A number of conservative people among the lower middle class and even the working class were monarchists, such as white-collar workers, artisans, and small farmers. One of the main weaknesses of the monarchist cause was the lack of a strong pretender. None of the Hohenzollern princes seemed suitable.

The most obvious candidate, the Crown Prince, was generally thought to be a weak individual; but he had just enough supporters and legitimacy to spoil the chances of any other princes.

In Bavaria separatism and monarchism went hand in hand. As Germany's chances of victory faded the supporters of the Bavarian Wittelsbach monarchy grew more numerous. Although support for a Wittelsbach king was strongest in the upper class there were monarchists at all levels of society, with strong support among the Catholic peasants in the countryside. The situation in Austria was similar to that in Bavaria with the number of Hapsburg supporters growing as German defeats mounted.

By 1944 there was considerable war weariness and pessimism in Germany. Food rations were continually reduced, and women had to stand in line for hours to get what little was available. The increased length of the workday, about ten to twelve hours on average, also put considerable strain on people. Why didn't the Germans revolt as they did in 1918? There were many reasons; first of all the food shortage never got as bad as it had been in 1918. Hitler was very conscious of public sentiment and saw to it that the Germans had sufficient to eat. It wasn't as much as they were used to, but no one was starving. The Gestapo was also more vigilant at nipping any resistance in the bud than the kaiser's police had been in 1918.

There were a few former labor leaders and Social Democratic politicians in the secret resistance groups, but there was no organized working-class opposition to Hitler. There was never a workers' strike against the mistreatment of the Jews or against the war. It must be remembered the Nazis had completely suppressed the labor unions and the Social Democratic party in the early 1930s, and many leading Social Democrats and labor leaders were still in concentration camps. There were a number of socialist-minded radicals within the Nazi Labor Front, but they were mostly loyal Nazis who spent their time attacking "reactionaries" rather than Hitler.

After the war some German historians tried to give the impression that the church was a hotbed of anti-Nazi resistance. Unfortunately, with a few courageous exceptions, most clergymen both Protestants and Catholics, passively went along with Hitler and the Nazi regime. For every one pastor like Martin

Niemoeller who, although an early supporter of Hitler, became an outspoken critic of the Nazis and ended up in a concentration camp, there were ten others who supported the Fatherland without question.

There were some clergymen involved in the small anti-Nazi resistance movements, but they could hardly undo the damage done by a man like Reich Bishop Ludwig Müller. A fanatical nationalist and vicious anti-Semite, Müller tried to unite all German Protestants into one easily ruled body. After a Nazi campaign of harassment to silence the moderate Protestant clergy, Müller was actually elected Reich Bishop by other churchmen at a national synod in Wittenberg in spite of his well-known extreme Nazi views.[11]

If some Protestant clergymen were guilty of collaborating with Hitler so were some of the Catholics. Cardinal Faulhaber, the leading Catholic churchman in Germany, was another extreme nationalist. Distressed by anti-Hitler sentiments abroad, Faulhaber ordered German Catholics to pray for the life and health of the Fuehrer. In 1936 Hitler invited Cardinal Faulhaber to the Berghof and talked with him for three hours. Although Faulhaber defended the church against government encroachments, he refused to join the July 20 plot. After Stauffenberg's attempt to assassinate Hitler, Cardinal Faulhaber publicly affirmed his personal loyalty to Hitler.

The only real popular resistance in Germany was a grumbling passive resistance of people fed up with the war. Their weapons were whispering campaigns against the luxurious lifestyles of Nazi party bigwigs and rumors about the incompetence of Nazi leaders. Jokes were another weapon of the passive resistance. One of the most popular was told about a German whose home was bombed out. The poor man complained in public saying: "One man is responsible for all this destruction and suffering." He was promptly arrested by the Gestapo. But when the judge questioned him and asked just who he meant was "responsible for the destruction," the man instantly replied: "Why, Churchill, of course! Who did you think I meant?"

Since Hitler was not to be overthrown by the Germans, the war had to be played out to the very end. After the failure of the July 20 plot the Allies had broken out of their Normandy beachheads, captured Paris, and pushed the Germans out of France. In the east the situation was no better for the Germans, with the Russians advancing on Poland and the Balkans.

In spite of recent defeats Hitler told Keitel and some other generals on August 31, 1944, that it was not yet time to try to arrange a negotiated peace. The moment for negotiations, he said, is when you are having successes. However, Hitler was not entirely pessimistic. "The time will come," he assured his generals, "when the tension between the Allies will become so great that a break will occur. All coalitions in history have disintegrated sooner or later. The only thing is to wait for the right moment, no matter how hard it is."

Suddenly Hitler's mood changed and he began to feel sorry for himself. "I think it's quite obvious that this war isn't a pleasure for me," he said. "For five years I've been so busy I've been cut off from the rest of the world. I haven't been to the theater, I haven't heard a concert, and I haven't seen a movie. I live only for the purpose of leading this fight, because I know that if there isn't an iron will behind our war effort, the war cannot be won."

Hitler's mood of self-pity vanished and his voice again became firm and determined. "I accuse the General Staff of weakening the morale of combat officers by their failure to set an example of iron will and determination. When General Staff officers go to the front they spread pessimism." His voice rose, as if he were addressing a large audience. "If necessary," he said, "we will fight on the Rhine. It doesn't matter to me. Under any circumstances we will continue this struggle until, as Frederick the Great said, one of our damned enemies gets too tired to fight anymore. We'll fight until we get a peace that will guarantee the life of the German nation for the next fifty to one hundred years and which, above all, does not stain our honor a second time, as happened in 1918."

Hitler's mood then quickly changed again from optimism and determination to melancholy and depression. Obviously thinking about the July 20 bomb plot, he said: "Things might have turned out differently. If my life had ended, I think that I can say for me personally it would only have been a release from worry, sleepless nights, and tremendous nervous strain. A split second and then you are free of everything and there is rest and eternal peace. But I am grateful to fate for letting me live."[12]

If Hitler was depressed and worried so were the German industrialists. They realized the greatest strategic weakness of German industry was the vulnerability of the Ruhr to enemy attack, due to its geographic location. Being almost on the French and Belgian border there was no protective geographic boundary, not even distance, to separate the industrial heart of Germany from the enemy. In World War I and again in 1940 the Germans were fortunate that the battles in the west were fought far from the Ruhr. However, by 1943 the industrialists saw to their dismay how vulnerable the Ruhr was to enemy bombers based in England.

The Allied bombing had deprived even the pro-Nazis among the German industrialists of much of their enthusiasm for Hitler's war. After all, what were all the rewards from Hitler, all the government contracts, slave laborers, and properties throughout Europe worth if your principal factories were being bombed to obliteration? By the fall of 1944 the tycoons of the Ruhr were faced with the additional threat of an imminent Allied invasion. The American and British armies were only miles away. The pro-Nazi industrialists were fed up with their partnership with Hitler. They wanted out. They wanted an immediate negotiated peace with Britain and America.

Even a former staunch supporter of Hitler like Albert Voegler, the General Manager of the United Steel Works, had had enough. While discussing the disastrous results of the bombing on the steel industry with Albert Speer, Voegler suddenly asked, "When are we going to call it quits?" Speer responded that Hitler was planning to stake everything on one last big offensive.

"But does he fully realize," Voegler continued, "that after that we have to call it quits? We're losing too much of our substance. How will we be able to reconstruct if industry goes on taking such a beating even for a few months more?"

"I think," Speer replied, "that Hitler is playing his last card and knows it too."

Voegler looked skeptical. "Of course, it's his last card, now that our production is collapsing all over the place."[13]

But Hitler was not ready to give up. He has been portrayed as being insane during the last part of the war, living in a fantasy world, refusing to accept the inevitable defeat, determined to take the whole country down with him to a fiery Götterdäm-

merung. However his military and diplomatic strategy was still
sound, even if the chances of success were slim.

On the evening of December 12, 1944, Hitler held a top secret
conference of his generals at his western headquarters in a
remote valley near Bad Nauheim. Still visibly suffering from the
effects of Stauffenberg's bomb, he walked stooped over, dragging one leg behind him. His face was puffy and pale. Although
he remained sitting throughout the conference his hands trembled and his left arm occasionally twitched violently. His mind,
however, had lost none of its evil brilliance. Hitler said:

> Never in history has there been a coalition like that of our
> enemies, made up of such heterogeneous elements with
> such divergent aims. . . . Ultra-capitalist states on the one
> hand; an ultra-Marxist state on the other. On the one hand,
> Britain, a dying empire; on the other, the United States, a
> colony eager for its inheritance. Each of these partners
> joined the coalition in the hope of realizing their own
> political ambitions and to cheat the others out of something.
> America wants to be England's heir; Russia aims to secure
> the Balkans, the narrow seas, Persian [Iranian] oil and the
> Persian Gulf; England tries to hold on to her posses-
> sions. . . .
> Even now these countries are bickering with each other,
> and he who sits like a spider in his web watching develop-
> ments, observes how these antagonisms grow stronger from
> hour to hour. If we can strike a few hard blows this
> artificially constructed common front may suddenly col-
> lapse with a tremendous clap of thunder.
> It is essential to shatter the enemy's belief that victory is
> certain. Wars are often decided by one side or the other
> recognizing that they cannot win. We must continually
> demonstrate to the enemy that no matter what he does he
> can never count on us surrendering. Never! Never![14]

Hitler decided his last-chance offensive would be a bold attack
in the west. He would drive through the Ardennes, cross the
river Meuse, and push on to Antwerp, the Allies' chief supply
port. This offensive would split the American and British armies
and if successful cut off the British forces just as the Germans

had done at Dunkirk in 1940. Hitler was sure that if his offensive was a success the Allies would agree to a negotiated peace. The decision to attack in the west rather than the east was a logical one for Hitler because of the distances involved. In the west a decisive battle was possible and could be accomplished using much less fuel.

On the night of December 16, 1944, German troops suddenly attacked out of the fog and achieved complete surprise against the weak American forces in the Ardennes sector. For several days the Germans relentlessly pushed the Americans back through the snow-covered hills and forests. But before long Hitler's panzers were running short of fuel and American resistance stiffened. The heroic stand of the American 101st Airborne Division at Bastogne, in the center of the Ardennes front, doomed Hitler's offensive. Nevertheless, on the northern flank of the battle area advanced elements of the Second Panzer Division came within three miles of Dinant and the river Meuse.

If the Germans had captured Dinant they would have cut all Allied communications and supplies running through the Meuse Valley putting all Allied armies in the north in jeopardy. Fortunately, Hitler's plan failed, primarily for a lack of gasoline and air support. Finally the skies cleared, and the American Air Force paralyzed the German troops. As always Hitler was slow to admit defeat but gradually the German forces were withdrawn from the Ardennes. Hitler had played his last offensive card; now the war would be fought on German soil.

After the failure of the Ardennes offensive Hitler's health deteriorated rapidly. He looked like a sick old man who could hardly walk. Most of Hitler's illnesses were probably caused by his addiction to drugs. Many of these drugs were prescribed by his personal physician, Dr. Theo Morell, who was considered a quack by some of his colleagues. By 1945 Morell was giving Hitler as least one injection almost every day as well as handfuls of pills every few hours.[15]

Hitler first became a patient of Dr. Morell in 1937. At the time Hitler was suffering from severe stomach cramps that several well-known specialists had been unable to cure. His photographer, Hoffmann, recommended Dr. Morell. Within a month

Morell cured Hitler. The grateful patient hailed his new doctor as a miracle worker. But unknown to Hitler one of the medications Morell had prescribed for him contained small amounts of strychnine. Hitler's other physicians felt the cumulative effect of the strychnine was gradually poisoning him.*[16] Morell also began giving Hitler numerous other medications and regular injections, "to increase his energy level."

Even before he met Hitler, Morell's practice had been a lucrative one. With his office located in Berlin's fashionable Kurfurstendamm many of his patients were prominent film stars and entertainers. Morell was a specialist in venereal diseases. In the 1920s many of his patients had been British, French, and American members of the Allied Control Commission, a fact that would later lead some people to suspect that he was an agent or dupe of the Allies.[17] To Morell's credit even after 1933 a number of his patients were still Jewish. This didn't seem to bother Hitler.

Morell's physical appearance was hardly the picture of health. He was obese with a huge potbelly, coarse features, dark swarthy skin, and an almost bald head. He wore thick round glasses. His personal hygiene also left much to be desired. His hands and fingernails were often dirty; his overpowering body odor indicated he bathed infrequently and used no deodorant. When Eva Braun, Hitler's mistress, complained about Morell, Hitler replied: "I employ Morell for his medical skills not his fragrance."

Morell treated Hitler with an ever increasing number of drugs. He gave him everything from vitamins and dextrose to stimulants on a regular basis, mostly by injection. "I have the greatest confidence in Morell," said Hitler. "I follow his prescriptions to the letter." Whenever Hitler felt tired or caught a cold Morell gave him an injection. Hitler became increasingly dependent on Morell's drugs. Several other doctors believed the number and mixture of drugs Morell was giving Hitler on a regular basis were dangerous. Over the nine years of Morell's treatment Hitler's health continually deteriorated.[18]

---

*A U.S. military intelligence report compiled after the war indicated that the pills containing strychnine may have been harmless because the quantity of strychnine was so small.

Finally Hitler was taking so many drugs that his valet had to carry a huge medicine chest with them wherever they went. Of course there were two sides to the relationship between Hitler and Morell. Hitler had an addictive personality. He encouraged and even ordered Morell to give him an ever increasing number of drugs. When on one occasion Morell was ill, another doctor prescribed a medication containing cocaine. Toward the end of his life Hitler stepped up the dosage of the medication containing cocaine from once a day, as prescribed, to ten times a day.

Hitler himself must bear the primary responsibility for becoming a drug addict. Dr. Morell probably genuinely feared for his life if he did not please his demanding patient. "I have always *had* to resort to crash treatments with maximum dosages," Morell once complained to Hitler. "I *had* to go right to the limits of the permissible, even though I might be condemned by many of my colleagues for doing so."[19]

Most of the drugs Dr. Morell gave Hitler, especially those produced by legitimate pharmaceutical companies, were useful medications that would have been safe if taken as the manufacturer recommended. However, Hitler abused some of these drugs. Although Morell kept a diary, it is believed that he did not always record the drugs he gave Hitler. Furthermore Hitler took some drugs without Morell's approval. Thus it is impossible to determine exactly the amounts and types of drugs he used. There is also the problem of the drugs Morell produced himself, about which very little is known. Some of Hitler's other physicians mentioned "mysterious medications and injections" Morell gave Hitler that no one knew anything about.

Hitler frequently exhibited the classic symptoms of drug-induced rage. His eyes would flash dangerously and he would become completely irrational. He would gesticulate wildly while shouting at the top of his voice.[20] A number of disastrous military and political decisions were probably caused by Hitler's abuse of drugs.

Hitler also exhibited a number of other symptoms that may have been due to the side effects of drug abuse. They ranged from puffiness of the face and trembling of the hands to more serious ones including an enlarged heart, a loss of balance, jaundice (which may have been a sign of permanent liver damage), and extreme mood swings. Even close associates said Hitler would sometimes suddenly behave like a different person.

Morell got rich from his association with Hitler. He acquired pharmaceutical factories, and Hitler granted him a monopoly on the use of his lice powder by the German army.[21] However, Morell had few friends. Most other German doctors considered him disreputable. Hermann Goering contemptuously referred to him as "the Reich Injection Master." A number of people in Hitler's entourage thought he was slowly poisoning the Fuehrer. Hitler himself forbade all criticism of Morell, but when his health continued to deteriorate after 1943, he too became increasingly suspicious of Morell. Once when Morell was chiding Hitler to take better care of himself he said, "My Fuehrer, it is my responsibility to watch over your health. What if something would happen to you?" Looking Morell right in the eye Hitler said very slowly and clearly: "Morell, if anything happens to me, your life won't be worth a red cent."

On October 1, 1944, Hitler passed out after a dose of cocaine. He had been taking cocaine for about a month. It was prescribed not by Dr. Morell but by Dr. Giesing, an ear, nose, and throat specialist. In the testimony Dr. Giesing gave to Allied interrogators after the war, he explained that Hitler requested another dose of cocaine. He clearly enjoyed the treatment as Giesing put the cocaine in his left nostril. He was speaking, but his eyes slowly closed and his face turned pale. Giesing checked Hitler's pulse. It was very weak. He asked Hitler if he was all right but received no answer. Hitler had passed out. The experience did not frighten him enough to quit the drug. Within a few months he was taking even larger doses of cocaine, this time without a doctor's supervision.

Hitler's drug addiction and his association with Dr. Theo Morell was an unexpected circumstance the generals and the pro-Nazi industrialists had not counted on when Hitler became chancellor. The Fuehrer's drug-induced mood swings made him impossible to control. It was even difficult to predict how he would react to any suggestion, since it might depend on what drugs he was under the influence of at the moment. The amount of drugs Hitler was taking could have made his personality unstable even under normal circumstances. Hence he was unable to cope with the strain of the continual defeats he suffered in 1943 and 1944.

Chapter 15

Hitler's Partners Turn Against Him

By 1944 Hitler's former partners in the army and industry were fed up with him and wanted to find a way out of the war. When Hitler became chancellor in 1933, his conservative ally, vice-chancellor von Papen, speaking for the militarists and the reactionaries, said: "We've hired Hitler." Indeed they had hired Hitler to resurrect Germany's military and economic power, not to lead the nation to defeat. Consequently in the last year of the war there were three revolts against Hitler's regime. Only the first of these, the so-called Generals' Plot of July 20, 1944, is widely known; however, the other two rebellions against Hitler succeeded. The success of these revolts saved hundreds of thousands of lives and preserved a significant portion of Germany's assets for the postwar reconstruction.

The second conspiracy against Hitler began soon after the Allies broke out from their Normandy beachheads. In Russia the Germans had followed a scorched earth policy as they retreated. All factories, bridges, and railroad tracks were blown up or destroyed so they could not be used by the advancing Soviet troops. In the west a different situation presented itself. The German industrialists now saw defeat as inevitable. If they destroyed French factories, the French might in turn want to destroy German factories after the Allies were victorious. Hitler, however, had no such inhibitions. He ordered the army in the west to destroy all industry, bridges, and transportation facilities before they were captured by the Allies.

Albert Speer, who was in effect the representative of industry in the government, became the leader of a small but influential group of conspirators who sought to frustrate Hitler's scorched earth orders. Speer contacted the commander in chief of the German armies in the west and told him the destruction "had no sense and no purpose" and "that I in my capacity as minister of armaments did not consider [it] essential."[1]

On September 5, 1944, Speer even issued instructions stating that "In any case provisions must be made that the Minette, the Luxembourg area, and also the other industrial districts, if they should fall in enemy hands, are only paralyzed by removal and transfer of any essential machinery, mostly electrical, without the plants themselves being damaged."[2]

During the confusion caused by the rapid collapse of the German forces in France, Hitler never realized his orders for the destruction of industries in France, Belgium, and Holland were being sabotaged. It was not until January 1945 that he became suspicious. At a conference he handed Speer a foreign press report. "You know I ordered everything in France to be destroyed. How is it possible that French industry is already approaching its prewar production only a few months later?" He stared at Speer angrily.

"Probably it's a propaganda report," Speer replied calmly.[3] Having used similar propaganda himself Hitler seemed willing to accept this answer and said no more.

Although Hitler had not been able to enforce his scorched earth policy in France and the low countries, he was determined that when the Allies invaded Germany everything would be destroyed before the German troops retreated. An editorial in the *Völkischer Beobachter* written at Hitler's instruction warned the German people what would be required of them: "No German stalk of wheat is to feed the enemy, no German mouth is to give him information, no German hand is to help him. He will find every bridge destroyed and every road blocked; nothing but death, destruction and hatred will greet him."[4]

Speer held a number of secret meetings with prominent industrialists throughout Germany. They decided that in view of the hopeless military situation, Hitler's scorched earth policy would only mean the needless destruction of their factories. By this time (January 1945) 90 percent of the German industrialists had abandoned Hitler and were hoping for a speedy Allied victory. They decided their objective would be to turn German industry over to the Allies in working order. This, they believed, would give them a good chance of retaining their property after the war.

Surprisingly the German industrialists were not alarmed by the Morgenthau Plan, proposed by the U.S. secretary of the treasury, Henry Morgenthau, to wipe out German industry and reduce Germany to an agricultural country. Hitler and Goebbels made great use of the Morgenthau Plan to frighten the average German citizen. The industrialists, however, had witnessed the failure of Nazi attempts to do the same thing in Poland and Russia. There was always a strong financial incentive to keep industry working and not to destroy it regardless of the ideological motives. The German industrialists correctly predicted that as soon as the war was over the Americans and British would need the output of German factories.

Speer's two principal collaborators in the plot to save German industry were Hermann Rochling, the steel king of the Saar region, and Walter Rohland, the panzer expert, both prominent industrialists who had formerly been staunch supporters of Hitler. It was a "curious phase" of the war Speer recalled: "In roundabout conversations, full of traps and detours, one man would probe another's views; groups of accomplices formed; and a candid remark on this subject might mean putting your life on the line."[5]

It was Speer's job to get in contact with sympathetic generals and secure their cooperation. He went to Upper Silesia to see General Heinrici, who agreed not to destroy the railroad network there that supplied coal for southeastern Germany. General Heinrici was a known anti-Nazi, so his involvement in the plot was understandable. Speer also received help from generals who were among Hitler's most loyal supporters, including General Guderian, the commander in chief of the eastern front;

General Jodl, chief of the operations staff of the high command; and General Model, the commander in chief of the armies on the western front.

In March of 1945 Speer attended a secret meeting of industrialists in the Ruhr to discuss the strategy for the postwar recovery of German industry. Naturally such meetings were illegal. Anyone who even casually mentioned the possibility of an Allied victory was labeled a defeatist and subject to immediate execution. Nevertheless, like medieval theologians debating how to get from this world to the next, the Ruhr barons were trying to extricate themselves from the last phase of the war with as little loss as possible.

At the March meeting one of the principal concerns of the Ruhr business leaders was the transportation network. If the factories and mines were saved but the railroad bridges were destroyed, all industry in the Ruhr would be brought to a standstill anyway. Transportation had to be maintained to get the coal and ore to the factories.

Speer immediately went to see Field Marshal Model. Model was furious at an order he had just received from Hitler instructing him to attack the American bridgehead at Remagen. He told Speer that Hitler simply didn't understand that the only German troops in the area had lost all their heavy weapons and had little fighting strength.[6] In such a mood Model readily agreed to spare important railroad bridges whenever possible. Speer also got General Guderian to issue an edict "forbidding the demolition" of any bridges that would hinder the supplying of the German population.

What Speer and his fellow conspirators were doing would have been considered treason by Hitler had he found out. Up until March 1945 Speer succeeded in tricking Hitler into helping prevent demolitions. He was able to do this by using Hitler's own optimism against him. Hitler always contended that any losses were temporary and territory captured by the Allies would soon be won back.[7] It was then easy for Speer to argue that if the lost territory was soon recaptured, then it was senseless to destroy factories before retreating. In an effort to discourage Hitler from issuing further scorched earth orders, Speer sent him a memorandum on March 15, 1945, bluntly stating Germany's hopeless situation:

In four to eight weeks the final collapse of the German economy must be expected for certain. After that the war cannot be continued. . . . We must do everything to maintain, even if in the most primitive manner, the basic everyday needs of the people to the last.

It must be guaranteed that if the battle advances further into the territory of the Reich nobody has the right to destroy industrial plants, coal mines, electric plants and other supply facilities, as well as traffic facilities, internal shipping routes, etc.

The blowing up of bridges to the extent which has been planned would mean . . . the removal of any further possibility for existence of the German people.

We have no right, at this stage of the war, to carry out destructions which would adversely affect the life of the Nation.

If our enemies wish to destroy Germany then this historical shame shall rest exclusively upon them.

We have the obligation of leaving to the Nation all possibility which, in the future, might help reconstruction.[8]

On March 18 Speer attended one of Hitler's military situation conferences, which were held in the underground bunker rather than in the great conference room of the Chancellery. Hitler was in a friendly but somewhat melancholy mood when he greeted Speer. "Ah, you know, Herr Speer, your beautiful architecture no longer provides the proper frame for the situation conferences." The most pressing topic of discussion was Patton's invasion of the Saar. Hitler was arguing with the generals that he could not afford to lose the mines of the Saar. Suddenly he turned to Speer for support: "Tell the gentlemen what the loss of the Saar coal will mean."

"That would only speed up the collapse," responded Speer. Under normal circumstances such a "defeatist" statement would have been considered treason, but Hitler let it pass. He was not so conciliatory later on, however, when one officer read a report from Field Marshal Kesselring that the German civilians in the west were not willing to help the troops defend their towns and villages against the Allies. Enraged, Hitler ordered that all towns near the front be evacuated, by force if necessary. When one general pointed out that there were no longer any trains to evacuate so many people, Hitler testily replied: "Then let them walk."

No provisions had been made for the relocation of these millions of people. If Hitler's orders had been carried out, thousands of people would have died from starvation, exposure, and disease. When the conference broke up at about 2:00 A.M., Speer decided he would not go to East Prussia as he had originally planned but would instead travel to the west to see what he could do to obstruct Hitler's evacuation order.

It was now March 19, Speer's fortieth birthday. As he left the conference Hitler wished him happy birthday and handed him a signed silver-framed photograph in a stamped red leather case. When Speer thanked him Hitler apologized for his handwriting. "Lately it's been hard for me to write even a few words in my own hand. You know how it shakes. Often I can hardly complete my signature. What I've written for you came out almost illegible."[9]

Speer then told Hitler he would be driving west that night to the Rhineland and the Palatinate. Hitler must have sensed that his minister of armaments might try to block his evacuation order because he insisted his chauffeur, Erich Kempka, go along to help Speer with the driving. Obviously Hitler had told Kempka to spy on Speer.

By the time the car was ready and Speer bid Hitler good-bye, the Fuehrer's mood had changed and he said coolly: "This time you will receive a written reply to your memorandum!" Hitler paused and then in an icy tone added: "If the war is lost the people will also perish. This fate is inevitable. There is no necessity to take into consideration the basis which the people would need to continue a most primitive existence. On the contrary, it would be wiser to destroy even these things ourselves, because this nation had proved to be the weaker one and the future belongs solely to the stronger Eastern Nation. Besides, those who remain after the battle are only the inferior ones; for the good ones have already fallen."[10]

With Speer at the wheel of his six-cylinder souped-up BMW, they drove out of Berlin and headed west on the autobahn. They had the car radio tuned to the air raid warning station, and Kempka had a grid map on his knees. Whenever R.A.F. Mosquito bombers were announced in their grid, they would turn down their lights and proceed slowly along the edge of the road. As soon as the radio announced their grid was free of enemy planes, Speer would turn on his bright lights and the yellow fog lights, switch on the supercharger, and roar down the highway.

Taking turns driving, they were in the Rhineland by morning. There was a protective blanket of early morning fog that grounded all Allied aircraft. Soon they reached Nauheim, where the headquarters of the German forces in the west was located in a picturesque little castle on the top of a cliff. At noon Speer met with Field Marshal Kesselring, the new commander in chief of the west, and tried to talk him out of carrying out Hitler's evacuation order. Kesselring was not interested in being involved in any "treasonous" plots.[11] But as he and Speer walked back and forth on the castle terrace, he did agree to suppress any further reports to Hitler on defeatism among the local German population.

After their conference Speer was invited to lunch with Kesselring and his staff. Just as the field marshal raised his glass to toast to Speer's birthday, the high-pitched whining sound of American planes descending on the castle was heard. Machine gun fire came ripping through the windows. Everyone immediately dropped to the floor, some crawling under the castle's heavy dining table. Bombs began to explode nearby. As the bombardment continued, Kesselring, Speer, and the other officers rushed through the smoke and falling plaster dust down a narrow staircase leading to the bunker below the castle. When the attack was over, they dusted off their uniforms and continued the conference.

By this time Hermann Rochling, a seventy-year-old industrialist from the Saar and one of Speer's principal collaborators in the plot, arrived to join the discussion. Rochling had formerly been a Nazi and a big contributor to Hitler, but now he wanted to end the war as quickly as possible. During the meeting Field Marshal Kesselring told Rochling that the Saar would be lost to the advancing Americans in a few days. Rochling, whose factories and mines were located in the Saar, did not seem upset. "We have lost the Saar once before and won it back. Old as I am, I shall see it returned to our possession again."[12]

Speer and Rochling left Kesselring's headquarters together

and drove through the Rhineland, meeting with important officials, trying to discourage them from carrying out Hitler's evacuation and destruction orders. On the drive Rochling "made it quite clear," said Speer, "that he thought it senseless fanaticism to continue the war."[13]

Everywhere they traveled there were signs of an all-pervasive mood of "defeatism" among the people. Everyone was anxiously awaiting the end of the war. Last-minute defensive measures by the *Volkssturm* (home guard) were confused and halfhearted. Hitler's evacuation orders were being completely ignored. S.S. General Hausser, the commander of the southern section of the western front along the Rhine, told Speer and Rochling that he thought Hitler's orders were irresponsible. Even Stohr, the Nazi gauleiter of the Palatinate, said he would refuse to carry out the evacuation order.

Hitler's power seemed to be breaking down completely. Isolated in Berlin he could issue draconian orders, but no one would obey them. Speer and his fellow conspirators were able to encourage disobedience to orders from Berlin because there was a power vacuum in the enforcement apparatus of the Nazi state. What was the S.S. and the Gestapo doing while the authority of their Fuehrer was crumbling? S.S. General Otto Ohlendorf, the former commander of S.S. Action Group D in Russia, was now chief of the S.D., the intelligence service of the S.S. He later said he was aware of the conspiracy to obstruct Hitler's destruction orders. Ohlendorf knew everything Speer was doing but did nothing to stop him. In fact some of the industrialists who belonged to Himmler's Circle of Friends, a group of wealthy contributors to the S.S., had been secretly discussing plans for a postwar Germany without Hitler for over a year. Furthermore Himmler was already plotting on his own to get rid of the Fuehrer.

Hitler was, however, not yet completely powerless. There were still Nazi fanatics and loyal soldiers willing to carry out his orders. To demonstrate his authority Hitler had four officers who had failed to destroy the Remagen bridge, executed. This was to serve as an example to "defeatists." It sent a shock wave through the army, and most officers now thought twice about disobeying Hitler.

On March 20 Speer was at Field Marshal Model's headquarters in a village inn located in the Westerwald. As they were discussing the preservation of railroad installations in the Ruhr, they were interrupted by a messenger. "This concerns you," Model said to Speer.

It was an order from Hitler that called for "the destruction of all industrial, supply, transportation, and communication installations" including gasworks, water-pumping stations, and electrical power plants. In this order Hitler also revoked Speer's power to oversee and thus obstruct industrial destruction. From now on the Nazi gauleiters were in charge of all industrial destruction, while the military authorities were responsible for destroying all bridges and railroad facilities including all locomotives and rolling stock. The object of this order Hitler frankly stated was to "create a transportation desert in the abandoned area."[14]

If this order from Hitler was carried out, the results would have been devastating. Without electricity, water, and transportation there would be no industrial production, employment, nor means of feeding the population; as Speer later said it would have thrown Germany back into the Middle Ages. However, as soon as Field Marshal Model read the order, instead of taking a stand against this vandalism, he immediately became very aloof and broke off the discussion with Speer.

After briefly returning to Berlin Speer was back in the Rhineland on March 24 trying to talk Ruhr gauleiters out of executing Hitler's destruction orders. Gauleiter Florian of Düsseldorf was particularly resistant. He intended to evacuate the entire population on foot and then set fire to the city. Several influential industrialists casually informed Florian that if he tried to set fire to the city "someone" might organize a popular uprising to instead burn the gauleiter, as might have happened in the Middle Ages. Florian prudently agreed to "delay" the destruction.

On March 25 Walter Rohland, the tank manufacturer, summoned the leading Ruhr industrialists who wanted to end the war to a meeting at the castle of Landsburg near Essen that had formerly belonged to Fritz Thyssen. Speer and about twenty powerful executives of the steel and coal cartels were present. The demolitions ordered by Hitler were scheduled to begin the next day. However, the Nazi gauleiters who were planning to blow up factories and power plants had two problems. First, they needed explosives, which they thought they could get from the coal mines. Second, they needed trucks to transport the explosives and their demolition squads. They planned to requisition the only nonmilitary trucks available, from Speer's Todt Construction Organization.

After a brief discussion, most of the industrialists at Landsburg castle were determined to resist Hitler's orders. They decided to take three steps immediately to stop any Nazi demolitions. First of all, any available dynamite, explosives, or blasting caps belonging to the coal companies would be dropped into the sumps of the mines. Second, Speer ordered the Todt Organization to drive all their trucks out of the Ruhr that night and either give them to the front-line troops or drive them until they ran out of gas.

Third, and most significantly, Speer agreed to give newly produced submachine guns to the industrialists and their workers, to defend their factories if necessary, from the gauleiters' demolition squads by force of arms. The factory police of many firms also possessed weapons. Finally, there was a will to use them. Some sympathetic generals also provided Speer and the leading industrialists in the conspiracy with bodyguard units of young officers with submachine guns. On the other hand the local police and Nazi party organizations on whom the gauleiters depended to carry out the demolition orders had recently turned their arsenals over to the army, so they were left with nothing but a few pistols.[15]

Speer arrived back in Berlin on March 27. The news was not good. General Guderian, the commander of all German troops in the east and the most powerful ally of the conspiracy, had just been dismissed by Hitler. When Speer reported to the Chancellery bunker, Hitler received him without shaking hands and came directly to the point. "Bormann [Hitler's private secretary] has given me a report on your conference with the Ruhr gauleiters. You pressed them not to carry out my orders and declared that the war is lost. Are you aware of what must follow from that?"[16]

There was a sharp bitterness in Hitler's voice. Then he hesitated, as if he had suddenly recalled something from the remote past. His body visibly relaxed and in a normal tone he said, "If you were not my architect, I would take the measures that are called for in such a case."[17]

Anyone else would have been sentenced to death for treason immediately, but Speer was Hitler's best friend, the man who shared his architectural fantasies. To Hitler, being an architect was the highest calling one could have in life. Some of Hitler's happiest moments had been spent discussing building plans and going over blueprints with Speer. "You are overworked and ill. I have therefore decided that you are to go on leave at once. Someone else will run your ministry as your deputy."

"No, I feel perfectly well," Speer responded. "I am not going on leave. If you no longer want me as your minister, dismiss me from my post."

"It is impossible for me to dismiss you," said Hitler. "For reasons of foreign and domestic policy, I cannot spare you." After a long pause Hitler finally sat down. "Speer," he said, "if you can convince yourself that the war is not lost, you can continue to run your office."

When Speer refused to commit himself, Hitler gave him twenty-four hours to think it over. On leaving the bunker Speer was undecided as to what to do. His coconspirators urged him not to abandon his post but to pretend to go along with Hitler and sabotage his demolition orders by delaying.

The next night at midnight Speer returned to Hitler's bunker under the Chancellery garden. When Speer was shown into the conference room Hitler looked up and tersely asked: "Well?"

"Mein Fuehrer, I stand unreservedly behind you," Speer answered.

Shaking hands with Speer, Hitler said, "Then all is well." His eyes began to fill with tears.

Taking advantage of Hitler's obviously renewed feelings of close personal friendship, Speer said: "If I stand unreservedly behind you, then you must again entrust me instead of the gauleiters with the implementation of your decree."[18] Hitler agreed.

Speer drew up a new decree on demolition that Hitler promptly signed.[19] Although this decree was worded like Hitler's original order, Speer inserted two loopholes. In some cases "crippling" of industries would be enough to deny their use to the enemy. Where "total destruction" of especially important plants was required, Speer himself had to give specific authorization first, which naturally he never did.[20] With his full authority over demolitions restored, Speer simply delayed giving any orders until it was too late and the rapidly advancing Allies had captured the important factories or bridges. All the conflicting orders issued on demolitions so confused local officials that a bureaucratic gridlock was created in which no one did anything, which is what Speer and his fellow conspirators intended. Later Hitler even conceded to Speer that a scorched earth strategy could not work in a country as small as Germany but was only effective in the vast space of Russia.

From the beginning of 1945 it had been obvious that it would not be a good year for Hitler or the Germans. On January 12 the Russians had launched a great offensive from the Baltic to the Danube.[21] They quickly overran Poland and most of Hungary. Soon the Russians were fighting on German soil in Silesia, the only industrial region that had escaped major bombing damage. During the later part of the winter and early spring the Germans were able to hold the Soviets on the Oder River. In the south, however, Vienna fell to the Russians on April 13.

In the west Hitler's armies had fared no better. In March the Americans and British had crossed the Rhine. One famous German city after another fell to the Allies. By April 1 the German troops in the Ruhr were encircled. A few weeks later they surrendered. This left a gap two hundred miles wide in the German line. The U.S. First and Ninth Armies headed for the Elbe River and the heart of Germany; there was nothing between the Allies and Berlin.

On April 16 the Russians crossed the Oder in force and began their great drive on Berlin. Heavily outnumbered, the German armies were not strong enough to hold them back. Berlin was in a state of panic. Everyone who was able was fleeing the city. The capital of the Reich had already suffered heavily during the war. About one-third of all homes and buildings had been damaged or destroyed by the bombings. Streets were littered with piles of bricks and rubble from the bombed-out buildings. In the center of Berlin the damage was particularly heavy. Few of the exclusive shops and banks on the famous Unterden Linden were undamaged. Many were gutted completely. On both sides of the

Wilhelmstrasse formerly magnificent buildings now lay in ruins, but Hitler's massive Chancellery remained standing. It was scarred from bomb damage with gaping holes here and there and many windows boarded up, but it was still habitable.

On April 20 the leaders of the Third Reich all came together for the last time in the Chancellery to celebrate Hitler's fifty-sixth birthday. In the years of Nazi triumph Hitler's birthday had been celebrated with regal splendor. A line of large black Mercedes limousines had brought dignitaries and foreign ambassadors in dress uniform to the Chancellery. By comparison this celebration was muted.[22]

The interior of the Chancellery looked like a building about to be evacuated. The paintings and tapestries were gone, and most of the carpets were rolled up. Much of the furniture remained, but there were conspicuous empty spaces where especially valuable pieces of furniture had been removed and put in storage. Dirty glasses had been left on the tables and discarded old newspapers in the chairs. Speer found the state of neglect in the rooms "a fitting framework for Hitler's own lamentable condition."[23]

Hitler received the birthday wishes of Goebbels, Goering, Bormann, Himmler, Speer, Ribbentrop, and others with little emotion. In the afternoon Hitler went out into what had formerly been the Chancellery garden, but what now looked like a pockmarked moonscape and junkyard from the bombing and debris, to award metals to a delegation of Hitler Youth troops. With the collar of his overcoat turned up against the damp spring chill, Hitler walked down the line of about twenty teenage boys, all war orphans from Breslau and Dresden, shaking hands and patting them on the shoulder. As soon as this ceremony was over, Hitler went back down into the underground bunker where he had been living for the past few weeks because the almost constant Allied bombing disturbed his sleep.

Later that day Hitler and all the military leaders assembled in the conference room of the bunker for the daily military conference. The Russian attack on Berlin was discussed. Soviet tanks had broken through north of the city and taken Oranienburg. This indicated the Russians were executing a great pincer move to encircle Berlin. Goering pointed out that only one main road out of Berlin to the south was still open and it might be cut at anytime. Almost everyone had been urging Hitler to leave Berlin and transfer his headquarters to Obersalzberg. For days Hitler had not been able to make up his mind. Suddenly he declared he would stay in Berlin and fight: "How can I call on troops to undertake the decisive battle for Berlin if at the same moment I myself withdraw to safety!"

Goering, pale and sweating, was sitting across the table from Hitler. He had just returned from blowing up his palatial home, Karinhall, on the outskirts of Berlin, to keep it from falling into the hands of the Soviets. He sent a convoy of over twenty Luftwaffe trucks carrying all the treasures of Karinhall, the paintings, silver, and tapestries, on ahead to Bavaria.[24] Goering had no intention of dying with Hitler in Berlin. As soon as the conference was over he told Hitler that he had urgent tasks in Bavaria and would have to leave Berlin that night. Hitler looked at him absentmindedly and shook hands. He gave no indication he saw through Goering's cowardly excuse to escape fighting. Probably he just didn't care.

Hitler decided to stay in Berlin because he was confident that the troops defending the city would be inspired by his presence to make heroic efforts. He was probably the only person who did not think the situation was hopeless. He had a plan. While General Krebs, the new chief of staff who had replaced General Guderian, was explaining the disposition of the German troops, he mentioned that S.S. General Steiner was reassembling his troops north of Berlin.

Hitler suddenly interrupted him and told General Krebs to order Steiner to attack south in the direction of Berlin within twenty-four hours. If successful Steiner's attack would cut off the Russians' northern pincer at Oranienburg. Hitler was also planning to order two German armies south of Berlin commanded by Generals Wenk and Busse to attack to the north toward Berlin and thus cut the southern Russian pincer.

Strategically Hitler's plan had merit. Berlin would provide the hard center that was drawing Russian troops like a magnet. Hitler would defend the city street by street. The Soviet tanks would be vulnerable and almost useless in the rubble, just as the German tanks had been at Stalingrad. While the Russians were thus tied down trying to invade and encircle Berlin, the German armies of Steiner, Wenk, Busse, and Heinrici outside the city would attack them from the rear and crush them against the hard central core of the Berlin defenses. "The Russians," said Hitler, "will suffer their greatest defeat of the war in Berlin."

There were several problems with Hitler's plan. First of all the German armies outside Berlin were not up to their full strength. They were particularly short of tanks and artillery. Many of their troops were reservists rather than front-line troops. Second, the commanders of the armies facing the Russians had no intention of defending Berlin or Hitler. Although Hitler didn't realize it yet, the third and final rebellion against his regime was already taking place. Many army units were deliberately retreating from Berlin rather than back to defend it as ordered.*

The leader of this last revolt against Hitler's authority was General Gotthard Heinrici, the commander of Army Group Vistula. Heinrici was a short, small, middle-aged man who looked more like a poor shopkeeper than a general. His clothes were always threadbare; his favorite winter outfit consisted of an old sheepskin-lined overcoat and World War I leggings. He hated the high polished boots popular with most other officers. But his mild, scruffy appearance belied his tough character. He was an expert at defensive warfare and made the enemy pay dearly for every foot of ground they took from him, while minimizing the loss of his own troops. His men proudly called him "our tough little dwarf."

Heinrici was from an old Prussian military family and was a cousin of Field Marshal von Rundstedt. A devout Protestant, he had never been a supporter of Hitler or the Nazis. On several occasions he was reprimanded by Hitler for publicly attending church services and encouraging his men to do likewise. Once, Heinrici had been relieved of his command and forced to sit idle for several months "for reasons of health." In the end Hitler had to recall him because his talents were indispensable. At last

---

*Heinrici's rebellion was not a plot to overthrow the Nazi government as the Generals' Plot in July 1944 had been. It was a spontaneous refusal to carry out suicidal orders. To what extent it was a conspiracy is difficult to say. The evidence seems to indicate Heinrici discussed part of his plans with a few other officers, and some of them were sympathetic.

Heinrici saw a chance to save Germany from Hitler and his final desperate gamble.

Heinrici's plan apparently was not to defy Hitler openly but to pretend to carry out his orders while at the same time ordering his armies to bypass Berlin and retreat to the Elbe. General Heinrici and his sympathizers seem to have had two or three major objectives.* First, they wanted to save their troops from dying needlessly for a hopeless cause. Second, they wanted to get their armies to the Elbe to surrender to the British and Americans rather than be captured by the Russians. Third, although it was probably never discussed, they wanted to put an end to the war as soon as possible.

At the General Staff military conference on April 22, in Hitler's bunker, General Krebs and General Jodl began by explaining the extent of the Russian advance. General Krebs said he thought Berlin would be encircled and cut off from the rest of Germany in about twenty-four hours. Hitler interrupted Krebs and asked where General Steiner and his attacking forces were. After some hesitation Krebs admitted that Steiner had not yet attacked. With an unexpected burst of energy Hitler jumped up out of his chair and began shouting and raving. "He turned alternately deathly pale and purple in the face, shaking in every limb," said Captain Gerhard Boldt, General Krebs's aide. "His voice cracked and he screamed of disloyalty, cowardice, treachery and insubordination."[25] He cursed and insulted both the army and the Waffen S.S. Finally Hitler's outburst subsided. He collapsed back into his chair and began sobbing. "It is all over," he said. "The war is lost. I shall shoot myself."[26]

For a moment there was complete silence in the bunker. Then all of Hitler's officers and associates tried to reassure him that all was not lost, although few of them believed there was much hope. Field Marshal Keitel and General Jodl volunteered to go to Steiner's and Wenk's armies and personally do everything they could to launch relief attacks to liberate Berlin. That night the

---

*It has never been determined exactly who General Heinrici's sympathizers were. The desperation and confusion during the last days of the war led many officers to have mixed motives. For example, even loyal Nazis may have preferred escaping to the west rather than dying for Hitler in Berlin.

two generals departed; General Jodl headed north to locate Steiner's army and Field Marshal Keitel traveled southwest to find General Wenk's headquarters.

After some difficulty and traveling miles out of his way to avoid the advancing Russians, General Jodl finally located Steiner's headquarters at Nassenheide, north of Berlin. General Heinrici also arrived at Steiner's headquarters at about the same time. The three generals began discussing plans for Steiner's attack toward Berlin. It was immediately clear that Steiner was trying to stall for time. He asked Jodl if he had seen any of his troops, the so-called Steiner Army Group.

"They are in first-rate condition," Jodl replied. "Their morale is very good."

Then Heinrici asked, "Steiner, why aren't you attacking? Why are you postponing again?" Heinrici wanted Steiner to attack, not to save Hitler in Berlin, but to slow down the Russian advance so he would have time to withdraw Manteuffel's army, which was the major component of his army group, to the northwest.

Steiner argued that he had only "a few" panzers and hardly any artillery. "I just don't have the troops," he said. "I don't have the slightest chance of succeeding."

"Well, Steiner," Heinrici said sarcastically, "you have to attack for your Fuehrer." Enraged, Steiner shouted back, "He's your Fuehrer too."[27]

Although Steiner was not an ally of Heinrici, he may have been refusing to attack in part because S.S. Chief Himmler had told him not to go to the relief of Berlin. Himmler had finally decided to betray Hitler and was trying to make a deal with the western Allies on his own. He believed his bargaining power with the British and Americans would increase as soon as Hitler was dead.

Southwest of Berlin Field Marshall Keitel's big Mercedes staff car pulled up outside the headquarters of General Wenk. Wenk had formerly been General Guderian's chief of staff, and at age forty-five he was the youngest general in the German army. A professional soldier, Wenk had no illusions about Germany's future. Tapping his field marshal's baton in his gloved hand, Keitel tried to impress on Wenk the importance and urgency of his attack. The fate of Germany was at stake Keitel said. By attacking north toward Berlin, Wenk's army would cut off the southern Russian pincer encircling Berlin.

Wenk was irritated by Keitel's arrogant manner and later recalled that the field marshal and his staff "strutted as if they had just captured Paris" while all around them the roads were clogged with pitiful German refugees and retreating beaten troops. Wenk, however, did not argue with Keitel and agreed to attack as soon as possible.[28] What he did not tell Keitel was that he thought it was impossible to relieve Berlin but would attack toward the northeast far enough to link up with the retreating Ninth Army of General Busse and then beat a hasty retreat to the Elbe to surrender to the Americans.*

Russian troops were surging into the suburbs of Berlin. They advanced carefully behind their T-34 tanks. There was no consistency in the defense of Berlin. In some places the Germans resisted doggedly; in other places the defenders broke and ran. The Germans' major problem was a lack of well-trained troops. The regular army, S.S. units, and the Hitler Youth fought tenaciously, but the poorly equipped *Volksstrum* (home guard) and reserves were easily overrun. The Russians used their artillery and rockets to good advantage, blowing down buildings where there was any sniper fire and setting whole city blocks on fire with phosphorous shells. Since there was no water in many neighborhoods and no one to fight the fires, the thousands of blazes cast an eerie glow throughout the city all night long.

As the Russian tanks penetrated deeper into the city, they encountered an unexpected problem. Boys of the Hitler Youth and determined civilians, including more than a few women, were firing *Panzerfaustes,* crude handheld antitank rockets, from basement windows and behind piles of rubble and knocking out Russian tanks. The *Panzerfaustes* were still being produced by a few Berlin factories and taken to the "front," which was often

---

*It is not clear whether Heinrici had given Wenk orders to follow this course of action or whether Wenk was doing it on his own initiative. Nevertheless, both Heinrici and Wenk deserve credit for saving thousands of men from dying needlessly.

only a few blocks away, in wheelbarrows. The Russians lost so many tanks to the *Panzerfaustes* that they finally gave up and ordered all tanks to withdraw from the city. This was the kind of resistance Hitler was hoping for. If the whole army had fought for Berlin, the city might have held out for weeks. But would it have made any difference? Certainly the death toll would have been higher and the destruction worse.

What difference would a few more weeks have meant even to Hitler? Some people accused him of trying to prolong his miserable life as long as possible, but he was playing for higher stakes. If the Russians failed to take Berlin quickly a split among the Allies might have occurred. When General Eisenhower decided the Americans and British would halt on the Elbe and let the Soviets take Berlin, the British were stunned. The British chiefs of staff declared that "letting the Russians capture Berlin was a grievous political and military blunder." Churchill was furious. He correctly recognized that the Soviets posed a mortal danger to the free world. "Berlin," said Churchill, "is the prime and true objective of the Anglo-American armies."[29]

Hitler was still personally commanding the Berlin defenses from his bunker below the Chancellery garden. The bunker was protected by six feet of earth and sixteen feet of concrete overhead. Inside it was cramped. There were eighteen small rooms with narrow corridors. Poor ventilation made the atmosphere dark and musty. Most of the rooms had nothing but bare gray cement walls. The air was always heavy with the smell of boots, sweaty uniforms, and mold. But the physical unpleasantness of the bunker was nothing when compared to the psychological atmosphere. There was a mood of gloom and hopelessness combined with hysterical fear. With the Russians in Berlin there was a danger that some of them might suddenly slip through German lines and get into the bunker. Some of the people in the bunker were women; Hitler's secretaries, cooks, and nurses, like all women in Berlin, were terrified of being raped by the Russians.

On the night of April 26, the Russian artillery zeroed in on the Chancellery. When heavy artillery shells landed nearby, the entire bunker would shake as the shock waves were absorbed by the sandy Berlin soil. The Soviet troops were only about a mile away now. Deep in the bunker Hitler was almost completely cut off from the outside world and reality. The information he was getting was increasingly unreliable and contradictory. He spent most of his time bent over the map trying to locate the remaining German armies outside Berlin and find out what they were doing. Hitler sent a wireless message to Field Marshal Keitel on April 28: "I expect the relief of Berlin. What is Heinrici's army group doing? What is happening to the Ninth Army? . . . What is the situation on the armored attack from the north of Berlin [Steiner]?"[30]

Field Marshal Keitel was one of the few generals still loyally following Hitler's orders. He set out in his staff car to find General Heinrici's army. To his surprise he soon encountered the Third Panzer Army, on the road going west in full retreat. This was the main part of Heinrici's forces. When Keitel finally met Heinrici a few hours later he confronted him angrily: "Why did you give the order to move back? You were told to stay on the Oder! Hitler ordered you to hold! He ordered you not to move!" Pointing his marshal's baton at Heinrici he shouted: "Yet you! You ordered the retreat!"

Heinrici calmly responded, "I cannot hold the Oder with the troops I have. I do not intend to sacrifice their lives."[31]

Hitler was being abandoned not only by General Heinrici but by some of his old Nazi comrades as well. Goering sent Hitler an ultimatum, by telegram, that he would take over as Fuehrer unless he received a response in a few hours. Even worse Himmler was secretly trying to negotiate with the Allies behind Hitler's back. Hitler immediately ordered the arrest of both Goering and Himmler and expelled them from the party. "Nothing is spared me," Hitler lamented. "No allegiances are kept, no honor lived up to, no disappointments that I have not had, no betrayals that I have not experienced."[32]

On April 30 General Wilhelm Monke, who commanded the troops in the Chancellery area, informed Hitler that the Russians were only four blocks away and he could no longer guarantee that his exhausted troops could hold out more than twenty-four hours. Hitler was prepared. He made his will and testament and selected his successors. In his testament he made one final denunciation of his old enemies the Jews, proving again just how obsessed he was with anti-Semitism:

It is untrue that I or anyone else in Germany wanted the war in 1939. It was desired and instigated exclusively by those international statesmen who were either of Jewish descent or worked for Jewish interests. I have made too many offers for the control and limitation of armaments . . . for the responsibility for the outbreak of this war to be laid on me. I have further never wished that after the first fatal world war a second against England, or even against America, should break out. Centuries will pass away, but out of the ruins of our towns and monuments, and the hatred against those finally responsible whom we have to thank for everything, International Jewry and its helpers, will grow. . . .

I also made it quite plain that, if the nations of Europe were again to be regarded as mere shares to be bought and sold by these international conspirators in money and finance, then that race, Jewry, which is the real criminal of this murderous struggle, will be saddled with the responsibility. I further left no one in doubt that this time not only would millions of children of Europe's Aryan peoples die of hunger, not only would millions of grown men suffer death, and not only hundreds of thousands of women and children be burnt and bombed to death in the towns, but the real criminals [the Jews] would have to atone for this guilt, even if by more humane means.

This was one of Hitler's few acknowledgments of his responsibility for the Holocaust; although, of course, the Jews were never "guilty" of anything, least of all of starting the war, and their treatment by the Nazis was never "humane." After his ridiculous accusations against the Jews Hitler went on to express his bitterness toward the army officers who he felt had betrayed him: "May it, at some future time, become part of the code of honor of the German officer—as is already the case in our Navy—that the surrender of a district or of a town is impossible, and that above all the leaders must march ahead as shining examples, faithfully doing their duty unto death."

After considerable self-justification, Hitler explained his decision to remain in Berlin: "I have decided therefore to remain in Berlin and there of my own free will to choose death at the moment when I believe the position of the Fuehrer and Chancellor itself can no longer be held. I die with a happy heart, aware of the immeasurable deeds and achievements of our soldiers at the front."[33]

In the second part of his testament, Hitler got his ultimate revenge on the army, Himmler, and Goering by appointing Admiral Doenitz, a navy man, as his successor as president of Germany. The navy had never played more than a weak secondary role in German politics. Now Hitler elevated it above the army. For his failure to carry out Hitler's orders of destruction Speer was replaced as minister of armaments by Saur, a Nazi party loyalist.

On the evening of May 1, 1945, German public radio interrupted its programming to tell its listeners to stand by for an important announcement. An hour later after a few notes of solemn funeral music, the broadcaster announced: "It is reported from the Fuehrer's headquarters that our Fuehrer, Adolf Hitler, fighting to the last breath against bolshevism, fell for Germany this afternoon in his operational command post in the Reich Chancellery. On April thirtieth, the Fuehrer appointed Grand Admiral Doenitz as his successor."[34]

Endnotes

CHAPTER 1: FINANCING THE 1933 ELECTIONS

1. Goebbels, *My Part in Germany's Fight*, 207–08.
2. Shirer, *The Rise and Fall of the Third Reich*, 19–20.
3. This was a spontaneous action of the marchers, not something ordered by Hitler or the Nazi leaders. In fact, when Hitler heard what was happening, he was alarmed that the French might use it as a pretext for an international incident. It was a perfect illustration of how widespread extreme nationalist sentiments were among the German people. Adlon, *Hotel Adlon*, 202.
4. François-Poncet, *The Fateful Years*, 48.
5. Fromm, *Blood and Banquets*, 74.
6. Papen, *Memoirs*, 261.
7. Fest, *The Face of the Third Reich*, 159.
8. Many of the officers liked what they heard. Admiral Raeder, for example, was particularly impressed. See *My Relationship to Hitler and the Party* by Erich Raeder, Moscow fall 1945. Document Statement IX.
9. Delmer, *Trail Sinister*, 158.
10. Bullock, *Hitler: A Study in Tyranny*, 221–22.
11. Hitler, *Secret Conversations* (hereafter referred to as *S.C.*), 405.
12. Irving, *Goering: A Biography*, 111–29.
13. National Archives Microfilm T 580, roll 85.
14. Hitler, *S.C.*, 407.
15. Extreme nationalism and antidemocratic sentiments were widespread

among the German industrialists. See National Archives record group
260 OMGUS papers 6234 5 1/11.

16. Speech of Hitler to leading members of industry before the election of
March 1933. Document D-203, Nuremberg Documents hereafter
refered to as ND.
17. Testimony of Hjalmar Schacht, 20 July 1945. Document 3725-PS, ND.
18. Toland, *Adolf Hitler*, 406.
19. Minutes of the first meeting of the Hitler cabinet, 30 January 1933.
Document 351-PS, ND.
20. Papen, *Memoirs*, 267.
21. For an eyewitness account of the Reichstag fire, see Delmer, *Weimar
Germany*, 118.
22. Toland, *Adolf Hitler*, 406–07, and Tobias, *The Reichstag Fire*, 50–51.
23. Delmer, *Weimar Germany*, 119.
24. Hoffmann, *Hitler Was My Friend*, 73.
25. Decree of the Reich President for the Protection of the People and
State, 28 February 1933. Document 1390-PS, ND.
26. Most historians think the Communists had no immediate plans for a
coup.
27. Hermann Goering, Speeches and Essays, Speech of 2 March 1933.
Document 1856-PS, ND.
28. Fromm, *Blood and Banquets*, 87–88.
29. Hitler, *S.C.*, 406.

CHAPTER 2: STEPS TOWARD DICTATORSHIP

1. Fromm, *Blood and Banquets*, 109.
2. François-Poncet, *The Fateful Years*, 61.
3. Rhodes, *The Vatican in the Age of the Dictators*, 176.
4. Ibid., 175.
5. For the so-called Enabling Act, see Law to Remove the Distress of
People and State, 24 March 1933. Document 2001-PS, ND.
6. Rauschning, *The Voice of Destruction*, 78–80.
7. Goebbels, *My Part in Germany's Fight*, 237.
8. Toland, *Adolf Hitler*, 424.
9. Ibid.
10. Manchester, *The Arms of Krupp*, 366.
11. For a complete discussion of Gustav Krupp's conversion to nazism see
Manchester, *The Arms of Krupp*, 366–71.
12. Ibid., 368.
13. Lochner, *Tycoons and Tyrants*, 122–23.
14. Manchester, *The Arms of Krupp*, 369.

15. Delmer, *Trail Sinister*, 114.
16. Ibid, 114–15.
17. Kubizek, *The Young Hitler I Knew*, 17–18.
18. Delmer, *Trail Sinister*, 156.
19. Goebbels, *My Part in Germany's Fight*, 251–53 and Lüdecke, *I Knew Hitler*, 632–38.
20. François-Poncet, *The Fateful Years*, 70.
21. Law concerning confiscation of property subversive to people and state, 14 July 1933.

CHAPTER 3: HITLER WAS GIVEN HIS ORDERS

1. For an account of Hitler's activities in Berlin during the second day of the purge, see Gisevius, *To the Bitter End*, 163–72; and Gallo, *The Night of the Long Knives*, 267–72.
2. Gallo, *Long Knives*, 238; and Heiden, *Der Fuehrer*, 770.
3. Rauschning, *Hitler Speaks*, 130.
4. Flood, *Hitler*, 196.
5. Infield, *Hitler's Secret Life*, 194.
6. Langer, *The Mind of Adolf Hitler*, 173.
7. Lüdecke, *I Knew Hitler*, 493–94.
8. Rauschning, *The Voice of Destruction*, 154–56.
9. Wheeler-Bennett, *The Nemesis of Power*, 310–11.
10. Baynes, *The Speeches of Adolf Hitler*, vol. 2, 556.
11. *Völkischer Beobachter*, January 2, 1934.
12. For the S.A.'s increasing involvement in military affairs and the army's reaction see Letter from Reich Military Ministry, 26 May 1933, suggesting that an S.A. branch and Reich Defense Council be united. Document 2822-PS, ND.
13. The S.A. was already in charge of "premilitary training." See Memorandum from Supreme S.A. Headquarters, 19 March 1934, concerning organization of the S.A. and collaboration between Wehrmacht and S.A. Document 2821-PS, ND.
14. Hohne, *Order of the Death's Head*, 88.
15. Benoist-Mechin, *Histoire de l'Armée Allemande depuis Armistice*, vol. 2, 553–54.
16. "Ten years, Security Police and SD" published in *Die Deutsche Polizei*, 1 February 1943. Document 1680-PS, ND.
17. Goering still exercised considerable influence over the Gestapo in Prussia. See Order of Gestapo Office, Darmstadt, 7 December 1938, concerning treatment of articles secured during protest action against the Jews. Document D-183, ND.

18. Padfield, *Himmler*, 151.
19. Bullock, *Hitler*, 290–91.
20. *Frankfurter Zeitung*, June 10, 1934.
21. Delmer, *Trail Sinister*, 231.
22. Strasser, *Hitler and I*, 186.
23. Delmer, *Trail Sinister*, 233.
24. Affidavit of Wilhelm Frick, 19 November 1945. Document 2950-PS.
25. *Völkischer Beobachter*, June 26, 1934.
26. Baur, *Hitler at My Side*, 77.
27. Hitler's address to the Reichstag, 13 July 1934. Document 3442-PS, ND.
28. Gallo, *Long Knives*, 207.
29. Noakes and Pridham, *Nazism: A History of Documents and Eyewitness Accounts, 1919–1945*, 178.
30. Payne, *The Life and Death of Adolf Hitler*, 270–74; Gallo, *Long Knives*, 212–13, and Noakes and Pridham, *Nazism: A History of Documents and Eyewitness Accounts, 1919–1945*, 178–80.
31. Gallo, *Long Knives*, 242.
32. Hitler's address to the Reichstag, 13 July 1934. Document 3442-PS, ND.
33. Affidavit of Wilhelm Frick, 19 November 1945. Document 2960-PS, ND.
34. Gisevius, *To the Bitter End*, 157–61.
35. Gallo, *Night of the Long Knives*, 269–70.
36. Hitler's address to the Reichstag, 13 July 1934. Document 3442-PS, ND.
37. Gisevius, *To the Bitter End*, 158–59.
38. Noaks and Pridham, *Nazism: A History of Documents and Eyewitness Accounts, 1919–1945*, 177.
39. Padfield, *Himmler*, 173.
40. Gisevius, *To the Bitter End*, 173.
41. Rauschning, *The Voice of Destruction*, 172–73.
42. Although Papen was detained during the purge, Hitler later publicly stated that he was innocent and a loyal member of the regime. See Hitler's address to the Reichstag 18 July 1934.
43. Craig, *The Politics of the Prussian Army*, 480.

CHAPTER 4: DID THE KING OF ENGLAND HELP HITLER REARM?

1. Hoover, *The Ordeal of Woodrow Wilson*, 234–42.
2. Speech of Hitler at November 23, 1939, Conference of Supreme Commanders. Document 789-PS, ND.

3. Unsigned. Schacht memorandum to Hitler, May 3, 1935, concerning the financing of the armament program. Document 1168-PS, ND.
4. Letter from minister of interior to minister of propaganda Goebbels July 20, 1934, concerning unauthorized press release about military affairs. Document 3581-PS, ND.
5. Minutes of second session of Working Committee of the Reich Defense held on April 26, 1933. Document EC-177, ND.
6. Unsigned documents found in official navy files containing notes year by year from 1927 to 1940 on reconstruction of the German Navy, dated February 18, 1938, March 8, 1938, and September 1938. Document C-23, ND.
7. Hitler's speech before the Reichstag, published in the *Völkischer Beobachter*, May 22, 1935. Document 2288-PS, ND.
8. Dodd, *Ambassador Dodd's Diary*, 51.
9. Directive for preparations in event of sanctions, October 25, 1936, signed by von Blomberg. Document C-140, ND.
10. Directive from von Blomberg to supreme commanders of army, navy and air force on June 24, 1935, accompanied by copy of Reich Defense Law of May 21, 1935. Document 2261-PS, ND.
11. Schacht, *Confessions of the "Old Wizard,"* 55-56.
12. Affidavit of Puhl, November 2, 1945. Document EC-436, ND.
13. Letter of January 16 with enclosure—article about Schacht in the *Military Weekly Gazette*. Document EC-383, ND.
14. Shirer, *The Rise and Fall of the Third Reich*, 441.
15. Toland, *Adolf Hitler*, 483.
16. Ibid., 484.
17. Shirer, *The Rise and Fall of the Third Reich*, 386.
18. Manstein, *Lost Victories*, 274–75.
19. Report from the ambassador in Great Britain to the foreign minister London, April 12, 1935. DGFP Series C, vol. 4, 48, 1506/E37333-35.
20. Interview of Goering by *London Daily Mail* concerning the German Air Force, March 1935. Document 2292-PS, ND.
21. Law of March 16, 1935. Reintroducing Universal Military Conscription. Document 1654-PS, ND.
22. Hitler's speech before the Reichstag published in the *Völkischer Beobachter*, May 22, 1935.
23. Shirer, *The Rise and Fall of the Third Reich*, 392.
24. Although the reintroduction of conscription was popular in military circles and probably approved of by the majority of Germans, Hitler was not confident enough to put the issue to vote as he had done in other plebiscites.
25. Bullock, *Hitler*, 334, and François-Poncet, *The Fateful Years*, 175.
26. Author's interview with Winfred Wagner.

27. The *London Times,* June 12, 1935.
28. Windsor, *A King's Story,* 254
29. From the *Morning Post,* June 13, 1935, quoted in Donaldson, *Edward VIII,* 207.
30. Ziegler, *King Edward 8th,* 385–86.
31. Hitler, *Mein Kampf,* 254.
32. Ziegler, *King Edward 8th,* 385
33. Unsigned memorandum sent by the duke of Coburg's chief of staff, Nord. Part III, Marked: "Strictly Confidential, only for the Fuehrer and Party Member v. Ribbentrop." DGFP Series C vol. 4, 1062–64, 5482/E382057-78.
34. Ambassador Robert W. Bingham to Roosevelt. London, January 5, 1937. Franklin D. Roosevelt and Foreign Affairs. Vol. 3, 568–69.
35. Ziegler, *King Edward 8th,* 385.
36. Order for Rhineland occupation signed by von Blomberg, March 2, 1936. Document C-159, ND.
37. Hitler speech in the Reichstag March 7, 1936, published in the *Völkischer Beobachter,* March 8, 1936. Document 2289-PS, ND.
38. Speer, *Inside the Third Reich,* 72.
39. Ibid., 72.
40. Hitler, *Secret Conversations,* 211–12.
41. Hesse, *Hitler and the English,* 21–23. Some historians question Hesse's account, however, it seems to be basically accurate.
42. Ambassador Hoesch to the Foreign Ministry. London, March 11, 1936, 10:30 P.M. DGFP Series C, vol. 5, 106, 6710/E506679.
43. Record of telephone conversation between Dr. V. Stutterheim and Paul Scheffer, March 18, 1936—12:45 P.M. Marginal note submitted to the state secretary and foreign minister. DGFP Series C, vol. 5, 193–94, 7609/E544945.
44. "The Strategic Position at the Beginning of the Fifth Year of the War," A lecture delivered by Jodl, 7 November 1943. Document L-172, ND.
45. Memorandum of conversation between William C. Bullitt, American ambassador to France and the German minister of foreign affairs, von Neurath, in Berlin, 18 May 1936. Document L-150, ND.
46. Hitler, *S.C.,* 515.

CHAPTER 5: WHO GOT THE CONFISCATED JEWISH PROPERTY?

1. Schleunes, *The Twisted Road to Auschwitz,* 86–87.
2. Ibid., 93; and Barkai, *From Boycott to Annihilation,* 17.
3. Gellately, *The Gestapo and German Society,* 101.
4. Barkai, *From Boycott to Annihilation,* 14.
5. Varga, *The Number One Nazi Jew-Baiter,* 217–19.

Endnotes

6. Ibid., 264–65.
7. Gellately, *The Gestapo and German Society*, 106.
8. Varga, *Nazi Jew-Baiter*, 215.
9. Noaks and Pridham, *Nazism: A History of Documents and Eyewitness Accounts, 1919–1945*, 531.
10. Laws were soon passed to bar Jewish children from German schools entirely. *Gesetz über die uberfullung deutscher Schullen*. Document 2084-PS, ND.
11. Shirer, *The Rise and Fall of the Third Reich*, 347.
12. *Der Stürmer*, no. 28, July 1938, "The Ritual Murder."
13. Children's book, *The Poisonous Fungus*, published by *Der Stürmer*.
14. This statement is in no way attempting to minimize the centuries of terrible persecutions, pogroms, and murders committed in the name of Christian anti-Semitism; indeed, Jews would sometimes convert only to be murdered anyway. However, by comparison, Hitler's racial anti-Semitism would prove even more terrible than any of the injustices and atrocities of Christian anti-Semitism.
15. Deverlein, *Hitler's Eintritt in die Politik und die Reichswer*, 202.
16. Steinhoff, *Voices from the Third Reich*, 42.
17. Barkai, *From Boycott to Annihilation*, 58.
18. Ibid., 54–109. Avraham Barkai proves conclusively that there was no "grace period" for Jewish business in Germany, even in the early 1930s.
19. Varga, *Nazi Jew-Baiter*, 262–63.
20. Disciplinary and Penal Measures for concentration camp Dachau and Service Regulations for camp personnel. Signed by Eicke, 1 October 1933. Document 778-PS, ND.
21. Lüdecke, *I Knew Hitler*, 717–18.
22. Schacht, *My First Seventy-Five Years*, 320.
23. *Gesetz zum Schultze des deutschen Blutes*. (Law for the Protection of German Blood.) 15 October 1935. Document 2000-PS, ND.
24. General Decree of September 10, 1935, on establishment of separate Jewish schools. Document 2894-PS, ND.
25. Dodd, *Through Embassy Eyes*, 28.
26. *Erste Verordnung zum Reichsbuergergesetz*. Document 1417-PS, ND.
27. *Time*, "Paradise for Blackmailers." November 25, 1933.
28. Dodd, *Through Embassy Eyes*, 28.
29. Schleunes, *The Twisted Road to Auschwitz*, 146–47; and Hale, 131–35.
30. For more on Hitler's secret ownership of Eher Publishing, see Chapter 6 of *Hitler and His Secret Partners*.
31. Hale, *Captive Press in the Third Reich*, 316.
32. Barkai, *From Boycott to Annihilation*, 72–73.
33. Fromm, *Blood and Banquets*, 264.

34. *Verordnung über die Ammeldung des Vermogens von Juden.* (Decree for reporting Jewish-owned property.) Reichsgesetzblatt, I, 414.
35. Barkai, *From Boycott to Annihilation,* 173.
36. Fromm, *Blood and Banquets,* 282–83.
37. Letters about anti-Semitic demonstrations of November 9, 1938. Document 3063-PS, ND.
38. Three Teletype orders from Heydrich to all stations of state police, 10 November 1938. Document 3051-PS, ND.
39. Steinhoff, *Voices from the Third Reich,* 55.
40. Thalman, *Crystal Night,* 64.
41. Anti-Semitic onslaught . . . as seen from Leipzig. Messersmith report, January 4, 1939. Document L-202, ND.
42. Pope, *Munich Playground,* 96–99.
43. Ibid., 98.
44. Statistics for damages on Crystal Night are taken from Schwab, *The Day the Holocaust Began,* 25–27.
45. Ibid., 28.
46. Reimann, *Goebbels,* 233–37.
47. Decree relating to payment of fine by Jews, 12 November 1938. Document 1412-PS, ND.
48. Decree on exclusion of Jews from German economic life, 12 November 1938. Document 2875-PS, ND.

CHAPTER 6: HITLER'S EXTRAVAGANCE AND CORRUPTION

1. Von Lang, *The Secretary,* 90.
2. Hoffmann, *Hitler Was My Friend,* 168.
3. Speer, *Inside the Third Reich,* 43–44.
4. Hoffmann, *Hitler Was My Friend,* 175.
5. Ibid., 179.
6. Ibid., 171.
7. Schwarzwaller, *The Unknown Hitler,* 183, states that Hitler paid 65,000 marks for *Venus and Amor* and "not less than" 24,000 marks for the other paintings.
8. Ibid., 183.
9. Ibid., 183–90.
10. Hoffmann, *Hitler Was My Friend,* 183.
11. Von Lang, *The Secretary,* 94–95.
12. Ibid., 98.
13. Ibid., 104.
14. François-Poncet, *The Fateful Years,* 280–81.
15. Von Lang, *The Secretary,* 100. Also see: Schwarzwaller, *The Unknown Hitler,* 178–79.

16. Speer, *Inside the Third Reich*, 60.
17. Hoffmann, *Hitler Was My Friend*, 189–90.
18. Figures are from Hitler's 1933 tax return. See Hale, Oron, "Adolf Hitler—Taxpayer," *American History Review*, 1965.
19. Speer, *Inside the Third Reich*, 86.
20. Krupp, Schacht, and Hess correspondence in 1933, regarding the Adolf Hitler Fund. Document D-151, ND.
21. Affidavit of 17 October 1945 concerning payments of Fried Krupp Cast Steel Works to Party and Part organizations. Document D-325, ND.
22. Hoffmann, *Hitler Was My Friend*, 179
23. Hale, *Captive Press in the Third Reich*, 21–33. Also see Schwarzwaller, *The Unknown Hitler*, 92–94.
24. Ibid., 317.
25. Von Epp papers, National Archives Microfilm T-84, R-24, FR.9692 and R-25, FR. 9695.
26. Hale, *Captive Press in the Third Reich*, 19–20.
27. *The Living Age*, "The Man Who Made Hitler Rich," December 1938, 338.
28. Lüdecke, *I Knew Hitler*, 403–04. On at least one occasion Hitler publicly denied that any shares of Eher Verlag were privately owned. Some historians have accepted this view. See Hale, *Captive Press in the Third Reich*, 20–21. However, it must be remembered that regardless of statutes and ordinances which stated Eher Verlag belonged to the NSDAP, Nazi Germany was a dictatorship and any secret trust agreement of the Fuehrer could override anything else. Documents that might have revealed that Hitler was the majority owner of Eher Verlag would have been one of the first things the Nazis destroyed in 1945.
29. Ibid., 403.
30. Speer, *Inside the Third Reich*, 34.
31. Ibid., 103.

CHAPTER 7: EASY PREY—BIG PROFITS

1. Gedye, *Betrayal in Central Europe*, 207.
2. Notes on a conference with Hitler in the Reich Chancellery, Berlin, 5 November 1937, signed by Hitler's adjutant, Hossbach, and dated 10 November 1937. Document 386-PS, ND.
3. The record of this conference is sometimes called the "Hossbach Memorandum" because Hitler's adjutant Colonel Hossbach took the notes.
4. Pauley, *Hitler and the Forgotten Nazis*, 172–216.
5. Von Schuschnigg, *Austrian Requiem*, 20. Also see Affidavit of Kurt von

Schuschnigg, concerning his visit to Berchtesgaden on 12 February 1939. Document 2995-PS, ND.

6. Unpublished diary of General Jodl. Document 1780-PS, ND.
7. Murray, *Change in the European Balance of Power*, 3–49.
8. Toland, *Adolf Hitler*, 596.
9. Gehl, *Austria Germany and the Anschluss*, 178–80.
10. Document signed by Hitler relating to "Operation Otto," 11 March 1938. Document C-102, ND.
11. Transcripts of telephone calls from the Air Ministry 11-44 March 1938. Document 2949-PS, ND.
12. Wagner, *Anschluss*, 174–81.
13. Quoted in Toland, *Adolf Hitler*, 622.
14. Letter presumably from Buerkel to Goering, dated Vienna 26 March 1938, concerning Aryanization of Jewish-held businesses in Austria. Document 3577-PS, ND.
15. Shirer, *The Rise and Fall of the Third Reich*, 477.
16. Ibid.
17. Order for Transfer of Austrian National Bank to Reichsbank, 17 March 1938. Document 2313-PS, ND.
18. Murray, *Change in the European Balance of Power*, 150.
19. Rauschning, *Hitler Speaks*, 9.
20. German Foreign Office memorandum, 19 August 1938, on payments to Henlein's Sudeten German party. Document 3059-PS, ND.
21. Affidavit of Fritz Wiedemann on Hitler's conference at the Reich Chancellery, 28 May 1938. Document 3037-PS, ND.
22. File of papers on "Case Green," kept by Schmundt, April–October 1938. Document 388-PS, ND.
23. Murray, *Change in the European Balance of Power*, 268.
24. Ibid., 269.
25. Affidavit of Gottlob Berger on the composition and activity of the Henlein Free Corps in September 1938. Document 3036-PS, ND.
26. Wheeler-Bennett, *Munich: Prologue to Tragedy*, 104–08.
27. Chamberlain's secret agenda for Czechoslovakia was apparently reported to Hitler by German intelligence in the fall of 1937. In his conference, at the Reich Chancellery, on November 5, 1937, Hitler said he believed England had "already secretly written off Czechoslovakia." Notes on conference with Hitler in Reich Chancellery, 5 November 1937. Document 386-PS, ND.
28. *Documents on British Foreign Policy*, Third Series, I and II.
29. Shirer, *The Rise and Fall of the Third Reich*, 565. Also see: Eubank, *Munich*, 207–21.
30. Gisevius, *To the Bitter End*, 326.
31. Testimony of Schacht at Nuremberg, 2 May 1946.

32. Testimony of Keitel at Nuremberg, 4 April 1946.
33. Shirer, *The Rise and Fall of the Third Reich*, 598–603. Also see German Foreign Office minutes of the meeting between Hitler and President Hacha, 15 March 1938. Document 2798-PS, ND.
34. *Wehrmacht* (German military magazine) article on the occupation of Czechoslovakia, March 29, 1939.
35. Decree establishing the Protectorate of Bohemia and Moravia, 16 March 1939. Document TC-51, ND.
36. Murray, *Change in the European Balance of Power*, 291.
37. Hitler's Reichstag speech, April 28, 1939.
38. Murray, *Change in the European Balance of Power*, 292.
39. Ibid., 291.
40. Benes correspondence quoted in Duff, *A German Protectorate*, 138.
41. Quoted in Toland, *Adolf Hitler*, 711.

Chapter 8: Victory and Looting in Poland and the West

1. Minutes of conference, 23 May 1939, Indoctrination on the Political Situation and Future Aims. Document L-79, ND.
2. Schmidt, *Hitler's Interpreter*, 464.
3. Guderian, *Panzer Leader*, 73–74.
4. Quoted in Toland, *Adolf Hitler*, 799.
5. Appendix to Goering's directive of 19 October 1939, concerning the economic administration of the occupied territories. Document EC-410, ND.
6. Frank diary, 1939, 25 October to 15 December. Document 2233-PS, ND.
7. Instruction for . . . law concerning property of Poles . . . seized and confiscated. Document R-92, ND.
8. Segal, *The New Order in Poland*, p. 118.
9. Thomas report, 20 August 1940, summarizing experience with German armament industry in Poland. Document EC-344-16 and EC-344-17, ND.
10. Segal, *The New Order in Poland*, 109–110.
11. Farben's VOWI report no. 3609, "The Most Important Chemical Firms in Poland," 28 July 1929. Documents NI-9151, NI-9154, and NI-9155, ND.
12. Segal, *The New Order in Poland*, 103–04.
13. Hitler, *S.C.*, 192.
14. Fischer, *From Kaiserreich to Third Reich*.
15. Hitler's speech of November 23, 1939.

16. Fischer, *Germany's Aims in the First World War*, 607–08.
17. Ibid.
18. Quoted in Shirer, *The Rise and Fall of the Third Reich*, 616.
19. Fischer, *From Kaiserreich to Third Reich*, 104.
20. Shirer, *The Rise and Fall of the Third Reich*, 641–42.
21. Directive No. 6 for the Conduct of the War, signed by Hitler, 9 October 1939; directive by Keitel, 15 October 1939 on "Fall Gelb." Document C-62, ND.
22. Hitler order for operation "Weseruebung," 1 March 1940. Document C-174, ND.
23. Manstein, *Lost Victories*, 94–126.
24. Manchester, *The Arms of Krupp*, 417.
25. Shirer, *The Rise and Fall of the Third Reich*, 977.
26. Speer, *Inside the Third Reich*, 171.
27. Quoted in Milward, *The New Order and the French Economy*, 71.
28. Development and position of French industry in area of military commander. France, 1941. Document EC-267, ND.
29. Milward, *The New Order and the French Economy*, 72.
30. Manchester, *The Arms of Krupp*, 427. The compensation the Germans offered the owners of such machinery was only a fraction of its true value.
31. Hoffmann, *Hitler Was My Friend*, 123.

CHAPTER 9: FOREIGN FRIENDS: KENNEDY, LINDBERGH, AND THE WINDSORS

1. Ambassador Dirksen to State Secretary Weizsacker, London, October 13, 1938. DGFD 2422/511576-81.
2. Blum, *From the Morgenthau Diaries*, 518.
3. Collier and Horowitz, *The Kennedys*, 94.
4. Lindbergh, *Wartime Journals*, 26.
5. Whalen, *The Founding Father*, 223.
6. Ickes, *Secret Diary*, vol. 2, 676.
7. Ambassador Dirksen to Weizsacker, June 13, 1938. DGFP 438/220953-62.
8. Lindbergh, *Wartime Journals*, 72.
9. Telegram from Ambassador Kennedy to Secretary of State Hull, London, September 28, 1938—noon. FRUS 760 F.62/1186.
10. Telegram from Kennedy to Hull, London, September 29, 1938—6 P.M. FRUS 760 F.62/1248.
11. Beschloss, *Kennedy and Roosevelt*, 241.
12. Whalen, *The Founding Father*, 244–49. Also see Beschloss, *Kennedy and Roosevelt*, 178.

Endnotes

13. Whalen, *The Founding Father*, 250. Also see Collier and Horowitz, *The Kennedys*, 96, and Beschloss, *Kennedy and Roosevelt*, 179.
14. DGFP 438/220953-62.
15. Collier and Horowitz, *The Kennedys*, 110.
16. Forrestal, *Forrestal Diaries*, 121.
17. Telegram from Kennedy to Hull, London, October 5, 1938—5 P.M. FRUS 840.48/Refugees/790.
18. Whalen, *The Founding Father*, 254–55.
19. Koskoff, *Joseph P. Kennedy*, 180.
20. Ibid., 221. Also see Beschloss, *Kennedy and Roosevelt*, 187.
21. Higham, *Trading with the Enemy*, 168–70, and Costello, *Ten Days to Destiny.*
22. Ibid.
23. Whalen, *The Founding Father*, 270. Also see: Beschloss, *Kennedy and Roosevelt*, 190.
24. Whalen, *The Founding Father*, 283–85.
25. *New York Times*, December 11, 1939.
26. Costello, *Ten Days to Destiny*, 101–25, 130–62. Also see: Beschloss, *Kennedy and Roosevelt*, 206–07.
27. Higham, *Trading with the Enemy*, 181.
28. *New York Times*, September 12, 1941.
29. Cole, *Charles A. Lindbergh*, 173.
30. Lee, *Henry Ford and the Jews*, 126–27.
31. *Der Stürmer*, no. 28, "The Ritual Murder," July 1938.
32. Cohn, *Warrant for Genocide*, 22, 55.
33. Author's interview with Sir Oswald Mosley.
34. Infield, *Hitler's Secret Life*, 115.
35. Donaldson, *Edward VIII*, 353.
36. Schmidt, *Hitler's Interpreter*, 75.
37. *New York Times*, October 23, 1937.
38. Higham, *Duchess of Windsor*, 269, and Parker, *King of Fools*, 180–81.
39. Orders postponing "A" day in the west, November 1939 to May 1940. Document C-72.
40. Higham, *Duchess of Windsor*, 46–49. Also see Thornton, *Royal Feud*, 56, 79.
41. Higham, *Duchess of Windsor*, 52–55, and Parker, *King of Fools*, 10–12, 63–67.
42. Some historians, including Charles Higham, *Duchess of Windsor*, and John Costello, *The Pacific War*, think Wallis could have been spying for the Soviets. Given her political sympathies, however, it is more likely she was working for the Japanese through her Italian friends.
43. Telegram from Ambassador Weddell to Secretary of State Hull, Madrid, July 2, 1940—noon. FRUS 740.0011 European War 1939/4357.

44. Telegram from the German minister in Portugal, Huene, to the Foreign Ministry, marked "Most Urgent—Top Secret," Lisbon, August 2, 1940—3:46 P.M. DGFP no. 276, B15/B002632-33.
45. Costello, *Ten Days to Destiny*, 302–16.
46. Telegram from Ribbentrop to the German legation in Portugal, marked "Most Urgent—Top Secret," July 31, 1940—6:30 P.M. DGFP no. 265, B15/B002617-18.
47. Telegram from Stohrer to Ribbentrop, marked "Most Urgent—Top Secret," Madrid, July 31, 1940. DGFP no. 264, B15/B002619-20.
48. Schellenberg, *Memoirs*, 109–11. Also see DGFP no. 265, B15/B002617-15.
49. Telegram, Ambassador Stohrer to the Foreign Ministry, marked "Most Urgent—Top Secret," Madrid, July 23, 1940. DGFP no. 211, B15/B002582-83.
50. DGFP no. 264, B15/B002619-20.
51. Telegram, Schellenberg to Ribbentrop, Lisbon, August 2, 1940—10:00 P.M. DGFP no. 277, B15/B002635-38.
52. Fulton Oursler, Jr., "Secret Treason," *American Heritage: World War II*, 58.
53. Ibid.
54. Notes on conference between Hitler and Oshima, 14 December 1941. Document 2932-PS, ND.
55. Toland, *Adolf Hitler*, 951.
56. OKW Order 24, initialed Jodl, signed Keitel, 5 March 1941, concerning collaboration with Japan. Document C-75, ND.
57. Hitler, *S.C.*, 123, 130.

CHAPTER 10: WEALTH TO BE WON IN RUSSIA

1. Extracts of General Thomas's unpublished report *Basic Facts for History of German War and Armament Economy*. Document 2353-PS, ND.
2. Stokesbury, *A Short History of World War II*, 154.
3. Top secret notes taken by Hamann of a discussion of the economic exploitation of Russia, presided over by General Thomas, 28 February 1941. Document 1317-PS, ND.
4. Top secret Fuehrer Order no. 21, signed by Hitler 18 December 1940 concerning the invasion of Russia. Document 446-PS, ND.
5. Hitler, *Mein Kampf*, 654.
6. Notes on a conference with Hitler in the Reich Chancellery, Berlin, 5 November 1937, signed by Hitler's adjutant Hossbach 10 November 1937. Document 386-PS, ND.
7. Thomas Document 2353-PS, ND.

8. Timetable for Barbarossa, approved by Hitler and signed by Keitel. Document C-39, ND.
9. Report on conference, 29 April 1941, concerning top secret plan for economic exploitation of Soviet areas (Oldenburg Plan). Document 1157-PS, ND.
10. Guderian, *Panzer Leader*, 200.
11. Thyssen, *I Paid Hitler*, 26.
12. Hayes, *Industry and Ideology*, 257.
13. Maser, *Hitler*, 216.
14. *Petroleum Times*, "The German War for Crude Oil in Europe," January 31, and February 14, 1948.
15. Irving, *Hitler's War*, 385.
16. Hitler, *S.C.*, 275.
17. Ibid., 259.
18. Speer, *Inside the Third Reich*, 195.
19. Ibid., 196.
20. Testimony of Field Marshal von Paulus at Nuremberg, 11 February 1946, ND.
21. Goralski and Freeburg, *Oil and War*, 84–85.
22. Hitler, *S.C.*, 20.
23. Hayes, *Industry and Ideology*, fn. 159, 254.
24. Reitlinger, *The House Built on Sand*, 200.
25. Hitler, *S.C.*, 57.
26. Ibid., 57.
27. Fischer, *From Kaiserreich to Third Reich*, 60.
28. Dallin, *German Rule in Russia*, 383–85.
29. Manchester, *The Arms of Krupp*, 434–35.
30. Economic policy directives for Economic Organization East. Agricultural Group Document EC-126, ND.
31. Letter of Rosenberg to Bormann 17 October 1944 concerning liquidation of property in the Occupied Eastern Territories. Document 327-PS, ND.
32. Goebbels, *Diaries*, 235.
33. General instructions for all Reich Commissars in the Occupied Eastern Territories 8 May 1941 found in Rosenberg file. Document 1030-PS, ND.
34. Gisevius, *To the Bitter End*, 200–01.
35. Clark, *Barbarossa*, 191.
36. Ibid., 192.
37. *Petroleum Times*, January 31, 1948, also Goralski and Freeburg, *Oil and War*, 182.
38. Goralski and Freeburg, *Oil and War*, 178–79.

39. Hayes, *Industry and Ideology,* 255–57.
40. Dallin, *German Rule in Russia,* 243.
41. Baur, *Hitler at My Side,* p. 153.
42. Toland, *Adolf Hitler,* 984.
43. *Petroleum Times,* January 31, 1948. For a slightly higher estimate of production see Goralski and Freeburg, *Oil and War,* 183.
44. Gilbert, *Hitler Directs His War,* 17–22.
45. Toland, *Adolf Hitler,* 985.

Chapter 11: Motives for Genocide

1. Musmanno, *The Eichmann Commandos,* 152–162. Also see affidavit of Paul Blobel, 6 June 1947, concerning extermination in Russia. Document No-3824, ND.
2. Stenographic report of the meeting on "the Jewish question" under the chairmanship of Goering, 12 November 1938. Document 1816-PS, ND.
3. Levin, *The Holocaust,* 103–04.
4. Morse, *While Six Million Died,* 212.
5. Ibid, 204–06.
6. Testimony of Rezsoe Kastner, Major Phases of the Persecution of Hungarian Jewry. Document 2605-PS, ND.
7. Rubin, *Hitler and the Nazis: The Evil Men Do,* 93.
8. Fleming, *Hitler and the Final Solution,* 17.
9. Hauner, *The Hitler Chronology,* 142.
10. Hitler, *S.C.,* 476.
11. *Völkischer Boebachter,* February 1, 1939.
12. Memorandum from Rosenberg file concerning instructions for the treatment of Jews. Document 212-PS, ND.
13. Frank's diary, 1939, 25 October to 15 December. Document 2233-G-PS, ND.
14. Fuehrer Decree, 13 May 1941, on court-martials and treatment of enemy civilians in district "Barbarossa," signed by Keitel for Hitler. Document 886-PS, ND.
15. Toland, *Adolf Hitler,* 915.
16. Dawidowicz, *War Against the Jews,* 166.
17. Ibid.
18. Directive on the conduct of troops in the Occupied Eastern Territories, 10 October 1941, signed von Reichenau. Document D-411, ND. Also see Dawidowicz, *War Against the Jews,* 167.
19. Affidavit of Otto Ohlendorf, 5 November 1945. Document 2620-PS, ND.

20. Letter from Goering to Heydrich, 31 July 1941, concerning solution of Jewish question. Document 710-PS, ND.
21. Jick, *A Story of Betrayal*, 89.
22. Frank diary, 1941, October to December. Cabinet Session, 16 December 1941. Document 2233-D-PS, ND.
23. Report by S.S. Brigade Commander Stahlecker to Himmler, Action Group A, 15 October 1941. Document L-180, ND.
24. Goebbels, *The Goebbels Diaries*, 175–77.
25. Regulation for the treatment of Soviet POWs, 8 September 1941, signed by Reinecke. Document 1519-PS, ND.
26. Letter from Rosenberg to Keitel, 28 February 1942, concerning mistreatment of Soviet POWs. Document 081-PS, ND.
27. Graber, *History of the SS*, 145.
28. Collection of four documents on execution by gas, June 1942, one signed by Dr. Becker, 16 May 1942. Document 501-PS, ND.
29. Minutes of the Wannsee Conference, 20 January 1942, Plans for the "final solution of the Jewish question." Document NG-2586-G, ND.
30. Toland, *Adolf Hitler*, 963.
31. Hitler, *S.C.*, 193.

CHAPTER 12: "GENERALS KNOW NOTHING ABOUT ECONOMICS"

1. Reitlinger, *The House Built on Sand*, 260.
2. Letter from Sauckel to Reichminister for the Occupied Eastern Territories, 5 October 1942, concerning mobilization of foreign labor forces. Document 017-PS, ND.
3. Sauckel order, 20 July 1942, concerning employment of foreign labor forces in Germany. (Section on transportation.) Document 2241-PS, ND.
4. Speer's conference minutes of Central Planning Board, 1942–1944, concerning labor supply. Document R-124, ND.
5. Testimony of Fritz Sauckel, 28 May 1946. International Military Tribunal.
6. Letter from Rosenberg to Sauckel, 21 December 1942, concerning labor in the east. Document 018-PS, ND.
7. Memorandum to Mr. Hupe, 14 March 1942, concerning employment of Russians. Document D-316, ND.
8. Affidavit of Dr. Wilhelm Jaeger, 15 October 1945. Document D-288, ND.
9. Manchester, *The Arms of Krupp*, 487.
10. Record of telephone conversation of the chief of the Economic Staff East, 11 March 1943. Document 3012-PS, ND.

11. Memorandum concerning evacuation of youths from the territory of Army Group Center, 12 June 1944. Document 031-PS, ND.
12. Himmler's speech to S.S. Grueppenfuehrers, 4 October 1943. Document 1919-PS, ND.
13. Baur, *Hitler at My Side*, 156–57.
14. Guderian, *Panzer Leader*, 308–09.
15. Speer, *Inside the Third Reich*, 243.
16. Directives issued by the Fuehrer and supreme commander of armed forces signed by Keitel, 7 December 1941, for prosecution of offensives against the Reich. Document 666-PS, ND.
17. Clark, *Barbarossa*, 188.
18. Speer, *Inside the Third Reich*, 315–17.
19. Maser, *Hitler*, 307.
20. Speer, *Inside the Third Reich*, 405.
21. Reitlinger, *The House Built on Sand*, 220.
22. Liddell Hart, *The German Generals Talk*, 67.
23. Manstein, *Lost Victories*, 504–05.
24. Speer, *Inside the Third Reich*, 294.
25. Goebbels, *Diaries*, 478.
26. Statement of Traudl Junge quoted in Galante, *Voices from the Bunker*, 112–13.
27. Goralski and Freeburg, *Oil and War*, 234.
28. Ibid., 242.
29. Borkin, *The Crime and Punishment of I.G. Farben*, 165.
30. Speer, *Inside the Third Reich*, 346.
31. Ibid., 348.
32. Goralski and Freeburg, *Oil and War*, pp. 247–48.
33. Ibid., 252–53.
34. Copy of order from Keitel to commanding general in France to cooperate with the Einsatzstab Rosenberg, 10 October 1940. Document 138-PS, ND.
35. Report of 8 August 1944 on confiscation up to 31 July 1944. Document L-188, ND.
36. Report on activities of special staff for pictorial art, October 1940 to July 1944. Document 1015-B-PS, ND.
37. Jaeger, *The Linz File*, 72–81.
38. Hitler, *S.C.*, 300–01.
39. Jaeger, *The Linz File*, 82.
40. Letter from Goering to Rosenberg, 30 May 1942. Document 1015-I-PS, ND.
41. Goering order concerning seizure of Jewish art treasures, 5 November 1940. Document 141-PS, ND.
42. Jaeger, *The Linz File*, 86.

43. Letter from Rosenberg to Schwarz, 28 January 1941, concerning registration and collection of art treasures. Document 090-PS, ND.
44. Report on activities of special staff for pictorial art, October 1940 to July 1944. Document 1015-B-PS, ND.

CHAPTER 13: WHO PROFITED FROM THE HOLOCAUST?

1. Field interrogation of Kurt Gerstein 26 April 1945, Describing the mass gassing of Jews. Document 1553-PS, ND.
2. Himmler's speech to S.S. generals at Posen, October 4, 1943. Document 1919-PS, ND.
3. Speer, *Inside the Third Reich*, 372.
4. Himmler's speech, October 4, 1943. Document 1919-PS, ND.
5. Letter from Goering to Himmler, 18 February 1941, on making more concentration camp workers available to Farben. Document NI-1240, ND.
6. Letter from Ambros to Ter Meer, 12 April 1941, report on Auschwitz construction and "our (Farben's) new friendship with the S.S." Document NI-11118, ND.
7. Affidavit of Rudolf Hoess, 5 April 1946. Document 3868-PS, ND.
8. Meltzer, *Never to Forget*, 91–92. For an insightful analysis of Farben's exploitation of Jewish slave labor also see: Jick, *Story of Betrayal*, 107–11.
9. Affidavit and testimony of Arnost Tauber, 3 March 1947. Document NI-4829, ND.
10. Borkin, *The Crime and Punishment of I.G. Farben*, 159.
11. Affidavit of Rudolf Hoess, 5 April 1946. Document 3868-PS, ND.
12. Ibid.
13. Shirer, *The Rise and Fall of the Third Reich*, 1263.
14. Deposition of Kurt Gerstein, Document 1552-PS, ND.
15. Affidavit of Rudolf Hoess, 5 April 1946. Document 3868-PS, ND.
16. Himmler frequently compared the killing of Jews to the killing of lice. Hoess may have picked up the idea from him; see Document 1919-PS, ND.
17. Hitler, *S.C.*, 269–70.
18. Ibid., 115.
19. Fest, *Hitler*, 80.
20. Maser, *Hitler*, 245–46.
21. Statement by Traudl Junge quoted in Galante, *Voices from the Bunker*, 97.
22. Fleming, *Hitler and the Final Solution*, 19–20.
23. Manchester, *The Arms of Krupp*, 450–51.
24. For more information on other industrialists who supported Himmler

and the S.S. see affidavit of Otto Ohlendorf, 28 January 1947, concerning the history of the Circle of Friends and its financial contributions to Himmler. Document NI-3510, ND.

25. Sworn statement of Dr. Wilhelm Jaeger, 15 October 1945. Document D-288, ND.
26. For an excellent analysis of the failure of the Allies to attack the death camps, see Gilbert, *Auschwitz and the Allies*, 299–311.
27. Ibid.
28. Notes on discussion between Hitler and Horthy, 17 April 1943. Document D-736, ND.
29. Letter from Himmler to Goering, 14 February 1944, on employment of prisoners in the aviation industry, marked "Top Reich Secret." Document 1585-111-PS, ND.
30. Speer's conference minutes of Central Planning Board 1942–1944, concerning labor supply. Document R-124, ND.
31. Affidavit of Dieter Wisliceny, 29 November 1945. Document Affidavit C, ND.

CHAPTER 14: THE "GOOD GERMANS" AND HITLER'S DRUG ABUSE

1. Gallin, *German Resistance to Hitler*, 7–16.
2. Stenographic report of the trial before the German People's Court on 7 and 8 August 1944. Document 3881-PS, ND.
3. Ibid.
4. Account of Traudl Junge in Galante, *Voices from the Bunker*, 114–15.
5. Wheeler-Bennett, *Nemesis of Power*, 635–94.
6. Bullock, *Hitler: A Study in Tyranny*, 749–50.
7. Report of People's Court trial. Document 3881-PS, ND. Also see Hart, *The German Generals Talk*, 261–67.
8. Report of People's Court trial. Document 3881-PS, ND.
9. Ibid.
10. Speer, *Inside the Third Reich*, 394.
11. Shirer, *The Rise and Fall of the Third Reich*, 324–33.
12. Hitler's military conference of 31 August 1944.
13. Speer, *Inside the Third Reich*, 416.
14. Hitler's military conference, 12 December 1944.
15. National Archives, Hitler Poisoning Rumors XE 198119, Annex II report on possible use of narcotics by Hitler.
16. National Archives XE 198119.
17. National Archives XE 198119, Annex III Observations on Hitler's doctors.

18. National Archives XE 198119, Annex II.
19. Irving, *Secret Diaries of Hitler's Doctor*, 231.
20. National Archives XE 198119, Annex II.
21. National Archives XE 198119.
22. Toland, *Adolf Hitler*, 827.
23. Ibid.

Chapter 15: Hitler's Partners Turn Against Him

1. Testimony of Albert Speer, 20 June 1946, IMT.
2. Speer's letter to Gauleiter Simon, 5 September 1944. Speer Document 025.
3. Speer, *Inside the Third Reich*, 434.
4. *Völkischer Beobachter*, 7 September 1944
5. Speer, *Inside the Third Reich*, 402.
6. Barnett, *Hitler's Generals*, 327–33.
7. For more on Hitler's optimism see Waite, *The Psychopathic God: Adolf Hitler*.
8. Testimony of Albert Speer, 2 June 1946, IMT.
9. Speer, *Inside the Third Reich*, 439.
10. Testimony of Albert Speer, 20 June 1946, IMT.
11. Barnett, *Hitler's Generals*, 286.
12. Speer, *Inside the Third Reich*, 441.
13. Ibid.
14. Hitler's March 19, 1945, Order for Destruction. Speer Documents 027 and 029.
15. Testimony of Albert Speer, 20 June 1946, IMT.
16. Speer, *Inside the Third Reich*, 451.
17. Ibid.
18. Ibid., 455.
19. Executionary decrees of Hitler, 30 March 1945. Speer Document 031.
20. Executive regulations of the Fuehrer Decree of 30 March 1945, concerning measures for crippling and destroying. Speer Document 032.
21. Guderian, *Panzer Leader*, 389–424.
22. Payne, *The Life and Death of Adolf Hitler*, 543.
23. National Archives XE 198119
24. Ryan, *The Last Battle*, 382–83.
25. Boldt, *Hitler: The Last Ten Days*, 117.
26. Ibid.
27. Ryan, *The Last Battle*, 446.
28. Mellenthin, *Germany Generals of World War II*, 269.

29. Breuer, *Storming Hitler's Rhine*, 286.
30. Testimony of Keitel, 28 September 1945, Keitel interrogation.
31. Ryan, *The Last Battle*, 448.
32. Interrogation of Hanna Reitsch, 8 October 1948. Document 3734-PS, ND.
33. Adolf Hitler's Political Testament. Document 3569-PS, ND.
34. O'Donnell, *The Bunker*, 368.

Selected Bibliography

The following bibliography comprises only works in English that are available to the public. Documents and German sources are cited in the footnotes.

Barkai, Avraham. *From Boycott to Annihilation.* Hanover, NJ, 1989.
Baur, Hans. *Hitler at My Side.* Houston, 1986.
Beschloss, Michael. *Kennedy and Roosevelt.* New York, 1980.
Bezymenski, Lev. *The Death of Adolf Hitler.* New York, 1968.
Boldt, Gerhard. *Hitler: The Last Ten Days.* New York, 1973.
Borkin, Joseph. *The Crime and Punishment of I. G. Farben.* New York, 1979.
Bracher, Karl. *The German Dictatorship.* New York, 1970.
Brook-Shepherd, Gordon. *The Anschluss.* Philadelphia, 1963.
Bullock, Alan. *Hitler, A Study in Tyranny.* New York, 1961.
Carell, Paul. *Hitler Moves East: 1941–1942.* New York, 1966.
Carr, William. *Arms, Autarky and Aggression.* London, 1972.
Ciano, Galeazzo. *The Ciano Diaries. 1939–1943.* Garden City, 1946.
Clark, Alan. *Barbarossa.* New York, 1965.
Collier, Peter, and David Horowitz. *The Kennedys.* New York, 1984.
Costello, John. *Ten Days to Destiny.* New York, 1991.
———. *The Pacific War.* New York, 1981.
Craig, Gordon. *The Politics of the Prussian Army: 1650–1945.* New York, 1968.
Dallin, Alexander. *German Rule in Russia, 1941–1944.* New York, 1957.
Davidson, Eugene. *The Trial of the Germans.* New York, 1966.
Dawidowicz, Lucy. *War Against the Jews.* New York, 1976.

Deakiin, F. W. *The Brutal Friendship*. New York, 1962.

Delarue, Jacques. *The Gestapo*. New York, 1964.

Delmer, Sefton. *Trail Sinister*. London, 1961.

———. *Weimar Germany*. London, 1972.

Dietrich, Otto. *Hitler*. Chicago, 1955.

Dodd, Martha. *My Years in Germany*. London, 1939.

Dodd, William. *Ambassador Dodd's Diary, 1933–1938*. London, 1941.

Donaldson, Frances. *Edward VIII*. Philadelphia, 1977.

Donitz, Admiral Karl. *Memoirs*. London, 1958.

Dorpalen, Andreas. *Hindenburg and the Weimar Republic*. Princeton, 1964.

Fest, Joachim. *The Face of the Third Reich*. New York, 1970.

———. *Hitler*. New York, 1974.

Fischer, Fritz. *From Kaiserreich to Third Reich*. Boston, 1986.

Fleming, G. *Hitler and the Final Solution*. London, 1985.

François-Poncet, Andre. *The Fateful Years*. London, 1949.

Fromm, Bella. *Blood and Banquets*. New York, 1942.

Galland, Adolf. *The First and the Last*. New York, 1957.

Gallately, Robert. *The Gestapo and German Society*. Oxford, NH, 1990.

Gallo, Max. *The Night of Long Knives*. New York, 1972.

Gedye, G. E. *Betrayal in Central Europe*. New York, 1939.

Gilbert, Felix. *Hitler Directs His War*. New York, 1950.

Gisevius, Hans B. *To the Bitter End*. Boston, 1947.

Goebbels, Joseph. *The Early Goebbels Diaries*. London, 1962.

———. *My Part in Germany's Fight*. London, 1935.

Goebbels, Joseph. Louis P. Lochner, ed. *The Goebbels Diaries*. London, 1962.

Goerlitz, Walter. *The German General Staff*. New York, 1959.

Goralski, Robert, and Russell Freeburg. *Oil and War*. New York, 1987.

Guderian, Heinz. *Panzer Leader*. New York, 1952.

Gun, Nerin. *Eva Braun*. New York, 1969.

Hale, Oron J. *The Captive Press in the Third Reich*. Princeton, 1964.

Heiden, Konrad. *Der Fuhrer*. Boston, 1944.

Higham, Charles. *Trading with the Enemy*. New York, 1983.

———. *Duchess of Windsor*. New York, 1989.

Hitler, Adolf. *Hitler's Secret Book*. New York, 1961.

———. *Hitler's Secret Conversations*. New York, 1953.

———. *Mein Kampf*. Boston, 1943.

Hoffman, Heinrich. *Hitler Was My Friend*. London, 1955.

Hohne, Heinz. *The Order of the Death's Hand*. New York, 1970.

Infield, Glenn. *Hitler's Secret Life*. New York, 1979.

Irving, David. *Goering: A Biography*. London, 1989.

———. *Hitler's War*. New York, 1972

Jaeger, Charles. *The Linz File*. Exeter, 1981.

Selected Bibliography

Jick, Leon. *A Story of Betrayal*. Cincinnati, 1954.

Keitel, Wilhelm. *Memoirs*. London, 1965.

Kirkpatrick, Ivone. *Mussolini*. New York, 1964.

Klein, Burton. *Germany's Economic Preparations for War*. Cambridge, 1959.

Koskoff, David. *Joseph P. Kennedy*. New Jersey, 1974.

Langer, Walter C. *The Mind of Adolf Hitler*. New York, 1972.

Laqueur, Walter. *Russia and Germany*. Boston, 1965.

Liddell, Hart B. H. *The German Generals Talk*. New York, 1979.

Lindbergh, Charles. *Wartime Journals*. New York, 1970.

Lochner, Louis. *Tycoons and Tyrants*. Chicago, 1954.

Lüdecke, Kurt G. W. *I Knew Hitler*. New York, 1937.

Manchester, William. *The Arms of Krupp*. Boston, 1970.

Manstein, Erich. *Lost Victories*. Chicago, 1958.

Manvell, Roger, and Heinrich Fraenkel. *Dr. Goebbels*. New York, 1960.

————. *Himmler*. New York, 1965.

Maser, Werner. *Hitler*. New York, 1975.

Meltzer, Milton. *Never to Forget*. New York, 1976.

Meskill, Johanna. *Hitler and Japan*. New York, 1966.

Milward, Alan S. *The German Economy at War*. London, 1965.

Milward, A. *The New Order and the French Economy*. London, 1970.

Morse, Arthur. *While Six Million Died*. New York, 1961.

Murray, Williamson. *Change in the European Balance of Power*. Princeton, 1984.

Musmanno, Michael. *The Eichmann Commandos*. Philadelphia, 1961.

Noakes, Jeremy, and Geoffrey Pridham, *Nazism: A History of Documents and Eyewitness Accounts, 1919–1945*. New York, 1990.

O'Donnell, James. *The Bunker*. New York, 1979.

O'Neill, Robert. *The German Army and the Nazi Party*. New York, 1966.

Orlow, Dietrich. *The History of the Nazi Party, 1933–1945*. Pittsburgh, 1973.

Padfield, Peter. *Himmler*. New York, 1991.

Papen, Franz von. *Memoirs*. London, 1952.

Parker, John. *King of Fools*. New York, 1988.

Payne, Robert. *The Life and Death of Hitler*. New York, 1973.

Pope, Ernest. *Munich Playground*. New York, 1941.

Price, G. Ward. *I Know These Dictators*. London, 1937.

Rauschning, Hermann. *The Voice of Destruction*. New York, 1940.

Reiss, Curt. *Joseph Goebbels*. New York, 1948.

Reitlinger, Gerald. *The House Built on Sand*. London, 1960.

Reitsch, Hanna. *Flying Is My Life*. New York, 1954.

Rudel, Hans Ulrich. *Stuka Pilot*. New York, 1958.

Ryan, Cornelius. *The Last Battle*. New York, 1960.

Schacht, Hjalmar. *Confessions of the "Old Wizard."* Cambridge, 1956.

Schlabrendorff, Fabian von. *The Secret War Against Hitler*. New York, 1965.

Schleunes, Karl. *The Twisted Road to Auschwitz*. Urbana, 1970.

Schuschnigg, Kurt von. *Austrian Requiem*. London, 1947.

Schwarzwaller, Wolf. *The Unknown Hitler*. New York, 1984.

Schweitzer, Arthur. *Big Business in the Third Reich*. Bloomington, Indiana, 1964.

Shirer, William L. *Berlin Diary*. New York, 1941

———. *The Rise and Fall of the Third Reich*. New York, 1960.

Speer, Albert. *Inside the Third Reich*. New York, 1970.

Steinhoff, Johannes. *Voices from the Third Reich*. Washington, DC, 1989.

Stokesbury, James A. *A Short History of World War II*. New York, 1980.

Strasser, Otto. *Hitler and I*. London, 1940.

Thornton, Michael. *Royal Feud*. New York, 1985.

Thyssen, Fritz. *I Paid Hitler*. New York, 1941.

Tobias, Fritz. *The Reichstag Fire*. New York, 1964.

Toland, John. *The Last 100 Days*. New York, 1966.

———. *Adolf Hitler*. New York, 1976.

Trevor-Roper, H. R. *The Last Days of Hitler*. New York, 1947.

Turner, Henry A. *German Big Business and the Rise of Hitler*. New York, 1985.

Varga, William. *The Number One Nazi Jew Baiter*. New York, 1981.

Von Lang, Jochen. *The Secretary*. New York, 1979.

Waite, Robert. *The Psychopathic God: Adolf Hitler*. New York, 1977.

Warlimont, Walter. *Inside Hitler's Headquarters*. Washington, 1964.

Whalen, Richard. *The Founding Father*. New York, 1966.

Wheeler-Bennett, John. *Munich: Prologue to Tragedy*. London, 1966.

———. *The Nemesis of Power*. New York, 1967.

Windsor, Duke of. *A King's Story*. London, 1951.

Wulff, Wilhelm. *Zodiac and Swastika*. New York, 1973.

Ziegler, Philip. *King Edward 8th*. New York, 1991.

Index

Index

Ciano, Galeazzo, 231
Cliveden Set, 218
Coburg, Duke of, 103, 227
Cologne, 106–07
Communist party, 17, 28, 32–39, 40
Communist revolution of 1918, 15–17,
  39, 271
concentration camps
  in 1930s, 55n, 123–25, 136
  Allied failure to attack, 338–39
  Farben factories in, 327–28
  gas chambers in, 319–20, 331–36
  German knowledge of, 336
  Krupp factories in, 337–38
  slave labor, 320–31, 337–38, 340, 341
  S.S. factories in, 329–30
  See also Holocaust
Crystal Night pogrom, 132–38, 266
Cuba, 271
Czechoslovakia, 94, 103, 106, 161, 162,
  175–76, 236, 266, 272
  invasion of, 186–89
  and Sudetenland conflict, 176–86,
    219–20

Dachau concentration camp, 124, 333
Daladier, Eduard, 183, 185
Darre, Walther, 62–63
Da Zara, Alberto, 231
Delmer, Sefton, 35, 53
Denmark, 204, 269
Dietrich, Otto, 153, 271
Dietrich, Sepp, 77, 79
Dirksen, Herbert von, 220–21
Dodd, Martha, 53–54, 128
Doenitz, Admiral, 380
Dollfuss, Chancellor, 94, 165
Duisberg, Carl, 348
Dunkirk, 208

Eagle's Nest, 145–46
Ebert, Friedrich, 14, 15, 16
Eckart, Dietrich, 154
Eden, Anthony, 68, 99
Edward VIII. See Windsor, Duke of
Eher Verlag, 129–30, 150, 152–55
Eichmann, Adolf, 264, 267–68, 288,
  289, 290, 340–41
Eisenhower, Dwight, 377
Eisner, Kurt, 14, 16, 17
elections, 26–27, 30–32, 39–41, 110

Enabling Act, 44–48, 51, 58
encirclement, 201
Engle, General, 261
Epp, General von, 70, 154
Ernst, Karl, 83–84
Ethiopia, Italian invasion of, 102
euthanasia program, 334–35
Evian Conference, 269

Farben, I.G., 31–32, 162, 250, 251, 252
  anti-Nazis in, 347, 348
  Auschwitz factories of, 325, 327
  concentration camp of, 327–28
  confiscation of businesses by, 198–99,
    212–13, 245
  synthetic fuel plants of, 309–10
Faulhaber, Cardinal, 350
Feder, Gottfried, 63
Flick, Friedrich, 255
Florian, Gauleiter, 367
food supply, 161, 241–42, 257, 310, 349
Ford, Henry, 225, 226
Four-Year Plan, 162–64, 165, 169, 177,
  210–11, 251
France, 90, 94, 95, 97, 98, 100, 180, 201,
  269, 271
  Ardennes offensive in, 353–54
  art thefts from, 314–18
  declaration of war, 195
  German attack on, 203, 205–09
  Normandy invasion in, 311–14
  occupation of, 210–15, 314–18
  and Rhineland reoccupation, 102–03,
    106, 108, 109, 110
  rivalry with Germany, 202
  and Sudetanland crisis, 181–82, 183,
    184
Franco, Francisco, 218
François-Poncet, André, 23, 146
Frank, Hans, 198, 276, 283, 289–90
Free Corps, 15, 16, 27, 90, 154
Frick, Wilhelm, 25, 26, 37
Fritsch, General von, 70, 76, 112, 160,
  163, 164, 281
Fromm, Bella, 131–32
fuel. See oil
Funk, Walther, 136, 165

gas chambers, 319–20, 331–36
Gemlich, Adolf, 121
Generals' Plot, 342–46

409

Index

Index

Index

Index

Index

414

Index